THE ESSENCE OF lightness

A Roadmap to Peak Performance and Self-Mastery

...and Also a Historical Fiction Kung Fu Action Hip-Hop Humor Musical Epic

Tom Fazio

Cover Design by Islam Farid
Meditation Art by Zhu HaiBo

ISBN: 1733062203
ISBN 13: 978-1733062206

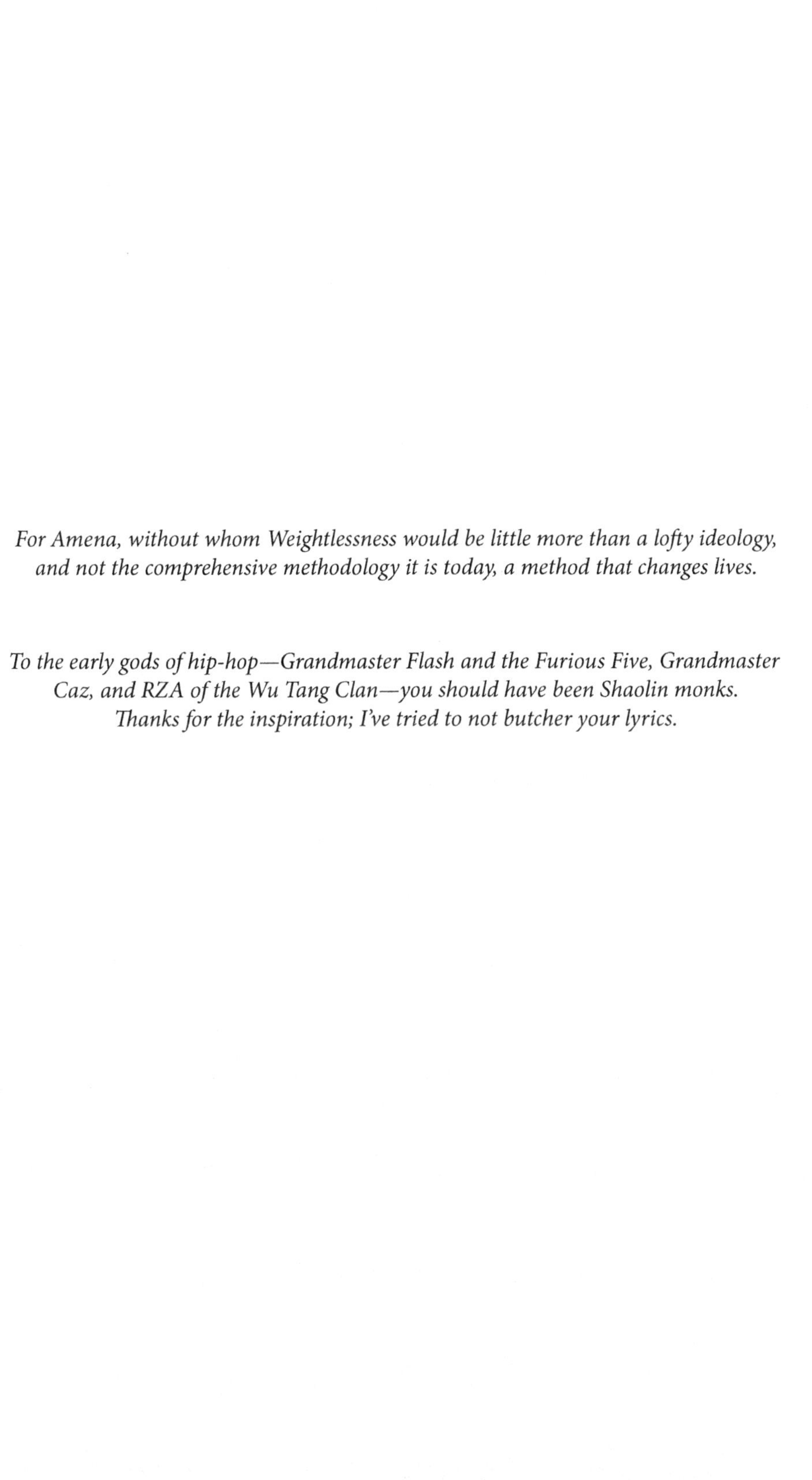

For Amena, without whom Weightlessness would be little more than a lofty ideology, and not the comprehensive methodology it is today, a method that changes lives.

To the early gods of hip-hop—Grandmaster Flash and the Furious Five, Grandmaster Caz, and RZA of the Wu Tang Clan—you should have been Shaolin monks. Thanks for the inspiration; I've tried to not butcher your lyrics.

CONTENTS

PART 1

The Essence of Lightness

> *Suddenly you're ripped into being alive. And life is pain, and life is suffering, and life is horror but my God you're alive and it's spectacular.*
> —Joseph Campbell

Once Upon a Time in Shaolin

Master Shi's stomp resonated deeply within the meditation hall. The reverberating tremors were prominent enough be felt, eerily so. A space of a basketball court constructed of mountain stone and concrete, human-sized crystal Buddhas lined the wall opposite the wide open entrance, adjacent to two centered, oversized, ornately carved wooden chairs fit for royalty—the Grandmaster himself.

In comparing kung fu skill, if we can claim that, his stomp obviously was the earthquake to my sledgehammer. It's common in China to request a show of kung fu skill. My twenty-five years of martial arts practice at that time wasn't a nothing-burger, but kung fu wasn't even my second language. I was a mutt, a polyglot of martial arts, and Chinese kung fu wasn't even in my top five most competent arts.

I wasn't a stranger to the technique Grandmaster Shi asked me to demonstrate, but I was no expert. The technique is central to most kung fu forms: a stomp that brings one foot to the other accompanied by a centering shift and drop in body weight. It's not terribly aesthetic, but it has function. It's an energy trigger, a lion's roar, a gorilla's chest pound. It's a test of a warrior's qi.

My stomp echoed loudly within our four walls. His stomp penetrated three meters of bedrock and sent tremors throughout the hall, tremors that could actually be felt extending from the floor up my legs, triggering a preternatural fear response that raised hair on the back of my neck.

"You stomp the floor, whereas my energy penetrates all the way through," said master Shi, pointing straight down and then waving his hands apart, indicating dispersion. "This is kung fu."

I had trained with Shaolin monks before, exceptional specimens all, as well as grandmasters of many martial arts, many of whom possessed inhuman power, including Master Su in the north of China, my first qigong and chain whip teacher. Master Wang, my second chain whip instructor, also taught me the foundational Shaolin weapons, as I started at the harder ones and worked backwards. And I trained under another Master Su, my meteor hammer instructor at the Shaolin Temple itself.

But this was the first time in nearly three decades I had witnessed *real* kung fu, the essence of martial arts, the deepest energetic skills that a human is capable of.

The journey to the Shaolin Monastery was an experience unto itself. It began with a cable car, a rickety old death trap full of rattles and bounces, that began not far from the Shaolin Temple. In my first visit to the temple ten years before, a friend and I hiked from the base and spent a full day to get to the monastery. The cable car dramatically shortens the hike but with a bit of fate tempting. After the car arrived, we hiked about an hour along cliff faces with concrete platforms jutting from the sides of vertical cliffs, passing through small caves, and climbing dense forest at points. The last point of passage was a new and improved version of what I recalled as a rickety drawbridge of wood and rope that I dared not cross ten years before for fear of an Indiana Jonesian calamity, with broken floor planks and frayed suspension rope. I was relieved to find steel cable and brand-new planks this time around.

This time, along the hike with my cohort, I had time to take in the views, eat fresh tomatoes sold by wayside vendors—best tomatoes ever—and pump myself up with a bit of old school hip-hop of the Wu Tang variety in anticipation of meeting a martial arts badass. Method Man feverishly spat:

> Yo RZA, yo razor, hit me with the major
> The damage, my Clan understand it be flavor
> Gunning, humming coming at ya
> First I'm gonna get ya, once I got ya, I gat ya
> You could never capture the Method Man's stature
> For rhyme and for rapture, got niggas resigning, now master
> My style? Never!
> I put the fucking buck in the wild kid, I'm terror

Razor sharp, I sever
The head from the shoulders, I'm better, than my competta
You mean competitor, whatever, let's get together

After I was asked to accompany my friend Katy, who called in connections to get us access to the part of the monastery walled off from the public, I did a bit of research on the man behind the walls. The YouTube videos of Shi De Jian, of which there are not many, show him practicing his martial patterns on slanted, narrow rooftops that fall into deep ravines, meditating on massive pointed boulders that also have no safe base, and translating animal forms for foreign visitors in a documentary.

It's very difficult to discern real kung fu by watching a video, as the presence of a master and the weight of his touch are needed for a real display of skill, but what I did see, and what you can see for yourself, is a highly skilled craftsman demonstrating a lost art. And martial elements aside, there's true beauty and bravery in his movements.

Among my first hours at the Shaolin Monastery I had witnessed the impossible, the power of a demigod. But over the following days, my own journey was not one of transcendence into a higher plane, but one of stillness, a grounding of sorts where the basics of life (organic vegetarian food, mindful movement, and breathing) took precedence. I trekked to Songshan Mountain in search of an insight that could catapult my skills further; instead, I learned to let go.

When men are direct pedagogical descendants in a lineage of warrior monks, each of whom selects a sole inheritor of their highest knowledge and skills, and then you put that man in a cave for over three decades, well… that man knows things. What he knows I cannot say exactly, but he knows things. His eyes beam with innocence, wisdom, and light. His concentration and conviction are unwavering. His life is exceedingly simple. And his power is legendary.

Master Shi was a monk of the old school, a path that required decades of training and discipline, and, in his case, celibacy, vegetarianism, kung fu, and Zen. I quickly learned that getting answers to questions of depth regarding martial arts skill or qigong was like drawing blood from a stone. Regardless of my query, Master Shi would insist the answer was to practice Zen and eat vegetarian. Oh, and don't fornicate; Buddha forbid.

This was one of those times in life that was both expected yet utterly unimaginable. When you seek out a warrior monk, one of the last true practitioners of Shaolin kung fu, you expect abnormalities. But what you don't expect is something so eerily normal, something so natural and innate that it feels like coming home. Time and space there seemed infinite. Nothing was urgent or unaccounted for, nobody rushing from one place to another or vexed with a mundane problem. Time stood still.

On day two, Master Shi gave us a tour of the monastery grounds, including his personal bedroom of thirty years, a cave at the top of the monastery itself. The local magistrate who was accompanying Katy and me wasn't sure if she would be allowed into the cave, because she's a woman and sometimes women bleed from their nether regions. So, he asked Master Shi, who replied confidently, "It's okay; she's not on her period."

Katy was a bit taken aback, but Master Shi later explained that since the tender age of fifteen he's been able to tell such things due to a very acute sense of smell and subtle shifts in energy. Apparently, if Katy were on her period, she would not have been admitted into the man cave. Katy leaned over to me and sardonically pointed out, "A true warrior doesn't mind getting his sword bloody."

His cave was as humble as caves get, a bed of rickety wood with a few sheets off to the right side, neatly folded. A wall to the left organized several weapons hanging from nails, including a straight sword, a curved sword, a thick chain whip, and thick steel spikes. These were real "live" weapons with sharpened blades and pointed tips, unlike those at the base of the mountain used by tens of thousands of kung fu students who live and train there.

In the back sat a large crystal Buddha that glowed in the dark when lights were turned off. After a few minutes, Katy and I were asked to leave. We weren't sure if the master and the magistrate were talking biz or maybe cave improvements and the need for donations, or Katy spontaneously started bleeding or having the thought of bleeding. It was none of the above. It turned out that Master Shi smelled something synthetic. My deodorant was messing up his cave qi.

Just atop of his cave was a paved concrete platform that served as both roof and private training area. About three meters by four, it contained five thick concrete pillars. Each was approximately three feet high and distanced a few feet apart, used for balance work above the ground, as well as for striking with the forearms and shins every morning and night. This type of training must be built up over decades, not just months or years, as the adaptations to tendon and bone must be made methodically and gradually.

At one point on the tour, Master Shi flexed his forearm and asked me to squeeze. Men that size shouldn't have forearms so thick and hard that you can't fit your full hand around them. They had become as hard as the pillars he struck daily. A second later, he asked me to feel his arm again and the concrete bulge he just demonstrated was replaced by a vacuum of soft tissue. I could feel straight through to the bone. He was able to display the full spectrum of tension and relaxation within a moment, and to a degree I'd never seen before. "This is kung fu," he reminded.

This secluded rooftop was one of several breathtaking locations on the mountain where Master Shi had been filmed practicing his forms on a pointed ledge overlooking a steep ravine. This spot can be seen in YouTube videos that show him practicing patterns and even locking and throwing disciples literally on the edge of death. His brilliant surefootedness requires several replays of the video to make sure what you're watching is real. It was. And it is.

At one point during our stay, the head of tourism of Henan province, the province hosting the Shaolin Temple, came to visit the monastery to ask Master Shi to stop training on these precipitous edges and tempting fate. His videos had gone viral in China and the government didn't want the flack for promoting reckless behavior with a natural heritage. He's one of a handful of authentic remaining Shaolin warrior monks; one misstep would risk the loss of ancient secrets that few, if any, could replicate.

Master Shi politely declined, telling me later that the fear of death is necessary to practice with true intention, "I don't want to die, so I practice real kung fu. Without fear, I might not grip the ground with my toes properly."

Later, sitting on the balcony of our recently constructed, modern accommodations and overlooking the concrete and mountain stone training platform before us, we sat with Master Shi watching his top disciples practice their forms as the sun was setting behind them. Master Shi shared with us the fantastical origin story of his monastery, as well as that of *his* kung fu, which were not independent from each other.

[Full disclosure, there were likely gaps in my full comprehension due to language and excitement; therefore, this retelling may contain a modicum of embellishment. But the story is basically the same and true, except for those places where it isn't.]

A Grandmaster's Grandmaster

F*or every legend, there are the ones they are born from that make them seem ordinary.*

Master Shi came to be the abbot of his monastery for two fascinating reasons. Technically he should have been the rightful heir, proper abbot of the Shaolin Temple down at the base of Songshan Mountain. Lineage is measured in both mentor line—who's yo masta?—and generation (i.e., who has the lower number next to their title?) Master Shi is two generations younger than the current abbot and, therefore, of more pure descent in the art, in theory.

But politics be politics, and modern kung fu be bastardized and watered down. At the base of the mountain, kung fu is far closer to gymnastics and parkour than it is mortal combat. This has been an evolutionary process since the most recent reconstruction of the temple post Cultural Revolution. It has become a factory for impressive aerial displays, lightweight, paper-thin weapons, and the illusion of Zen heritage. Master Shi, always wholly committed to the monastic life, settled for his magical monastery in the hills, a castle of sorts he rebuilt with his own two hands, the support of his devout followers, and a renowned Swiss architect to honor his master's dying wish that the monastery be rebuilt.

The dilapidated monastery was a lost heritage that Master Shi's master felt a strong affinity for and a deep sense of loss over. It was also the home of Master Shi's cave site for decades. Master Shi moved bedrock, raised pillars, and carried 100kg bags of concrete up endless stairs that scaled vertically from the base of the hills into the mist until he reached the peak. For twenty years, he honored the dying wish of his master to rebuild the monastery until he'd completed the most beautiful hermitage you'll never see.

But you're not alone. Most will never see it. They keep it rather guarded and open the doors only to those with invitations. Katy had very well-connected friends and family who granted us access to a full week with Master Shi. Otherwise, I too would have only known him from YouTube and would not have learned the tale I'm about to tell.

Master Shi De Jian came from a line of authentic kung fu masters, many of whom were in close connection with the temple, though not always monks themselves. It's been complicated for a long time, with kung fu being a forbidden practice off and on for extended eras. Master Shi, the disciple of Yang Guiwu, the disciple of Shi Degen, himself the disciple of—screw it, I always get lost in these lineages. Add two more grandmasters and we've got our man Shi Jiqin 1820-1917. Let's call him Grandmaster Flash.

Grandmaster Flash, at the origin of the story of our last remaining warrior monk on the mountain, was another warrior monk.

One hundred and fifty years ago, ordained protector monks took vows of devotion to the temple and to the ten laws of Shaolin. Once a monk, forever a monk. You don't get to dabble in the mystic arts of Shaolin and trade down to become a YouTube star or Instagram influencer. There were rules.

So, Grandmaster Flash, barring copyright infringement for a badass hip-hop moniker, grew irreparably discontent at the growing corruption and degeneracy rising among the upper ranks of Shaolin. This was nothing new. The Shaolin Temple had been at the center of political drama for millennia with repeated cycles of moral degradation and spiritual cleansing that flowed in and out like the tides. This era was one of the former, and its conditions were worsening year after year. The vows that Flash committed to were no longer those practiced by the Shaolin council or the abbot himself.

After painstaking, careful deliberation and soul-searching, Grandmaster Flash decided he could no longer tacitly ignore the materialism, greed, prostitution, and political favor that were becoming the norm. Flash decided he would forego his temple vows and depart on his own in order to practice in full commitment to his values—the deteriorating purist values of Shaolin. But as I mentioned, monkhood is a one-way process. Monks are all about compassion, until you decide to leave the brotherhood.

Grandmaster Flash knew that while giving up his monkhood was a forbidden act, there was in fact one loophole. While frowned upon, it was honored by the Temple as sacrosanct and would not put him at the butt-end of Shaolin sentinels not employed in action in his lifetime at least. Flash could fight for his freedom.

To be perfectly clear, the monks of Shaolin were not prisoners. It wasn't like that. They were free to venture out of the temple as needed, albeit with a bit of oversight and regulation, but they were not captives. As long as they returned at night and kept their vows, they were protected. But should someone leave in a more formal way, disavowing the Temple and ceasing their responsibilities and commitments and answering only to themselves thereafter, this was different. It created risk to the Temple order, as well as created the dangerous possibility of the dissemination of Shaolin knowledge. This could not be allowed. This could not be granted. But it could be fought for.

This fight would be no ordinary death match, no humane survival of mortal combat against evenly matched odds. No, in this case, the odds were 18 to 1. If you wanted to leave, the door was open. The only catch was that there were 18 of the most powerful Shaolin warrior monks who ever lived—The Guardians, brothers and mentors that you grew and trained with—standing between you and that open door. And they took betrayal of their vows personally.

The Guardians

The Guardians were straight out of legend. And I mean that. Temple monks were not even sure they were real, *if* they were real. They weren't ordinary protector monks of the Shaolin temple. I say ordinary here, but let me clarify a bit. Protector monks had reputations as being first in class in the combat arts, not merely in Henan, but across all of China. They were commissioned on many occasions by Emperor's past to assist in squelching uprisings or suppressing aggressive warlords.

The Guardians were the very best among the protectors, and what's worse, their identities were never disclosed in times of peace but for two cases: an all-out attack on the Shaolin Temple itself, or in the rare case of an internal challenge for freedom from the temple pledge, a challenge that was almost never made.

Both of these held risks to the Shaolin arts: the destruction of Shaolin knowledge and heritage in the first case, or the dissemination of Shaolin secrets in the second. These secrets were partly responsible for their allure and political influence, along with their overflowing coffers from collected alms. Further, a successful departure without penalization could lead to a mass exodus of monks and their return to normalcy. These could both be considered crises worth dying for from the perspective of the elite 18. Their entire worlds were at stake.

How badly do you want your freedom, young Grandmaster Flash?

Grandmaster Flash knew, as any rational monk would, that he was no match for the Guardians. Flash was, in fact, an extraordinary creature of combat, elite in technical ability with Buddha given talent and a fight IQ second to none. But those odds were not to be taken lightly. Despite them, he didn't feel his cause was entirely lost. Something in his gut told him there must be a way. But again, those odds… how can one navigate such insurmountable odds?

Flash determined to fight, live or die, for the alternative, ignoring the rotting stench of avarice around him and live a lie of false devotion, was just another form of death. And he had an idea, however crude and delusional. Eighteen men can be aligned, albeit clumsily, around an adversary. But they cannot effectively be organized defensively around a gate and offensively around an adversary at the same time.

The only reasonable plan would be for the Guardians to give Flash their utmost attention rather than focus fully on defending the gate as an exit, which would divide their ranks and stack their formations in compromising ways. Sure, a few guardians may guard the gate as a last resort, but that couldn't make up the entirety of their strategy for all.

No, Flash would be circled, he surmised, at least on three of four sides. And as he is circled, the numbers in direct line between him and the door would diminish. Interpretation: he shouldn't need to fight 18 Guardians, ever. If he prepared and strategized well, he might be able to reduce the numbers of direct contact to half, hell, maybe even a third of their ranks, due to natural limitations in effective attack-formation.

Could he defeat nine guardians, nine of the most powerful warriors on the planet? Unlikely. But it's far more probable than beating eighteen. That's at least something. But was that glimmer of hope really enough to bet his life on?

He would need time to prepare, daily, full on. He speculated six months could get him in position to face this challenge if every waking moment were dedicated to not only surviving the battle but also developing an edge. This wasn't a battle he could win in haste; the consequences were too severe. He could not, in such a short time, out-train career Guardians at what they do, Guardians who themselves are commissioned to remain in peak condition and who each essentially represent older, wiser versions of Flash himself. To do that would require eighteen lifetimes, which he clearly didn't have.

No, Flash would need an edge, a highly specific approach suited to the constraints of his escape, an approach that would require more time for the Guardians to adapt than him to implement. And he thought he found it.

There were two skills that Grandmaster Flash figured would save his life and ensure his escape: Dian Xue (more commonly known in the West as Dim Mak or pressure point incapacitation) and Qing Gong (Lightness Training).

As I listened to Master Shi recount this story, I inched to the edge of my seat with the giddy intrigue of a ten-year-old listening to the retelling of his favorite hero's tale, one that would never get old, one that would only get better with each successive embellishment.

As if the story wasn't visceral enough, Master Shi looked at me during this pause with a bit more intensity than he displayed to date, holding his index and middle finger together and displaying their sheer density, if not deformity. "Do you believe I could put my fingers through your sternum?" he asked without an ounce of irony or jest. I chuckled nervously.

This was the origin of one of the very few life dictums that I live by. It's very straightforward and easy to apply:

If a warrior monk asks you if you believe he can kill you with his finger, always say yes. This is better than saying no and challenging him to prove you wrong.

Admittedly, this isn't a frequent occurrence for most in life. But I would have thought the same before that day. It's one of those black swan occasions that, while highly improbable, bears such steep consequences that the mere off-chance possibility should be given careful consideration and a heuristic of its own.

"Yes. Yes I do," I replied with a placating smile. "But she doesn't!" I declared, pointing to Katy.

This is the origin of another of the very few life dictums that I live by. It's also very straightforward and easy to apply:

If you get the chance to watch a warrior monk put his fingers through someone else's sternum, always say yes. 'Cause, you know, life stories.

The Monks Retreat

The Shaolin army was commissioned for centuries, starting in the Tang Dynasty circa 620 A.D. when 13 warrior monks rescued the son of the Tang emperor from enemy forces, to defend the Emperor and support local militias in times of war, on standby as last-resort protectors. They were a super team of battle-hardened special forces.

Consider that today most military men receive basic training that lasts up to a few months, while elite special forces training carries on for another year and a half to three years.

Shaolin protectors, monks who from the age of, in some cases three to five years old and all the way to adulthood, have practiced the combat arts for four to six hours a day, every day, for over a decade. They could, and did, chase down pirates on multiple occasions over tens of miles and multiple weeks, hunting, fighting, hunting, until they were all vanquished. It's not hard to envision the sheer inequity of these monks in combat, and easy to envision them doing just fine when outnumbered 10 or even 20 to 1. They were superior specimens. And they knew that kung fu.

In their last reported battle, which occurred just prior to the great Temple burning of 1732 under the Yongzhen Emperor, the general of the protector monks became disillusioned with their commissioned work and concluded that his army wasn't being utilized for righteous purposes, but instead were being exploited with devious intentions.

Standing over their fallen prey, a field of bodies, blood, and lifeless steel, the protectors surveyed their plight and together knew with one mind that they were not doing Buddha's work. When the commanding general of the Emperor's army ordered them to finish every last wounded soldier, take no prisoners and aid no injured, the Shaolin general defied him, dropping his blood-stained saber. The Shaolin protectors took their cues immediately; all aligned and feeling the same sense of guilt and regret, they dropped their weapons where they stood. That was the last time swords, spears, sabers, axes, hammers, lances, bull whips, chain whips, rope darts, and meteor hammers were all buried with the blood of fallen armies.

It was the last time they were wielded in full-blown combat, period. It was a right shit-show of blood, guts, and steel. Monks meant business when they did business. But the protectors were done.

The general pulled his protectors from battle and they returned to their monastic lives. Despite their battle acumen they were then instructed to utilize their kung fu for spiritual advancement only and focus all efforts on their Zen roots. They were to return to the path of compassion and maintain only the foundational fist forms, the animal forms, and their classical weapons training for purposes of mind-body development, grit, and fortitude. They were to focus on higher mind and energy practices, meditation, and vegetarian nutrition.

This triggered backlash from the emperor who was personally offended by the treacherous withdrawal of the warriors from his battalion. What followed was not the first or the last burning of the Shaolin Temple, but it was the most devastating and took the lives of master and junior monks alike who refused to break their recently revived vows of nonviolence.

The monks who survived resolved to uphold their newfound commitment to nonviolence and retreated deep within the mountains many hours hike from the base of the mountain on foot. It was, at points, a treacherous hike, but their destination was known for growing potent medicinal herbs and being well fortified on all sides by steep cliffs and deep ravines. A rickety drawbridge of wood and rope was the only way to access what would become the second home of Shaolin, The Monastery, where the purist roots would be reborn and remain pure to this day, the very place we sat and listened to this tale.

While sojourned on the mountain, all monks were equal again. There were no nonviolent cliques and no warrior factions. All ate and trained together. They returned to their humble, vegetarian diets, harvested right there on the monastery grounds. The warriors, having no immediate need to perform in battle, surrendered their diets with meat, reduced their physical training, and blended in with their brothers in standing and seated meditation, taking in the fresh mountain air and cultivating deeper energies that pulsed through their veins.

In the years that followed, the protectors, along with the nonmartial monks of the temple, constructed spartan accommodations, digging out caves and constructing humble buildings of wood, earth, and stone for living and meditation. During their seclusion, monastery scouts were sent periodically to survey the original temple site for signs of Imperial spies. This lasted for nearly a generation, and despite the predominately quiet expeditions, they played the side of caution and remained hidden far longer than may have been necessary. The pain of their lost family was very hard to let go.

When the emperor was overthrown, the monks of Shaolin were notified by his replacement that their good standing was returned in the eyes of the throne. They were not only allowed to return to rebuild their temple but also requested to return as a symbol of spiritual rebirth for the nation and a guiding light for the people. But they should refrain from weapons training, a request signifying lingering fears of their abilities and one intending to suppress their power. The monks complied.

The monks of Shaolin returned to the temple area at the base of the mountain to reconstruct their home and live in full compliance with the laws of Shaolin. Or at least that was the aim. It wasn't long before greed, fame, and fortune tempted the council of Shaolin to exploit their clout once again with the selling of their arts to highest bidders. The protectors were left with no choice but to comply. Conditions were deteriorating, and some of the monks took notice. Enter Grandmaster Flash.

Wisdom of the Ancients

The most important part of the temple, The Wisdom of the Ancients, didn't burn with the rest. It was hidden in plain sight within the pagoda forest, the Shaolin Temple graveyard of antiquity, hosting hundreds of beautifully designed pagodas that bore similar structures: thick-based, tiered towers with multiple ascending eaves. Therein lay a mausoleum no more striking than the rest, which didn't diminish its beauty, protected like the others by superstition and reverence.

This room was protected only by its seeming lack of significance. The monks assumed most invaders would honor the dead, but if they didn't, they were unlikely to dedicate the same attention to the devastation of a graveyard as the living and praying quarters. There was nothing on the exterior that made this pagoda stand out from the others. But within it was a dug-out corridor descending steeply into the ground and opening into a dingy, mold-ridden, unlit room. It smelled ancient, that's for sure.

The forest grounds and the mausoleum entrance needed to be dug out from under a bit of fallen rubble (though some of it was strategically placed preraid to hide the site), but it took mere minutes with the help of a dozen or so monks to clear. They were relieved to see the ancient library and its temple scrolls, the true treasures of Shaolin, were untouched.

This was the very room that Grandmaster Flash now cautiously paced through, illuminating one small subsection at a time with a glowing oil lamp. Grandmaster Flash was at that time just a master, exceptionally skilled in martial arts and a respected teacher. Despite his youth, a man of midtwenties, athletic build, deep black eyes, and a face that carried no tensions betraying stress or insecurity, he'd long graduated from the ranks of junior monks and was recognized as a monk of great virtue yet youthful vigor. An enthusiast learner and a patient teacher, Flash was a sponge for the Shaolin arts. And he was here on a whim, a well-informed hunch from long-held memory.

Flash visited the temple archives in search of that edge we discussed, sifting through scroll upon scroll for well-kept secrets. He wasn't blindly searching the archives but pursuing a vague recollection of legend: The Masters of Lightness, early predecessors of Shaolin with extraordinary skills cultivated mostly in times of war, but that fell by the wayside for centuries in times of peace. He suspected that if the legends were true, remnants would be here in the archives.

While the ancient library was relatively organized with scrolls rolled neatly and segregated by small shelves with etched labels carved onto their facades, not all scrolls were included in the general Shaolin canon. Energy cultivation, nutrition, herbal medicine, meridian studies, temple history and lineages, and animal forms, to name a few, were considered indispensable cornerstones of Shaolin heritage. All monks were exposed to their teachings, to varying degrees. But those that were extracanonical and lesser known were relegated to a side room collecting more dust than the rest.

These scrolls were racked in no particular order like those in the larger of the two rooms, but at least they maintained an etched label and clear categorical segregation on the shelves supporting them. For the most part, they were too obscure to classify but too precious to burn.

Carefully passing his lamp, one etching at a time, he scanned dozens of ambiguous titles dancing in the flickering light like choir soloists waiting for their chances to shine, barely peeking through ages of dust. Many of these texts could easily be lumped into the broad category of esoteric, if not mystical knowledge: *Taoist Alchemy*, *Golden Elixir*, *Buddha's Dark Sermon*, and the *Time, Change*, and *Transformation* scrolls.

Flash would have lied if he said each title wasn't titillating in and of itself, but they weren't his focus. Each title would require months to years of dedicated study and reflection to internalize, and he had mere months for a mission that wouldn't entertain distraction. Toward the back of this small, cloudy, cobwebbed room where presumably only the obscurest of the obscure texts resided he found what he was looking for, *Qing Gong*—Lightness Training.

The character Qing was also stamped into the wax that sealed the scroll itself in addition to the etching beneath it. Why was it sealed? None of the others carried a seal. The answer was as obvious as the question was frightening. Its contents weren't meant for all eyes.

He'd heard this text referenced only once or twice from his Grandmaster. After blowing a lungful of blanketed residue from the scroll's topside, he carefully removed an edge of the wax seal. Flash couldn't help but feel guilty; for what, he wasn't quite sure. Similar perhaps to the feeling of trespassing on guarded property, he wasn't sure what the consequences of this act would be, but he was committed, nonetheless, to playing it out.

Flash figured if there were to be consequences, he might as well take in as much as he could, as quickly as he could. He carefully unrolled and skimmed the entire work with the intention of diligently studying each line later from a safe place. He felt a surge of adrenaline, well aware that he was likely one of the few monks alive who even knew it existed, and certainly, he was the only monk to crack its seal in decades.

Near the end of the scroll, Flash found several stains of blood. He hovered his lamp carefully over the stains and was stunned to find that he recognized the chops of three names, each stamped within a blood stain of its own in a line of many more. All names were neatly filed under the heading "Qing Gong Shi Fu"—The Masters of Lightness. The masters had all stamped the scroll with their own blood. If the gravity of breaching the seal didn't hit him like a punch in the gut, this sure did.

His eyes widened with a curious skepticism as he surveyed these three names; they were those of his master, his master's master, and his great grandmaster. The only reason he didn't recognize the prior names was because his master hadn't shared more of his own direct lineage. Story time was a revered, but infrequently practiced art. Flash's history of Shaolin lineage was strong up to a century, and weak thereafter. Then again, perhaps it was just never relevant to his development.

What was relevant, what made the hair on his arms stand tall, was that he knew of Lightness only because his direct lineage were the keepers of this secret, the ones decreed by abbots past to master and pass it on to their own disciple of choice. This didn't mean a master couldn't teach whom he pleased whatever he liked, but it did mean only one inheritor would be selected to carry on the authority of that message.

This was a common process. Most monks knew that the temple traditions were far too extensive for one man, or even one lineage to master the wide spectrum of Shaolin arts and skills. But if each generation had at least one master who could advise the council in times of need or teach savants in case someone showed extraordinary capability to adopt rarer techniques that they could wield responsibly and teach in true form, then the arts would survive in their purity.

It just so happened that those scrolls in the large room that fit neatly into standard categories of development were heavily emphasized for all monks. Several lineages within the temple became chosen carriers of the

Shaolin canon: the core body of scriptures detailing herbal medicine, Zen Buddhism, and kung fu knowledge. All monks were required to study them as part of their general curriculum, to varying levels of proficiency. Only the truly obscure skills, the ones that nobody knew what to do with, perhaps the ones most relevant at times of war, or the truly esoteric ones that postulated immortality or the dark arts were kept as the tight secret of one lineage alone.

This meant that Grandmaster Flash's master was a master of Lightness, and his master before him, and his before him. It also meant that Flash's master, while truly a generous albeit strict mentor, didn't deem Flash ready to inherent these secrets. But why?

Flash wrapped the scroll and tucked it into his robe, lest he get caught red-handed pilfering old texts. But this wasn't all he came for. The other document he needed was closer to common knowledge, at least theoretically, and had earned a place on the shelves under the category of *Meridian Theory and Martial Applications*. It sat adjacent to the classic Yi Jin Jing (Muscle Tendon Change Classic), the perfect complement to Dian Xue (Dim Mak). He grabbed them both and left without a trace.

Safe and secure in the confines of his room, Flash began to scrutinize the scrolls before him.

C.R.E.A.M.

RZA lazily sauntered over the nearest hilltop and into view, wearing loose robes, a faint cloud of smoke hovering behind him, mumbling rhythmically to himself:

> "Fusion of the five elements to search for the higher intelligence
> Monks walk around celibate, living irrelevant
> The most benevolent king, communicatin' through your dreams
> Mental pictures bein' painted, Buddha's heard and seen
> Everywhere, throughout your surrounding atmosphere
> Troposphere, thermosphere, stratosphere
> Can you imagine from one single idea, everything appeared here
> Understanding makes my truth, crystal clear"

RZA was Flash's closest friend; had been for over fifteen years. When they weren't training together, they were usually hanging and discussing whatever monks do. RZA was a powerful protector, but he didn't really fit the mold. His robes were always a little too big, almost baggy. They seemed to hang off of him in a way that completely hid his warrior physique. He could have easily been mistaken for a bum if he weren't forced to keep his robes clean and stitched and his head freshly shaven like the rest. His eyes carried a slight droop to the outside, his speech a slight drawl. And there always seemed to be a few random scraggly mustache hairs that never got reigned in. He pulled this persona together with a cheap conical hat like those worn by farmers nationwide.

RZA was also one of the temple's most skilled herbal healers, with a personal stash of medicinal herbs second only to the official apothecary. This affinity might have branded him an eccentric healer only, if he weren't so damn gangster with a sword. He earned his place among the warriors, despite a lingering disapproval of him by many who strictly followed customs.

"RZA! Ma monk," called Flash.

“You’re lucky it’s just me and you up on this mountaintop. I see you jumpin’ in and outa holes and shit. If the Guardians saw that… hell. Or maybe you want ‘em to, get ‘em thinking your head ain’t in the game. That shit’s comical.”

To date, RZA was the only one who knew of Flash’s intentions to place a formal challenge before the council in a few months’ time, a secret he would keep close to his chest until it was officially issued.

“Didn’t know you’ve been watching, RZA, but thanks for keeping it between us.”

“No thankin’. You know we tight. Ever since I got here, you had my back; now it’s time I get yours. You always had some crazy in you, I know, but this is nuts. I see you poking trees too. Is that that Dim Mak stuff? I heard about that,” RZA said, furrowing his brow and poking the air with his forefingers.

“What did you hear about it?” Flash goaded RZA, knowing RZA was just as familiar with it as he was.

“My uncle, an old dirty bastard, got poked by that Dim Mak once. Right in his chest. It was devastatin’.”

“Seriously? What happened to him?”

“What do you think happened? He died, man! That shit’s no joke. Got into an altercation with some dude over dumpling spice, didn’t know the guy was kung fu. Dude tap-tapped my uncle right here,” RZA pointed to Flash’s sternum, over his heart. “Thirty years later, to the day, enjoying some rice wine and pork dumplings at dinner and telling old tales—BLAM! Died right then and there on the spot. His qi just stopped flowin’.”

“That… sounds pretty hardcore, RZA. Preeeettty powerful kung fu.” Flash was struggling to tell just how much RZA was messing with him. RZA was rarely serious. The challenge, even for Flash, was usually telling just how much of what he was saying was true versus mostly true. He balanced madness and measure in ways that left a monk wondering if maybe he actually knew more than it seemed.

“Yo, look man, you know I gots to come clean on something. I don’t want to see you go. But I got your back on the outside.”

“You got my back? What haven’t you told me?”

“I got a method, man. Let’s just say when I came here as a young blood, it wasn’t by accident. You know Shaolin keeps tabs on the outside clans. Well some of them keep tabs on us. I haven’t exactly been isolated here.”

“What are you talking about? Wu Tang?”

"Yo, I can't confirm, nor disconfirm anything about the Clan. But if you make it outa here—"

"*When* I make it out," Flash cut in.

"When you make it outa here, have your people call my people. My peoples… they some bad motherfuckers too."

"If you can do that, why don't you come with me?"

"My job ain't done here yet, but one day… Look, I can't get you outa here, not even sure if you can get you outa here, but I can make sure once you out, you stay out, and you be gone. If the council don't honor your challenge and they send sentinels after you, you ain't gonna be alone. I promise you that. There are tensions brewing here; we all feel it. The powers that be ain't as secure as they seem, and they're tightening their grip. This place lost its essence a long time ago. Now it's all politics and coin. The abbot is eatin' five courses and we're fighting for scraps. He's crappin' in gold bowls and we're squattin' in dirty holes. Next thing you know, he'll be sending us to war."

"So much for the laws and virtues of Shaolin, huh, RZA?"

RZA reflected aloud,

"It's been twenty-two long hard years, I'm still strugglin'
Survival got me buggin', but I'm alive on arrival
I peep at the shape of the temple
And stay awake to the ways of the world 'cause shits an example
Council man with a dream with plans to make C.R.E.A.M.
No joke I got woke at the age of 15
A young monk beggin' and such who never had much
Trying to get a clutch at what I could not
The temple played me short, now I face degeneration
Pacin' going deep hate's my destination
Handcuffed in back of a caste, truth has amassed
Life as a shorty shouldn't be so rough
But as the world turns, I learned life is hell
Living in the temple no different from a cell
Every day, I escape from Masta givin' chase, countin' kills
Smokin' bones in the hills
Though I don't know why I chose to smoke sess
I guess that's the time when I'm not depressed
But I'm still depressed, and I ask what's it worth?
Ready to give up so I seek the Old Earth
Who explained training hard may help you maintain

To learn to overcome the heartaches and pain
We got mistreated kids, corrupt abbot, and bad habit
Straight jacket, blinds young monks from whole planet
Leave it up to me while I be living proof
To kick the truth to the young monk youth
But shorty's running wild swinging sword spinning spear
And ain't trying to hear what I'm kickin' in his ear
Neglected, for now, but yo, it gots to be accepted
That what? That life is hectic"

"Copper rules everything around me. Get the money. Copper copper coins ya'll,"

RZA rapped melodically as if he'd rehearsed it.

"Cause it's all about the money, ain't a damn thing funny
You got to have a con in this land of milk and honey,"

Flash spat back.

They bumped forearms to acknowledge the sick flow.

"And besides," continued RZA, "This sticky icky shaolin kush ain't too bad, neither. If it wasn't for this green right here I'd have ghosted a long time ago."

"I'm with you there, but it's not like we've got a free pass. I didn't exactly challenge the head cook to push hands. The stakes are a bit higher. Thanks, though, I owe you, RZA."

"Just don't get caught. If you get caught, I get got. Know what I'm sayin'?"

"I do. And the offer stands to join me. Two vs. eighteen betters the odds by 50%," Flash joked.

"Yo, I love ya, but I ain't gonna fight shit. I ain't gonna do shit. I'm good right here on this mountain," he chuckled, knowing they both knew he didn't fully mean it. After a long, chilled out, pensive pause, RZA passed the joint. "What the hell you doing in that hole anyway? It *IS* comical."

"Check this out, man," said Flash, reaching under his man-satchel of fabric and leather ties and pulling out a scroll. He handed it to RZA, who unraveled and quickly skimmed the first section of it. His movements were always a little erratic, seemingly uncoordinated or wild, which gave Flash immediate concern for the future of the scroll as RZA stretched it out. Then his wits came back to him and he remembered his brother's skills. This wild touch is what always made him seem dangerous and, no doubt, made it harder for his opponents to read him in combat.

RZA's eyes were likely the only extra-lineage eyes ever to fall on this scroll. To RZA's stoned-out mind, it seemed cool and all, but Flash could see the lines weren't quite resonating as he read them aloud with his gangster slur.

"Da Pillas a Lightness"

[The reading to follow should be cross-shot with parallel action of the training montage mélange. I believe Master Shi would have wanted it that way. Shot selections associated with each pillar should be accompanied by visuals of Flash training during RZA's voice-over narration of the four pillars, which in and of themselves might seem pedantic. At least now we've got some badassery, where Flash is lifting and running and getting suited up and… well, I'll explain as we go.]

RZA read the pillar of strength aloud,

> *The student of Lightness approaches strength as a skill, not as a capacity. It must be practiced religiously against increasing resistance, in degrees of effort that are reproducible after short bouts of recovery. The legend of Wang Zi demonstrates this principle, as from a young age he carried a bull calf several meters each day without fail. As the calf grew, so did Wang Zi, until he became the strongest man in China.*

[I imagine here we're seeing a rapid evolution scene; a boy struggling to carry a calf becomes a man confidently carrying a bull. I don't know how exactly you'll manage that without it looking hammy, but if you can make Superman fly and Aquaman swim, you can figure it out, Hollywood.]

> *Our concerns exceed the strength of skeletal muscles, looking deeper to the elastic spring potential of soft tissue. Tendon and ligament strength require more time than muscular strength to develop, and must be conditioned against heavy resistance within short efforts. Volume adds risk to connection points in the body. This is well documented in the Yi Jin Jing.*

> *Lift heavy things. The duration of maximum strain should not exceed a count of 15, but should exceed a count of 5. If effort can conceivably exceed a count of 15, resistance is not adequately selected. Progressive skills should be comprised of a select few compound movements within five vectors of force: push, pull, squat, press, and twist. Attempts per session should not exceed five, and vectors per session should not exceed two. Strength should be practiced four to six days per week.*

[Flash, with upper robes drooped and secured around his waist, revealing his carved, sinewy body, shoulders full of blood with pronounced vascularity. He's fireman-carrying two cement blocks molded around steel bars, and he's walking with intense strain that wobbles the knees and limits his movement. Next, he's performing a handstand in perfect balance, the camera pans down to see that he's supported only atop two fingers extended from each hand.

Cut to an epic planche-hold on the peak of a lone mountain boulder, likely accompanied by a close-up of his intense focus, background blurred with a beautiful soft bokeh, followed by a circling wide-angle drone shot showing just how dangerous this feat is, with careening drops on all sides into a steep ravine.]

RZA: Yo, I get that. Less is more and whatnot. Lift heavy things.

FLASH: That's a slight oversimplification, but yeah. I think the information we're looking for is between the lines. It's not just about what to do; it's about what's intentionally not prescribed, what's discarded. Keep reading.

RZA continued,

> *Dynamic Flexibility is a skill native to the Shaolin arts and mastered by all protectors who bear the name. But it is a skill we cannot be complacent about, for the stressors of strength training in conjunction with ballistic weight training creates unique strains on the body that must be counteracted and conditioned with dynamic stretching.*

The 5 foundational stretches must be maintained: front, rear, inner crescent, outward crescent, and side rising kicks. Practicing these skills with added weight will take dynamic mobility and joint resilience to profound heights. They will bulletproof the body from sprains and tears and allow for the loading of greater elastic forces within explosive movement.

[Flash demonstrates the foundational kicks of Shaolin. At first, he's performing each individually, with slow pacing and deep focus. Each extends with an explosive pop, but he patiently transitions into the next. After a few seconds, and as RZA gets further along in his description, Flash starts adding height, speed, and power to his kicks.

As his legs rise rapidly without compromising his erect spine and physical structure, his opposite hand extends to receive the power and spring load the kick's recovery. There's a loud crack on each impact like a shotgun as dust clouds pop off his shoe. It's likely there wasn't that much dust in reality, but this can be added by the stagehand just prior to each cut for maximum visual impact like in those old kung fu flicks.

As his speed increases, so too does the complexity of his movement, going from single to multiple kicks, rearranging them in combination, even adding leaps and turns to them.]

RZA: So, basically, what we be doing already for years, plus weights.

FLASH: Seems so… but like the strength component, I'm not sure yet how small of an adjustment adding weight to them really is. We both see what we know, but we may be missing what we don't know.

RZA: Sure.

RZA continued,

Energy work is generally considered the height of Shaolin practice. It is only approached after the Shaolin curriculum has been mastered over a minimum of ten years, and the student has the fortitude, awareness, and self-discipline for deep work. Shaolin masters are no strangers to energy work, but because the myriad

Shaolin lineages are kept pure in advanced training, there is no primary Shaolin system of energy work.

Therefore, the master of Lightness will receive that of the Lightness lineage, a well vetted progressive sequence of qigong practices that are fully compatible with Lightness protocols and higher-mind skills. This sequence is as follows:

1: Accumulation—The Hollow Man

Extend conscious awareness to and throughout a hollowed body devoid of soft tissue to enliven sensitivity as if the body is breathing through all areas. Once natural pulses are well identified, draw your concentration to your lowest sea of energy—the dan tian. Keep it there until the fire is lit and the well is filled. This is done through deep concentration within the hollow man.

2: Distribution—The Small Universe

Distribution occurs by one of two streams—spontaneous and willful. When the well is full, it may overflow with no additional effort. But it may not. And spontaneous flow may not become volitional control.

Focus on the lower dan tian until it is charged. Then coordinate your inhale with focus on the lower dan tian, and exhale with focus on upper dan tian at the center of the forehead. Repeat for 30 slow breaths, drawing energy in through the nose to the lower dan tian, and upon exhale, down past the perineum between the legs, up the spine to the crown point, and resting in your third eye.

3: Channeling—The Collapsing Room

This is an exercise in visualization. You sit in stillness, with channels open and alive. Imagine the room around you closing in on you. Your arms should be extended before you, extremely relaxed with a significant bend that fluctuates slightly within your efforts.

Draw energy into your lower dan tian as you inhale. As you exhale, resist with your utmost intention—devoid of physical tension—the wall pressing in on you. Resist with your mind, and channel your qi. Empty body. Empty mind. Full intention.

There may be unique applications and variations passed from master to disciple stemming from his own understanding of the base principles and experiential successes, but these three progressions cannot be neglected without compromising or dramatically slowing progress.

The inner mechanics of qigong will be discussed further in the Energy Analects to follow.

[Overlaying this reading is a rather perfunctory meditation montage. You know, the kind seen in every martial arts movie ever, where the hero is forced into solitude to find himself, and therein, the specific tools needed to overcome his adversary. So that's happening here, basically. But that doesn't mean it can't inspire.

Telescopic zoom edits take the viewer from a full frame shot of the meditator straight into and through his body to show the inner workings of his lungs, followed by the energy conversion occurring in cells, where ATP is formed through cellular respiration. This would be his foundational practice.

For the accumulation practice, we have a 3D rendering of bioelectricity conversion within the cell membrane as the sodium-potassium pump in the cell produces charge. This starts within the mesentery—that electrically conductive outer casing around the intestines that make the area act like a conductor—and then disperse throughout his small universe channels with what looks like emanating static charge.]

RZA: Yo, that's tight. I'm gonna try that shit. Why they gotta make this energy stuff so complicated? My master had me standing under a cold-ass waterfall and breathing backwards. That ain't natural. He got that inner fire and all, but...

FLASH: Ya, I thought this was good too. Caz always had me on the opposite; giving me far less and always sending me back to the basics. He's only ever had me on passive qigong, telling me whatever I could learn and develop could be done through that practice alone. And that was most in accordance with higher spirituality. He never went into detail, but hinted a few times at the power issue, like the pursuit of those skills can make you chase them not for spiritual advancement but for the power they give you over others. I think he was wary of me losing the essence in there. But no doubt, looking at these progressions, he's held me back. Or maybe I wasn't ready for more. Not worthy. Whatever it was, he kept this from me.

RZA continued reading,

> *Ballistic Weight Training is the integration practice within Lightness Training. It is analogous to standing meditation in the general curriculum, which balances the mind-body and imbues it with symmetry and antigravity lift. What standing meditation develops statically, ballistic weight training cultivates dynamically.*
>
> *Ballistic weight training:*
>
> *1) Removes tensional hindrances, thereby improving sensitivity and coordination.*
> *2) Conditions soft tissue and neural signaling to that of a heavier person. These, together, generate the capacity for effortless speed and reduce the risk of injury.*

Method:

Dig a hole 3 feet deep.
Add 3lbs to each ankle.
Begin in a calm, relaxed state.

In leaping add 10lbs to your torso. Release all tension with the mind, breathe into the abdomen and relax the shoulders. Leap and exhale in sharp, concerted effort. Incrementally increase resistance on the body and depth of the leaping hole. Maintain awareness at all times.

When running, begin only with weight added to the ankles, 3lbs to each. Set your relaxed pace for five to eight minutes, lightly jogging in place or for distance. Complete the session with one full-effort sprint to fatigue—never failure. And finish fresh.

If your ballistic effort lasts longer than forty seconds to one minute, the weight is insufficient or your effort is lacking. While sprinting, the mind should remain clear and relaxed, and breath should be comfortably settled in the abdomen.

If you cannot manage the above, reduce resistance, slow your pace, and humble yourself. Applying the same aggressive force of prior training will reap no results here. You must be empty of self, and as consciously aware of internal and external sensations as you are when standing. You should be conscious of the energy pulsing through you at all times.

[This parallel montage begins with a slow motion dressing of body weights—the weight vest and ankle weights. RZA is in the blurred background looking on. We cut into a close-up of him blowing a big ol' cloud of smoke and nodding with gangster approval. We see Flash close his eyes in relaxed focus, tension falling from his face, connecting with his breath. And, in one explosive effort, he leaps from a hole.

This footage quickly rewinds in rapid sequence, unwinding his training protocol to the beginning, where he and RZA trekked into the hills,

Flash with shovel in hand implying the leaping occurred after this scene. The steel hits the earth and tears a chunk out of it. Dirt is piled. A hole manifests.

Cut to Flash breathing naturally, a close-up of his face with rapidly transitioning and blurred background. This widens to reveal he's in an effortless, steady jog before an awesome mountain scape. He spontaneously kicks into high gear, sprinting all-out as hard as he can. For the run, he's not wearing the vest, only the ankle weights. Then we see him throw a few weighted kicks before throwing the weight vest on, most likely in dramatic slow motion, and falling into the hole to begin his leaping routine.]

RZA continued,

> *Efforts within Lightness training test maximum intensity, but they do not exhaust capacity. This leads to consistent, yet slower progress, yet constant readiness. For the master's game is not one of performance-based targets, but one of readiness for unexpected volatility in life. The disciple feels accomplished when he cannot do more. The master feels accomplished when he can.*
>
> *This subtle balance is captured in Lightness protocols, discussed below.*

RZA: Yo, I get this. It's like that old lesson of the two bulls, where the young bull says to the old, 'Let's *run* down this hill and fuck one of those cows,' and the old bull is like, 'Naaa, let's *walk* down and fuck 'em all.'

FLASH: Whoops…anyone ever tell you that you have a way with words, RZA?

> "Cock back my tongue like a hammer, my head is like
> A nickel-plated bammer, spit forty-five caliber grammar,"

RZA confirmed.

Flash spent the next four weeks putting into practice the pillars of Lightness, implementing them according to protocol guidelines outlined later in the scroll. RZA spent the next four weeks keeping on, smoking a bit, and supervising the master-in-training. Much of Flash's training was performed alone in the hills, so as not to raise suspicions of those residing on temple grounds. He'd need to take this training as far as possible before his formal challenge was issued, for he wasn't sure how things would proceed, and by whose timeline thereafter. In his mind, the clock was ticking, and he had less than six months to earn his freedom from the kept façade of purist ideals, freedom from his home.

The Essence of Lightness

"I know what you're doing," Flash heard before he matched the speaker to the voice. Flash, catching his breath from an intense set of leaping and rewarding himself for his efforts, was startled and quickly turned to face his voyeur. "I know I can't stop you. At least I can make sure you stand a chance to survive," said Grandmaster Caz, Flash's long-time mentor and, as he recently discovered, the only living keeper of the Art of Lightness.

Grandmaster Caz was watching from a distance, somewhat concealed by a tree, watching Flash attempt a basic Lightness protocol. As a warrior monk, Flash was an extraordinary specimen already. His kung fu was at master level. His physical conditioning was bar none. But he, like everyone who attempts Lightness, was making novice mistakes. Caz could see, even from a distance, that Flash's cadence was off. This meant his breath was off, and he was using far too much effort, creating far too much tension. Caz gave him the space to spend himself, to make his mistakes, just like Caz's Grandmaster did for him. For if you never feel the futility of fruitless effort, you'll never be humble enough to discard what you think you know.

"Master Caz, I…"

"It's okay. I'm not mad at you. Well, not anymore. I was at first. But I understand."

"How did you figure it out?"

"It wasn't that hard, actually. You've been more distant, secluding yourself more frequently. The scroll has mysteriously disappeared from the archives. And with the growing discontent around here—"

"RZA told you," Flash interjected.

"RZA told me," Caz confirmed. "He's worried about you, and rightly so. He pleaded with me, in fact, to at least speak with you. Claimed you were out in the woods *employing madness to accomplish the impossible*."

“He’s got a way with words,” Flash sarcastically noted for the second time, scrunching the right side of his lips. “Why would you help me with this, Caz? Why now, when you’ve been *the man* all this time?”

“Cause there’s too many tears, and too many sides
Too many “we gonna miss hims” and too many goodbyes
Too many flowers for baskets, too many caskets
Cause there’s too many shootings and not enough ass kicks,”

replied Caz. “In some ways I might even be jealous. This cloth is red for a shameful reason; it hides the blood. And it’s seen far more than it should. I’d be lying if I told you I didn’t have the same thoughts, a similar plan, and if my master didn’t speak sense into me once upon a time.”

“Thank you, Caz, it means more tha—”

“Your technique is wrong, by the way,” said Caz matter-of-factly.

“Excu… my technique? How long have you been watching me?”

“Long enough. And RZA is right. You’ll get yourself killed if you keep training the way you’ve been. The Guardians are no joke. No backyard tactics will give you a chance with them. Their kung fu is too deep. You need real skill, the kind that cannot be gamed or replicated quickly. And it starts with your breath.”

Caz pivoted 180 degrees and lunged three steps in sprint, and then four more.

Vertically.

Up a tree.

He took four steps up its thick trunk as effortlessly as a cat in chase. Before Flash knew what happened, Caz was sitting on the lowest hanging branch a clean fifteen feet above the earth. He sat there, looking down on Flash with a cocky smile, “Now you try.”

Flash’s mind started playing games with him. How, Flash wondered, did Caz, a man who must be well into his fifties, manage a feat that not even the younger peaked-out protectors could manage? Monks always wear robes. Is it possible Caz is stacked like a lion under those, ripped muscle atop ripped muscle? How? How? Was it really technique? And breathing technique no less?

“Waiting,” Caz nudged from above.

Flash lurched at the tree in what he felt was similar fashion, taking two aggressive steps up the trunk before sliding clumsily back down. The soles of his shoes tore bark off in a clear line the whole way down, and his palms gathered splinters as he tried to control his descent. He stumbled back but caught his balance. Frustrated and confused he attempted again with even more aggression. This time he landed a third step. Well, kind of.

In order to make the third point of contact, Flash needed to lean heavily away from the trunk. In so doing he managed to touch the tree a third time, just enough to kick himself away and drop eight feet onto the flat of his back. It was a good few minutes before his wind came back and he was able to face Caz, who now sat next to him, with a newfound respect.

"There is a lot more to Lightness than speed and power," Caz explained. "Those are byproducts but not the essence. Lightness isn't just more of the same. A common mantra in Shaolin is to relax, but when we say "relax," almost everyone hears "more power." The intention to generate force is willful and, as such, is at cross-purposes with the nature of things."

"But, Caz," said Flash, "with all due respect, there isn't anything in the scroll… I mean, the pillars; there's nothing new there…"

"Lightness didn't invent anything… lightness reinvented everything," replied Caz. "Lightness isn't about what you do, the specifics; it's in how you do them. Lightness permeates every aspect of life. It gives life."

"So what am I doing wrong?" Flash inquired in earnest.

"Will creates tension, and tension resistance, frequently in body but always in mind. Tension is who you think you should be. Relaxation is who you are. Yin is the key to Lightness. Not yang."

Ugh, Flash thought, rolling his brain-eyes. But he spoke more respectfully, "Please go on."

"These are dialectical forces, yes, but not independent of one another. The Tao of power is in understanding that tension that leads to power is not antithetical to relaxation but sprouts from it. This is a spectrum of performance capacity, not a static state. Most of our training produces tension in body and mind, despite all efforts to counteract it with flexibility, meditation, and conscious awareness. This is simply because when you finish meditating, you return to the conscious and unconscious structures that allow you to interpret your experience and make meaning in your life. This is the source of will—your identity.

"There are natural limits to tension," Caz continued. "But the relaxation from which it is born is near limitless. Most of your training to date has focused on tension, on yang.

Harder.
Faster.
More effort.

But the other, emptiness, is where Lightness dwells. Emptiness is not so easy to access. It can only be attained when thought is present, when breath is coordinated with movement, when movement is free of tension, when channels are open, and when action is empty of self. When you focus on emptiness over effort, you're practicing Lightness."

"Caz, man, I just want to kick some Guardian ass, not learn the essence of all things everywhere," Flash poked appreciatively.

Caz, in all gravity, replied, "Let's hope, for your sake, that isn't the same challenge.

A Naked Man Floats

Flash comfortably reclined at the base of a twisted cypress, cattycorner to the abbot's room. Sometimes, the safest deceit is to hide in plain sight, he figured. He covered his precious secret with another scroll on the history of temple diet like an abashed monk on a carriage ride from Dengfeng to Guangzhou, covering *Fifty Shades of the Emperor's Feisty Concubines* with *The Buddha's Last Sermon*. Nothing to see here. Just reading the classics.

Flash carefully studied the Energy Analects, the second section of the scroll. It contained a series of short appendices to the larger bodies of work on qi cultivation with specific notes on their application to the art of Lightness. Many of these texts can be nail bitingly obscure and impossibly indecipherable. Flash was pleasantly surprised at how grounded the language in this scroll felt, overall. Where many of the other texts on the topic deviate from the language of science and either enter more of a philosophical, if not mystical explanation for those things that lie beyond known biology and physics, herein lay an extremely practical framework for the application of qi.

This made sense upon reflection. If this were intended to prepare warriors for combat, what use is metaphor and flowery language? You need simple, unmistakable descriptions, reproducible experiments, and concrete instruction on implementation if survival is on the line. The simplicity of the document and its coherence and integration of many components generally considered ancillary or disparate topics came together with great clarity.

> *Qi, if we are to make any practical sense of this energy, is of organic origin and purely exists within the natural order of things. The human body is a battery, one that both generates and stores energy. This energy is no different from that of lightning or the spark that leaps space from metal to skin.*

Flash was amazed to see that these most basic principles were even diagrammed, formulas written for energy conversion, which, despite their archaic descriptions, made perfect empirical sense. His experience found a rational home in their descriptions.

> *The character Qi is unmistakably the composite of two other characters—rice and air (or vapor).*
>
> *These (rice and air) are the foodstuffs of energy in the human battery. The quality and quantity of both dramatically impact energy conversion and accumulation. Nutrition from the gut and air from the lungs converge in blood to create qi. Therefore, the health of the gut and the strength of the lungs together define the power of the man.*
>
> *But here, one must not overlook nature's profound rule of purification through pressure. The diamond is born from pressure; the warrior is born through fire. The human battery is enhanced when stressed.*
>
> *Quality of nutrition trumps all. A vegetarian diet without the addition of toxins or excitatory herbs and chemicals [garlic, onion, soy, caffeinated tea, coffee, alcohol] is essential for your internal burners to upregulate. Meat should only be consumed if ample supply of vegetables and rice aren't present to support energy and power. The sensitive master will know when that is.*
>
> *Second to quality is deprivation and excess. Fasting depletes storages, but it triggers greater conversion and storage capacity. When diet is restored, more of its nutrients are utilized. Excessive rice consumption energizes the body and stores energy.*
>
> *Quality of breathing trumps all. The regulation of breath, including pace and depth, is preeminent. Some call this rediscovering your natural breath. It resides in the liberated abdomen, not the upper chest. This should be at an intuitive level before manipulations within energy work can be fruitful.*

Second to quality is breath manipulation: hyperventilation, hypoventilation, and retention. Hyperventilation accumulates energy and excites the body. Hypoventilation and retention release energy and depress the body. These practices are internal to Lightness qigong progressions. Breath manipulations trigger profound supercompensations not unlike cold, heat, high elevation training, and extreme fatigue that stimulate healing, resilience, strength, and capacity.

There is no other source of qi in the human battery: rice and air. But in advanced Lightness practitioners, will alone is enough to augment and manipulate energy conversion within the body for healing or martial purposes. This is only possible, however, once the battery is charged, the channels are open, and the central nervous system is without inhibition; this is the Essence of Lightness.

With every paragraph, with each successive reading, Flash felt he was drifting further into uncertainty of the art. The language was relatively straightforward, yes. But his gut told him there was far more between the lines that could only be lived. This "capacity" the masters spoke of wasn't intellectual; it was biological. Real work would have to be done and the window to do it in was quickly closing. Thus began a series of experiments that integrated fasting and binge cycles, cold exposure, and hyperventilation.

Flash sat with RZA on the platform looking into the open temple courtyard, watching the other monks pass by on the way to the food hall. Flash's stomach rumbled with hunger, but the whites of his eyes were crystal clear, exuberant. RZA patted him on the shoulder in solidarity, and then left him to catch up with the others. No sense in both of them suffering.

***

Over the following weeks, Flash exposed himself to greater extremes and noticed rapid shifts in his energy and physique. His head was far clearer throughout the day, despite a voracious appetite that was exceedingly distracting at first, but which fell back within a manageable, though sustained hunger.

Watching the others head to breakfast and lunch was frustrating at first, but after a week or so, he didn't miss them at all. It also helped that he stopped watching them. He had bigger things to occupy himself with, and if the loss of a meal or two could defeat him, what the hell was he doing challenging the Guardians?

Forcing himself to train on empty, so to speak, was a whole new thing. It was torturous at first, but, again, after the first couple weeks, he felt a deeper surge of raw power that grew week after week. Those sessions on empty ensured his body drew from reserves, both in muscular capacity as well as body fat, and tapped every last resource he had.

He also felt the metabolic ramp-up that occurred during his post-training binge sessions. After getting his fill of fresh veg and occasionally meat or fish, which was integrated in this era for protector monks, he forced down a couple bowls of rice to top it off. Fellow monks looked on with confusion as he downed his entire day's ration in a single sitting. He could feel his muscles swell and his nervous system relax, which, on a full belly in need of digesting, made for some of the best nights of sleep he ever had.

Upon waking, Flash was surprised at how fresh and alert he felt. Though he was a man of mid-twenties he felt like he'd rebounded like a man ten years younger. And the shifts on the outside were just as pronounced as those inside. The fasting, training on empty, feeding, and resting cycles triggered something deep. The undereating phase of the day emptied his gut and carved what little fat he had stored to the bone, while the calorie surge at night restored his energy, healed damaged tissue, and swelled his muscles with deeper glycogen stores.

Flash frequently closed out his training sessions by testing himself beneath a cold mountain waterfall, standing within the fall's cascade in serene focus as beads pelted his head and shoulders. His hands pressed one another in front of his chest in common prayer formation. His lower abdomen oscillated at rapid pace to elevate his metabolism, draw in more air, and keep him warm and connected. His face was free of tension, carried away with each passing drop, as he embraced his immediate experience rather than numbly transcend it, bearing the cold with full presence and nonjudgment.

RZA, his faithful brother in arms would float naked in the still pool at the base of the waterfall, spittin' rhymes and drifting about:

> "Yo, don't waste your mind on time, don't chase the blind
> Don't eat swine, don't play yet neglect the grind
> Don't quote weak rhymes
> If you approached by a brother in need, give him shine
> Show him light, don't get emotional, son, don't fight
> Unless it's self-defense, to break the savage backs
> So he's crew could be convinced
> That any time you cross the line, we snap spines
> Split ya melon, down to the rind
> You be fucked up, yo.
> From the way I talk, no tellin' what you might hear
> BOODOODOODOO
> The words of wisdom is like a magnet to the ear"

***

Daily and weekly, Flash was beginning to see the shifts in mental acuity and physical performance that he assumed would coincide with Lightness Training. He dramatically reduced his total volume of training after chastisement from Caz, and it resulted not only in greater power within his short protocols but also far more energy in general, the walk-down-the-hill-and-fuck-em-all kind of energy.

This was counterintuitive at first, the idea that more is less, and less is more. The monster athletes the temple produced had stamina of Olympic caliber in general, so earned by running for hours, practicing fist forms until they couldn't stand, crawl-walking on hands and feet down endless stairs from the great Buddha statue to the temple, and fighting rounds upon rounds against challenging brothers. Their reputations preceded them, and for good reason.

But Flash could tell for many years that progress in strength for many monks capped young, in their late teens or early twenties before reaching a point of diminishing returns. They still grew in strength, but gains were far slower and harder fought for. The same went for skills, which generally peaked out in mid to late twenties under the same pattern. But there were no Shaolin theories of training that explained why the efficacy of their practices needed to plateau when they did. It was just the way things were done. More was considered better.

Flash's reduction in volume, new breathing practices, and oscillation of nutrient intake with heavy training coming just prior to feeding were like tapping a new well of energy, and systems that had grown dormant were revived. He was gaining muscle at a rate he hadn't seen in nearly a decade when his hormones were peaked in puberty. So too could he feel his pulse, constantly pronounced and smooth. He never needed to touch a finger to his wrist or neck; he could feel from any region his pulse from within that region itself. And beyond his pulse was another form of movement, augmented week on week within his breathing sessions, sometimes heat, sometimes cool, but always a tingling flow of energy.

Rice and air—glycogen and oxygen—the foodstuffs of qi. One thing was clear; Lightness was about balance. The Tao of power as Caz called it, but it wasn't balance in the way Flash first envisioned. It wasn't about the middle path, but about testing boundaries and maximizing capacities. Balance was arrived at through one's biological homeostatic response to extremes: *The diamond from pressure, the warrior through fire.*

Lightness hadn't added anything new in the sense that techniques were created or changed… but the way they were applied changed everything. All monks ate but they didn't eat like Flash. All monks breathed but they didn't breathe like Flash. And all monks trained, but they didn't… well, time will tell if this tree bears fruit.

Despite his explosive progress and despite Caz's agreement to teach, Flash continued to scratch a persistent itch, to ruminate on that question that first arose in the Wisdom of the Ancients, one that seemed to imply something of his readiness—why had Caz waited so long to teach him the art?

A Vessel With Holes

"Focus!" ordered Caz. "Patience!" Young junior monk Flash's legs trembled with strain, his brow furrowed, face winced, and structure began to collapse. Monks learn to fight through the pain early, because the pain that accompanies a quitter is far worse. But that doesn't mean training was anything short of excruciating at times.

Flash was practicing stance and footwork with his small cohort under the tutelage of Master Caz, who was known even then as a compassionate monk but a severe teacher. Caz watched his young cohort (one of several classes under his guidance), this one ages five to eight, strain and struggle and cry following their orders.

Caz understood what they were going through, and he knew there was no other way. So, while he felt their suffering, he showed no empathy. When his pupils cried out from their trembling horse stances he only replied, "Stay focused."

What made this session more defeating than normal for young Flash was their close proximity to another class of just slightly more experience, practicing skills that looked far more fun. They were rotating through acrobatic sequences, practicing jump spinning leaps with long pauses of rest in-between, and occasionally adding in flashy kicks here and there. Flash's eyes were fixated on some of the boys to distract himself from the pins and needles in his legs.

One at a time, Flash's classmates started to drop, and, in due time, Flash did as well. The point of this drill wasn't for them to sustain but to fail. They learn that failing is inevitable, and then they're taught later, after the strength forged from failing efforts begins to surface, that failure isn't acceptable. But all in due time. The boys felt ashamed and defeated, but they had each other and knew they weren't alone in their shame.

"Why can't we practice what they're doing?" Flash called out boldly. The other boys scooted slightly away from him. They all wanted to do the same but were too timid to ask.

"Why would you like to do that?" Caz inquired.

"It looks more fun," replied Flash.

"Do you want to learn kung fu? Or do you want to have fun?" challenged Caz.

"Can't we do both? Aren't they practicing kung fu?"

"It would seem so, wouldn't it? Tomorrow, I'll give you another lesson, Flash, one that may help explain the difference."

Flash's classmates scrunched their faces and cowered for what they imagined that lesson might entail. And though he asked what all of them wished to know, they didn't wish for the outcome.

The next morning at five a.m., as instructed, Flash arrived at Caz's living quarters. He found that it was more or less the same as his; only there was one bed instead of four, and two potted orchids on his windowsill. They were quite striking and captivated his attention, drawing in light and emanating florescent light-green petals with a splash of dark red on the lips. The stems seemed to be of miniature bamboo, with clearly defined green and brown alternating segments. Flash had never seen this flower before.

"Choose one," insisted Caz.

"Choose one for wh—"

"To take care of."

"Really? But why?"

"Because I need help looking after them. Well, help with one. These are very special flowers—Tiěpí shíhú (Dendrobium officinale). Aside from their aesthetic beauty, they have powerful medicinal properties that can heal deep disease and replenish lost qi. You're going to help me look after one of them for a few weeks. You just need to choose which one."

The orchids were quite similar. Both healthy with a similar number of stems. But their vessels could not have been more different—one an ornamental porcelain pot with hand-painted floral designs, and the other a tired-old wooden box that looked as if its functional days were numbered.

"I choose whichever I want?" Flash confirmed.

"Correct."

"I choose this," Flash said, pointing at the glossier of the two. "How do I take care of it?"

"Come by my quarters once a day after breakfast. Add a teacup of water. And that's all. I'll take care of the other flower myself. You just need to make sure you water it daily. Got it?"

"Got it," replied Flash with a straighter back and pushed out chest. His spirit lifted with new responsibility, with what felt like Caz's confidence in him.

Morning after morning, day after day, young Flash arrived on schedule and watered his flower. He beamed with reward of his choice, the glistening porcelain that he and only he got to look after. He knew it was far more valuable than the wooden box, for it was shiny and expensive-looking. And he couldn't be happier watching the flower grow for the first week. But something changed halfway through week two.

Flash was still showing up daily, watering his flower as instructed. He'd even seen Caz water the other plant in similar fashion. But clear differences between the two were beginning to surface. Flash's flower began to wilt. Not altogether, but some of the petals curled in on themselves. Some of the stems stood less boldly. And, with time, the differences grew. Caz's flower only looked more and more vibrant in that shoddy old box, while Flash's flower was clearly suffering. Its color was lackluster; its posture was tired. It was dying.

When reality set in, Flash experienced a spectrum of emotion, from sadness to guilt, from anxiety to fear. He'd failed Master Caz in the most basic of tasks. What had gone wrong?

Caz found Flash sitting with head in hands, back against the wall beneath the windowsill that supported the pots. He was trying to sob quietly but failing. Caz put his hand on Flash's shoulder and told him it was okay. He told him that *this* was his lesson.

Flash peered up behind watery eyes, confused. "My lesson? To kill your flower?"

"You didn't kill the flower, Flash. I did, even before you chose which one you wanted to care for."

"But, wh-how?"

"Add four teacups worth of water to each pot."

"But that's too much."

"Give it a try and watch what happens." Flash followed instructions. "Now wait a minute and watch."

After a minute, water began to flow out from under the porcelain pot. And only the porcelain pot. Flash waited a minute longer. And another. The wooden box lost nothing. The porcelain pot was sitting in a pool of sediment-soaked brown water.

"Pick it up, Flash, check the bottom." Flash did so to learn that his pot had minor cracks and gaps exacerbated by the pressure of the soil and the moisture added daily, compromising the structure of the pot as the roots grew. He picked up the wooden box, and it was thoroughly protected.

"Why did you give me a pot with holes in it?" asked Flash angrily.

"I didn't; you chose it. *Why*...did you choose it?"

"Because...because it looked more special I guess. Full of holes... the flower is dead." Tears began to cloud his sight again.

"For something as precious as this orchid to flourish, it must be contained in the right container. If forced into the wrong one, both the flower and the vessel will be ruined. A vessel with holes is no place for something precious."

"Do you have something else that's precious to look after?" asked young Flash.

"I have. I have."

Weeks later, Flash was called from his room in the early eve by a fellow student. He was asked to report to the room of a Shaolin councilman. Upon arrival, he learned the elder was very ill. Caz was beside him, checking his pulses. "Flash, I need you to fetch me the orchid, as well as a mixing chalice and pestle." Flash did as he was told and brought the surviving orchid in the tired old box along with the mixing chalice and pestle to the councilman's room.

Caz held the base of a stem at the soil and slowly twisted and pulled until it broke. He placed the stem and it's flower in the chalice and began to slowly grind away at it. Moments later another young monk arrived with freshly boiled water in a teapot. Caz dropped the ground orchid into the boiled water and let it steep for a couple minutes, cooling just slightly, before pouring a teacup worth for the sick man next to him.

On Flash's slow walk to return the remainder of the orchid to Caz's room, he recalled his week's worth of care for the wrong flower. He realized if he'd chosen more carefully, not distracted by aesthetics, that he could have nurtured the flower that now gives life to the sick.

The following day, suffering in horse stance, Flash's strain was no longer in protest to the training he wanted to escape at all costs like his brothers beside him, but only in the fierce focus and heartfelt desire to seal all holes.

It Begins with Hope

"How long has he been preparing?" asked Councilman 3.

"We're not certain," replied one of Councilman 3's personal guardians. "Reports are somewhere between three and four months of abnormal training habits, though his progress seems to exceed that length of time."

"This is Grandmaster Caz's student?" followed Councilman 3.

"It is, but as far as we can tell, he's gone rogue, minus that droopy-eyed dolt that smokes more than he trains," said the second guardian present.

"This isn't anything yet, Councilman, it's just that—"

"You suspect a formal challenge."

"We do."

"Is this *Flash* mentally deranged?" asked the councilman with a sarcastic bend of Flash's name. "You aren't actually concerned he could challenge the Guardians and win, are you?"

"No, Councilman, that's not our concern. Our concern is that he doesn't lose shamefully enough to squelch any similar thoughts of dissent that may exist in the minds of discontented monks."

"Discontented monks," the councilman smirked. "Discontented for what? They live peacefully, eat amply, and have no concern for the necessities of life."

"Respectfully, Councilman, there is having no concern for necessities, and then there is having no concern for necessities with the comforts of cuisine, coin, and influence."

"Despite their vows, Councilman," said the other guardian, "the minds of the monks are free to drift where they please, and they please to see inequity. We cannot wrong them for that."

Councilman 3 chuckled. "Inequity. What inequity? They have everything in life taken care of, and all the space and freedom one needs for spiritual development. They don't understand, cannot understand or appreciate the lengths the council goes to protect them."

"That may be so, sir, but let's be candid. The temple is not a classless society. We are not here with you to shake the system or judge the actions of the councilmen. But the monks see what they see, and they're not wrong in doubting the integrity of temple leadership. There are… inconsistencies."

"What we're trying to say, Councilman…" said the other, "What we're trying to ask is… do you want us to squelch the rumors before they grow further. Before a formal challenge is issued. Accidents do happen."

"Break this down for me. Make it crystal clear. You don't believe this *Flash* poses a real threat to the 18. But you fear…?"

"We fear he doesn't die quickly enough. Flash is a formidable talent; we have observed him for fifteen years. It's unlikely an average protector would pose a challenge for him in a one-to-one match, especially now. And we cannot say with certainty any individual guardian would fare better."

"So...?"

"So, the sight or hearing of Flash taking down even one or, as unlikely as it is, several of us within a challenge before he's killed may be enough to instill hope in the minds of others. It all begins with hope, sir. Once that challenge begins, our identities will no longer be a secret to this generation and the veil of mystery will be torn. Plans and strategies can be made to address us with specificity."

"I can't believe I'm hearing these petty fears from the best warriors the temple has to offer. We have failed you in that."

"Sir, we're just—"

"I've heard enough. You think you've been trained to steal a life in the night? You're our Guardians, and nothing will prevent a mutiny better than you showing up in full force and performing the task you've been charged with. I've heard your concerns and I take them. For now, no issuance has been made and no blood will be shed. Should he challenge for his freedom," Councilman 3 shook his head with utter disbelief at the sound of his own words, "you'll prove your reputation is no trivial thing to be challenged ever again. You'll do it in front of all eyes that find a peering hole in the courtyard walls so that all ears in the temple hear of the foolishness, the futility, of challenging the Guardians of the Shaolin Temple."

"Yes, Councilman."

"Yes, Councilman."

The Craftsman's Reveal

The *Essence* section of the Lightness scroll opened with a parable about a farmer and the uncertain events involving his son. It was paradoxical in the way it revealed events, and there was no interpretation given for it. What followed seemed entirely dissociated from it, or was it? Regardless, Flash read on:

> *The essence of Lightness is the coalescence of three key forces: dedication to protocol, heightened sensitivity, and a mind that deals in probabilities. These forces further balance and enhance the efficacy of the others. Dedication without optionality is death. Optionality without consistency is psychosis.*
>
> *Lightness protocols are minimalistic compared to Shaolin foundations, which successfully cover the wide spectrum of human development. Lightness assumes this foundation, a foundation that cannot be shortcut or bypassed. Protocols of Lightness are sublimit, minimal training windows that integrate with the rest of life.*
>
> *The objective is simple, but not easy: to attain the body-breath where thought, action, and breath are integrated without inhibition. In such a state, the master's movements become poetry and his thoughts hurricane winds, where he safely resides in its still eye.*
>
> *This requires the removal of the perceived stress of training, as well as the compulsion to "do more." Lightness protocols are an exercise in reducing one's attachment to training, for most of the volume and technical training must be given up if Lightness is going to take hold.*

Lightness protocols are not designed to exhaust but to energize. They are conscious windows of sensitivity practice, rather than forceful expressions of will. The concentration required, therefore, trumps all efforts that come prior, many of which can be cheated with wavering attention. Lightness is a byproduct of the practice of quality.

Quality of movement. Quality of thought. Quality of breath.

How to execute the protocol: relaxed abdominal breath - ballistic weight sequence - dynamic stretching sequence - strength sequence done prior to qigong or at other short intervals throughout the day. Qigong practiced immediately post-protocol aids in minimizing residual tension from strength efforts and exploits the residual energetic after-burn.

The master of Lightness must always remember that his domain is not training. His domain is life. His purpose is not to train for the sake of training, but to train for balance in life. If his energy is spent in training, he has only enough energy for more training. If his training is integral to life, just enough to trigger environmental adaptation, then he retains his energy and has ample in stock for uncertainties ahead.

Sensitivity is the birthchild of structure and awareness. Physical structure is the conduit of relaxation, relaxation the vacuum from which awareness accesses information. The sum total of all structural training, standing meditation, and stance work, all aim to remove the pressures of gravity on the human frame. Without the pull of gravity, physical tension has no purpose. Without tension, the body comes alive in health and power.

A Shaolin master will be versed in the theories and structures of power born from tension. This is foundational practice. The master of Lightness will know the other, the vacuum from which power stems. There are natural limits to the power potential of skeletal muscles, due to size, conditioning, and technical proficiency. But the other, relaxation, is a near bottomless well of energy. It is the yin from which yang is expressed in its greatest degree.

The master of Lightness, therefore, is not concerned with maximizing immediate power expression, but is focused on the other side of the spectrum, the well of relaxation. For in that state of relaxation, sensitivity comes alive and energy permeates every cell in the body. When overcoming the resistance of added weight, relaxed, ballistic effort tonifies fascia in the body and heightens sensitivity and intuitive coordination.

Sticking points in movement reveal themselves in ballistic weight training just as standing meditation reveals imbalances and overcompensations in tensional forces. For this training to be effective as not merely a speed or coordination exercise, but to be a conduit of heightened sensitivity and spiritual development, speed and tension should not exceed awareness of the body breath – that is the pulsing wave of effort that creates movement. This is the physiology of Lightness.

Sensitivity is a qualitative state. But quality in this case is not independent of the volume of data. Sensation in the body is an extension of the mind. It can be augmented in relaxation or stifled in tension. The nervous system is a circuit that collects environmental feedback and distributes information stemming from thought. This is a dynamic system alive in reciprocity and adaptation.

Awareness of sensate information in its purity must be trained beyond the limits of bias. Bias is dictated by the unconscious patterns in thought and action that excite here and numb there. A master of Lightness is fully alive, not merely alive in a subset of experiential phenomena. This nondiscrimination of sensate information and the master's coordinated response to it is the height of human-environment fitness. This is the aspiration of the student of Lightness.

The psychology of Lightness is that of unbridled, creative freedom. Sitting atop a structured foundation of Lightness protocols that anchor the student to place and time, randomness and optionality are buoys that keep him afloat. Nonattachment is a foundational skill of Zen well cultivated by the master of Shaolin. But there are deeper freedoms accessed only through the unpredictability of chaotic environments – like that of war.

This chaos can be replicated with devices of chance that allow for the random expression of multiple selves at once. A mind that isn't bound by what it knows is free to know all. A mind that is free of compulsion to filter probability can access possibility. This is training that requires mentorship, for to access the deepest freedoms of mind, those attachments that bind it to fixed notions of self must first be broken.

If the mind becomes untethered from a grounding protocol, it can drift wildly in the winds of uncertainty. This is the risk of the highest practice. There is darkness in it. This darkness will not only be illuminated in the mind, it will manifest dark realities. Chance does not discriminate; neither will the unraveling mind of the student of Lightness. Therefore, the greatest point of caution in the application of chance is grounding to protocol, for it's the tether that prevents Lightness from becoming darkness.

Flash set the scrolls down at this point, that sense of being in over his head growing to a point of asphyxiation. This wasn't training. This wasn't some technical shift or insight that was going to allow him to declare victory. This was life shit with something all too real at stake—the potential loss of self.

The swell of reverence one feels in the presence of a true craftsman grew within Flash, that awe-inspired humility that creates natural order where elders have wisdom and youth have energy and there's just so much beauty in it all. Sitting cross-legged by candlelight on the dimly lit floor of his concrete block of a room, scroll splayed out before him, he felt the magnitude of meaning within the words he studied.

This isn't the grand victory, he realized. *It's the beginning of my journey, if I choose to partake. I can't hack this. I can't game this. And I cannot know this, not fully, without living it.* He recalled Caz's words:

Lightness isn't about what you do, the specifics; it's in how you do them. Lightness permeates every aspect of life. It gives life.

It hit like a White Lotus fist. Flash had experienced *the craftsman's reveal* many times over through his martial and meditative practices. Things he thought he understood rather quickly were revealed only later to be partial and perspectival, if not altogether flawed, as the depth of massively complex topics and skills unveiled themselves in thorough practice. This phenomenon, the interplay between mastery and ignorance isn't linear, Flash reflected. Those who skip from craft to craft and interest to interest in life without long-term commitment to a thing are blind as to their own process of becoming, which is relational, not solipsistic.

The smartest monk in the room is very quick to criticize and judge and determine the veracity or appropriateness of a thing, but he often speculates in a void of indeterminacy, and not one of direct experience. Many are quick to judge and *get* the thing, never to realize they're at the front-end of a competency curve, and that true depth of understanding is a long-tail process. It's a process that requires delusion-confronting experiences that cause crises of confidence. It requires skin in the game.

This chasm, the one between perceived knowing and actual comprehension, is one of nonrationality. This only the craftsman truly understands. The masters of Lightness understood this.

Flash understood the very first day he practiced standing meditation that it was a laboratory of integration. He felt present and was able to quiet his mind. He felt relaxed and was able to sense the interconnected parts of his frame with little inhibition. He thought he *got* it and so proceeded. albeit knowingly, for years. It was only after thousands of hours of standing still that his consciousness grew to envelop even the tips of his toes and the internal structures of his frame. It took years before he realized that presence and life are synonyms, as the more present one becomes, in the sense that increasing volumes of sensate data are accessible to immediate consciousness in real time, the more life one actually experiences.

Sure, this was accompanied by your general structural cues, the external rotation of shoulders and hips, the straight feet and semitucked tailbone, the lifted Crown Point and tongue pressed to palate. But these were not the thing itself; they were conduits to the thing. The summation of parts did not equal the whole. They were triggers that allowed access, keys that allowed the door to open. They all made sense from day one. They were not truly comprehended for years… the craftsman's reveal.

He felt a churning in his gut along with a faint nausea. He was like a big fish in a small pond transported to a larger pond, realizing just how distorted its perspective was. *I'm not at the top. I'm at the bottom. Again.* This is a feeling the craftsman rarely forgets, because he understands that art evolves. He also understands there are consequences to sustaining false assumptions. But the pedant, the person who thinks *getting* is *knowing*, will forever have small-pond delusion as the big pond is thrust upon them, again and again, without recognizing their persistent choice of standing dead center on the train tracks. Such is life. Flash relished the reminder.

The Long Game

Four months in, and two months out from his moment of truth, Flash began to see what he suspected was between the lines of the scroll all along after his first reading. RZA had brashly concluded the pillars were rudimentary enhancements of the more-of-the-same camp and failed to see that the larger insights lay more in what the masters weren't saying than what they were. That is, the key lay in doing, and doing only, the protocol as prescribed.

Flash had worked his way up to more than eight pounds on each ankle when running, and over fifty pounds added to his torso when leaping from his gradually deepening leaping hole. The difference in ease of dynamic stretching and footwork drills with added weight had been bridged. Naturally, he was slower wearing weight, but the inefficiencies of movement that the weights first highlighted had been smoothed out. But when he took the weights off—oh, when he took the weights off—the same monk he was not.

The integrated approach to breathing, relaxation, and ballistic training transferred better than he could have ever imagined. What was a lumbering hike to his training local in the hills at first was now an effortless, spring-stepped jog where no part failed him. His lungs had ample air, his legs ample strength. And, more importantly, his body was alive with information. He was constantly aware of his breath, his pulse, the subtle tingling of energetic power, and the effortless, efficient interrelation of his bodily parts. It was a feeling he wanted to share, a power he wanted to demonstrate. But it wasn't time. He needed to carry this as far as possible to buy himself as much of an edge as possible. That was the game.

Flash had discontinued his other training almost altogether to devote himself to the path of Lightness. To his pleasant surprise, on the occasions where he would revisit this or that technique, this or that form, they hadn't regressed in the slightest. In fact, most had improved, as did his perception of the time in which they took place. When he picked up his whips, he noted how far mentally ahead he was in a sequence or pattern, even to the point of innovating new patterns on the fly. And all this without losing his sense of presence and sensitivity within his body.

While the others could not feel what he felt, they could see the marked improvements in his fluency and articulation with his weapons when he'd wield them. Eyebrows were beginning to rise. Rumors were starting to spread.

Flash had learned many fist and weapon forms over his career, and one of the greatest challenges, perhaps the defining characteristic of a master in the making versus a serial novice, is in their ability to suspend what they know to immerse themselves in the *other*.

Fist forms are narratives, interpretations of the complex domain of combat. Each reflects the sum total of knowledge that it's originator had as an integrated approach. The problem lay in the nature of combat itself. No two warriors had identical experience. So, despite decades of conscientious research and application, what holds true for one may not hold true to the same extent for another. Forms may, however, be a great guiding light, and that's what all protectors take stock in, until that day comes when their own internal form coalesces and manifests organically.

Inherent in this process is the knowledge that each form teaches something essential, but it doesn't teach everything. This instills in the mind of the young monk that there's always something more, and the other likely contains what I'm missing. So, the hungry warrior voraciously consumes form after form, filling in gaps and complementing the whole. And it works. It works extraordinarily well, in fact, hence the reputation of warrior monks worldwide. There's only one problem.

It's impossible to discern which habitual patterns of thought and action are at cross-purposes with new methods. Flash was gifted in this domain. He was able to absorb new information and movement like a sponge because he could empty himself of who he was and what he knew with relative ease. He was able to train without fixation on outcome. This delayed his fighting ability when he was young because he refused to filter out what did not work immediately (which was largely context dependent) and, therefore, failed to apply the ready and relevant as rapidly as the others, who learned only to one end: to gain an immediate edge. But by the time Flash's repertoire began to complete the circle, his foundations were so strong that his abilities catapulted his performance in combat well beyond his peers and into that of protectors several years his senior.

This was a long-game approach that Flash was gifted with due to his temperament, and nothing more. It was coincidental. But it gave him insight into the relationship between the practitioner and the forms that few others had. Forms, as independent interpretations are coherent and pure. But in the mind and body of a student, they create glitches like incompatible algorithms. And the only workaround that Flash had identified through natural proclivity was suspending all other algorithms to master the one. This meant not judging a fist form prematurely, and certainly not judging it against other forms. This is far easier said than done, especially when weekly fighting sessions pushed them to their psychological edges to find the fastest routes to domination.

In many cases, the tools you've come to rely on are the very ones that scramble their possible superior replacements after sufficient practice. And the student is incapable of seeing this internal conflict just as a finger cannot point to itself and an argument cannot assess its own coherence.

Yin is the key to Lightness, Caz told him. And Flash had tasted that truth. The weights on his body acted as mirrors, reflecting points of tension back at him, and triggering conscious awareness of all sticking points within his movements. This gave Flash the opportunity to address them one after another and release them altogether. And as he learned to let go of these sticking points as a matter of habit now, his mind became accustomed to auditing his thoughts and applying the same practice to his mind.

Points of stress and fixed judgments were quickly identified and released just as he would release a muscle knot and improve the coordination of his movement. His mind gained similar coherence as he learned to release judgment with a mere breath, like a spread out bed sheet that eliminates all crimps and creases with a single splay.

A master of Lightness is fully alive, not merely alive in a subset of experiential phenomena.

The constant state of awareness Flash experienced, his sensitivity to environmental information, and his ability to coordinate and integrate holistic responses was a state altogether new to him. It was a state that he could only describe as pure life. It was a state so rewarding that it alone, his personal survival and escape aside, would motivate him to commit to this path for its own sake. The performance benefits were extraordinary, but the renewal of life Lightness granted was as close to a drug as a detoxified mind could know.

While Flash discontinued nearly all other training, he did throw in regular attempts at scaling that damn tree. The memory of his dramatic humbling persisted despite his awesome developments of late. He'd truly taken his power, speed, and agility to new heights but remained baffled by the effortlessness of Caz's demonstration months prior.

Flash was currently at three clean steps, which either ended in a controlled descent with shoe on bark friction, a devil-may-care reckless fourth touch that pushed him away from the tree and into uncontrolled free fall (he didn't try many of those), or a dive onto the branch of Caz's perch, minus the grace and with twice the oomph. He was getting closer, but not nearly close enough. And every attempt revived that vivid image of Caz staring down at him… waiting.

As far as Flash had come, he was consistently reminded of how much better Caz was, and this spurred him on with inspiration and resentment.

A Boy's Superstition

Flash and Caz stood shoulder to shoulder in the spacious council hall. The room had large wooden doors to the left and right that could open the room up into a well-lit indoor-outdoor space, but which were now closed and letting in little light through window like slits. Torches were lit on the platform before them, on both sides of nine empty chairs. They exchanged a few quips while waiting for the council.

"Know I wanna see if you can rock my beat.
now all hip-hop beats go boom tap
so check this out.
b***on number one is boom
and b***on number 2 is tap.
now here comes the beat,"

said Flash.

Caz wasn't having it, though.

"I don't like to boast that I'm better than most
But if you try to get beside yourself, I'll roast you
And your boy, or any MC toy
If you think that you can mess with the Real McCoy!"

They bumped fists and straightened at attention as the council entered the room and took their seats. Caz called together the council on Flash's behalf, something they agreed upon in advance. Done improperly, leaving the Shaolin order is the highest crime. Leaving in full compliance with the law was an acceptable honor. Caz wanted to make sure that Flash's challenge would be fairly considered. He also wanted to get a personal sense of whether, on the off (very off) chance that Flash won, he'd be hunted down postchallenge by temple sentinels.

Councilman 5, centered among them, spoke first, "Do I understand you're here today to challenge for your free passage from Shaolin?" His bald head and long white beard added a sense of solemnity to the procedure. His eyes were warm, but very sharp, giving the impression of a man of high intelligence and depth. And his movements were well calculated. In a way, Flash felt reassured in his presence.

"Yes, Grandmaster," replied Flash.

"May I ask why you want to surrender your vows?"

"Yes, Grandmaster, I… I don't believe the temple has maintained its commitme—"

"Who are you to judge us?" shouted Councilman 9.

"Let him speak," said number 1.

Flash continued,

"A child is born with no state of mind
Blind to the ways of mankind
Buddha is smilin' on you but he's frownin' too
Because only Buddha knows what you'll go through
You'll grow in the temple livin' second-rate
And your eyes will sing a song called deep hate
The places you train and where you stay
Looks like one great big alleyway
You'll admire all the number-book takers
Thugs, pimps and pushers and the big money-makers
Drivin' big carriages, spendin' copper and gem
And you'll wanna grow up to be just like them, huh
Smugglers, scramblers, burglars, gamblers
Pickpocket peddlers, even panhandlers

Turned faithless kid, but look what you done did
Got set up for a lifetime bid
Now your manhood is took and you're in a funk
Spend the next fifty years as a spiritless monk
Bein' used and abused to serve like hell
Til one day, you was found hung dead in your cell
It was plain to see that your life was lost
Heart was cold and your body done paid the cost
But now your eyes sing the sad, sad song
Of how you lived outcast and died so young"

"High Council," continued Flash, "I humbly request the opportunity, which is my right, to challenge the Guardians for my freedom. I'm not here to cast judgment on you, but to choose my path. I have strong conviction that the direction of the temple and my personal values are no longer aligned." Caz was impressed that Flash spoke so bluntly. You never know what will come out when face to face with the council.

Number 2 inquired, "Flash, we know who you are. We know you're a monk of virtue. Some of us understand your discontent. I would just like to implore you to consider that if you remain, you can be a force for change. Leaving, should you succeed, solves only your problem. This is your right, yes. But if you proceed and fail, there will be no change here of the type you desire, and your life may be cut short."

This appeal was unexpected, and a reasonable one at that. Flash had always seen solidarity in temple leadership. He'd never even considered if the corruption and degradation of values was uniform. This was his first hint that even among the council, unresolved issues and discord existed. And on a personal level, what does this decision say about his commitment to compassion if he's unwilling to be a part of the solution?

"To be honest, Councilman, I'm not hopeful that I can affect the change I desire. And perhaps I selfishly want to focus on a narrower scope of influence."

"Selfish indeed," chimed in number 6.

"Let him fight," followed Councilman 3, leaning aggressively forward. "It's his life, his funeral. And it'll be good for the Guardians to sharpen their teeth again, so to speak. If he can fight, let him fight."

Councilman 5 stepped back into the conversation. "Grandmaster Caz, do you take responsibility for your senior student here? Do you find him of sound mind and able body to participate in mortal combat against extraordinary odds?"

"I do, Councilman," replied Caz. "I only request that the challenge be set six weeks from now, to allow both master Flash and the Guardians to prepare sufficiently."

The council burst into uproarious laughter. "Six weeks for *the Guardians*?" said number 3. "Sure, let's do that. They'll need all the time they can get." Laughter exploded a second time. It exploded from all but one—number 5.

Councilman 5 knew something the others didn't. He knew that the man vouching for this mad challenger was the only living master of Lightness. And as his panel wiped their eyes and held their guts, number 5 stared deeply into Caz's eyes, those unwavering beads of ice and light, and he felt something he hadn't felt in many years—fear.

He reflected inward and allowed himself a moment of meditation to address this lingering superstition, a trigger for an emotion long abandoned. He recalled, as a young monk of fifteen having a campfire chat with his grandmaster and listening to the legends of the masters of Lightness, men as powerful as lions and light as feathers. The masters were no ordinary protectors.

"When attacking, you strike vapor; when defending you meet a hurricane," was how the old adage went, referring to the purported futility of fighting a master of Lightness. There was a time when the 18, as well as the highest-ranking protectors, were all required to study the art. Some were so proficient in skill and free in mind that they entered battle with no weapons at all; for battle would provide them the weapons they would need, as they would need them.

No army led by masters of Lightness could lose, or at least that was legend. All monks aspired to qualify for this highest of tutelage, as did Councilman 5 as a young monk… until it was forbidden. He remembered clear as day, as if it were yesterday, his grandmaster's reply when he asked him, "By what fist (style) would you fight a master of Lightness?"

His master replied without making eye contact, staring into dancing flames as if reliving a moment of deep impression, "You cannot fight a ghost."

And here now sat Councilman 5, a man of eighty years of age, carrying the superstitions of a boy. *This journey of transcendence is never truly complete,* he reflected. *The student is well alive in the master and the two shall never part.* Yes, he felt fear for what might become of the Shaolin temple.

"Six weeks!" Councilman 5 shouted over the laughter. "Six weeks to the day. Notify the Guardians. Good luck, young master Flash. You will need it."

Word travels fast of a formal challenge, and it travels very fast when one rogue monk is ballsy enough to challenge the Guardians. After Flash's meeting with the council, incredible hype and excitement circulated. Flash was not only of sound mind and able body. His skills were such that, though he certainly couldn't win, the monks pondered if he could. Many were dead-sure it was suicide. But some who had known him, judged him to be someone not to underestimate. And that made things interesting.

Five such monks, formidable protectors in their own rights, got to talking. They knew that Flash was a monk of high moral character, nearly above reproach and disciplined to the tilt. If he were making a challenge like this, perhaps it was for good reason. Perhaps it was even for the same reason that each of them had considered the same at one time or another—seeds that didn't flower. Either way, this was, by far, the most charged moment in recent temple history, and their minds were elated with the mere possibility of victory.

***

Flash spent months training in the shadows, preparing in secret so as not to raise suspicions of his grand intentions. Now that the challenge had been issued and what-if-he-does-this scenarios dominated temple conversations, Flash had passed the point of no return. He was in it now, exposed and committed. And while he'd made profound gains in performance to date, he had yet to address the obvious problem of strategy against the many.

Flash, in the middle of a set of weighted leaping, turned to spot the source of shuffling and crunching forest brush to find a confident Caz with five furious protectors behind him. As prescient as ever, Caz anticipated the urgent need for resilient bodies for Flash to run combat simulations with.

Fighting many is vastly different than facing only one. And five reaches the upper limit of effective engagement before things get too messy on the side of the many. Space is required to strike, and five would complete a circle of attack. The Furious Five would teach Flash to push the boundaries of multiplayer combat. Caz called out to his weighted disciple to introduce his new sparring partners, five of the most capable protectors the temple possessed, "I've got fresh meat for ya!"

A Device of Chance

"Listen to me, Flash," said Grandmaster Caz, "The Guardians taught you everything you know. But they didn't teach you everything *they* know. Do not commit the mistake of assuming what you see is all that there is. It's not possible for you to beat 18 guardians. It isn't possible for any man alone to beat them. That's why this rule exists. No one leaves Shaolin…at least not according to the rules."

"I don't need to beat them all, Caz; I just need you to help me survive long enough to make it through that gate."

"That's a bigger request than you realize. I won't leave you to face them unprepared. I promised you that. But be warned, this isn't a promise of victory. Answer me this: if someone knows everything you know, if they know everything you could conceivably do, what's the only reasonable option left?

I don't know," Flash chuckled nervously, "Is not being me an option?"

"Not bad…" Caz smiled. "It is. It's THE option." Caz reached into his robes and pulled out a wooden die. "You've read the scroll. You know that randomness is the third practice in the Essence of Lightness." Caz placed the die in Flash's hand, lingering with intention before retracting, "Take this practice seriously, as if your life depends on it, as it just might."

"I'm lost now. I was joking when I asked if not being me is an option. I don't know what to do with this," he said, studying the die.

"That confusion you feel right now, that voice in the back of your head that's pulling you back, is the same critic that stops you from doing everything that doesn't fit with your framework of the world, with things both important and trivial. Consider—for the last fifteen years you've been molded, mentally and physically, by the greatest warriors who've ever lived. They taught you the most powerful ways to move, the most relevant tools for an extraordinary volume of problems, and the most reasonable filters for solving new combat puzzles. Those have become tacit solutions and rationales, affecting your decisions but doing so from the shadows of your deep mind."

"Okay… I follow you, but…"

"But that cube in your hand contains everything you weren't taught. It contains all possible options, not merely the best, the most rational, the most efficient or effective. Just as your mind and body are conditioned to exploit opportunity with cold efficiency, so too are the Guardians conditioned to assume you will do so. They will not be prepared for what doesn't make sense."

"This is insane…"

"In a way, yes. But there's not such a great divide between insanity and enlightenment. True freedom is freedom from. Freedom from selfish desire. Freedom from compulsion. Freedom even from the most reasonable, the Good. We are men of the cloth. We are bound by the laws of Shaolin and committed to the Good. But that doesn't mean we surrender hidden potential by negating the *other*, the nonsensical, the nonrational."

"Let's assume for a second that I fully follow, which I'm not so sure of anymore. But let's assume I do. I have students of my own and I see the programming you speak of. Mental and physical programming, they all have it. They embody my thoughts and movements as well as those of their other teachers. It's clear as day. They are stronger for it, but… but they'll never defeat me should they ever need to, not so long as they move like I move, and think the way I think. I suppose my thoughts and movements are just as transparent to the Guardians… to you."

Caz rapped,

"I'm not sixty-five, I'm not retirin'
A legend in the old school, better today
I bust a sucker in a battle, the same old way
I did when I used to, I got the juice to
Put the best you got against and they'll lose to
The Grandest-master"

They did a complicated slap-handsy bro-five combo to acknowledge the tightness of the rhyme.

"Isn't this fundamentally what meditation is for?" questioned Flash. "Ego destruction, elevated consciousness?"

Caz snickered, "In theory, yes. But meditation practice has no carrot and no stick. We're talking combat here, where the stakes couldn't be higher. You think sitting in silence is enough to free your mind when the Guardians are closing in on you? It's not. And your biology knows the difference, whether or not your mind does. You'll revert back to habitual patterns in panic, just to survive. And they'll read you like a book."

"So, you're suggesting that gambling for choices—"

"Not gambling, no, we are still monks. The path to Lightness requires complete acquiescence to the possible, without your will imposing constraints. I'm suggesting you roll for options—options good, bad, reasonable and unreasonable. I'm suggesting you embrace the random so that you can learn to think and act in ways that you normally would not."

"I'll be learning to not be me."

"Yes."

"That sounds as dangerous as facing the 18."

"Between you and me, it is more dangerous. While you're not gambling, you are risking a great deal when you take to this practice. Right now you have a clear notion of the Good, of who you are and what you want. Like you're taught when you hold your first bamboo staff, any weapon you wield can be used against you. But when that weapon is held by a master, it becomes an extension of self. The die is no different. It's a tool. It can liberate you from the voice that constrains your potential. Or it can destroy you. And I mean that with no hint of hyperbole. It will shut doors and open windows. It will open your heart and expose your mind. But I'm here to help guide you through the process, at least as well as anyone can."

"How do I begin?"

"We'll do your first roll together, right now. We'll start with only two simple options, ones that you can execute right here and now. Say the first two things that come to mind."

"Shouting, 'Fuck da head abbot' and kicking that tree over there."

"Weird, but fine. They'll work. 1-3 on the die, you shout. 4-6 you kick. Roll the die."

Flash rolled a 2. "Fuck da head abbot!" he shouted.

"Louder," Caz prodded.

"Fuck da head abbot!" he shouted louder.

"Again!" Caz pushed.

"Fuck da head abbot!"

After a few moments, Flash asked, "How is shouting and kicking going to help me defeat the Guardians? This seems like child's play."

"It is child's play. You're a child. You haven't even begun to see what's possible, but this is a start. Question—Why, if these thoughts were so readily available… why didn't you do them of your own accord? Why did you place them as options on the die?"

"They were the first two things that came to mind. But they don't seem very meaningful. I suppose that's why I wasn't already doing them."

"Exactly! They weren't meaningful. Farts in the wind. And nobody outside of an insane asylum would consider them so, including myself. No offense. I could not have predicted those options and consequent actions. They were wholly unscripted. When you have managed to place those options along with every seemingly lesser random thought on the die and silenced the inner critic, you'll be able to do what you would not do, and act in a way the Guardians could not possibly anticipate. Then you will have a chance at surviving them."

Caz started Flash off with more of the same, accessing the immediate, rolling for the trivial. But he did this without stakes ongoing.

Run or walk? Teach the students this skill or that? Eat or fast? Rice or noodles? Meditate or study? Two options floated on a whim, given equal weight on the die.

Flash rolled dozens of times a day, and the more he rolled the more he became aware of the constant habit of choice suppression. It has always been there. It has never seemed to matter. But for the first time in his life, he realized how automated it was, *he* was, and just how much "Flash" was the outcome of automated decision making—direct programming.

The more he rolled for things he was unlikely to do on a whim, the more awareness he gained of his own impulses—right or wrong, good or bad, reasonable or unreasonable—and the fresher his actions felt. But they felt less and less like his.

One week later, Grandmaster Caz qualified the practice further. "Over the next week, you'll continue your current dicing. But, one roll per day, you'll add a third option. You'll choose at least three of the following four and create an option for each:"

1 — Practice a technique you deem vital for your survival 1,000 times.
2 — Disobey a standard protocol.
3 — Perform an act of kindness.
4 — Do something that scares you.

"Each option can be weighted as you like. Each could carry an equal weight of two out of six, or you could give option 1 just one number on the die, option 2 two numbers, and option three 3 numbers, for example.

You'll keep tabs each day. If you fail to do exactly what the die says within twenty-four hours, you'll receive ten lashings from me."

"And if I succeed?"

"Then your odds of surviving the 18 improve."

Over the next seven days, the adventures of Flash were increasingly perplexing, to RZA, at least, who observed what he could and inquired about what he couldn't when they had time to catch up and recline atop their mountain. To RZA's chagrin, Flash stopped puffing in order to follow the strict guidelines for qi development in the scroll. Unless of course the die told him to, in which case, he only hit it once. Unless the die told him to hit it more than once.

Over the course of the week, Flash practiced his Dim Mak technique 3,000 times based on three distinct roles. He mediated an ongoing conflict between some of the junior monks, one of whom was being severely bullied and who desperately needed an advocate. Everyone knew it. No one was intervening. And he washed the feet of one of the elderly council members and then took a dump in his toilet without washing it down. This was a two-fer he decided on at the last minute after he'd rolled the act of kindness, and then decided to roll again on his way out of the elder's room.

He also replaced the dry bricks used for brick breaking practice with the wet ones left out in the rain, which made them damn near unbreakable and hilarious to watch as he and RZA stood on the sidelines in the late afternoon before dinner. First the junior monks failed in their attempts. Their teacher then rebuked them. They tried again. Failed again. Then the master stepped up to the bricks and let out that Shaolin scream of death as his chop landed on an uncompromising stack of blocks. He stepped back in bewilderment, scratching his head. Flash could see pretty clearly that if this process didn't open his creative channels and silence the inner critic, it would sure place him in prime running for Temple Degenerate.

He did fail to act on one roll, which was boldly enough to leave the temple right then and there, no trial or tribune, no honor or ceremony, just disappear in the night. He didn't sleep a wink that night, lying in bed, gazing at the ceiling of his concrete block of a room, body flooded with adrenaline—the freezing kind, not the fighting or fleeing kind. But it wasn't so much that he feared the consequences of getting caught, but the irreparable damage it could do to his own sense of honor. He chose honor and reflected all night on the true power the die held over him.

He received ten excruciating lashes from Caz for that decision. But after he'd received them he felt exonerated of his failure, and free to start anew. He knew after the first lash and before the second that the reason for the penalty was not only punishment for the misstep, but to remind him that the true consequence of noncompliance, the true consequence of listening to the inner critic could be death itself. While Flash was able to bottle the pain for the first few, latter lashes extracted his deepest wail.

Caz reeled inside with every strike. It made him sick to his stomach. To show mercy now could be tantamount to a death sentence for Flash. It was one of those rare moments where deep compassion and merciless torture were one and the same. He too knew the consequences of noncompliance. He received his own lashes once upon a time. But only once. It was all he needed to respect the die. It was all he needed to gain the visceral understanding that the die was there for one purpose: to align thought and action. It was there to annihilate anything that caused friction or hesitation.

This lashing was an initiation of sorts, one that proved to both Flash and Caz that they were serious about this process. From then on, dicing became more focused toward specific ends, with less tolerance for noise. Options grew within key contexts such as first active practices of the day, training technique emphasis, and exploring multiple opponent strategies with the Furious Five, to name a few.

Over the next four weeks, Flash regained his sense of focus, and went from assuming Caz had handed him an inane child's practice to realizing he'd given him a key to unlock the deepest parts of himself and, most importantly, a sledgehammer capable of crushing all hesitation and fear.

For Flash, the message had become crystal clear. We often know what we want. We rarely know how to get it. Let randomness be your guide. And she was.

Dicing was a way of practicing transitions, the sticking points in any endeavor. Most people can scheme and vision. And many, given the right resources, connections, and knowledge, can finish. But that in-between is where rules and theories are tested with real skin-in-the-game. The in-between either kills or empowers.

"In battle, my young Master Flash, nobody knows what they're doing," Caz reminded. "Those who say they do are selling you something. You still gotta fight."

"Speaking of which," Flash inquired, "Is there any way to uncover who the Guardians are ahead of time?"

"Not a chance, Flash. I'm sorry. This is truly guarded information, something neither the Guardians nor the council would ever reveal, especially before combat. It's not hard to speculate on a few of them I suppose, but the Guardians are not normal protectors. They only reveal the current cohort when the temple itself is under attack… or in this case, Shaolin secrets are at risk of exposure. Their identities are one of the temple's deepest secrets."

"No one knows who they are? How can one properly prepare for an enemy they know nothing of?"

"The council knows, naturally, as each guardian is heavily vetted and assigned to protect a council member, each member receiving two guardians. But in terms of general temple population, masters or otherwise, this information isn't shared. If it were to get out, who these 18 are, there's a risk that they can be targeted to fracture the temple army before an attack. Without that specific knowledge, adversaries will have to assume they need to attack the entire Shaolin army, including the 18. This is a deterrent we all want to remain in place. This is protection for everyone, not only the council and the guardians themselves.

"But as to your second question on preparation for the unknown, you cannot," Caz continued. "At least you cannot prepare if you define these 18 as your enemy. They are not. And you shouldn't assume you'd defeat them with tricks or gimmicks geared toward individual weaknesses. You won't find them. There is only one strategy of preparation that will stand, and that's to make yourself the very best kung fu man you can. And for this, you have only one enemy to contend with: yourself."

The Die is Law

Young Master Caz lay awake in the early morning hours, staring through darkness at the white, mold laden ceiling of a windowless room. His head rested in folded hands with his shamelessness exposed. Next to him was a young woman of similar age in deep sleep, the kind of restful sleep one falls into after a long day and a job well done.

Caz lay there overflowing with energy and excitement. He'd broken his vows and committed an indiscretion that would either stay a forbidden secret between him and his new acquaintance or would become an enduring stain on the young monk's reputation that would prevent his ascension to the council one day. But this didn't need to be sorted immediately. He could decide later how to play this.

What he was contemplating rather was *why*. *Why* did this act of forbidden deviance feel antithetical to how he imagined? *Why* was there no guilt? *Why* did he feel, from head to toe, better than he'd ever felt at any time throughout his pious life to date?

He replayed the events of the day, a day in a long line of equally puzzling days, though the others were less threatening to his existence within the Temple. Returning from a communications run between his master and a neighboring town, Caz came across the brothel by chance. He'd run that path many times and could do so effortlessly, even with added weight to his ankles. His breath wasn't even challenged anymore.

To add some variety to his journey he rolled for new directions home. 3—left. 6—right. 2—left. And there, down a road he'd never taken was a temptation he'd always avoided.

2 — Enter.
4 — Accept the offer.
4 — Don't bargain.
1 — The first girl in the lineup.

He was pleased with his chance-dictated option. She was very alluring and had kind, inviting eyes, wearing little but a thin silk slipover.

It didn't feel as dirty as he would have thought. She took him by the arm with a bounce in her step and an impish smile. She was happy to be chosen, it seemed.

There was a dissociation of action in it that Caz had become very familiar with. The die would speak. He would listen. And in so doing, the *actor* seemed absent. There was the act, but there was no ownership. An act without an actor. It often felt like remote viewing through another's body, a surrogate of his own mind. There was the strangest combination of egoless nonattachment, while simultaneously feeling fully alive, with screaming senses and novel curiosity.

Caz lay there in full relaxation feeling this very paradox alive and living in him again. He should have felt an unknown shame. He should have regretted his decision. But he wasn't the one choosing his own actions from a place of personal meaning. He played no degenerate impulse, honored no habitual thought.

He could have just as easily rolled a different girl – one in six – rolled to decline the offer – four to two against – rolled not to enter – fifty-fifty – and rolled to turn right – fifty-fifty as well. Chance could have sent him any way at any point. It was indifferent.

On top of the titillating insight that his act had felt more like enlightenment than damnation, he also considered the odd shift in his understanding of obedience since the day his master, the master of Lightness, handed him a wooden die. His life prior to that moment had been one of strict discipline, strict obedience to the Laws of Shaolin and to the dictums of those who outranked him. But his master and mentor of nearly two decades had turned tutelage on its head and placed a new master in young Caz's hand. He made the lesson clear:

"The die is law. It is the highest law for the duration of your training. Wheresoever there is conflict between the die and dictums of the cloth, the die retains ultimate authority."

"What if it tells me to neglect my temple duties?" asked Caz, perplexed.

"Try harder, ask what you want to ask," replied his master.

"If I consider an option that's immoral, do I still give it a chance?"

"Getting closer. And perhaps good enough for now. The die is law," his master confirmed.

Caz felt his master was looking for more from him, a deeper understanding or application of the process, but this would take time.

"Where does this end?" Caz asked one more time.

"Only the die knows," replied the master, deferring all responsibility to chance, "But… but if you fail to listen, there are consequences. Severe consequences. You will taste them at some point, no doubt, but the die will teach you how to play over time. If you don't break, you'll find balance born not from obligation but wisdom."

And if it tells me to kill you? Caz thought, but dared not speak. As the thought occurred, he felt a surge of power, but also simultaneous fear. That was his first taste of *the paradox.*

His master smiled as if reading Caz's thoughts. A deviant smile, the honor among thieves type. The type that implied *the die is law*, BUT, *if you step to the master, you'd better be prepared to die, and not the chance kind.* That tacit warning was palpable, so much so that Caz's legs felt weak.

Caz's master had raised him like a son. He'd taken special interest in Caz from a young age just as Master Caz would take interest in young Flash many years later. Caz was left at the steps of the temple, dirty and cold, but not broken. His eyes were always bright, and his intelligence and natural movement acquisition was altogether unique. His master knew since their first meeting that he'd found the inheritor of Lightness.

And since that day, Caz had been groomed to be a true practitioner of Zen first, a healer second, and a martial artist third, or, at least, that was the aim. Caz absorbed each of the three treasures like a sponge. His capacity for emptiness, for stillness, made him a remarkably quick study in the meditative arts. His sensitivity, cultivated in stillness, allowed him to sense the energy within, as well as that of those in close proximity. He could feel the vibrations of plants and herbs and match their frequencies to counteract qi perturbances in the sick by mere intuition alone.

But the anatomy of healing is not a one-way street. Those who can heal can also harm, and harm well. The best warriors of antiquity were always healers.

This intuition of the qi of others made him an indomitable kung fu man, for he didn't fight the surface of a man, he fought his essence. He could sense faster, see deeper, and react with deep intelligence. Caz was a mad force of nature when he fought. But he was always contained, always knew his place and respected the law.

Now he held in his hand the anti-law.

He held a trump card, a key of caprice, a vehicle of chance.

Caz now looked into his mentor's eyes, torn between a license to kill and a will to love. He had always loved his master, but not without a hint of resentment. That same resentment felt by all phenoms who catch a glimpse of their own potential before they have the wisdom to fully control it. Phenoms who feel their talent exceeds that of their mentor yet are forced to bottle it out of duty. He had carried that resentment without letting it show for years, but this moment changed everything.

Now he had license to ignore duty and consider options that would be condemnable. He received this license by the man himself. And that power in his hand that became fear in his legs tore a veil of ignorance from his mind. He saw something in his master's eyes that he'd never seen before: darkness.

He realized in that moment a delusion of confidence. The game Caz played, the one he thought he superseded his master in, was not the real game. There were no stakes, only abstract metrics and contrived objectives.

Staring a lifetime at shadows, Caz turned to see the darkened silhouette of the man who created them standing in the light. And the tables turned. He realized he was not only in the presence of one of the greatest Shaolin warriors alive, if not ever, the man who fixed his stances as a child, handed him his first weapon, and more recently, taught him that gravity doesn't mean shit. Caz realized he didn't know his master at all. He had only seen the shadow cast. He had no idea what this man was really capable of. What he'd done.

Siddhartha Fucking Gautama, what had the die told him to do in his day? he contemplated.

The paradox. The master of Lightness had no loyalties, not even to Lightness itself. *Could this really be true? He was the best friend, father, and mentor a person could ever wish for. Was this all an illusion? No. What then? Does mastery of Lightness require one to embrace lawless evil so as not to be confined by the light? Can we even consider it evil if there is no selfish impulse driving action? If there's no actor?*

> Too many of us still thinkin' like slaves!
> Time to break the chains and the ties that bind
> And elevate ourselves to a greater state of mind...

Caz chuckled to himself spontaneously from a deep, dark place, louder and louder with maniacal undertone until his resting company began to shift from her slumber. He recalled where he was, what he'd done. Her soft skin, her playful touch in a world without rules and consequences. *Keep it together,* he consoled himself. *Between darkness and light, there is still choice.* He rolled toward her, draping his arm around her waist, embracing his random act as long as possible, watching his mind unravel into a million voids.

Shadows in the Night

Fall was coming, and Grandmaster Caz was taking advantage of the cool temperatures for an evening meditation session. He was within the vast temple grounds, just on the outskirts of the pagoda forest. Breathing there gave him a sense of paying homage to those who sacrificed for the perpetuation of Shaolin knowledge and skill, knowledge for which he couldn't be more grateful at this particular juncture.

The challenge had been issued and the Temple had become charged with energy. Caz had taken a great deal of flack for supporting the challenge of monastic vows, but he reminded all, one after another, that nothing that had transpired was in breach of Shaolin law. Their ways had been honored and laws had been complied with. This didn't console any of those passing judgment, for despite all attempts at airtight jurisprudence, it's damn near impossible to cover the spectrum of moral rectitude with comprehensive law. They felt in their hearts this wasn't right, but there was nothing more they could say.

Caz too carried that energy. It buzzed through him in orchestral levity as the moon's glow warmed his back and cast his shadow forward. He felt truly alive despite the unprecedented times of uncertainty. He had long relinquished control and judgment over Flash's decision and had resolved to play out this charged game, in which he was merely a pawn. At this moment, he was free of it all: the drama, the fear of losing his best pupil and friend to death or freedom, the excitement for change that broke the mold. His mind was empty of it all and full of the cool night air, the soft moonlight, his internal pulses, and his soft, subtle structure that gave him effortless lift yet firm roots that merged him with the earth.

An anchored buoy, the master of lightness is suspended yet grounded, containing polarities and contradictions and floating between them with fierce artistry. Permeating it all, a lightness of being.

Without opening his eyes, Caz could feel shifting of the moon's continuity on his back, the heads of five shadows enveloping his own before him. His energetic lightness fell back to earth with energy of a different kind, dark energy charged for action, if need be.

"You've made waves, dear brother. Awakened the dragon," said one of the voices behind him.

"How can I help you, my friends?" inquired Caz, suspiciously. "There must be something important if you're convening together."

"Your disciple, Flash. We would rather not be in this position in the first place, but we did not set the ball rolling. Out of respect to you and you alone, we want to know if you would have us take mercy on him. To show restraint and leave him his life when the time comes?" asked another voice.

"The odds are not in Flash's favor, for certain, brothers. But this may not be the simple challenge you anticipate. I caution you to take your preparation seriously. He should not be underestimated."

"You're preparing him then? You're preparing him to fight… us? Should we assume the reserved Master of Lightness has finally chosen an inheritor?" asked the first voice.

Caz didn't bite the hook but opened his eyes to see the heads of five shadows. Five dark patches amid the illuminated ground brush and tracked dirt glistening in the moonlight.

"Is this really what you're here to ask me?" Caz jabbed.

"Your intuition was always something to be noted, dear friend," a third voice observed. "You're right, we're not here to offer mercy. Our loyalties are to the temple, the highest mercy is shown to those who will carry on their vows and fight for its future. We're here to know where *your* loyalties are at this time. We need to know if, when the time comes, we can count on you to do the right thing."

"Dear brothers, I am as devoted to Shaolin today as I have been my entire life. The temple is my home; its inhabitants my brothers and friends. Nothing will prevent me from honoring my vows, adhering to the laws, and protecting the temple."

"We are happy to hear that, Grandmaster Caz. We're sorry to have disturbed your practice," said a fourth voice as the shadows retreated from the casted moonlight.

That Tai Chi Tho

Flash had pulled the random thread, and, with it, the tapestry of his mind began to unravel. The die had unlocked parts of him that he didn't know existed, if he could even claim them as his. One week to game time and Flash no longer recognized the reflection looking back at him. Head dripping from a cooling rinse in the still pool beside the falls, Flash slowly placed his index finger through the surface, forming the center of emanating circular ripples that blurred his features, but not fully. He felt as though *he* were dispersing with each ripple, not just witnessing a reflection. *Who am I? Who is Flash?*

The Furious Five were each finishing up their own washing, some with a splash, and some a full dunk with robes drooped around their waists. All had earned their cool-down after the last of regular training sessions since their commitment to help Flash prepare. What started with heated one-on-one rotations, trading in fresh blood for battered bone, with Flash receiving no rest between bouts, evolved into more elaborate fighting sessions that integrated dice-dictated random scenarios.

The puerility of early dice rolling had organically evolved. The fruitlessness of whimsical options lost intrigue for Flash as his fate drew closer, and without effort his selections became more focused and performance oriented. This unlocked an array of creative solutions to complex combat puzzles.

While Lightness is not independently a combat art, he realized that it was a tool for generating one's own. It was a system built for all arts whatever. Flash's style had evolved rapidly as the die taught him to release his forms and experiment under pressure with unorthodox movements, strategies, and solutions that he would not have done otherwise.

This could only have evolved with monks like *the five*, formidable masters all, and who soon grew to be the closest of brothers. They knew each other in and out, each session, every technique relaying a deep intention stemming from the depths of their minds. Enough movements, enough hits, and you see the mind behind the movement. You begin to read your opponent like the back of your own hand and treat each engagement as a game of mahjong. Each master trying to outwit an opponent who knows him intimately, looking for not just gaps in skill, but gaps in psychology—a weakness.

When readings became so transparent that fighting sessions stretched due to familiarity and conditioned hesitation, Flash took to rolling for scenarios, handicaps, and just about anything they could collectively think up to remove Flash's sense of prediction and consequent reservation. He would learn to rely on his flexibility and adaptation over static approach. He would learn to fight from his heart, not his head.

He'd frequently roll for uneven odds, perhaps the most reasonable option given his fate—two to five opponents in simultaneous engagement. This didn't go well at first. Flash had a few close calls that nearly took him out of the game altogether, but he healed, and he learned. He learned things in those simulations that one couldn't merely postulate given man-to-man sparring. He learned how to cut the middle, and he learned how to align the many to fight the one. Strategies changed with each additional opponent, and he grew grateful for the willingness of the five to subject themselves to this brutal process with nothing to show for it but a personal sense of honor.

He rolled for types of terrain: flat, inclined, unstable, obstacle-laden, in shallow water, on loose earth, and on and on. He rolled for handicaps: one arm tied behind his back, a prefatigue exercise, a hard punch to the gut to take his wind, even RZA's Shaolin kush hits, anything to put him at further disadvantage and force him to rely on nothing but his ability to adapt and integrate, to call on every tool he had, no matter how big or small, to rely on himself.

He rolled for acupoint strikes on himself and the five, testing angles, depths, and forces required to cause loss of consciousness, nervous system shutdown, energy shifts, loss of lunch, and even release of bowels, which were by far the least fun for the five and eventually led to testing these without pants to save on unnecessary laundering.

He even relinquished control and accepted options conceived and rolled for by the five, truly at the beck and call of randomness. And the result of it all was a Master Flash like no one had ever seen before, an absolute titan of martial arts. But it was not without the fallout that Caz had forewarned.

Who am I? Who is Flash? Are these questions for which answers are needed? Or is the desire to answer them yet a deeper layer of self that needs to die?

Does it even matter? My former self was an illusion. I see that now. Do I need to fill that void with yet another, more comprehensive notion of self? Or can I live in this void forever?

Thoughts rippled across Flash's mind as did his reflection before him.

With the dissolution of Flash's identity came deep uncertainty of purpose. If he were an illusion, so too was this grand charade of discontent at the degradation of his beloved home. The temple didn't belong to him. Nor did the actions and values of temple leaders. Nor did the intention to resist it all and fight for change.

Here, Flash was trapped in an illusion of self that he'd meticulously molded since childhood, an illusion without meaning sprouting from delusional self-importance. *I'm just like them,* he observed, *drifting in the winds of capricious impulse*. The die had not only managed to silence the critic, it burned his entire world down and left him with a handful of ashes.

Caz passed the five as they dripped and moseyed back to the temple for dinner. They seemed exhausted, broken in body, but alive in mind, fulfilled with a sense of purpose. They showed their respects and gave Caz conscientious bows with prayer-drawn hands in passing. He gave them subtle nods and an elevated knife hand before his chest in return, a general's casual salute to his infantry's precise one.

"If you look real closely I'm told you can see the faint outline of an idiot in there. Legend has it the ghost of a monk crazy enough to challenge the 18 still floats in that pool," Caz teased.

> "Don't push me 'cause I'm close to the edge
> I'm trying not to lose my head
> It's like a jungle sometimes
> It makes me wonder how I keep from goin' under,"

replied Flash without looking up from his dispersing silhouette.

Caz knew that all too familiar look well. It was like seeing an old flame cross your path unexpectedly, at once feeling that pure romance in all its fond memory resurface right beside the brutal pain of loss that accompanied its demise. The most nonrational of complex human emotions perhaps, that of simultaneous love and hate. And while it pained him to see his disciple in this lawless state, he reminded himself that it's always darkest before the dawn, and that Lightness requires that other thing.

Yes, he knew that look very well.

"Come, brother; there's no time to give in to the void. Not yet, we still have work to do," said Caz. Flash turned slowly to face him, finding Caz in push-hands posture with his left arm behind his back and his right arm extended in wait.

Flash immediately relaxed and came to, feeling gratitude for the true friend and mentor who stood before him, a mentor who'd been there from the beginning, a friend who was giving him a chance at life. No words could express something so complex. The best he could do was demonstrate to Caz that his wisdom and skill was alive and well in his dedicated student.

Flash mirrored Caz's stance and placed the outside of his extended right forearm, with palm inward facing, against Caz's forearm. No other ceremony was needed for this game, this game that became a regular test of skill and deep sensitivity.

At first, Caz's version of Tai Chi push-hands was a disaster for Flash. It's one thing to cut a brick with your bare hand and bear the deep burning pain of a horse stance. It's another to face a Master of Lightness in a game of sensitivity, where he reads every inequity in your structure, even misalignment of your smallest toe through the slightest pressure of your arm.

Caz's skill in this domain was altogether foreign to Flash, who quite frankly didn't even know it existed, at least not like this. His first experience of it months prior felt like an eerie demonic force that overrode Flash's most sophisticated structures and intentions. It was like fighting an automated machine programmed to counteract every move with subtle one-upmanship so as to make him feel snuffed out, suppressed, mentally defeated, all the while his body was fresh and able. He was powerless to express his will. It was total humiliation that trumped even the tree run demonstration.

Week after week, Flash grew in sensitivity as the bodyweights highlighted every loose wire and shoddy connection in his neural circuitry, as his breath enlivened, energized, and integrated, as his mind-map sprawled to encompass dormant data receptors, as his qigong became more rooted and stances became more stable, as the holes in his vessel were sealed and his push-hands improved.

Flash came to see the sophistication in what first seemed like a demonic imposition of will by a superior being. It now seemed like the only assessment that truly mattered, for it didn't only express dominance over others, but depth of development of the whole self. This wasn't a game that could be hacked. It was for the lifers, those with skin in the game, the proper gangsters.

Like a multiplayer experience on a Ouija board where movement manifests spontaneously and everyone denies responsibility for dictating the device's direction, so too does the conversation of push-hands spring from nothing but first contact. Neither player is solely responsible; both are lost in the subtle give and take of energy being exchanged.

When playing with a master of Caz's caliber, this conversation often starts before first contact as his surface qi extends well beyond his skin, attuning to electromagnetic shifts in the space beyond his body. This created that ghost-like, if not demonic sensation of being seen without seeing, being known without knowing. Caz was a ghost at first, ever present but always out of reach. This gap was bridged slowly to where Flash now displayed near similar sensitivity to contact.

And with sensitivity came speed. As data flooded in on minute levels and inefficiencies in neural signaling were snuffed out, the read-in speak-out conversation of push-hands became lightning fast, though to the information-filled minds of the warriors, time slowed to a snail's pace. They saw everything, felt everything.

The conversation always began on a subtle level with short oscillations, pulsations of slight pressure back and forth, and quickly expanded to full range pushing, accompanied by an extended stance from one. The other received this force on the back of his wrist with a rearward shift, 'ghosting' until his opponent's energy was on the fringe of over-extension. This is when the cycle rapidly reversed and retreater turned attacker.

The extension, the aggression, the forceful pressure of this game was something Flash had mastered long ago in basic training. It's also what compromised his structure and exposed him time and time again to Caz's immaculate sensitivity. He had to learn a new theory of power… of being. *Yin is the key to Lightness.* Not exactly a lesson one can learn without the sensitivity to experience it. *Emptiness is where Lightness dwells.* These elusive dictums lay in wait for the vessel that could contain them, for intellect alone could not comprehend such living absurdities.

Retreat, redirect, shift, push, rebalance, rinse, repeat. The cycle started fast and grew even faster. What many see and experience in push-hands, the slow exchange between two static fighters, is a very preliminary application. Caz's version was anything but soft, quickly escalating from one arm only to two arms supported to a free-moving, fast-stepping hurricane of a conversation. Contact was always kept to keep the flow of information and corresponding force in constant flow, until it wasn't.

Each warrior pressed, listening, shifting, spinning, and sensing those subtle imbalances in structure of their opponent, until opportunity to exploit them surfaced. In the early days, these attacks took the form of pushes, shoves, throws, joint locks, and pins. These were still the desired outcomes, but Flash's response-time and articulation of force had gotten to a point of near immediate response. And with it, their conversation grew to the deepest depths of their minds, looking for any gaps in consciousness: fears to exploit, attachments to sever, compassions to manipulate.

But there was no *Flash* left to dissect and manipulate. He'd become a ghost.

For minutes, they tore that secluded section of forest up with neither of them gaining clear advantage over the other. The conversation came to a close with the same lack of intention with which it began. And they clasped hands and supported that union with their others, eyes fixed with gratitude and admiration on both sides. "Now for what might be your biggest challenge to date, to do absolutely nothing for the next seven days," said Caz.

"Nothing?" Flash asked in surprise. "Surely the Guardians are preparing. How can I rest knowing that my opponents are training to destroy me?"

Caz grabbed a branch and put it to the earth in a series of lines. "What's this?" asked Caz.

Flash turned to view it from Caz's perspective. "That's a temple," replied Flash.

"And this?" asked Caz after further etchings.

"A monk," replied Flash, looking at a bare-bones but masterful formation of lines that suggested each.

"Why are they not the same?"

"I'm not sure what you mean..."

"Why is the monk not the temple?"

"That's a strange... uh—"

"Each is a series of lines, no? Nothing more. How do you know the temple is not a monk?"

"Because of the way the lines are drawn. They're distinct. The space between them gives them form," offered Flash.

"You've filled out your forms, articulated your lines," explained Caz. "Your technique and conditioning are on-point. For mind-body coherence to evolve, you need negative space. You need rest. Do nothing for the next seven days. While your opponents practice yang, you will prepare with yin."

"Not even protocol?"

"Literally nothing. The protocol is in you now. Lightness is in you. A few more days will make no difference. Light movement and breathing are acceptable. But you've done the work, now you must let it all go. Do not carry what you know forward into that challenge. For whatever you are lacking will be revealed in action, not with more willful training. You'll need your freshest, most creative self to fill those gaps and find solutions in real time. Trust in the work you've done and rest."

A Walk Down the Hill...

Without training, Flash found a world of time and space. Days were much longer than he remembered, eliciting fond memories of childhood play. He didn't quite know what to do with himself for the first forty-eight hours. He spent a good bit of it relaxing with RZA, sauntering around and chatting about whatever popped into their heads.

"Yo, Flash, remember the poke-n-poo?" RZA questioned. They both laughed, reminiscing about their first exposure to Dim Mak, a vivid demonstration by Caz to discipline one of their unruly classmates. It was more a coincidence than a direct lesson. Caz was discussing meridian theory in the context of standing meditation, specifically, the dan tian as prime energy generator in the body. One of their classmates was messing around a bit, distracting other classmates in the process. And when Caz called on him to point exactly where his dan tian sits, the student failed to mark the point precisely.

"Not quite," Caz corrected. "It's slightly lower, right here." To make the lesson one of the most memorable, especially for a crew of adolescent boys who were always looking for new things to joke about, Caz drove his forefinger and index finger together into the student's dan tian, also known more colloquially in amateur homeopathic circles as the poo button for its laxative effect. The boy dropped his brown, learned his lesson, and gave his classmates the most vivid demonstration of Dim Mak possible.

They rolled through dozens of fond lessons, as well as those they wished they could have unexperienced. Life in Shaolin was tough, and it made for tough warriors. But they accepted a lot of abuse in ignorance because it was the status quo. And they were destined to carry some of it forward because they were products of their environment.

Flash spent time with the five, who were anxious to continue their riverside battles, but content, nonetheless, to connect with Flash in relaxed conversation. They'd all been as close as any monks in the temple, but the last six weeks had bonded them in ways none of them would ever forget. A loyalty had formed, perhaps even stronger than that of their temple vows. They were with Flash. And he was with them.

He made drop-ins to his respected elders and long overdue catch-ups with old classmates, all of whom knew their fellow monk had less than a week to live. His challenge had become a liberating cancer, one that carried a senseless shame, but also free license to forego formalities and pretense, and delight in the simple things. Old reminiscences sparked appreciations long neglected, reminding everyone why they were really there, what their vows really meant. Monks forget. People forget. We forget what matters when the monotony of life overshadows life itself.

There was an air of absurdity and speculation in it all as well, for no one knew which 18 would be facing Flash in a few short days; no one but the 18 themselves, that is. And he may have been spending precious moments with them as well, none the wiser. He had this thought in passing but didn't dwell on it. He just wanted to make the most of his time left there. Would they be sizing him up, looking for gaps in structure, lapses in awareness? Or would they, like him, forget which side of the challenge they were on for a few short moments to connect with another soul?

These were some of the best days of Flash's life, free of stress, full of life. It's a shame that all it took was his impending death to break down barriers and make meaning of life.

Flash also noticed, without the constant push for performance and granting himself the respite of rest, that the in-betweens were different. Or he was different. One way or another there was specialness in the very basics. Meals with his brothers were more impressionable: the taste of tea more pronounced, listening with deep connection, even feeling the processes of digestion taking place. Strolling slowly around the temple, he was conscious of every step, the tensional forces within his body that generate natural lift well balanced, his eyes guiding him with soft focus.

Lightness isn't about what you do, the specifics; it's in how you do them. Lightness permeates every aspect of life. It gives life.

It was a lesson, one last lesson perhaps, of the true domain of Lightness. Sure, it made protectors indefatigable demons of war, but that was a byproduct. For the first few days of Flash's *walk down the hill,* he experienced doses of doubt over whether he was squandering his remaining hours on…nothing at all. That anxious impulse to do, to constantly push forward, was deeply ingrained. It was even stronger now with the pressures of his challenge bearing down on him, a suffocating pillow. But after months of training to release the thoughts as quickly as they arose, Flash discovered not just something to fight for, but also something to live for.

It's everywhere, in everything. It pulses through me. Life is beautiful.

He released his focus of fate. He relinquished control, relinquished even his desire to survive. He accepted this very moment as being the gift he'd always yearned for. This had nothing to do with temple politics or a degenerate state. This moment held no baggage of the sort. He was free. And with that freedom surged a flood of power.

Flash was ready to beat some Guardian ass.

Shame on a Monk

All monks dined together on the eve before the challenge as they did most nights. It was a custom that was reinforced by the council a few days prior to maintain solidarity and avoid possible factions. The reason made sense, but only sort of. They grew together. Trained together. Perhaps because they were supposed to be family. Or perhaps because it was the last chance to gain a psychological edge or discover a tacit weakness before life was on the line.

Only two were bold enough to sit with Flash publicly, Grandmaster Caz and Master RZA. While others had wished for the courage to share a last meal with him, the optics of it would have been terrible, and they alone would have to face the consequences after Flash was dead.

There also wasn't much for anyone to say at this point. The air of tension was so thick in that room it could have been cut with a knife. It wouldn't have surprised anyone if things popped off right then and there in anticipation, but the monks had just enough restraint to honor protocol. This experience was uncharted for all of them. Making sense of it wasn't easy.

RZA, in cynical manner, hunched over his rice bowl in full protective embrace like a prison inmate protecting his meal, eyeing the room suspiciously. While he surveyed the room, he noticed combative postures and, from a few, malicious looks. His mind ran simulations of which among them might join the ranks of Guardians within twelve hours. And he couldn't shirk a visceral hunch that something was afoot. He muttered:

> "Shame on a monk who try to run game on a monk
> who buckwild with the chain ball sickle."

"Eeeasy RZA," Flash calmed, despite his veins also pumping with adrenaline. "This is my battle to fight. It doesn't need to be yours too."

"Something don't feel right, yo." A crazed darkness manifested in RZA's eyes:

> "I come with that ol' loco, style from my vocal
> Couldn't peep it with a pair of bi-focals
> I'm no joker, play me as a joker
> Be on you like a house on fire, smoke ya
> Crews be acting like they gangs, anyway
> Be like, "Warriors, come out and play, yay"
> Burn me, I get into shit, I let it out like diarrhea
> Got burnt once, but that was only gonorrhea
> Dirty, I keep shit stains in my drawers
> So I can get fizza-funky for you
> Murder, taste the flame of the Wu-Tang, rah!
> Here comes the Tiger verse Crane
> I'll be like wild with my style
> Punk, you play me chump, you get dumped
> Wu is coming through at a theatre near you
> And get funk like a shoe
> What?"

As RZA whispered, Flash's eyes began to droop. His qi sank to the floor. Grandmaster Caz sensed it immediately and reached under Flash's arm to lift him to his feet before everyone else noticed. In moments, they shuffled out of the room, Caz dragging, Flash stumbling, and RZA taking cue and chasing after.

In the hallway, just out of sight of the others, Caz held Flash's head steady and read his eyes. "Poison," he announced.

"I knew something was foul," spat RZA. "Come on, Caz, let's get him to my room; you know I'm good with those herbs."

The two of them carried Flash, supporting him under each arm, and Flash laboriously struggling to move his feet at their pace. His proprioception and control were quickly deteriorating. The passageways that he knew like the back of his hand blurred, morphed, and twisted into labyrinthine channels. Lights flickered and hazed. He felt the worst possible thing that could happen. He was losing control.

Once they got him settled, sprawled out on RZA's bed, Caz looked again at his eyes for particulars. Simultaneously he held his arm gently, thumb pressing on the inside of Flash's wrist, surveying one after another of Flash's six organ pulses: heart, lung, liver, spleen, kidney, and vital gate. Surveying each for abnormalities and corroborating with Flash's eye color and pupil dilation for about thirty seconds. He diagnosed, "Kidney—his qi is knotted."

"I'm on it," said RZA, opening his wall-to-wall makeshift cabinet of herbs. Shelves lined bowl-to-bowl and stacked shelf bottoms to tops with dried herbs, RZA was considered by many to be the Temple's backup apothecary, hosting the largest private stash outside of the official one. His collection was predominately collected from around the Song Mountain area, but some were collected and saved from Temple visitors. He snuck samples when he could.

"They didn't try to kill him," asserted Caz, still feeling the characteristics of his kidney qi, "but just weaken him."

RZA dexterously threw several different herbs into a stone mixing mortar. He pressed and ground with the pestle until finely mixed, then spit on them to hydrate and congeal his remedy. In moments, he held a sticky green-brown paste and placed it in Flash's open mouth, which he retained little control over.

"Don't swallow," RZA told him. "Just keep it there and let it absorb slowly." Then he lit a spliff with half tobacco, took a deep hit and blew a long, slow, trail of smoke into Flash's face. "This will open the lungs and activate the antidote faster," he explained.

Flash extended his frame with what little energy he had, aligning his channels and letting the antidote take hold. He peered down past his nose with a slight, sloppy tilt of the head at a body completely dissociated from his mind. He could see his feet peaking above his torso and none of it felt like his. He was peering through another man's eyes. The toxin hit him deeply.

With his last bit of strength Flash began to breathe heavily, deeply, in rhythmic hyperventilation, flooding his body with oxygen. His abdomen oscillated with each breath, concave to convex and back. He watched his visions of success the morning to come begin to fade away from him, scenes he'd rehearsed and practiced in his mind dissolving like burning filmstrip.

But he didn't give in to despair, not fully. He carried on for several minutes while his friends looked on. He lit the fire in his abdomen and fanned the flame with more oxygen until waves of heat flushed his body. Once he felt his energy rise and his eyes clear marginally, he knew there was still hope. He surrendered to the toxin and relaxed into a deep sleep.

A few hours later, Flash awoke with a violent cough and spit out the herbal wad on to the floor, gumming his mouth like a toothless senior with a mouthful of peanut butter. The aftertaste was something truly awful, sour and corrosive.

"What happened?" asked Flash, whose eyes were now steady, but who's body had yet to regain strength.

"Poison," said Caz. "Wasn't meant to kill, but to weaken. They'll be expecting a weaker version of you tomorrow. If it weren't for RZA here—"

"Ya, you'll be weaker," interjected RZA, "But not by much. Caz caught this quick. And you know I know my herbs."

Flash faintly nodded with appreciation. "The Guardians did this?"

"Unlikely," said Caz. "Could have come from the council. Anything *not* to lose face. I don't believe The Guardians would want to face a weaker version of you tomorrow. They have their pride. And despite this setback, you can use this to your advantage, if you choose. The optics—"

"Optics!" RZA cut in, more aggressively than he should have in the presence of a master of Caz's caliber. "You want my man to play possum? Buddha dammit! I say we fight toxin with toxin. I'll give those guardians some real hurt. Bumps, tremors, the fear of Buddha too. Spike the well tonight, give the whole temple an early morning surprise."

"I'm not happy about this either, RZA," replied Caz. "But we're here now. Flash will need every advantage he can gain tomorrow, even if that means deceit."

Flash and Caz exchanged a deep, knowing look with one another. They both knew he wasn't going to defeat 18 guardians in less than twelve hours, especially not with this setback, the severity of which had yet to be determined. But they also knew that that wasn't exactly Flash's game plan.

The Morning Of

RZA and Flash sat, leaning backs against the brick wall of the courtyard and gazing out over the drawn-out valley. Between them was a pot of tea, distilled all night by RZA to be extremely strong, containing copious amounts of one of nature's most potent performance enhancers—caffeine. It was instilled with another of nature's performance enhancer's, one quite foreign to the monastic diet but which would add an incredible surge of energy—sugar. Together they would hit hard like nitrous oxide through a race engine. And by the time Flash hit the wall and crashed from the stimulants, he'd either be dead or free.

Flash didn't know much about sugar beyond its flavor enhancing and preservative qualities, but he trusted RZA implicitly when RZA told him the combination was deadly, in a good way, to the detoxified mind. They were reserving it for the minutes preceding the challenge, approximately one hour away.

Flash assumed, after six months of grueling prep, including six weeks of maddening dicing, that he'd feel his surest in these very moments, but he didn't. That fight or flight response gripped him and was unlikely to release him before things kicked off. Adrenaline pumped through his veins, swelled his muscles, and weakened his knees. He remained present as best he could, sustaining abdominal breathing to ease his pulse and calm his nervous system, but fear is a powerful drug.

Everything was real now. His first glimpse of this reservation occurred standing before the council, but hadn't manifested much before or since. That was nothing compared to the flood of energy and skepticism overtaking him. *Have I made the right decision? Why ask at all, nothing can be done now. But have I? What if I fucking die?*

His mind was racing a mile a minute even without the caffeine-sugar punch waiting for him. His mind saw the events of the last six months, the events since he decided to challenge the Guardians for his freedom, splayed before his eyes like a slowly extended pictographic scroll: His discovery in The Wisdom of the Ancients. His confession to RZA. His failure scaling the tree with Caz. Issuance of his official challenge. Training with the furious five. Dice practice and subsequent lashing. Push-hands. Even his toxic episode the night before. Snapshots of brilliantly colorful moments, all so pronounced.

And then there were the projections, the far-fetched visualizations of life beyond the temple. These were somewhat off limits to him before, challenging his focus with unnecessary distraction. *Keep your eye on the prize. Focus on what's in front of you and the rest will take care of itself,* he figured. But now, now things were far clearer. The objects of his focus were finished. There was no more prep to be had. No more work to be done save for the challenge itself. There was only open space… nothingness.

Flash, for the first time in his life, felt that most human of sensations, deep uncertainty. Since youth, his life had been one of status quo without concern for necessities: food, shelter, even care and camaraderie. These were designed into monastic life in a way that kept him sheltered from the realities of fending for himself. If he were victorious, the necessities became just that, and Flash had no plans in place. What if life were harder out there? What would become of him if he had nothing, no one, and couldn't rectify that condition?

Feeling his impending need for the basics made him feel not only inadequate, but also foolish, two foreign emotional states that would have been more useful six months before. And he felt foolish that he felt foolish, that he managed to take on so much, to face a challenge so great that life was on the line; and here he sat with his best friend and a pot of tea between them feeling foolish. There's a real lack of dignity in these moments of uncertainty, moments that stand between who one is and what they'll become. There's a lack of reason in them too, a void of nonsense scatterbrained last-minute doubts and questions for which there's only one answer—action.

Awareness of a moment, torn between today and tomorrow, drifting in uncertainty. Flash contemplated the meaning of this moment that carried significance insofar as the fear of future consequences invaded his sense of momentary peace. *To face uncertainty, naked and afraid, without grasping for the oxygen of delusional certainty, this must be the crucible of change,* thought Flash. Growing pains for which there is no balm but time.

Flash deepened his breath and straightened his back. He surrendered to the overwhelming energy tossing his thoughts like a dinghy on rocky tides. Resisting it was futile and risked him falling into self-deceit. Nothing was all right. The risks were real, and the clock was counting down. And nobody could reassure him with positive outlook of a fate he alone had only marginal control over.

This was chaos, and chaos cannot be contained. Let it go. Breathe.

"Yo, Flash," RZA compassionately broke the silence. "You remember when I arrived here, that first beating them young monks put on me?"

"I do," recalled Flash.

"I do too, man. It was four-on-one until you stepped in. I was hurtin' real bad. I could fight a bit coming into the temple, but not four-on-one fightin'. It could have gone a few ways man. If you wasn't there and steppin' in, I don't know which way I woulda gone here. That creates terror in some young monks' minds, the kind that don't go away. Training and breathing for years is just gauze on an open wound. It coats it, but that healing doesn't happen. But you gave me a chance to heal, man 'cause you showed me I wasn't alone."

"You're not alone, RZA," said Flash.

"Funny you saying that at this particular time, given the circumstances… but I know you mean that. And who knows? Maybe one day, after you beat these chumps and I retain full bragging rights among the brothers, maybe I'll be seeing you."

"I hope so, RZA."

"Do you remember what you said after you whupped those four dickheads?" continued RZA. "After they ran off and you helped me up, I asked you why you stepped in. You remember that?"

They both chuckled and Flash recited their fifteen-year punch line, "I was so afraid and angry at the same time, I didn't know what to do. I told you I felt like puking and beating some ass… and I already puked."

"I already puked," RZA repeated. "That's cold… and weird." RZA picked up the pot of tea between them, unstacked two small porcelain teacups and poured them with care. RZA hid it well, but he was deathly afraid this would be that last cup of tea he'd share with this best friend. He placed one in Flash's hand, the other he held up to clink. "I suggest you get to puking my good monk, 'cause this shit's gonna prepare you for the other thing."

Two cups deep and Flash's pupils dilated along with his veins. Caffeine was triggering adrenaline, which was triggering rapid metabolic churn, converting that infused sugar into ready energy. His veins started to bulge, his vision sharpened, and the valley before them glowed with a cornucopia of vibrant colors. The butterflies fluttered and spread in a fierce second and Flash jolted forward and lost his guts.

Time was barreling in and his mind settled into a state of calm presence. The jitters that had his legs shaking and knees weak minutes before were now redirected and concentrated on the task at hand: opening the floodgates of Lightness and reigning hell upon the 18… or die trying. RZA let Flash release his demons and sipped his own tea, checking that first item off his mental list. "Yo, you ready now, my monk?" Flash wiped his mouth on his golden lapel and rapped,

"I dress like a pimp and I work like a ho
And Shaolin is the only life I know
I get respect on the street wherever I go
And they only get respect when they doin' a show

Cause I never had a fright when I'm on the fight
I beat a bum like them up just the other night
When he opened his eyes all he could see
was the referee, the ceiling, and me

My teachers were martial arts masters and monks
My class was survival and school was the slumps
Math was counting copper, large coffers no doubt
And my homework was knocking sucker monks out"

The door to the courtyard, mere meters away, opened from the inside, and Flash was called in to face his fate.

An Open Window

Flash and RZA stood at the rear entrance to the training courtyard. They were both charged to the tilt; Flash trying to sustain his readiness and RZA his righteous anger. RZA worked Flash's arms, one at a time, extending his wrists with one hand and massaging his biceps and inner arm with the other—relaxing, loosening, quickening. He was the best corner man a monk could wish for: fierce, focused, concerned, probably high, and willing to inflict Flash's opponents with the hurt he felt inside, an ambition that required painstaking counterargument by Caz the night before.

Caz. Caz was nowhere to be seen. After everything they'd been through, Flash would have thought… didn't matter. He had been there through and through, done enough, gotten Flash to the ledge. He alone must take the leap.

Flash turned to RZA one last time before entering, quite likely to say thank you and share that bro-moment, but RZA, in RZA fashion, cut in with a final reminder, "Remember my monk, the eyes is the groin of the head."

"Eyes are the groin of the head," Flash confirmed, making severe eye contact and linking forearms in the manliest of ways, quite likely the way Vikings would do just before a proper pillaging.

The council was perched on solid marble thrones that shined in the sunlight, themselves atop a solid brick-earthen platform that spanned the perimeter of the courtyard. This platform was the base of fortified walls of fifteen to twenty feet, constructed of thick vertical wooden beams and filled in with packed earth. From Flash's current vantage he was flanked on each side, left and right, by four and five councilmembers respectively.

Councilman 5 occupied the middle of five seats with the same austerity and innocence Flash observed at their last encounter. His presence alone carried a great sense of meaning that continued to give Flash unexpected reassurance. The councilmen dressed uniformly in ceremonious dark brown robes with yellow peeking out at the ankles and wrists. They were sitting in calm anticipation, sheltering whatever disdains or excitement they might be harboring. Proper stoics.

A beautiful sweeping roof of red and blue and yellow geometric designs protected the platform on the sides hosting the councilmen, somewhat stifling the feeling of spaciousness the courtyard otherwise created. The center of the yard was predominately set-stone, an open court for training, with landscaped patches of green life, young trees, and stone pathways enveloping the center.

Flash had seen this training field more times than he could count. He'd sweated, bled there as well. But today was the first day he'd felt its majesty. He wasn't sure if it was the exceptional light or his caffeine-charged brain, but the courtyard glowed brilliantly. The colors leapt at him with vivid definition. The landscaping and architecture felt like a true embodiment of Zen, meticulously cared for but extraordinarily balanced. He wanted to thank the gardeners, whom he'd taken for granted. He realized this was an odd time to have such thoughts of gratitude, but he wanted to share his sense of awe with the caretakers of this oasis.

There were a few cracks and gaps in the walls, and while Flash could not see them, they were blocked from behind by the eyes and bodies of temple monks dying in anticipation to watch the monk who challenged the 18. Was he insane? Was there any chance he would survive?

Yes… the 18. How had their presence not been the first, the only thing he noticed upon entering? The mind does funny things when pressure is applied. It was as if they weren't even there, likely due to their statuesque stillness. Their readiness.

They looked on Flash with a variety of emotions. Many felt personally affronted by Flash's decision to leave Shaolin… to leave them. And they knew that a man in his position, trapped and cornered with life on the line is a feral cat with claws drawn and fangs ready to penetrate. A man with nothing to lose is as dangerous as a man with something to fight for. They just weren't sure which one of those men was standing before them. If they didn't bring their A-games, they too were in danger. But their strength was in numbers.

Flash could see the door ahead of him, his vision narrowing, telescoping through scattered legends dressed in warrior robes of blood red, sleeveless and taut, revealing their strength, suctioned to the calves and ankles with leather ties to avoid snags. To see his brothers' poise, power, and focus made him feel proud in a way. They were an awe-inspiring force, the product of millennia of Shaolin science and alchemy in flesh and blood. And he may have become one of them at some point… not now.

A second shot of nausea and nerves, weakness hit his knees as it did when he was first handed the die. There, standing between him and the door to freedom was Grandmaster Caz. He was the last line of defense of the treasures of Shaolin. Decked out like the rest from head to toe in battle robes. It was actually breathtaking for Flash to see his old master among the cohort before him. It felt wholly appropriate for the Master of Lightness to stand supreme among the Guardians themselves.

Like the others, Caz's red robe glistened in the sun. It was fastened tightly at his calves, cross-wrapped with thin yellow ribbons braided against leather ties that formed a stylish zigzagging X on the front and rear lower leg to prevent tripping or being caught and pulled. His muscular arms extended from a sleeveless top, lined as well with yellow lapel that extended shoulder to hip, fastened at the waste with a thicker yellow sash.

Caz looked twenty years younger in combat robes, as did the other 17 Guardians surrounding him. Seeing him in this form made sudden sense of the effortless tree scaling months back. He truly looked the part with ripped, sinewy shoulders and arms, frame stacked in effortless symmetry. He chastised himself for letting the robes betray his perception, for believing the crow's feet dignifying Caz's eyes. Foolish. Short-sighted.

Flash did a brief scan of the field. He knew all of them to one degree or another, a few very dear teachers but most to a much lesser degree. All of them were known to be elite in some form of Shaolin combat: White Lotus Fist, Plum Blossom Style, Explosive Style, Flood Style, Mind Style, and Leopard Fist, among others. The one consolation he had to relax his nerves was that weapons were not permitted. Had they been, it would have been game over within seconds, and not in his favor.

He noticed, about halfway between Caz and himself, the longstanding Grandmaster of Master RZA, whom RZA usually referred to as Masta Killa. Killa was indomitable with a straight sword. Some of the Guardians may stand a chance with him using their own weapon of choice, some of which included spears, but Flash would not have made the cut of survivors had arms been allowed. His swordplay alone would have dominated the engagement. That's one… and the seventeen others?

After taking in what might be the most elaborate and well-attended funeral any monk in his lifetime was privileged to, his eyes refocused on Caz.

He was a Guardian all this time? Why didn't he tell me? Was this all a game? Was he with the council all this time, keeping them informed of every move I was making? Was he scrambling my mind with the die so the Guardians would make easy work of me and send a lasting lesson to the rest of the brotherhood? Did Caz himself poison me?

Flash quickly worked through alternative happenings, scenes behind scenes, seeing in his mind's eye the sinister Caz concocting and sneaking toxin into his water when he wasn't looking. He saw him taking a great laugh with various councilmen as he reported the absurd practices he'd been occupying his insolent student with, a student who needed the harshest of lessons in the most public of settings.

Caz's placement here was far more unsettling than Flash would have imagined. *Could* the poison have been one last lesson for him? Was Caz, the reliable mentor and brilliant strategist, giving him one last lesson on uncertainty—the importance of focusing on outcome, but flexible on method? *Who you are on your best day is not who you really are,* Flash recalled Caz's cryptic message one session. *I am not my strongest self. I am not my best-laid plan. A plan based on my strongest self being present to execute it is a plan doomed to fail.* Was that it?

If so, what a Buddha-damned lesson.

Caz knew. He knew the poison wouldn't kill me. He knew what it was within moments. How could he be so sure? He's a master of toxicology and herbal medicine, he would know. He would know regardless.

Caz was the only one in Flash's corner. Was it all a lie? Was this some nefarious plot to squelch not only him but also every potential dissenter who might challenge the 18?

No, it doesn't need to be him. Flash shook his head. *Don't get stuck there. Not now. Is he here… is he here to help me see this through? Or to stop me?* Get present.

GET PRESENT.

"Siddhartha Fucking Gautama," Flash spat under his breath. He'd felt for the first time that he'd signed his own death warrant and 18 of the baddest dudes on the planet came to collect. He recalled one of Caz's gems—a Law of the Die as he called them—*If you're playing mahjong and you're not sure who the mark is, you're the mark.*

And then he saw it.

The Guardians all stood with perfect poise and stoicism. All but one. Flash surveyed them again to be sure, eyes scanning them up and down quickly, leaping from one to the next.

Nothing.

Nothing.

Nothing.

Nothing.

Caz!

Caz had a slight leftward lean. This would mean nothing to anyone if that man had not whipped Flash personally into understanding the importance of observing protocol, one part of which is constant observation of physical structure and alignment. Constant readiness.

This would be the most ironic of incompetencies if it were unintentional. Flash carefully looked at Caz's attire. Nothing. His face. Nothing. No expression. His hands, placed right over left before his dan tian. Wait. His right index finger was not flush against his left hand as his other fingers were, as all fingers were by every other Guardian. It was ever so slightly extended. It was pointing. It was matching the direction of his leftward lean.

Flash's eyes followed Caz's subtle cue to Caz's left, Flash's right. They screened an inch of the courtyard at a time until a speck of red caught his eye. In the rightmost corner from Flash's vantage was a splash of red the color of robes ever so subtle amidst the cornucopia of ornamental color of the adjacent roof. It wasn't clear what it was, but it was out of place. Or rather, it was indicating a right place, cutting the corner where a gap in the pagoda roof lay.

The courtyard earthen walls were more than fifteen feet tall, but they felt like one hundred. The pressure of the Guardians breathing down his neck would compound the difficulty of anything he would attempt. But he knew now what was going on. Caz was clear, "You cannot defeat the Guardians in combat." Flash now finished the sentiment that was never spoken, "But you don't need to."

The law states that you must fight the Guardians for your freedom. You must fight in order to leave. It does not state anywhere that you must defeat all of the 18 or that you must leave through the front door, especially when the cohort's formation is organized to fortify that exit before all else.

Caz knew this from the beginning. He knew...

Caz made it depressingly clear that it isn't possible for any man alone to beat the Guardians. That's why this rule exists. No one leaves Shaolin… at least not according to the rules. *Not according to the rules… The die will close doors, but open windows.*

And the die. The die. That whimsical vehicle of chance that would teach Flash to see what he wasn't seeing, think in ways that he would not, and act without hesitation.

"Options good, bad, reasonable, and unreasonable. I'm suggesting you embrace the random so that you can learn to think and act in ways that you would not."

That corner at the end of Caz's index line was the only option to escape the gauntlet alive—a corner the height of the lowest hanging branch. He mustn't hesitate. His first lesson on hesitation cost him 10 excruciating lashes. This time, his penalty would be dea—

A Tip of the Hat

. . . the battle began unceremoniously with surreptitious attack to the neck of Flash's closest adversary, his nearest brother in the cohort. He felt his index and ring finger together penetrate the conditioned neck of his neighbor, compressing his carotid artery and causing a temporary loss of consciousness. By the time his body hit the ground, there were two more like him, limply collapsing. He caught them off-guard. Fifteen to go.

Flash did some more of that speedy monk stuff, that dim mak jazz, and dropped two more of those within the distance of his outstretched fingers. He stabbed vagus and sciatic nerves, pinched tracheas, and blocked qi flow at key acupoints, all so quickly, the Guardians didn't know what hit them. He exploited the element of surprise, a very simple lesson that his fallen brothers would relive the rest of their lives with embarrassment, at least insofar as they remembered it. They wouldn't remember much.

At this point, there were no questions left as to whether this challenge would go down. It had already begun, and Flash was in the black. His momentum was rising faster than a celibate monk's morning wood. But were his skills sound enough to sustain it?

The next line of warriors, made up of six hungry aggressors who hadn't tasted blood in decades, began to circle while those farthest prepared in formation to block the gate by any and all means. He had mere moments before those he attacked first would regain their composure and seek redemption.

After his initial assault, the battalion realized Flash didn't intend to play fair. They surmised very quickly that included means of escape. While they could indeed protect the temple gate with their lives, they could not possibly guard every inch of the wall enclosing the training yard. They adjusted as quickly as a flock of birds in flight, spontaneously and in perfect synchronicity closing in on him from all sides and blocking a possible retreat to the walls of his entrance. One door closed.

They quickly reoriented under the misassumption that he would try to flee as far as possible from the proper gate, as far as possible from Caz. This would have been reasonable. It would have been safer. It would have been his most likely decision.

Observing the rapid reorientation of these six, with three blocking his retreat, and three blocking his advance, Flash did the unexpected and did indeed rush toward the main gate, attacking the center of three guardians directly in front of him before needing to face the six remaining at the gate itself, Caz calmly in their center.

In striking his sixth adversary Flash's luck ran out. It was too good to be true, too easy. Who was he kidding, making such easy work of five guardians with stealthy backyard tactics? Now the element of surprise had run its course, the remaining guardians shifted into high gear and a true display of skill was imminent. Flash's crane fist strike was caught in midflight on the inside of his wrist, gripped so tightly that power drained from his arm. In a second, his brawny challenger threw a complex combination of low sweep (evaded), neck chop (blocked), and full-body blow (landed hard), followed by a whipping throw that Flash could not prevent, but which he was able to blend with.

He listened to the force and in mid-air rotated into a controlled aerial cartwheel and reversed the lock, using the leverage of his bodyweight to pull and throw his adversary into a headlong roll. The roll was rough but contained as his adversary glided between two other guardians and rolled to his feet. Flash leapt so quickly, the triad was caught off guard by both his stunning speed and his brashness. Wasn't he supposed to be the attacked?

He spread the two in front apart simultaneously with a flying split kick—hitting one, meeting the block of the second but still applying penetrating force, but missing the third, who stepped back just out of range of Flash's third mid-air kick. His opponent, the same man who struck and threw him moments before, reentered his space and attacked ferociously while the other two recouped and looked for an opening.

Flash had just enough wherewithal to know this persistent monk who was giving him so much trouble was *the* Masta Killa, RZA's longtime mentor. Apparently, he wasn't *just* a stellar swordsman. His qin na (locking and controlling skills) were just proven to be extraordinary. Flash couldn't let this monk get a hold of him again… it would be all over. He knew that if he got caught up here for even a moment longer, he'd be swarmed and bludgeoned.

Killa attacked first with a drop-sweep to Flash's front foot, which was in the process of finding the earth as he landed from his split-triple kick. He caught it successfully, but it didn't have the impact expected. Masta marveled at how light and agile Flash was in recovery, blending with Killa's force and spinning with it. He found his footing just before Killa's follow-up, an aggressive Lotus fist combination that left gaps in his guard.

Flash recalled the many times RZA laughed and joked about Killa's gastrointestinal problems—he loved those spicy noodles—and made no attempt to hide it when teaching. Killa's flatulence was notorious amongst his students as he'd make no effort to hide or curtail its power. "Qi flows," he'd often announce as the toxic fumes watered the eyes of fearful students struggling to maintain their horse stances, adding insult to injury.

Amidst Killa's flurry of strikes Flash saw a straight line to the bowels of Killa and took it, penetrating his lower abdominals three finger-widths below the navel with his Dim Mak. He burrowed straight to conception vessel 6, the dan tian, the ol' sea of energy, the infamous poop button. This triggered a shock wave of nerve pain throughout his body, a massive drop in qi that buckled his knees, and the effusive release of bowels full of spicy noodle digest. Councilman 3 slapped his own forehead.

This was a stroke of poetic genius that gave Caz an internal chuckle. But Flash had wasted time with this stubborn adversary and the two he separated, only marginally stunned, were now firing a barrage of kicks and punches for which Flash had to address in ambidextrous blocking and evasive footwork. Time slowed, and Flash dismissed the flurry, fifteen or more techniques, with the clarity of a man who reads intentions and merely waits for the techniques they form, at least until one of the two reached for Flash's robes to initiate a throw, likely drawing inspiration from Killa's near-success moments earlier.

As soon as contact was made, however, Flash became hyperaware of his own structure. He felt his channels open, the instantaneous shifts in pressure applied from his opponent, and he felt the earth beneath his feet. He was ready this time and sensed it as it came. An ever so slight gap in his adversary's grip was all Flash needed in order to sense a subtle imbalance in his structure, to deleverage the technique with a forward step, and, blending seamlessly with his opponent, spin 180 degrees to reverse the lock and to throw, sending him heels-over-head into the other attacker.

Flash flooded with confidence, recognizing the fruit of his countless losses and laborious push-hands efforts with Caz. Flash could sense the all through the one. But his footwork, well, that was well vetted and derived from his sessions with the Furious Five, when Flash learned to line and stack his opponents, rather than remain exposed to the flurry of many.

The master of Lightness contains multitudes. He left his forms and strategies behind, but his skills seemed more than readily ample. His empty cup was full of options. It was an impressive display that all guardians took note of. The three who retreated to the rear wall (plus three of those first fallen and revived) under false assumption were now closing back in, pressing Flash from behind cautiously, because no one imagined Flash would get this far. Cautiously because they didn't want to shit themselves like Masta. No one imagined this but one, that is, the monk enjoying his top student's display of kung fu, his masterful display of the power of Lightness.

After the poke-n-poo technique and the two-on-one flurry that followed, Flash ignored the six on his tail altogether, for to engage them would reduce his probability of survival to zero. Instead, he faced the gate and the six plus Caz protecting it. Caz was grooving move for move, strike for strike with Flash, feeling his flow, sensing his thoughts. *That's my monk*. Caz tipped the conical hat in his heart to his remarkable student and friend and said goodbye with a proud sense of loss.

Flash, with a runway that wouldn't inspire, exploded from his concave in the battle at Caz and company, juked left with an aggressive faint, forcing the guardians to commit in that direction with him. Then he impetuously turned right with the agile traction of a leopard that left them all off-footed and stumbling. All except Caz that is, who remained stoically centered minus the gangster lean.

Flash bolted toward the marked corner with a few light, rapid steps before leaping at the intersection of the two walls. All eyes widened in surprise, including all those peering through the cracks in the courtyard walls and the few who managed to peer over the top, bodies stacked feet upon shoulders. Two council members stood without realizing it. All bodies were pulled forward toward Flash as one feels the impulse to reach for a stumbling child or catch a falling glass.

Flash's right foot touched the right side of the corner first at abdomen-height, giving him a great deal of leverage to kick up and to the left, touching the left side of the corner at head height with his left foot, a third step higher still, feeling the pull of force through his toes and connection throughout his being, four times total and gone.

An Impudent Chop

Councilman 3 along with his personal guardians, Masta Killa and the guardian thrown viciously heels-over-head, entered Flash's room with heads hung low in search of answers. Everyone wanted answers. This news would spread quickly and would stain the reputation of Shaolin for eras to come.

One, just one monk could challenge and make fools of the 18 Guardians of Shaolin? Impossible. Well… impossible no more. The Guardians were real. And they were mortal. This was no longer up for debate. And Lightness. Lightness will find its place, not among the greatest styles, but among the higher methods of spiritual advancement. The Guardians saw no new techniques or tactics; they just felt the presence of a superior person. They'd been outwitted and outmatched.

The room was bare, as most were in the monks' quarters: an oil lamp on a wooden desk, a wooden bed with a woven bamboo pad for softer sleep, a single bed sheet neatly folded at its foot, and a note pad lying atop it. Masta opened the pad and saw what seemed at first glance to be poems or koans. Councilman 3 snatched the notepad and aggressively began to read the first page aloud:

> "Grandmaster come faster
> Than any known cell to the bone
> Full grown, he's a one of a kind
> And Flash is gonna rock your mind, huh"

Councilman 3's eyes widened in bewilderment. Page two:

> "Cause I never had a fright when I'm on the fight
> I beat a bum like them up just the other night
> When he opened his eyes all he could see
> was the referee, the ceiling, and me
>
> My teachers were martial arts masters and monks
> My class was survival and school was the slumps

Math was counting copper, large coffers no doubt
And my homework was knocking sucker monks out"

And the third:

"Aaaaaaah!
I'm the King of the Temple Y'all
What, what, what are you?
What are you? What are you?
What, what, what are you?
What are you? What are you stupid?"

Councilman 3 tore the pages loose and slammed the notebook on the ground. He and his guardians were altogether baffled by the inane scribbling's in the book. Was Flash insane? Who was he writing to? For? For what? How could the author of this madness humiliate the Guardians? Each page added greater confusion and served only to fan the flames of anger and frustration they felt.

Beneath the bed heals-over-head monk discovered two scrolls. The first they knew all too well, that of Dim Mak. As sole recipient of the poke-n-poo, Masta Killa's shame painted his face red and elicited a snort and chortle from the others. But the second, Qing Gong, was far more unexpected and hit like an eerily familiar erhu riff. They connected the dots immediately: Flash's speed, his sensitivity to touch and reaction time, his effortless wall-scaling escape, his creative spontaneity.

It all made sense now. And it occurred to all in tandem that Flash had had help. No one could have translated this scroll alone, could have interpreted the simple outline into that living ghost who bested the best. But what would they have had Caz do instead? He had his duties to the temple and to his disciple. And he broke no rules, technically.

Surveying the entire scroll top to bottom, line by line, they determined that this scroll would never again see the light of day. They also determined that as soon as it was locked away they would take it for themselves in secret. It had some cool shit in there.Toward the end of the scroll, examining it for anything that stood out as abnormal, any hints at what was going on in the mind of Master Flash, they noticed a fresh stain. More brightly colored than the rest, Flash's chop stood out like a sore thumb, taunting them, both the impudent act of adding his chop without permission and the frivolous revision beneath:

Be weightless, bitches.
Grandmaster Flash

PART 2

The 9 Scrolls of Weightlessness

Time
Uncertainty
Change
Transformation
Weightlessness
Process
Integration
Lightness
Mastery

Foreword to Part 2

How to Read This Book

This book is a reverse mullet. The mullet, as you may know, is a haircut with short, spikey trim in the front and long, trailing hair in the back. It's a haircut that says, "business in the front, party in the back." It's an attitude that says, "I'm easy going, but if you spill my beer we're gonna have a problem."

The reverse mullet says the opposite. First discovered, I imagine, by the first college bro to pass out while his drunk friends decided to shave the back of his head with short clippers. It's also an attitude, one that says, "Oops." But that's not all. The reverse mullet is the life of the party, but it waits until the last guests leave to hang out with the host and discuss philosophy until the sun comes up.

I hope you enjoyed the story; it's time to get down to business.

In the pages that follow, we'll explore a wide range of topics that I would place under the mind-body domain, not as that domain currently is, but as it should be. We'll explore the relationship between ourselves and our complex environments, extrapolating science-based tools and robust strategies that manufacture a sense of weightlessness in life—power, presence, and the toolkit necessary to unburden ourselves of the weight that holds us back in life.

This is not a one-stop shop for positive thinking and superficial self-help. It's a roadmap, one that will evolve with you over time and prescribe the tools you need as you need them.

The remaining sections of this book are not linear, which is to say that they're intended to stand-alone and address specific (yet integral) aspects of mind-body development and performance. I wrote the book as it is because mind-body concepts and tools age in us like a fine wine. Time is a key factor in assimilation. And context creates meaning. If this book earns a spot on your shelf, it will speak differently to you every time you refer back to it.

As for *The Essence of Lightness* short story in Part 1, well, I'm a firm believer that facts are great, but we learn better through narrative, and better still when we see ourselves within it. The story provides context; the scrolls provide the deeper discussion and insights. If you are to give the story a reread after you've digested some of the principles on the pages that follow, it too will speak to you in new ways, for it embodies key insights and principles of performance and mastery throughout.

The scrolls may be read from front to back (there's a natural progression in them) but they can also be read in any order whatsoever. While each scroll's theme is an integral aspect of your larger growth story, the reverse mullet has no rules. Enjoy the story if that's your thing. Delve deeper if you're a lifer in the mind-body game or looking for that edge in life. It's okay to have your dessert first on occasion, just don't overlook the meat and veg.

For the serious mind-body and peak performance enthusiasts, I hope the scrolls will serve as focused discussions on specific subcomponents of personal transformation and self-mastery.

And while these nine scrolls comprise a narrative in and of themselves (your narrative of personal transformation and self-mastery), for those looking to study and implement the methodology of Weightlessness yourselves, you'll find the theoretical framework in The Weightlessness Scroll, its implementation (assessment and workouts) in The Process Scroll, its application to life beyond training in The Integration Scroll, and advanced theories and practices in The Lightness Scroll. The other scrolls (Time, Uncertainty, Change, and Transformation) serve as underlying philosophical and science-based discussions that inform the system.

You'll also find that The Lightness Scroll refers directly to key sections and chapter titles from *The Essence of Lightness* story, delving rather deeply into key performance principles behind the narrative.

For the Heroes

This book is long. As much as I would have loved to add images that detail various exercises, it would have been too much. Additionally, this work has turned out to be largely philosophical and principle-based. So, rather than try to adapt it to a general "how to" manual, I'm leaving it awesome.

BUT! For those who want to delve deeper and implement Weightlessness, or if you'd merely like to stay connected and see what else Weightlessness has to offer, you can visit www.weightlessness.co and join my free newsletter, where a supplementary e-book will be sent to you that accompanies this book, containing some of the demonstrative material that didn't fit here.

As always, be weightless.

Key Definitions:

- Weightlessness (The *method*)—Also referred to as Weightlessness Training, Weightlessness is an integrative model of personal growth, mind-body integration, and peak performance. Also known as "The Art of Unburdening," Weightlessness aims to unburden you from all that holds you back, while empowering you to navigate uncertainty in life with a sense of power and grace.
- weightlessness (The *experience* - with lower case w)—A momentary state of experience marked by sensations of nonjudgmental awareness, embodied presence, and personal power.
- The Tao of Weightlessness—A polarity stemming from the perception of passing time—torn between the desires for both an awesome tomorrow and a weightless today. These outcomes are best manufactured through antithetical practices—those of applied stress or cultivated sensitivity.
- Stress—That which challenges, either in mind or body, our sense of homeostasis. Stress is cumulative (as well as relative), so one might consider a compounding effect of volatility at work, a diet with excessive sugars, and long cardiovascular sessions as placing undue pressure on the mind-body complex at the same time, while only one of those factors alone might be perfectly manageable. Stress is not merely a psychoemotional phenomenon but a holistic and systemic trigger for breakdown or transformation.
- Sensitivity—The capacity to intuit or receive environmental (including internal sensation) information. This too is not merely a reactive or hyperemotional state but speaks to the degree of holistic awareness one has cultivated. People have countless points of data reception via the nervous system; sensitivity aims to access them, generally through awareness of the five senses plus thought.

- Meditation (the *practice*)—That which cultivates awareness, concentration, and nonattachment as skills comprising meditative experiences.
- Meditation (the *experience*)—A preintellectual, nonjudgmental state of awareness of one's immediate experience. Meditative moments comprise the richest, most flavorful experiences in life, the ones that make life worth living. Meditation IS life.
- The Weightlessness Spectrum—The foundational, prescriptive model of mind-body integration and peak performance within Weightlessness. It informs the allocation of key tools and practices across three pillars: strength, flexibility, and meditation.
- Lightness Training—Advanced protocols designed to augment sensitivity, adaptability, and mind-body weightlessness. It designs the living balance between stress and sensitivity within daily practice, integrating four key pillars: strength, dynamic stretching, qigong, and ballistic weight training.

The Time Scroll

Time is a game played beautifully by children.
—Heraclitus

”

The Time Scroll addresses the flux of time, and our illusive perception of its continuity. It introduces the Tao of Weightlessness—the violent dialectic that lives in your mind and mine as we choose presence over preparation and vice versa. Are you present to the passage of time and the novelty it contains? Or are you busy preparing for the future? Weightlessness transcends this inescapable paradox by fully embracing, even augmenting the polarities of resilience to stress (preparation for an awesome tomorrow) and awareness of the present (experience of a weightless moment).

Moments within Moments

The ancient Greek philosopher Zeno presented a paradox over two thousand years ago that even today annoys philosophy students worldwide, or at least it did during my studies. He presented a series of puzzles, essentially demonstrating the perception we have of movement as illusory. In one of his classic examples he proved that an arrow shot through space could never actually reach its target, for to cross any amount of space it would first have to traverse half the distance. For the arrow to reach the halfway marker it would first have to reach the quarter marker. And to reach that point, you guessed it; it would have to again bridge half that distance.

The problem, Zeno identified, is that space is infinitely divisible, and it is physically impossible to traverse an infinite number of points, thereby rendering our perception of movement in general, and the trajectory of an arrow in particular, an illusion. Fortunately, for us in the modern world, we learn that Zeno was an idiot by age five when we crawl and grab and punch and poop. Stuff happens when we will it. But we can't seem, through any form of analysis, to bypass this divide completely.

There are moments, in time and space, and there are timelines (or narratives), and the latter is not merely the sum of the former… Time is movement, a magical force that manifests like a tapestry from thread or a film from a series of snapshots.

An extraordinary phenomenon occurs when we learn to simply remain still, innocent of egoistic judgment, and aware. We start to notice things; details, colors, and sensations that were there the whole time in each passing moment, but that we'd overlooked. We begin to notice moments within moments, the infinite data points in an arrow's trajectory.

We have common measures of time. All of us have watches, clocks, or smart devices that keep us in tune to seconds passing. We measure our ages, relationships, and careers in years, our illnesses in days, and our schedule in hours. But if we lost our watches and calendars and just had experiences, that is, if the relationships of things defined our perception of time, then interesting patterns emerge.

Remember your first year at college? How about your first experience abroad? Time seemed to have passed so slowly at those points, whereas in later years, our experience of time flew by. When things are novel, when we have no previously established filters or no overbearing ego that rapidly associates the new with the old, then we experience more of the present. We take in more information. And time slows down.

Time is the change-relationship between things.

Alternatively, once things become familiar in life, years pass without even noticing. The first few months of a romantic relationship might feel equal in length to the following four or five years after the honeymoon phase has fizzled.

Time flies by, not when we're having fun, but when we "get it," when we know what to expect, when we embrace routine and stop taking chances. If we removed objective measures of time, it would be reduced to the evolving relationships of things. As we observe less change in life, as we neglect to see the moments within moments, the stuff of life directly before us, time flies. Linear narratives are created from cherry-picked key moments, just as historians chronicle the winners. But this is just a story.

Yet, when we slow down in stillness, when we listen and feel without judgment, we have a far richer experience. When we experience more within a unit of time through cultivated sensitivity (nonjudgmental awareness) we experience more. And when we experience more data per unit of time, we live more life.

We don't, as of yet, have the ability to travel back in time or extend our lives considerably (though that will change soon). But we do have the ability to live more life right now, to experience the richness of many lives if we simply breathe and open ourselves to the infinity of experience that exists within each passing moment.

The Rebirth of Weightlessness

Several years back, I attempted to scale up what was, at that time, a flourishing personal training business. I relocated to a larger space in Shanghai, took on double the overhead with double the space, and failed to bring in the right trainers and partners to extend my reach. It turned out developing a business based on one's craft is a very different game than scaling said business beyond the scope of the craftsman.

I put all I had and then some into the move, and the stress and pressure of survival became ever more real by the day. I started relying heavily on coffee for the buzz, and alcohol for the release. I was never a big drinker, but one to two drinks a night is more than enough to turn a trainer into a hypocrite. You can't outrun your fork as they say, or in this case, your drink.

One of those mornings felt a bit heavier than usual, as I watched the toilet bowl turn red instead of that color we expect while going number two. I hate doctor visits with a passion and will be at deaths door before dragging my cynical ass there. At this time, however, I had to think of more than just the internal bleeding; I also had no health insurance, IN SHANGHAI, and was torn between spending my money on a colonoscopy or feeding myself for the next three weeks. Not a terribly fun call to make. But I reasoned, after three days of watching the toilet turn red of varying luminescence, that if I didn't get checked, there might be no body to feed for three weeks.

So, I did, and it was confirmed… you actually have to take care of yourself if you want to be healthy.

I've always known my body and coffee don't quite get along. I love coffee. I think it's one of those things that truly makes life worth living. The aroma, the buzz, the environment and culture of coffee drinking that steels you out of time and responsibility for a while, but which stimulates you to think, create, and do.

But the acid… the acid just wages war on my gut, and I need to use it in moderation if I'm going to sustain strong digestion and keep inflammation down. The doctor found nothing that I couldn't fix without medication and a little more discipline. So I fixed it. I cut coffee, cut alcohol, and fasted to let my body do what it has evolved to do, heal. But this didn't fix my overall state of mind; it just bought me more time to suffer the fear and shame of ongoing struggle.

At that same time, I joined my dice buddy and accountability Nazi, Michael, for our weekly Friday night burger, beer, and dice-for-the-future meetings. We had a tradition at that time of sporting for each other every other week and didn't mind running up the bill. I remember one of those nights feeling nervous about going, as I had two weeks before my $6,000 rent was due. I had to pay two employees, and that very morning I woke up with less than $150 to my name and no immediate solution to address my situation.

To this day, going and showing up at that absurd tradition was probably one of the worst financial decisions of my life, but it might have saved my soul. We are defined by our choices. We create ourselves every time we decide to honor a commitment, and even more so when we have something at stake, something to lose, skin in the game. And I had.

That night, I told Michael, likely with watering eyes of self-pity, about my situation. To which he coldly yet compassionately reminded, "So, you said you were going to write a book this year. It's the cusp of June. I'm no expert, but I would imagine if you don't roll the dice tonight to place the option of starting that book on the table, it's not going to happen."

I told him I was one day from bankruptcy and he asked if I was going to man up and roll the dice on one of my yearly targets and lifelong bucket list items—to tell the story of Weightlessness. He called me out on my own personal objectives, which I can confirm is the single last thing anyone experiencing depression, self-pity, and self-doubt wants to hear or feels capable of processing.

But warriors aren't made on the playground. They've got more scars and demons than civilians can understand. This hurt as much as the most severe hits I'd taken over thirty years of martial arts training. But

Michael was right. I didn't place that personal target on my list with the caveat that I'd write a book if I didn't get sick, or I wasn't busy, or if the stars aligned and everything was perfect in life. No, my goal was to write a fucking book. And life throws you curveballs.

He was right. And the truth hurt that day, and it made me stronger the next and thereafter. What I'd been doing wasn't working. It was time to try what I wasn't doing, what I was neglecting.

The very next day, I decided to make a new commitment to myself. My health had not yet fully recovered. And I was indeed on the verge of bankruptcy. We even had an acronym for it that allowed us to share quick updates on proximity to death—DTB—days-to-bankruptcy. I acknowledged, as we all must do at some point, that life is fleeting, and while I could spend every waking moment hustling, there was never a guarantee hustling will, in fact, pay off. This is a probabilistic illusion that stems from hindsight bias in all of us. I delve into this illusion in The Uncertainty Scroll next.

Successful people work hard. They usually hustle. And so their lesson to you is hustle and work hard and you too can have your wildest dreams come true. But they conveniently neglect to mention their networks, capital, knowledge, immediate access to relevant resources, and strong partnerships. This is more than sour grapes excuse making. It is an existential problem with success narratives. Context matters.

Two people can work equally hard, take similar risks, make similar sacrifices of family and friends for career, and no matter how you cut it, someone born in Venezuela at exactly the time of this writing, is at a greater disadvantage than someone born in New York in achieving the same financial goals. Technology is bridging that gap, no doubt. But life is unfair, so we deal.

So, I decided not to hustle, against all common reason, for the outcome wasn't under my control. I decided, instead, to release what I felt was fifteen years of pent up passion and reflection on my personal treatise of mind-body development—Weightlessness Training.

I became obsessed. Every morning that I wasn't coaching I was usually waiting outside Starbucks before the doors opened in order to get in four hours of writing before noon. I had good days and bad. Passion-filled passages one day and mindless dribble the next. But I showed up. I kept showing up. And in this absurd twist of events, in the commitment to do what had to be done one way or another before I die, and affirming there is no better time than the present to do such things, I started to heal in mind as well as body.

My mood improved by the day, and this certainly presented a different energy and impression on clients and friends. I opened the door to my deepest interests again and, in so doing, opened the door to passion, personal growth, and indefatigable focus. I embraced the fear of failure, the fear of death. And I relinquished control. I didn't throw caution to the wind or bury my business, I merely reoriented my focus, refusing to give negative emotional energy to worry and, instead, fed my spirit.

Four and a half months later, the first draft of *In Pursuit of Weightlessness* was complete. I'd turned my business around and moved from 1 DTB to a whopping 60, which felt like the heavens opened and showered me with cash flow. My health and body were back intact and ready to coach effectively again without breach of integrity. Weightlessness healed me. And life got better.

For the second time in my life, Weightlessness became my saving grace. I tell the origin story of Weightlessness in *In Pursuit of Weightlessness*—the unexpected outcome of three months of solitude in the jungle of Phangan island, Thailand, where I set out to internalize and integrate for myself the disparate elements of mental and physical development I'd studied prior. After three months in the jungle, I was weightless… burden free, focused, and in peak physical condition. It's not hard to understand anymore how surrendering to Weightlessness for a second time killed the man with blood in his stool and water in his eyes just four months prior and released the lion yet again.

The remainder of this book is the story of Weightlessness, and the comprehensive mind-body system it has become since that bold decision to honor the die over reason.

The Tao of Weightlessness

The not-so-hidden reveal of this story is that it isn't really about me. It's about you. It's about all of us. There comes a point for all of us—hell, there may be more than one—when we need to boldly decide if we're going to sacrifice these precious moments in the hope of better moments in the future, or whether we're going to throw caution to the wind and embrace without restraint the beauty that is before us, the life that is passing with every single breath.

Now I'm not suggesting, and this is important, that life improved after that decision *because* of that decision. Things could have developed very differently, if not disastrously. The need to make decisions in spite of complete uncertainty as to how events will unfold is very much the topic of the next Uncertainty Scroll.

But what I hope my story does is highlight the extremely prominent yet polar selves within all of us that battle for dominance. We're all torn between the desire for an awesome tomorrow and a weightless today, between enjoying quality, weightless moments now or sacrificing those same moments to invest, to strive, to fight for immediate survival in hope of a brighter future.

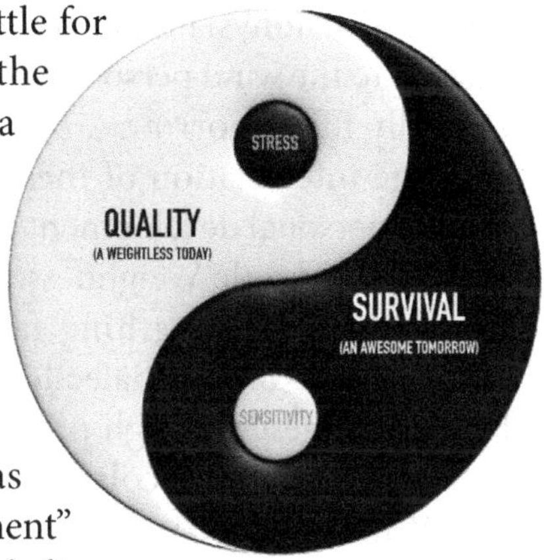

It's an existential dilemma if there ever were one. And it isn't as simple as "being responsible" or "living in the moment" as many coaches or gurus would have us believe.

Join me in a quick thought experiment. Let's say you know with certainty that you have exactly thirty years to live... to the day. Now, close your eyes for just a few seconds and feel through your three biggest priorities in life. After you've identified them, allocate an ideal percentage of your daily or weekly time to those priorities. Write them down.

Now, imagine you have exactly one week to live, to the minute. Close your eyes, and feel your way through your three biggest priorities, as well as how much time you'll ideally allocate to each. Write them down.

Everyone I have ever asked this, with rare exception, has had very different answers to each inquiry. This is both reasonable and troubling at the same time. Presumably, they're not schizophrenic. And it's unlikely their personal values have changed in the mere one-minute between each question, or their identities or personalities, yet if you're like the rest of us, you have very different answers too, either in terms of composition of priorities or time allocation you'd give to each. For many, the biggest difference lies in time allocated to family versus work, with family and friends winning out in the one-week scenario, while work gains a greater percentage of time in the thirty-year scenario, for example.

This is, for some, so glaringly self-explanatory that the gravity of it is missed altogether. But it's not nothing. You are not one person. You have at least two personas, each with a different opinion of how time affects the value of things.

You can lump most systems of ethics and, for that matter, most religions into one of two camps: those that place more weight on tomorrow than today (Christianity, Islam, etc.), and those that place a greater emphasis on the ephemerality of life (Zen, Taoism, etc.). We all have both Dionysian and Apollonian natures, a devil may care, throw caution to the wind persona, and a responsible, rational self that prepares carefully for tomorrow.

The interrelation of these two selves is the essence, the absolute crux of personal development and transformation. For those who "get it" and want to bottle Weightlessness into a be-in-the-moment philosophy, it isn't. There's something far more comprehensive here, a way of making sense of two dialectical timelines (the now and the future) and balancing these through prioritization and foundational training and developmental protocols.

When was the last time you said you were going to eat right and hit the gym three days a week? How long did it last? Most New Year's resolutions make it to the 2nd of January before being overridden. Apollo understands the value of health, of a strong body and a focused mind. Dionysus says, on no particular eve: *this little bottle of champagne is for a special occasion, and that occasion is NOW.*

Here's the challenge for us all: if you will die in exactly one week, Dionysus's is the only reasonable perspective. Only in the context of hope, longevity, and legacy does Apollonian thinking pay off.

We're torn between two selves, both of them brilliantly insightful. If only we knew exactly when our last breath would come. We're charged to live amidst complete uncertainty and to, nevertheless, make decisions with real consequences based on completely unsubstantiated beliefs about the timeline for payoff or failure. This is absurdity manifest. And it won't change. Uncertainty is our greatest certainty.

Weightlessness addresses this haunting dilemma by embracing it in full, not denying the value of one timeframe or the other. Both matter. Weightlessness accepts that we have to act and make meaningful decisions from positions of ignorance, partial or complete, without knowing how much time is left.

So, the only logical conclusion is to improve the hardware that governs both timelines: the quality of one's experience of the present and one's resilience to hardship (and with it, exposure to upside in the future).

Warriors are not made on the playground. Our bodies and minds are built to grow in response to stress. When muscle is torn from weight training, it becomes bigger and stronger. When you're injected with a vaccine containing the virus you're trying to immunize, your body creates antibodies that make you immune to that virus. When you find yourself in a foreign country where no one speaks your native language, you learn that new language at lightning pace. It is stress (the appropriate kind) that makes us stronger, that immunizes us against the stresses and uncertainties of tomorrow.

On the other hand, the mind that can perceive and feel this present moment is not one built from stress alone but one that has cultivated awareness of and sensitivity to the data of passing time.

How loving and sympathetic are we to those we care about when we feel stressed, when we're worried about our jobs, when we're in pain, when life doesn't pan out the way we expect? How optimistic and focused are we when negative news or the pressures of work come closing in on us? The mind that relies on judgments and the ego that holds on to fixed notions of the Good cannot fully love a child, empathize with a partner, perform well at work, sooth nerves, release tension from the body, and simply be present to beautifully fleeting moments in life.

The role of Weightlessness Training is not to alter or correct your values or present a different version of reality, but to empower you to flourish amidst uncertainty.

I don't know what decisions you'll need to make tomorrow, but I do know that your probability of making intelligent, unbiased ones that don't stem from fear, and executing on them day after day goes way up when they're supported by a strong, lean body and a focused, unburdened mind. You'll have the greatest chance at having strong relationships when you're not self-absorbed. And you'll stand the greatest chance of exploiting opportunities if you survive hardship that's sure to present itself along the way.

Embracing only one side of this equation, sacrificing tomorrow for today or today for tomorrow, is an untenable position that leaves you vulnerable to negative events: sickness, poverty, isolation, depression.

Life must be lived today, and tomorrow must also be prepared for. We must embrace the stress of physical training to prepare for unforeseen hardship tomorrow, and we must cultivate sensitivity to the present in order to extract as much joy and peace today.

To be truly weightless, we're playing a game of probabilities, accessing deeper levels of sensitivity and performance, so that those things that motivate us to be our best, whether they're career, family, or passion oriented, are actualized with greater effectiveness, ease, and speed, and with fewer burdens holding us down.

It's About the Other 23...

In the pages that follow, I'll discuss the notion of "showing up." I'll talk about commitment and compliance to protocol to the tilt. You'll likely find me extreme at times. But when I'm not talking about the cold and calculated details of effective programming, I'm talking about life.

This journey is not for the fainthearted. It will test you in every way. It will pound your body and invade your mind. It will show you how little you truly know yourself. And it will show you who you really are. But please, don't mistake the forest for the trees.

Weightlessness is not about that grueling hour in the gym, it's about the other 23.

It's about the other 23 hours a day where the stuff of life happens. That's what we're training for. Weightlessness is about extracting the greatest personal payoff in life. It's about covering your bases, the essence of who you are and how you show up to the world, so that your experiences in life are rich and fulfilling. This cannot be bought. It can't be gamed. It requires conscientious commitment to being better tomorrow, in body and mind, than you are today.

And when you consistently bring a better machine to the race, one that's well calibrated and optimized for performance, you're far more likely to win, regardless of how you define winning.

In the coming pages, I'll discuss the psychology of performance. And in those conversations, I'll examine the frustrating paradox of discipline vs. discretion in decision making. Most of us feel a sense of control and freedom when we get to choose what to eat, how to train, and how to spend our time. It feels great to choose that ice cream over a salad, to choose that TV series over diligent work. This sense of control is an illusion that blinds us to true freedom and self-expression.

I've seen this demon more times than I can count. He always rears his ugly head between weeks five and eight of committed training programs. He's the demon that says: *You've done good work thus far; a little dessert won't hurt. Skip your training this morning; you can always make it up tonight.* But you don't.

It feels so good to relieve that pressure. It feels good, ironically, to unburden ourselves of the structure and discipline of training, diet, and development… for a time. And that's the kicker. By the time you start to deteriorate and feel a loss of focus, softness around the midsection, and a general loss of personal control in life, it's too late. And it's unlikely you'll correlate that feeling with a lack of training because you're not immediately penalized for those decisions. Deterioration takes time. And then the excuses come.

I don't have enough time to train (even though you experienced ample time for all things with prior discipline). *I don't have the energy to train* (even though you experienced a dramatic increase in energy from prior training). You forget that structure bought you freedom, that constraint bought you time. And now you feel that training impedes both. You forget that adding weight made you feel light.

This is the grand paradox of Weightlessness—we must add weight to unburden.

For those who don't understand Weightlessness, this is a laughable paradox. It's ironic and counterintuitive. *If Weightlessness is about removing burdens, why do I need to take on burdens to be free?*

This comes down to perception and expectation in the end. It may require a reorientation of how we view the world and ourselves. It may require a reorientation of how we view time, its value and its passing. It may require us to reframe burdens altogether.

Those who are hungry for a sense of immediate control stemming from their right to choose what they want right now are not focused on the big picture. They're not giving a great deal of thought to the other 23, those precious and fleeting moments of time where life is.

Those who are willing to relinquish a sense of control (for discipline) find their greatest sense of it. Focusing on immediate comfort, avoiding stress, and triggering serotonin release with sweets or social media is about as close to living that rockstar lifestyle as possible without actually doing cocaine (though some have made the case that sugar does more damage to the body, takes more lives, and is far more addictive than cocaine). But there's nothing left in the moments thereafter but a deeper hole and a stronger craving to fill.

This paradox—accessing peace through discomfort, or adding weight to unburden—disappears when you engage in the current moment with full presence. This will be revisited in the context of Lightness Training and self-mastery in The Lightness and Mastery Scrolls.

You find power in personal resilience and beautiful moments within moments. We must train, all of us. We must train if we desire greater payoff and presence, but the training isn't the point! Don't assume that all you see when experiencing the discomforts of training, or the burdens of life, is all there is. A world of opportunity and beauty awaits you on the other side. The path to peace is through discomfort. The path to weightlessness is through the taking on of intelligent, prescriptive burdens.

When is Weightlessness?

In my last tribe in Shanghai, I had an interesting exchange with one of the tribers. The tribe of six plus me, which made seven, were sitting in a circle and discussing the principle of nonattachment and, with it, the path to unburdening. This was after four or five weeks of training, well past the window of excitement and well into the grueling shit of personal development.

Nonattachment is an interesting topic because individuals process it's meaning in many ways. It's very easy to see the superficial application, which is the removal of negativity or burdensome thought that prevents us from problem solving or merely feeling good about ourselves. But there's a deeper layer that strikes at the essence of who we are, that speaks to the *I* in *my* experience.

As we'll discuss in The Transformation Scroll, our identities are constructs, partly volitional, yet mostly circumstantial. Over a lifetime of countless experiences, sensations, learnings, and associations, we wind up with the fallacious assumption that there is a constant "I" behind our experiences. We feel and sense, and even express ourselves from the perspective of a fixed, static entity that goes through the world and thinks and feels stuff.

But a great reveal from both classical Buddhism AND contemporary neuroscience is that there's no man behind the curtains. This experience of self is merely an illusion of centrality extrapolated from the immediate, fleeting phenomena within conscious experience.

Many resources are out there for those who want to delve deeper into the science of consciousness or the classic thought proofs of nonattachment stemming from various meditative traditions. I'd recommend Ramachandran for the former, and Sam Harris or Jiddu Krishnamurti for the latter. But that depth really isn't within the scope of this book. My agenda is different.

My agenda is to give you something nontheoretical and wholly practical, stemming from that information, to integrate it into an actionable framework of personal development that makes sense of the many disparate aspects of human performance. With that, I start and end with a question:

Are You Weightless?

I have said for many years now that meditation is both the means and the end of weightlessness (the momentary phenomenon, not just the system). We'll delve much deeper into why that is later in The Weightlessness Scroll. But it's important, as a starting point to approach the journey ahead with right focus. It's extremely common for people to get into my programs and after four to six weeks mistake the trees for the forest and conclude that the grueling, high-stress training regimen is the core of Weightlessness. It isn't.

If I could do away with the physical training altogether, believe me I would. But it is, as will be proven, a necessity. For the mind is hard-pressed to discover true freedom and grit without a strong body. Thus, it's important, as you and I walk through the narrative of Weightlessness, the story of your own personal growth and self-mastery, that we don't mistake the forest for the trees. We must continuously reorient ourselves around the big picture, and not forget why we're here.

When I asked Z that very direct and basic question—*Are you weightless?*—leaving it open to interpretation, her response was a simple "No."

I investigated a bit, "Why is that?"

"I've just got so much going on at work," she explained.

"I see..." I continued, "Well, how about now? Do you feel weightless now?"

"No," she replied. "I just explained that things with work are shit."

"Ah... okay. Got it. How 'bout now?"

"No, now I'm thinking about this other thing..."

"And now?" I pushed.

"Why do you keep asking me that?" she questioned with a bit of frustration. The other tribers were looking on with a chuckle, as some of them saw where I was going with this. And I tried one more time, "Z, I understand the work situation, the lack of sleep, the sore and tired body. I understand all of these factors. I'm asking something different, however. I'm asking you if right now, in this moment, you're weightless?"

And without a pause, "No." So strongly attached we can be to the stories we build for ourselves that we cease to see there is a difference between the reliving of memories and all the thoughts and emotions associated with them, and the potential to see what's directly in front of us here and now. In this present moment, the moment before thought or analysis, there is no suffering as such. And if we can commune with the present without judgment for even a few moments, to see and feel with a sense of fullness, we feel unburdened and free. We feel weightless.

I ask this question repeatedly over the course of my programs not only to remind tribers of the big picture, but also to catch their pulse. Their responses demonstrate exactly how they interpret the question, and to what degree they understand the meaning of nonattachment. It's common for novices to associate weightlessness with an abstract, static state the way they might do with Happiness (capital H). Those making great headway might understand the question but may not yet be able to release their burdens, connect and sense throughout an integrated, relaxed frame, and meditate there and then.

And the masters-in-making hear the question, correct their posture, and with a mere breath enter the present unencumbered. They look at me and feel the room and their senses come alive. Their mind, body, and breath integrate for a few moments and they are free. They are weightless. They just needed a reminder.

There is a bit of trickery implicit in this question-and-answer game. I'm never looking for an answer. I'm looking for a shift in immediate experience, for a shift in perspective. For it's not just that the response is wrongish; it's that it's a trick question. The question isn't implying arrival at a final destination but rather acts as a trigger for immediate connection to the here and now. Are you burden-free and empowered… right now?

There is no grand arrival in life. There's no transcendence to a permanent state of freedom and nonattachment. There is the long-term struggle, and the short-term peace. There is stress and sensitivity. And neither of these is more important or more meaningful than the other. They are both inextricably entwined, combatting, supporting, and compensating for one another.

We don't get to live in this world in any normal sense and avoid the stresses and pressures of life outside of our control. That's life. But we do have the option, albeit with a lot of preparation and conscientious training, to step beyond the attachments of the ego and experience this world, our loved ones, our passions, and this very moment with complete, unbridled freedom.

We can define weightlessness, what it is, and how to cultivate it. But if we don't remind ourselves constantly, if we don't ask the question:

Am I Weightless? Then we forget that the gap between burdened living and weightlessness lays predominately in the will to see and feel this very moment.

Weightlessness is now.

We'll study many principles and techniques that require a lot of time and discipline to master, techniques ultimately designed to facilitate a greater sense of power, performance, and integration. Techniques that improve your capacity and wherewithal to be present. But your arrival needn't wait for any metric or outcome. At any moment, you have the choice, the freedom, to be weightless.

Are you weightless?

Time and Uncertainty

As important as living in the now is, it isn't all there is. For decisions in life must be made in these moments to address future moments, and the consequences of those decisions are largely blind to us beforehand. In order to gain greater confidence and control in the present we try to bottle the future in coherent systems, methods, ideologies, and personal plans to allay risk.

If bottled well, tomorrow can be awesome. If bottled poorly, then uncertainty will be the end of us all. For amidst uncertainty, the mind and body are exposed to great personal suffering. To be weightless, we must have a robust approach to navigating uncertainty in life.

The Uncertainty Scroll

> *If you look around the poker table and you're not sure who the patsy is—you're the patsy.*
> —The Guy With All the Chips

The Uncertainty Scroll addresses cognitive bias stemming from perspective limitations inherent in all complex domains. We don't know what we don't know. And we often assume that all we see is all there is. Half the battle in navigating uncertainty is identifying the nature of the domain you're operating in; the other half is personal approach to risk management. Through right orientation to systemic risks and design of robust strategies, one can bulletproof themselves against personal ignorance and position themselves for more frequent good luck.

Parable of the Farmer's Son

One day in late summer, an old farmer was working in his field with his old sick horse. The farmer felt compassion for the horse and desired to lift its burden. So, he let his horse loose to go to the mountains and live out the rest of its life. Soon after, neighbors from the nearby village visited, offering their condolences and said, "What a shame. Now your only horse is gone. How unfortunate you are! You must be very sad. How will you live, work the land, and prosper?" The farmer replied: "Who knows? We shall see."

Two days later, the old horse came back now rejuvenated after meandering in the mountainsides while eating the wild grasses. He came back with twelve younger and healthier horses that followed him into the corral. Word got out in the village of the old farmer's good fortune, and it wasn't long before people stopped by to congratulate the farmer on his good luck. "How fortunate you are!" they exclaimed. You must be very happy!" Again, the farmer softly said, "Who knows? We shall see."

At daybreak on the next morning, the farmer's only son set off to attempt to train the new wild horses, but the farmer's son was thrown to the ground and broke his leg. One by one, villagers arrived during the day to bemoan the farmer's latest misfortune. "Oh, what a tragedy! Your son won't be able to help you farm with a broken leg. You'll have to do all the work yourself, How will you survive? You must be very sad," they said. Calmly going about his usual business, the farmer answered, "Who knows? We shall see."

Several days later, a war broke out. The Emperor's men arrived in the village demanding that young men come with them to be conscripted into the Emperor's army. As it happened, the farmer's son was deemed unfit because of his broken leg. "What very good fortune you have!" the villagers exclaimed as their own young sons were marched away. "You must be very happy." "Who knows? We shall see!" replied the old farmer as he headed off to work his field alone. As time went on, the broken leg healed but the son was left with a slight limp. Again the neighbors came to pay their condolences. "Oh, what bad luck. Too bad for you!" But the old farmer simply replied, "Who knows? We shall see."

As it turned out, the other young village boys had died in the war and the old farmer and his son were the only able-bodied men capable of working the village lands. The old farmer became wealthy and was very generous to the villagers. They said: "Oh how fortunate you are, you must be very happy!" To which, the old farmer replied, "Who knows? We shall see!"

Complexity, Uncertainty, and the Models that Navigate Them

I like to claim that Weightlessness provides life tools for navigating uncertainty. The thesis for that claim will be presented and defended throughout this book, but to do so, a little track laying is necessary. To assess the cogency of a formula, method, or philosophy of living that allows us to navigate uncertainty with power and grace, we need to agree on what uncertainty implies about the nature of reality. Without this, it's very easy to claim *what works for some doesn't work for others.*

I believe we can do better than that. I believe we can go so far as to say that while we'll never be able to fully interpret the complexities of life, we do know enough about the nature of complexity that holds true for all people at all times to design meaningful models, however minimalistic, at least in theory. And this is where I'd like to start.

Uncertainty exists when complexity of a system or domain exceeds one's ability to model it—exceeds the limits of understanding, personal, social, or scientific. It is such that the reconstruction of composite parts can never quite reconstruct the whole, like the position points along the trajectory of an arrow. Models may allude to it, but the model itself can never fully reproduce the original phenomenon. But as long as we're aware of the theoretical limitations of a model prior to implementing it, it can likely shed invaluable light into the reality that it maps.

The role of models is very simple. They ought to say something accurate about an underlying reality and provide accurate predictions of future events based on specific, repeatable patterns. Uncertainty arises when one's models of X fails to provide practical or actionable insight toward managing X – a bad model. It also arises if we don't effectively apply model X correctly – human error.

To fully unpack the issue of complexity and the necessity in life of needing to act despite assured uncertainty, I've discovered a few principles that must be kept front and center when dissecting complexity, abstracting key truths, and modeling it. If we can do this with complexity in general, we can begin to formulate a model that allows us to face life with a much greater degree of nonattachment (to things in flux) and personal power (to change our thoughts and actions), rather than delusional optimism, false confidence, or fear.

Below, I'll refer to a few prominent chaos navigators—traders and fighters—in juxtaposition to those who dominate domains in closed systems: surgeons and mechanics. My aim is to present a clear picture of different types of complexity so we can understand the nature of uncertainty arising from each as well as a reasonable way to approach modeling or systematizing them.

Life is complex. And without clear insights into the nature of its complexity, one has no hope of meaningful decision making and effective planning.

Surgeons make shitty traders.

Understand the nature of your domain.

Surgeons are notoriously shitty traders. The reason for this is rather simple once we begin to examine the domains in which surgeons operate versus that of a stock or commodities trader. To do this, we must look at types of complexity each are facing daily. As stated above, by virtue of dealing with complex things at all, we are faced with unknowns. This is given. But is there a difference-in-kind between types of complexity and the applied systems that model them? I believe so.

While we are a long way from fully understanding the human body, doctors can perform in certain subdomains with a relatively high rate of success. Surgeons have an awesome understanding of how skin heals after its been cut or burned, how anesthesia sedates the mind and relaxes the body, how tendons can be reattached to bone, how bones can be reset, and how bullets can be removed. If you're ever shot, you should go to a surgeon over-and-above a reiki healer. They're more likely to get the bullet out.

This doesn't mean that surgeons are miracle workers, but perhaps they're something better (at least the good ones); they're scientists. They have extremely strong models of their subject matter and meticulously test that model in controlled environments through countless repetitions. We might describe gross physiology and the domains in which it's applied as a relatively closed system, where inputs or efforts (incisions or reconstructions) have a very strong correlation with outcomes (healing).

An example of a closed system could also be an engine. Parts can be exchanged and altered without dually affecting the rest of the component parts. But if one part is extracted without being replaced, the system stops working altogether. We might also describe this system (any subdomain of surgery: orthopedic surgery, cardiac surgery, neurosurgery, etc. or the wide range of mechanical work) as a static one, in that the body of knowledge surrounding the topic doesn't change dramatically from day to day, and, therefore, models of how to operate in said domain don't change dramatically over short periods of time, barring significant, paradigm-shifting breakthroughs.

I need to qualify one thing here; I'm not speaking of all surgeons, I'm comparing the best in class against the best in class traders and fighters below, and I'm arguing for a different underlying complexity to both domains. It does no good to compare an awesome surgeon with a shitty trader and vice versa. Let's say both survive, if not flourish in their domains, by their systematic approaches.

Some things are outside of the surgeon's control. A cardiac surgeon in attempting to save a life may make the best possible decision, but that life could still expire. We're looking here more for the correlation of cause and effect. And we can say, for example, that a good cardiac surgeon performing a routine bypass surgery has an exceedingly high rate of predictive accuracy over and above a professional trader in their respective domain.

Likewise, an orthopedic surgeon would have an excellent grasp of the pros and cons, prep, and recovery of a routine hip replacement. The reason for this is simple… shitty surgeons don't survive the game. Those who aren't good kill or maim patients. And this isn't by a little bit that they are good, it's by a lot. They're rockstars. They understand the causal implications of most of their actions to a very high degree.

Compare this to the dynamic, open system of a stock or commodities trader, one of the most uncertain occupations and volatile domains there is. A further example of an open system might be the weather, or the universe. The butterfly effect stipulates that a butterfly can flap its wings in Brazil, and somewhere else, through irreducibly complex causal sequences, a typhoon forms in Southeast Asia. You cannot affect one part of the system without unpredictable consequences unfolding.

The markets are open systems. Very few good traders actually study the underlying fundamentals of the markets they trade. They don't research the companies or global supply and demand stats of the stocks or commodities they trade. They don't follow geopolitics and congressional hearings that relate to their assets. They consider this information noise.

Novice traders, on the other hand, spend an inordinate amount of time researching, following news and chat groups, and obsessing over price. And this is easily understood when you see that every financial news channel reports price movement as a correlate of known news, as if they have some causal relationship. "Crude oil falls $2 a barrel as OPEC deliberates output increases." In truth, most price movement is random and unpredictable in the short term.

The great secret to trading like a pro is that the game isn't about being right; it's about not dying when you're wrong. Most elite traders are wrong, a lot. Most report predictive accuracy of around 50% if they're lucky. Can you think of any other domain off the top of your head where you could be considered elite in your craft yet be right in your assumptions (and actions) 50% of the time?

That means, just to be clear, you're wrong half the time. That's terrible. And despite this disastrous record, elite traders consistently pocket millions to billions year on year with track records that challenge the random nature of markets. How they manage this we'll address shortly, but, suffice it to say, the complexity of this peculiar domain rivals that of the domains of combat and love.

So, what happens when surgeons, after years of high-stakes operations in which lives are on the line, decide to retire and put their hard-earned savings into the markets? Generally speaking, they bomb, notoriously so.

They bomb big. Just to be clear, I'm not intending to rag on surgeons. Most people bomb big who attempt to trade their stakes regardless of their backgrounds. But surgeons, presumably, are highly intelligent, highly educated masters of their domains. It just so turns out that their greatest assets, when placed in the domain of trading, become their biggest vices. This can be reduced to one primary factor, that of devastating domain confusion.

Surgeons are used to being right. They rely on their depth of knowledge and experience to provide concrete, actionable decisions in this moment that will correlate with a successful outcome. When they move from their static, closed domain to the dynamic, open domain of trading, in which cause and effect are as loosely correlated as wine and diarrhea, they experience the greatest crisis of confidence in their lives.

For you can study technical analysis. You can follow the news twelve hours a day. And you can study every bull, bear, consolidation, fractal, reversal, and crash chart pattern in existence, and still have no clue how to predict where the market price of your chosen asset will go today. It just ain't that game.

We must then define our domains. Are we operating in a closed or open system? Is it static or dynamic? I will argue that life with a capital L falls into the category of a dynamic open system and will, therefore, require certain strategies and methods that would seem asinine in a predictive, static-closed system like that of the surgeon or mechanic.

ANYONE Can Win (or lose) a Fight

The person who thinks in terms of certainties is not to be trusted.

When the notorious Conor McGregor fought the wild card Nate Diaz in a mixed martial arts event for the first time, Diaz stepped in with only eleven days' notice. McGregor, at this time, was world champion of a slightly lighter weight division, so his title wasn't on the line, and good thing for him it wasn't.

He had an impeccable winning streak preceding this fight, in which he intimidated and psychologically emasculated his opponents prior to their fights, a kind of verbal and psychological warfare rarely implemented with such humorous and derogatory rhetoric. He also predicted, to the round and, in some cases, with what technique, he would end his fights. He predicted specific outcomes of several fights. This is no easy feat, one that earned him the nickname Mystic Mac among others, and it's incredible considering the fight game is an open system.

But when Nate Diaz, pot loving, vegan, black sheep gangster of the UFC stepped in and received the same barrage of insults leading up to the fight, as well as considerable underdog Vegas projections, Diaz walked McGregor down, giving up very little space, eating straight shots over and over. McGregor, oddly enough, wasn't conditioned for a real fight that goes the distance, one where his opponents could receive his power and not fall immediately unconscious. He wasn't used to the pressure, and even received sloppy unorthodox shots that slipped through his guard. So, he fatigued. And to reduce the volume of shots taken, McGregor did the unthinkable against his legitimate Brazilian Jujitsu black belt opponent and master of the ground game. McGregor took Nate to the ground. Within moments, Nate manipulated and pressed until Conor gave up his back, and Nate choked him out in the second round.

No one, including McGregor, could believe the lanky, awkward, unprepared, and inarticulate Nate Diaz would best the champion within two short rounds with a mere eleven days' notice. It truly shocked the mixed martial arts world. And while McGregor is, without a doubt, a formidable talent, the UFC has had several extraordinary fighters.

What made McGregor truly unique was his ability at that time to speak outcomes into existence, outcomes that relied on infinite complexity, and he predicted them to a T. It was a phenomenon that snowballed, backed with greater accuracy and far greater confidence if not delusions of grandeur with each successive bout. McGregor believed his victory was not merely likely but certain. This… was a misunderstanding of the nature of an open-dynamic system, and a lack of awareness of a cardinal rule of said systems: ANYONE can win a fight.

In static, closed systems like that of an engine, models can be extrapolated that predict causal relationships to an extreme if not absolute degree. In dynamic, open systems, complexity exceeds our ability to interpret or model it to a high degree. We can try, and perhaps believe we understand said domains, but this is, I'm sorry to inform, pure delusion. And I hold this conviction as someone with thirty years of martial arts experience. Fighting is such a domain, as is trading, love, and life with a capital L.

Other, more nebulous domains that often confuse our sense of certainty, but which have low predictive correlation might be astrology, climate change, and religion. This isn't to say that these models are wrong, but it is to say they overstep and apply a sense of absolute causal realities where there are mostly correlations. These are chaos systems. If you understand them as such, and work to mitigate the fallout from misapplication or ignorance of realities beyond the models, then they might serve one's interests to a high degree. Again, this doesn't mean they're wrong, it just means we cannot be certain they're right, regardless of how strongly we believe them to be.

But I digress. The principle that ANYONE can win or lose a fight is really an issue of psychological attachment to a specific narrative. If we are first aware of the type of complexity, i.e. static-closed, or dynamic-open, then we can begin to orient our psychology around that domain to create an edge. Closed systems can be mastered to a high degree with the acquisition of knowledge and technical skill. Open systems require those same assets, but can be dominated only with extreme self-discipline, risk management, and emotional control.

We may know a great deal of the components of an open system, but we may have little understanding of their causal relationships. And if we choose to play in domains of open complexity, this is where we must be psychologically prepared for the unpredictable. We must understand that despite how thorough our analysis and understanding, we don't know all, and ANYONE can win a fight. We must, therefore, have a strategy that speaks to human error and implementation just as much as system dynamics.

First Principles (primary assumptions) Must be Falsifiable

If there are no conditions under which your god can theoretically be proven nonexistent, I have no use for him.

This principle will certainly chap a few hides, but it's a critical one that stipulates what kind of principles are acceptable in the first place. And this matters. I don't expect you to take my word for any of this. You should be able to investigate these principles independently and draw similar conclusions. That said, this principle might require a bit of mental masturbation to finesse its essence out into the open.

First principles should not be divinely asserted or blindly accepted. After all, we're looking here for a model that can serve us in navigating uncertainty and impacts virtually every aspect of life. The tools and principles we implement ought to be empirically verifiable or self-evident. Religion and science are systems of faith. But the means by which they derive their precepts are diametrically different.

Theistic religions assert as first principle a prime mover or God. Period. *We don't know how it all got here. Therefore, God did it. Now, let's figure out what he wants us to do with homosexuals.*

Science too has first principles, treated as law, but which, sadly, are imperfect. The law of gravity and the speed of light for example, two *facts* that we accept as indelible, are both inconstant. Yet we treat them as static laws of the universe on faith. The difference here, however, between this scientific application of first principles and those of religion, are that one could, by applying the scientific method, create a hypothesis or speculate on necessary conditions that could prove these laws false. There's that, and also… they work.

If they cannot somehow theoretically be scrutinized for their veracity, then they cannot be held as true.

Why is this important? Because without the ability to theoretically falsify principles within a model of an open system, like that in theistic religions, the model can never grow to more accurately encapsulate the complex realities that it purports to describe. There's no way, in other words, to vet information from noise, fact from speculation, truth from falsehood. The model gets stuck in time. While pointing at an open dynamic system, the model itself is static closed. The model doesn't change as the system does. This is like mistaking a photograph for the landscape within it. It's a snapshot, and perhaps accurate to that time and place. But time isn't kind to fixed snapshots.

This is a massive problem for anyone seeking truth. It's like looking outside through a keyhole, assuming that everything one sees is all that there is. This issue is pervasive among theists during discussions of the origin of the universe. It's quite common to hear from theistic apologists that because you cannot explain what preceded the big bang, and because something cannot come from nothing, that, therefore, God is the origin of the universe. They usually ignore the obvious follow-up that if something cannot come from nothing, where did God come from? But let's focus on the core argument itself.

This logical fallacy is known as an argument from ignorance. You assert something is true because you personally are unable to prove it is false. Your proposition (God exists) is true because of a lack of evidence to the contrary. This argument has been around for ages because it sneaks up within a domain of irreducible complexity, and quite frankly, it's a lot to sift through.

But we can very easily show, regardless of whether there's a God, that the argument itself is nonsense because its structure is identical to: *The tides come in, the tides go out; therefore, Poseidon. There is pain and suffering in the world; therefore Bob*. Can you prove that not-Bob? No, you cannot disprove an absurd statement. I cannot prove that God does not exist any better than I can prove that unicorns absolutely do not bathe in leprechaun feces. We're just less anxious to attribute the tides to Poseidon and suffering to Bob because physics, biology, and sociology do a decent job of modeling those domains without the need to posit mystical forces. There may come a time soon when we see well beyond (or before) the big bang, and understand whether something came from nothing, or whether something was always there.

The main takeaway from this tangent is that if first principles are not falsifiable, then we have only to rely on the authority of someone who thinks they know everything about everything. I'd rather not bank on *that* someone personally. Too much is at stake. To be clear, this doesn't mean God doesn't exist or unicorns don't bathe in leprechaun feces: it just means we can't know whether they do, and that our ability to interpret and model their domains sucks.

The ability to challenge principles and assumptions gives us the power to adapt and redesign our worldview ongoing. It gives us the power to test and try our assumptions without the fear of said principles failing under intense pressure or scrutiny or tearing apart the core of our being.

We're approaching life with a sense of innocence, because we know that anyone can lose a fight. There are no guaranteed wins. We're not playing in a closed system of binary, right-wrong understanding. We're dealing with a dynamic environment where things can constantly improve, can be more right than they are now. The model that doesn't limit adaptation and growth, even of its own tenants, is a more robust model than one that does.

You Will Get Hit

Success cannot depend on being right, for volatility doesn't mind your plans.

All things break down in volatility.

This principle is the ugly stepchild of the second principle, but rather than assert the win-loss scenario as binary, it acknowledges there are degrees of success and failure within specific decisions. This too speaks to the nature of complexity exceeding our ability to model it. It means that while, best case scenario, we have an edge in a complex domain, and that may be enough to win, it may not be enough to not get hit and possibly hurt. And if this isn't life, I don't know what is.

In dynamic, open systems, one cannot rely on being right as a means of navigating the complexities of that system. Mike Tyson said it best: "Everyone has a plan, until they get punched in the face."

This acknowledges the reality of complex domains, the reality that anyone can win a fight, and it addresses further the psychology of engagement within that domain. I'd like to submit that the largest difference by far, from my experience as a martial artist and a prior trader, is that unsuccessful people in open-dynamic domains generally implement static-closed models… and they fail. In other words, they're bringing knives to gunfights.

And in a gunfight, there are no rules. It's domain confusion at its worst.

What does this mean in practical terms? It means that if you want to party in complex games, such as self-defense, financial speculation, love, and life at large, you should assume that winning these games comes with a lot of losses. Being wrong is a probabilistic certainty. So how do fighters and traders, those weathered navigators of chaos, survive the long haul to join the ranks of champions? They build strategies that facilitate victory BUT also assume hits and losses.

Their edges are not merely better understandings or implementations of fundamentals; they apply a Spartan psychology of indomitable spirit.

It's one that designs (not merely insinuates) that if you strike me, I'll hurt you; if you hurt me, I'll maim you; and if you maim me, I'll kill you. It assumes striking and hurting are possible, if not probable from the onset, so there are no surprises. Now where's the victory party?

When Tyson shared his iconic line on strategy, and one that truly permeates all complex games from entrepreneurship to love, he wasn't speaking about the quality of said strategy, he was talking about the psychology that implements it. A psychology that is determined to win but knows and accepts the likelihood of getting hit is a formidable one. It's hard to break.

The fighter who steps into a ring and assumes he'll make an easy show out of a weaker opponent, taking no abuse and rushing off to the after party is a perfect candidate for a shocking identity crisis. Even though he might be stronger, physically and technically, his mind has no room for adaptation. It's the concrete approach one often takes in a static-closed system. That rigid strategy and mentality are easily fractured. Loss is inevitable, for reality never fully conforms to expectation.

We'll discuss the origin of this problem along with possible fixes in The Transformation Scroll under neural plasticity, where I highlight the benefits and dangers of egocentrism. At its core, identity is an infinitely complex arrangement of associations: associated ideas, values, memories, and emotions. The tighter our particular strategy or general worldview is wound, the easier it is to pull one single thread and watch the entire tapestry unravel.

This has a lot to do with one's need for control or comfort within uncertainty. The good news is that these different states can be conditioned (reconditioned) in the mind and designed into models.

I imagine, some might reasonably argue, "If I have to engage in something intimidating or risky, wouldn't I be better off with the supreme confidence of a person who believed that victory was a certainty? Wouldn't entering a ring, knowing I'll get hit, trading commodities with the knowledge that 50% of my positions will be wrong, or falling in love, knowing that it will lead to deep hurt at times, make me more likely to cower, hide, or simply not even try?

Yes.

That's a possibility for many. But it doesn't change the reality of complex domains. Many people choose delusion. And you can too. And if the context of your environment is tightly bottled and controllable, that strategy may not expose those perspective gaps, those rogue threads that if pulled, tear your mind, or your life apart. But I hope you can see that, regardless of what makes one feel more comfortable today, clear and present dangers exist in embracing blindness to risk.

Relinquishing your sense of security and embracing the reality that you'll get hit sets the stage for two invaluable edges. The first edge is risk management: a humility and honesty regarding the partiality of your model and the risks inherent in complex domains. This both allows and forces you to look for some other edge, that is, an edge that doesn't require perfect understanding. This edge is often found on the fly in the heat of battle through experience-based insight and creative problem solving.

This will seem odd to those who gain their sense of security in life from their perceived ability to control the circumstances of their lives. But for those who operate in volatile environments, this will be self-evident, whether or not you currently implement this principle proactively. Merging the desire to survive and win with the realities of complete uncertainty of future events, one must learn to mitigate risk. The ability to minimize risk increases the likelihood of survival and, therefore, success. And this—this is an edge.

An edge is something that couples known market or environmental information and your own unique perspective in the world (or in your domain) into a strategy that's wholly unique. It's something that, quite possibly, would only work for you. This doesn't mean that your model or governing framework isn't the same as your neighbor's; you both could be Weightlessness practitioners for example. But it does mean that the application and evolution of Weightlessness in your lives will be different. Principles can remain the same if they're worthy, but expression and implementation may vary dramatically.

For a trader or a poker player, that edge is sometimes an underexploited yet repetitive price pattern. These occasionally provide massive opportunities but they rarely last long as other participants catch wind of them. But the true edge of the trader is effective betting strategy. And while some consider all betting gambling, something is very honest about this practice that accurately describes the nature of complex domains.

Elite gamblers and traders know that. They both know that banking on being right is a fool's game. They know they'll often be wrong. So, they expose themselves only a little, knowing this trade or this hand could go their way or not. If successive cards increase the probability of success, or if price action confirms the position by moving in the right direction, then bets increase as risk-reward profile improves.

This is counter to what most investors do, who dollar-cost average on the way down and take profits gradually on the way up. Where the classical investment mantra is buy low and sell high, the trader's secret is to buy high and sell higher.

The investor says, "The price has to go back up." The trader says, "Um, yeah, okay… but the price IS falling." They look for inflection points, points of support and resistance that correspond with psychological battles among countless market participants. These points are memories, battlefields where certain people won and feel good, and others lost and don't want to get burned again.

The price itself is innocuous, meaningless. But what it represents is fear and hope. And when those battles are fought on high volume (large numbers of contracts traded), they leave in the minds of those traders involved lessons on whether they want to stand for that position, long or short, again. They remember the hurt, and they shy away. Or they remember the glory, and they double down. The reason I find trading psychology and strategy so fascinating is that it's no different from self-defense. And it risks almost as much.

Models will always present the danger of an individual mistaking the finger for the moon. Most people are familiar with the classical metaphor of a man pointing to the moon and stating, "Look at the moon." The person he's speaking to doesn't see past the man's finger and assumes the finger *is* the moon. Models are fingers. Many people mistake them for moons and, in so doing, are blind to the moon itself. And this is tragedy because the moon, first of all, isn't contained in the model, and second, contains immediately relevant information. It's dynamic and changing. And if we don't look clearly without preconception, we miss truth manifesting.

The surgeon with a track record of being right and backed by chart patterns and technical analysis has a very hard time interpreting counter movements when speculating in the markets in time to allay risk. When that individual buys a stock, and the market moves down past their risk point, they believe that it's only a loss if they sell. They can wait, and the market will come back up to prove them right. *Or what if I sell, take a loss, and then it rebounds? I'd look a fool by both being right AND losing money at the same time.*

Experienced traders aren't married to any position. There are points of inflection one can consider as good entry points due to low risk exposure, but if they take a position and are proven incorrect, good traders takes their loss very quickly. Losses are frequent and many, but they're small. They don't hurt them, and they don't take them out of the game. When the market reinforces a position and there is sufficient profit within the trade, good traders don't liquidate (take profits), they add to the position, resting on a cushion of accumulated profit, all the while raising their stop losses to secure more profits and prevent large losses.

The key difference here is that the novice investor trades on the assumption that they know something about the stock or the market, and so they stop listening to the market. The master trader assumes they know little. They apply their model as a means of minimizing risk, but then they listen, watch, are sensitive to what the market tells them its doing, and flow with it. When they're wrong, they take their boat out of the water. When they're right, they ride the current to its end.

The finger gets them to the moon, but once there, they discard the finger and listen very carefully to what the moon is saying.

Fighters spend years preparing for competition and longer preparing for real combat. They acquire a small number of highly robust techniques. They condition their strength and stamina. And they develop motor reflexes and strategies that add insight into the realities of hand-to-hand conflict. But against an equally strong opponent, this isn't enough to win. These things do, however, mitigate risk, like the entry and stop loss strategies of the trader. They DO NOT guarantee victory.

And this is where many martial arts practitioners who have little experience in full-contact fighting often drift into delusion. They become experts at abstraction. They focus on strictly confined simulations with creative and often complex solutions in if-*they-do-this, you-do-this* scenarios that guarantee victory over some unnamed back-alley foe. And this works, as long as the opponent only does this one thing and nothing else in the same way and preferably holds the punch in the air and freezes so you've got time to whup him.

Otherwise, you'll fry your robot circuitry and your brain explodes when confronted with an infinite number of possible options under high-stakes scenarios.

I once knew a martial artist who recalled in his younger years hearing the sounds of domestic abuse emanating from the apartment above him. In his chivalry and valor, he marched upstairs and, upon seeing a beast of an abusive man in front of him declared, “I’m a black belt.” This was true, insofar as someone else with a black belt gave him one too. But this wasn’t the confined training scenario of a martial arts studio. This was an angry, aggressive, jacked athlete who didn’t give a shit about the rules. And he ruthlessly pummeled the martial artist and mentally scarred him for life.

The only good thing about this scenario is that the martial artist didn’t quit that day. He took that hard lesson, accepted market feedback, saw the moon as it really is, and he redesigned his martial framework. That wasn’t going to happen again. He didn’t see the moon before. But he does now.

Perhaps the best piece of advice for those who want to play in or prepare for high-stakes complex games is to take as many hits as possible in training, under pressure, in a variety of ways, so that when reality hits, there are no surprises. Not intentionally getting hit, mind you, but accepting that risk within the training process. The trader should not paper trade and at the same time think they know what they’re doing. They must trade with real money, ideally small amounts at first, and feel the fear and hope that accompanies decision making with something at stake. They must put skin in the game.

The martial artist must test their system under pressure with full contact and with a variety of opponents, at least some of the time. For declaring oneself a black belt may not be enough to survive a life-or-death situation. They must put skin in the game to test their system ahead of time. And if they, the trader and the martial artist are fortunate in make-or-break moments, they’ll be dancing with the moon and not distracted by the finger.

Pattern Recognition is (must be) Possible

Have we met before?

In order to model a complex system, patterns must be present. In static systems, we might be able to map or model up to 100% of the patterns or parts therein. The more complex or dynamic the system, the more that percentage drops precipitously. But that doesn’t mean that we ignore the finger because it isn’t a perfect reconstruction of the moon.

We’re often much better off understanding the right implementation and limitations of a model than we are with no model at all. But let’s assume for a second that we don’t fully understand the domain at large; how do we determine whether we can actually create a model that will offer any value whatsoever and not merely cloud our reality with complete gobbledygook?

Millenia ago a tribal warrior walked off a battle field of dead brethren and enemies, and he thought to himself: *all men who wielded their weapons in their right hands, swung from my left to center, or lunged straight on during their initial strike.* He thought about this over and over. He analyzed his responses, some similar to one another, some different. He analyzed not only their efficacy in dealing with the assault, but also, like a chess master against a novice, which decisions placed him in a better position for his next move or confrontation. He recalled positions he found himself in that supported defensive and offensive blocks and strikes. And he started to see patterns. He shared these patterns with other warriors and, while not identical, their experiences corroborated similar patterns of enemy assault. That man entered the battlefield a tribal leader, and he left a martial artist.

On the chance this battle might repeat itself, the martial artist and company wanted to be better prepared. They looked at those patterns that occurred a high percentage of the time and consolidated them into series of if-then scenarios. And they looked at those that happened rarely and put them into two categories: patterns that were rare but deadly, and patterns that were rare but had little impact. And they included those with deadly consequences, and they rejected those that seemed random or inconsequential.

Then they ran simulations and tested these if-then propositions with physical reenactment. And they learned that many did, in fact, occur as remembered, and they learned that some, while relevant at the time, just don't seem to make sense upon deeper analysis. In other words, they learned that some responses were far better than others. And they discussed this, re-examining patterns, formalizing their model of combat. And the first martial art was born.

A few generations later, after long episodes of peace, the new generation of tribal warriors received a model of combat that was even more elaborate than that following the first battle. It contained movements and positions that didn't seem natural. It had coherence and made a great deal of sense out of a messy topic. But the young tribers had no personal experience from which to judge this system. They had to take it on faith and test it as much as possible with their friends and teachers under a bit of pressure. But there wasn't much fear of death in these training sessions, for they were all on the same side.

The most gifted among them could see beyond the patterns to the underlying problem they were trying to solve. They understood through learning a variety of defenses to a variety of techniques that the method they were studying wasn't as abstract as it seemed. There are only so many ways a human arm, generating force from the hip, can swing with killing power.

There are places on the body that are more vulnerable than others. And there are psychological thought patterns that inform technical assault, some more aggressive than others, some more calculated, and some of pure fear. The least gifted among them, well, they were a different story. They mistook the finger for the moon, and when war broke out, they declared, "We're black belts!"

Models acknowledge patterns. And good models acknowledge patterns that can be tested under high-stakes scenarios in real time.

Complexity is noisy. The difference between a master and a novice in any craft is that the master can distinguish information from noise, wheat from chaff. And for masters-in-the-making, models will have to suffice in reducing complexity and information into coherent, learnable pieces. Throughout the growth process, one's relationship with their chosen model or system often goes through many phases, from blind trust, to blind doubt, to respectful skepticism, to an understanding of implicit depth, to understanding it isn't the moon but it's a damn good finger.

The master has two forms of pattern recognition in his toolkit: an abstract, formal set of patterns that have been passed on to him, ideally containing key insights into the most meaningful elements of his domain, and an intuitive set of patterns that arose by virtue of stepping into the void of his domain, albeit with skin in the game. His kit of intuitive patterns is alive, and the perfect merging of formal understanding and immediate experience.

These are often unique solutions born of one's unique psychology and, in the case of martial arts, unique physicality, movement patterns, and technical strengths/weaknesses. These patterns would be virtually useless in the hands of anyone but the holder himself. There's no need to design these; they arise organically through conscientious application of formal methods and processes.

For our purposes here of lifestyle design and therein models for mastering oneself and succeeding in life, both are essential, but the former is the domain of Weightlessness – self-mastery and performance. All good models focus on common threads, not individual differences. Good models point directly at the moon, using sound scientific evidence and airtight reasoning. They do not fill in all gaps or paint fully finished paintings.

This isn't possible, as we've discussed, and it increases the probability of propagating inaccuracies. But they do the next best thing, they give us a small subset of coherent, consistent, and verifiable *truths* that allow us to play the game. And the more we study them, the deeper our knowledge of our domain becomes. As we accumulate life experience, strong models integrate themselves in many ways, elucidating complex experiences and providing a formula for navigation.

Pattern recognition is more of a precondition to modeling than a principle of designing or modeling itself. But they are the insights one needs to filter information from noise and learn to dominate in complex domains.

Show the Fuck Up

No model delivers 100% of the time when it's implemented 70% of the time.

Discretion is the enemy of growth. Compliance is the beginning of conversation.

Compliance to protocol or method is perhaps the hardest part of this whole equation. It's explored in-depth in both The Change Scroll and The Process Scroll. Many assume the game is best played, and upside maximized by seeking the perfect model, the best martial art, the most sophisticated trading method, the best coach. And while filtering information and refining assumptions around your complex domain is critical for long-term progress, they're not where most go wrong.

The human factor is the loose cog in most complex machines. It is said that a good student can learn from even a bad teacher, and this is a great frame with which to view all models. It's the frame of personal accountability. It's the willingness to adhere to set rules and principles, good days or bad, rain or shine, sick or healthy, until the merit of that system becomes internalized, while the weakness of it becomes illuminated and minimized.

It could be a terribly rainy day, but you're not going to elect to not-fill your gas tank if its empty because the system breaks down. It could be a high-pressure day at work, but you're not going to elect to not go because the system breaks down. But you're a bit tired? *Fuck it, I'll work out tomorrow instead.*

We might also assert the antithesis: not even a strong model can help a shitty practitioner. You must own your own path. The only way you can truly measure the value and applicability of a model is if you adhere to it uncompromisingly for a time.

A good model will also provide context for reinvention or reiteration of itself.

When dealing with complex systems, the more minimalistic the model, generally speaking, the more robust, universal, and applicable it is. Thus, it might not be comprehensive enough to guide all followers. The more filled out and detailed a model is, generally speaking, the more fragile it becomes, and it runs the risk of being highly context dependent. We find this with many religions and even economic systems. The world is full of paradoxical scenarios that aren't right-wrong, or good-bad, but are instead bad-terrible, or average-excellent.

These types of scenarios blow gaskets off of complex machines (systems) without extraordinarily skilled interpreters. Theists claim it's wrong to lie, always. But…what if a Nazi is at your door and you've got a family of Jewish refugees in your basement? Life dictums that are cut and dry are rarely useful. Those that allow for hierarchical thinking in complex situations tend to provide more insight in real time. They just, by definition, don't answer all questions. They can't.

If accurately identifying the domain we're dealing with, static-closed, dynamic-open, one can conform their expectations to an appropriate degree of insight. And this is powerful. A highly detailed system is likely to fail in important ways when describing dynamic-open domains, whereas they excel at describing static-closed domains. The opposite is also true, that sparse, lean models do a poor job of describing static-closed systems, but do a better job pointing the way to the moon within dynamic-open ones.

But keep in mind; they make no claim of concrete, universal description. That isn't their function—to track as close as possible to the specific patterns of the past. They're beacons of light that insinuate direction, not concrete maps with which to navigate all waters seamlessly.

Given that lean models are incomplete, and detailed models are wrought with inaccuracy when navigating complex domains, and given that due to the nature of complexity as discussed this is as good as models get, that leaves us with our ability to use said models to develop ourselves or master our environments.

It means we may need a model for dealing with models. And while we don't need to outline anything extensive, suffice it to say that if you want to test a model, or reap the rewards of a tried and tested model, you must actually adhere to it unquestioningly for a time. You must assume that your understanding as a novice is partial; that your perspective is limited, and that your judgment is uninformed. You must empty yourself, so to speak, if you wish to be full of new, true insight.

And in so doing, you must avoid five delusions of noncompliance:

- **It was only 1 slip-up**. This is the slippery slope of noncompliance. Actions generate momentum. The more we comply, the easier it becomes, and the faster results compound. But if we skip that healthy meal, that workout, that opportunity for counterattack, that trade suggested by our model, the more likely we are to do it a second, third, fourth time, until everything falls apart. It's never only one slip up if it wasn't merely an accident but a discretionary choice to deviate from one's plan.

  There is also another, more perfidious problem here, which is that a system that recommends 10 actions to elicit results but only receives 9 won't perform.

- **I'm strictly complying... basically**. I'm showing up 80% of the time, but not seeing results. Many assume that 80% compliance = 80% results. In dynamic, open-complex domains we don't have the luxury of assuming a percentage of effort or compliance corresponds with an equal percentage of results. Life isn't an SAT test where questions are equally weighted and payoff is determined by tabulating accurate steps and developed skills.

  Complex systems are chaotic, and payoff is nonlinear. This means that there is often a compounding effect of seemingly unrelated parts, where together they generate momentum unfelt and unseen without serious commitment. In other words, if you're building an engine, then following blueprints 80% of the way will get you to 80% of an engine.

  In life, combat, love, and trading as we've seen, this correlation is nonexistent. One shouldn't make the SAT or engine fallacy when dealing with life. If you love your partner 99% of the time, but one day get drunk and beat them, it's enough to undermine the other 99% loving relationship. That's just life.

It's quite possible that 70% compliance might get one only 50% of the results sought. This is commonplace in the fitness domain. Without a high enough degree of stress and shakeup of homeostatic nutrition and exertion, next to nothing happens. Once higher degrees of compliance are implemented, results skyrocket. So, to further those percentages, it's possible that 85% compliance gets one to 70% of the projected results, and 90% to 100% compliance gets you into the 95%+ results arena.

- **The method sucks**. *I'm not perfect, but I'm trying and not seeing results... the method must be wrong, I'm gonna try something else.* Many assume they know enough to determine the relevance of a rule or protocol when they've only just gotten their feet wet in that domain. It should work even if I don't work it.

  They're proud of themselves for doing more than previously, but disheartened and frustrated that the game ain't over yet, and it's certainly harder than expected. But poor execution of a good plan is like filling a cup full of holes. Water seeps right out. Efforts are totally wasted. No progress is made. Zero insights are gained. The method itself cannot be assessed because it hasn't been applied.

- **I've got an awesome excuse**. I've got reasons for noncompliance. The dog ate my homework. I was at a business dinner where alcohol was required and carbs were shoved down my throat. My hotel didn't have a gym. I thought my opponent was going to do something else. I didn't place a stop loss this time because I had that damn lucky feeling.

  Belief in one's excuses is one of the subtlest, but most powerful delusions. It's complicated because they're often reasonable and, in some cases, more reasonable than the method, rule, or protocol you're meant to follow. There will always be black swan events and freak occurrences that force a change of plans. But! Most of the time, you're just too lazy to anticipate the obvious and factor in additional space, time, and energy to deal with small, unforeseen obstacles and still adhere to plan A.

  For example, if you're traveling on work, CALL THE HOTEL and ask what kind of gym facilities they have. Flying and on a strict diet? PACK A LUNCH! Worried you'll get punched in the face if you follow the rules? MAN UP. Your model will only work so long as you work it. You can either prioritize it, or you can take comfort in your excuses once you've failed.

- **I've got that lucky "knowing" feeling**. I know my body, so I altered the workout today. Many believe they know, feel, or see something in current context that the system, coach, or protocol must not have anticipated, and, therefore, they'd better play the renegade and start controlling things themselves.

  If you're not a relative expert in your chosen complex vocation or domain (and cannot unequivocally identify those who are) don't play the cowboy. This has serious fallout. It will generally 1) lead to a lack of results if not pain and suffering and 2) give you zero insight as to the veracity of rule x or principle y, resulting in no personal or empirical evidence to support whatever opinions you take away from the experience.

  As Nassim Taleb explained in *Black Swan,* "When you develop your opinions on the basis of weak evidence, you will have difficulty interpreting subsequent information that contradicts these opinions, even if this new information is obviously more accurate."

  If you could trust your intuition in complex domains without training, you'd be a shit-kicking billionaire badass with enough time to save animals from extinction and harass nuns (just cause). Everything you've always wanted would have been last year's footnote. It wasn't, so empty your cup and just say no to discretion... for a time. When your model points one way and your gut points the other, hit yourself in the gut to silence it... for a time.

As a coach, I often tell my clients that if nothing else, compliance is the beginning of conversation. Commonly, a remote client will deviate from their protocol due to travel or unexpected work/life issues without telling me ahead of time. When they return, they often comment that they're struggling with stress, not losing weight, or not gaining strength. They ask if they should change something in the program, but mind you, THEY HAVEN'T BEEN DOING IT. Sure, you can change whatever you want, but unless you stick to something 90-100%, we have no idea what's working and not working with any particular workout prescription.

Compliance is the beginning of conversation. If you want to grow, you need data. If you want data, you must apply a method as prescribed with little to no discretionary changes. This isn't a dabbler's game. It's the path to mastery.

And a note to the overachievers: this goes just as much for adding work as it does for missing it. There are some elements of training that benefit from greater volume, flexibility and meditation for example, when done correctly. Others don't necessarily benefit, strength training and conditioning for example (and therein, fat loss and energy recovery). This is an aspect of understanding your domain.

Does your model give you necessary and sufficient conditions for growth? If so, how do you measure the efficacy of your program and, therefore, understand the degree of stress required within each workout to elicit adaptations and growth, if you have added 20-30% *more* work than prescribed? If you got results, well, something worked. But what was it? If you didn't get results, well, then either nothing worked, or the additional work has impeded the stress-adaptation and recovery process and kept you from actualizing stimulated gains. Either way, you're none the wiser. You don't know. You can't analyze, discuss, alter, or proceed. You need to start over, be humble, and show up. Do the work, and ONLY the work.

Embrace the Void

The expert complies. The master abandons.

After an individual has mastered a model, they must then learn to see beyond it.

When navigating complex environments, psychology often trumps method.

Embracing the void is a bit of a floating paradox, meaning that one needs to embrace a contradiction regarding the relevance of modeling in principle and in practice.

The role of training is to mold the body and mind (depending on domain) to the principles of that domain. In practice or application, the mind must relinquish trust in that model enough to see beyond it. This is challenging for all of us. It requires a form of blind faith in the training process, and then a healthy skepticism when it actually matters.

This is a contradiction in principle, but not in practice. In the real world, it gets results.

An example of this paradox in action may be a martial artist who feigns injury to bait an opponent. In principle a fighter should carry a high guard, one that protects the jawline or ribcage without inhibiting view. They should strike a balance between defensive capability and offensive potential. They should project a sense of security, a safe that isn't easy to crack.

I recall one fight in particular in which a fighter received a kick to his right floating rib, and he immediately caved in to protect it. This was accompanied by a cringe and a cry along with stumbling footwork. He was a wounded animal beginning to cower.

His opponent saw his opportunity to finish him, and he charged aggressively, recklessly, with his gaze blood-hungry and his guard down. He only needed one shot to his defenseless opponent's temple. And as he wound up for the strike, his coiled opponent, whose eyes remained fixed on his opponent despite his injury, released everything he had and beat his assailant to the punch, knocking him unconscious.

I'm not denying that the fighter was indeed injured, but he wasn't incapacitated as his movements suggested. This lured his opponent in with a false sense of security, of victory.

The wounded man, remaining in a compromised posture, temporarily discarded theoretical rules of survival: keep your hands up and protect yourself at all times. But in so doing, opportunity arose. His wounded posture convinced his opponent that there was no threat left for him, no risk to finishing the job quickly. And because the wounded man's arms were wrapped around his midsection protecting his rib, his head was fully exposed and unprotected. But hands only provided one form of protection. Insight and awareness are by far the supreme protectors. Seeing clearly what one's opponent does is a better defense and weapon, far better than merely keeping one's hands up.

In that split second, he saw the essence of what that cardinal rule was indicating, he saw the moon that the fingers of training were pointing to. He saw that true security wasn't about his physical guard; this was merely an embodiment of a deeper law. The truth is in the perception of strength or weakness in his opponent's mind. He was able to use his opponent's implicit bias and blood thirst against him. He knew that his posture was vulnerable, but he also knew that the only reasonable option left for his opponent would be a strike to his head with a power straight.

And because of this serendipitous reduction in complexity, all things came into focus and his solution became obvious. Slip his opponent's power right, turn on the heel, and strike into the gap. And he did. There was no room left based on optics for his opponent to consider him anything but a wounded victim. He certainly didn't consider a counteroffensive attack a possibility. And the wounded man won, by breaking and exploiting one of the cardinal rules within their models of combat – keep your hands up.

An example from the world of trading comes from the antiprinciple known as The Hounds of Baskerville, named after the Sherlock Holmes novel. In this novel, Holmes was called to the scene of a murder, a wealthy man's estate. After rounds of interviews, Holmes noticed a recurring theme. Despite there being a watchdog on the premises, nobody reported having heard any suspicious sounds the evening of the murder. This brief dialogue elucidates:

Gregory (Scotland Yard detective): "Is there any other point to which you would wish to draw my attention?"
Holmes: "To the curious incident of the dog in the night-time."
Gregory: "The dog did nothing in the night-time."
Holmes: "That was the curious incident."

For Holmes, the absence of expected evidence, that a watchdog would bark at the sight of an intruder, indicated that the theory of the murderer coming from outside the property was false. This *negative* fact, the absence of an expected fact, is sometimes more meaningful than all other facts supporting a case.

Alexander Elder in *Trading for a Living* translated this notion to the domain of trading. This odd anti-principle has been implemented by rogue traders in the past to not only save them from bad positions, but also to generate extensive profits after they liquidated their poor positions, reversed them, and doubled down. This might occur for example on a suspected market reversal, where very high volume seems to confirm that a long-term trend reversal is underway.

As we discussed, volume indicates the size of the battle and, therefore, the number of independent psychologies that have been burned or rewarded by being right or by being caught on the wrong end of a large move. Occasionally, all signs are present for trend reversal, and, despite a significant correction, price regresses back to the high or low in question, it tests it, and the support fails.

If this were a suspected market low and a trader went long (bought shares) relying on his technical analysis and a variety of factors, yet the market revisited and fell through support, a trader might take this negative fact of price weakness over and above all other indicators. He might then go short (sell short), for example, because all reason pointed long, and the market simply didn't confirm that, despite his personal beliefs or technical indicators.

The market is never wrong.

Many investors aren't equipped with such a versatile and fast-moving psychology. In the mind of most traders, if I'm right, given X number of technical or fundamental reasons to be long (to buy) this market, and the price goes lower, then it's an even better buying opportunity. There's only one problem, there's no telling how low price can go, and for how long. There's no rule in life that stocks or real estate always go up. Many go to zero in many countries, despite the long-term uptrend in stocks and real estate in the United States.

The nimble trader, against common investment advice, would reverse his position and SELL into a cheap market, reasoning that if they're wrong, larger forces are at play that exceed the interpretive value of their model... for now. Remember, we only know what we see. It's often the factors we overlook that make the largest impact. This is not a trading lesson; it's a life lesson.

Markets are not cowering opponents. Even in boxing, it's the shot you don't see that gets you. As I said several times now, complex domains cannot be fully modeled. If you're not right, then you might be *really* wrong. It's possible your model is wholly inaccurate in this particular case, and should be abandoned...for the moment.

This ability to nonattach to model or method at times when reality (the moon) exceeds pattern recognition (the finger) is a defining attribute of mastery. The rules and principles are both context dependent and outcome oriented, and the true master knows that there are times when even the best models fail (his model is giving false signals), and one must rely on hard-earned intuition (built upon years of skin in the game and personal trial and error) to make what might seem like an absurd move, i.e. the feigned injury counterattack, or the hounds of Baskerville position reversal.

It makes no sense to practice such discretionary decision making for most of us in most cases, as 9 times out of 10, they'd put you in the grave or give false reads. Habituating feigned injury is tantamount to suicide. But once in a while, when complex realities don't adhere to your model of it, and you truly understand the intricacies of your model, you ought to burn the model and act from the gut.

From Uncertainty to Certain Change

While this scroll has taken turns and tangents that I hope create a clear picture of the risks and opportunities inherent in complex domains, the single most important takeaway should be this: In life, we're forced to make decisions that have consequences, and we're largely blind to those real consequences ahead of time. If we seek certainty and the world does not conform to our expectations, weightless moments give way to anxiety and depression.

If we want to apply this harsh reality to the domain of personal growth and development we'll need to find a model, a process that acts as a lighthouse illuminating the path to shore. It won't be perfect, and it will have waves and blind spots. But if we can remove the biggest kink in most chains, the risk of human error, by complying with a tried, tested, and well-researched process, then change is probable.

In The Change Scroll, we move beyond the role of models and systems and look at our personal ownership of the commitments we make. When we're floating in uncharted waters, our ability to adhere to and trust the lighthouse often determines whether the shore is found, and whether growth is manifested or regression occurs.

The Change Scroll

> *The snake which cannot cast its skin has to die. As well the minds which are prevented from changing their opinions; they cease to be mind.*
> —Friedrich Nietzsche

Change is a long process that occurs in a moment. Change is the process of showing up when times are hard. Change is the process of adapting who and what we are to the realities imposed on us in that complex domain called life. The Change Scroll addresses personal implementation of method and the psychology of success.

Life is Chaos, and Weightlessness is a Model for its Navigation

Weightlessness first found its home in a small, boutique training studio nestled into a side alley in Shanghai's French concession amidst a tribe of six individuals committed to becoming weightless in body and mind. The studio had blue matted martial arts floors, dumbbell racks and a pulley machine lining the walls, and a tree, a proper tree, growing up through the center of the floor and up through the ceiling.

Mirrors lining one wall reflected the entire setup, including Japanese sliding doors, one that segregated the kitchen from the gym, and one that led to the bathroom. It was small. It was quaint. And it tested, broke, and nurtured the hearts of true warriors over the course of three years, during which Weightlessness became what it is today.

After writing *In Pursuit of Weightlessness,* the philosophy of Weightlessness was quite fleshed out, but the specific methodology that led people from states of mind-body burden to a sense of personal freedom and power was, well, all in my head in a jumble of disparate tools and principles. At that time, Weightlessness was more a philosophy of life. Today, it's a comprehensive, minimalist approach to mind-body peak performance in the game of life.

The level of precision and detail within, I think, would surprise many practitioners of the mind-body arts, as it provides very concrete prescriptions for a plethora of starting points, conditions, and imbalances. And before we get into the nitty-gritty details of Weightlessness Training in The Weightlessness Scroll, we need to have a heart-to-heart about the journey ahead for those considering *the path*.

When I took on my first tribe, I took on a commitment to community and individual alike in a form I wasn't quite used to. I had, prior to that time, facilitated a wide array of transformative programs, several of which I outline in my last book. But none of them went to the depths that my early tribes explored, some to the depths of despair and personal breakdown, and some to the heights of existential self-empowerment.

I knew the power of Weightlessness Training firsthand, but when I saw the power it had to break or enlighten the minds of others, I knew this had to continue. There was no shortage of fatigue, self-doubt, excitement, fear, optimism, psychological break down, and transcendental moments. We ran the gamut of human emotion and expression as I tried and tested the paradigms of all tribers and held the mirror of Weightlessness before them.

Weightlessness has a purity about it that inspires many and frightens even more. It refuses to coexist with delusional views of self and other. It doesn't allow us to have ideologies that cannot be tested by fire and redesigned as needed. It doesn't allow us to have unfounded convictions and blind optimism. But it does give us the tools and insights to face our greatest fears, to conquer our demons, and to enter the void of uncertainty with extraordinary poise and focus.

Weightlessness is at once a mirror that reflects our true selves, in all our insecurity and strength, as well as a beacon of light for what we can become in quantifiable, concrete terms.

In my first tribe alone, we had a wellness innovator who overcame lower back disk misalignment (spondylolisthesis) with the deadlift. One triber was an executive mentor-coach who wanted to take his personal development to the next level and integrate mind and body. He did so on the very last day of the program with the aid of a shot of whisky when he sliced two bricks in half with his bare hand for the first time. Another was an entrepreneur who was faced with the pressures of this commitment and forced to reassess how much value he really placed on his own health and performance. He didn't make it through. A fourth was a fitness coach who faced her anxieties and mind-body dissociations by learning the suspended splits, a technique that required unified mind-body-breath in training and execution.

We had an artist and brand designer who had a crisis of confidence, yet who regained his center and found a focus and stillness he didn't know possible through the implementation of an elite-level concentration practice, one that breaks most practitioners. The last was a focused executive seeking balance and the confidence to overcome a recurring herniation in the lower back, which she proved with 300 jump lunges in fifteen minutes in the last week of training.

Along the way, I encountered patterns that I was only loosely familiar with beforehand. These patterns became so clear that by my fifth tribe orientation, I told everyone on Day 1 exactly what to expect in terms of emotional and psychological struggle and distraction according to each week of the program. I had discovered the patterns that led people to stay the course, and the patterns that derailed a program early. I had discovered the attitudes and behaviors that created personal crisis, and those that lead to massive breakthrough. And I had learned, oddly enough, that we're all not so different in the ways we navigate uncertainty. We may have different thresholds for stress, but the nature of breakdown and breakthrough are the same for all. It's just a matter of when and to what degree.

While these patterns are not at all unique to Weightlessness practitioners (they are consistent for everyone engaged in a highly committed process of change), they do provide critical insight as to potential pitfalls that could prematurely end one's growth process, as well as the tools required to reach one's overarching goals.

You're not special.

All of us tend to think we're unique. We think that we have special circumstances that make our excuses or criticisms more valuable than the recommendations of an experienced coach. But we're wrong most of the time. This is a critical point. You may be unique. Congratulations. But until you've paid your dues and know clearly what makes us all similar, you should not expect anyone to care or acknowledge your individual differences.

You have to first do the work, to lay the foundations of mind-body performance, and to understand the principles therein. If you cannot manage this due to reasons outside of your control, then you're not yet in the game. I'm here to tell you that few reasons outside of your control are legitimate. Ninety percent of them can be managed with preemptive scheduling. Is your issue the type of restaurant you ate at due to work? Well…schedule someplace else. Or order a chicken salad. Or eat beforehand and tell your boss you've got diarrhea and are sticking to water for now. Own your choices fully.

The other ten percent requires an honest look at who you are. It's convenient to think that the advice and guidance of experts in the personal growth domain may not be relevant because you're special. But you'll never know if that's true unless you relinquish control, stop embracing your own excuses, and surrender to the process or method you're considering.

One hundred days is a great minimum commitment target. It's short enough to stay the course, yet long enough to test the full spectrum of self-doubt and confrontation that will occur when the tools that got you to today aren't sufficient to get you to tomorrow.

This self-confrontation is the precipice of breakthrough, and it's met with either psychological suffering or with an open, conquering mind. It's my priority to help you achieve breakthrough with the latter and avoid the former. To do so, we'll need to explore the requisites of change in a bit more detail.

Confidence is a Byproduct, not a Prerequisite for Change

We'll discuss in The Transformation Scroll the concept of neural plasticity. In particular, we'll look at its role in psychological unburdening. But regarding change in general, it's important to keep in mind that who we are is very much a result of what we've done.

A lot of people wait for inspiration. They wait for convenience to start. They believe that some people succeed because they're strong, because they're confident, and they miss the personal narrative that generated those attributes in those people. Strong people got strong; they weren't born that way. Confident people nurtured self-confidence by acting until successes occurred.

If someone is highly confident yet they haven't accomplished anything that could signify competence in domain X, they're delusional in domain X. In psychology, this delusion of false confidence is known as the Dunning-Kruger effect, a bias that stems from having limited skill or perspective (low competency), so one lacks the perspective to assess how competent they really are. There's no glory in that. If someone lacks confidence and hasn't accomplished anything, they're a reasonable person who can change in dramatic ways, so long as they're willing to take action. They're just not going to know that or feel that until they blindly leap into a process that challenges their perspective.

You don't need to be strong to start. Just start. Strength is the byproduct of working through the uncertainties, fears, and challenges that crop up along the way. You don't need confidence to achieve awesome things. You just need to be willing to fail and get back up. You do that enough times and winning happens. Confidence is a byproduct of competence. Get good at the thing and feel good about yourself. Today is the day. Whether you're ready or not, confident or not, today is the day.

Manage Your Expectations

Your perspective on the commitment at hand is as meaningful as the commitment itself in regards to your transformation. Understanding the nature of the domain is critical for orienting yourself appropriately for the journey ahead. The nature of your domain, the contents of which is static-closed or dynamic-open, has a lot to do with how much you ought to seek understanding or control over that domain, as we discussed in the last chapter. There may be a justifiable place for confidence and ego in the first (closed-static) domain, whereas such things can easily derail a more dynamic and potentially chaotic domain.

I once taught a women's self-defense workshop where, on day one, we covered a few key principles of self-defense, as well as the not-so-happy nature of it all. I showed several videos from YouTube of assaults on women. None of them ended in death. None of them were wartime events, which would have likely been far worse. But they were shocking in terms of the speed and intensity of the assaults.

Watching a woman being thrown over a desk and kept from escaping her office, or another being stalked, thrown to the ground, and head repeatedly smashed into the pavement, are challenging even for someone who more frequently thinks of preventing such circumstance. Every woman in the group was shocked. One was in tears. After thirty years in martial arts and very serious training undertaken under a variety of experts around the world, ranging from Shaolin monks to Navy Seals instructors, I'd like to think of myself as nondelusional in the domain of self-defense. From my experience, however, few in the martial arts world understand and present the realities of self-defense to their students accurately.

Self-defense isn't a static-closed domain that can be easily bottled. It's chaos. And a balance must be struck between the tools and principles assimilated through training, and a willingness to put skin in the game and test said principles by fire. This is absolutely critical to prevent the delusion of guruesque pedagogy.

On Day 2 of the series, we tested the techniques we'd practiced on Day 1 to make sure we were applying them correctly. This was early in the class and we were still working with only the foundations of a wrist grab escape. It's not a difficult technique, but it's hard to apply when your opponent is considerably stronger. The woman who became very emotional when viewing the videos on Day 1 was butchering the techniques I taught her.

She wasn't applying the highly leveraged, full-body effort that reduced the need for muscular strength and mechanically releases the grip. She found that difficult and, instead, wrenched her arm with full might in a way that applied no leverage and would only work with someone weaker holding her. I asked her why she wasn't applying the technique she learned. She stated that it didn't work for her. Yup, after one day and less than fifteen conscientious repetitions, she'd determined the technique was broken.

I explained that nothing in the world of self-defense would work without practice. Period. Anyone who tells you self-defense is easy is lying to you. This stuff takes practice, and it takes practice under pressure. How could one possibly determine after ten to fifteen attempts that the technique is flawed? I hope the reason for this case study is obvious. This is a case where a person approached a dynamic domain with the mindset of someone learning a static-closed system. She thought she could learn a few things and they'd work and that's that. Simple.

I pointed out that her technique would get her injured and wouldn't work with a strong hold. That even if it took 1,000 reps to learn the correct technique, it would be time well spent. This is your life. If it's ever truly threatened, do you want to be armed with a sharpened sword or a random, ad hoc weapon you just borrowed from your ass?

She continued to practice it her way with her training partner. So I stepped in to test her technique. It failed. We tried again. It failed. And again. Failed. Not only could she not loosen the grip even a bit, she nearly tore her shoulder out with the force she applied to escape.

When navigating dark, chaotic waters, trust in the lighthouse.

She was embarrassed. She was angry. She reacted the way petulant children do when they don't get their way. It was someone else's fault. This was a person who was used to controlling her environment and getting her way. She was used to playing in static-closed environments that lacked volatility, where her experience served her well.

I explained to her that self-defense is the single most difficult thing to do in life. Period. Nothing is harder. It requires 100% of your being, your insight, your memory, your intuition, your concentration, your physical strength and conditioning, your technical proficiency, if any, and your integrated response under the pressure of injury or death. That's the starting point. And I asked her, "Can you name one, just one other challenging domain in life, anything, like a lawyer or a doctor, military man or firefighter, where you can show up to a survey class, practice a few basic techniques, and expect to handle yourself under real pressure in the environment of that expert without countless hours of practice?"

Not one.

We here, you and I, are approaching a wide open domain, one that does indeed have a lighthouse, but has, at the same time, some of the most treacherous waters and ominous skies. In the domain of personal development, we have to contend with both the scientific foundations and existential speculations around the better versions of self, as well as the dubious relevance that various tools, skills, and habits may offer in the context of our real-world environments, which, as you guessed it, is an open-dynamic clusterfuck of a domain.

Before we start out on a life-altering journey together, we must orient ourselves around the realities of this domain. We must take very seriously the known science of human health and performance, and we must be humble and disciplined to stay the course as life itself tests our principles and our resolve, for we are not playing in a domain that's easily dominated. We're playing in a domain, like self-defense, that can break your body and fracture your mind or allow for the expression of your greatest strength, passion, and purpose.

Trust the Process

Trusting the process generally goes hand in hand with the perspective an individual has when engaging with a new domain. Master learners are able to empty themselves of preconceptions and approach a new subject with innocent curiosity, drawing on their prior knowledge bases only when necessary. There are very few master learners.

Most who attempt new things in the personal development camp have experience with the personal development camp or have had successes in life that have made them acutely aware of their strengths and weaknesses. So, they think if they can merely fill in the gaps and grow in ways X, Y, and Z, they'll have a greater chance of future success.

This approach leads to process rebellion when a competent and capable professional, a leader in their own domain who has more or less risen to the top of their field and controls their own environment, is confronted with a process that requires a different modus operandi. This is generally a disaster. In my last two remote tribes (which last three months rather than the 100-day immersions I taught in Shanghai), a woman quit at Week 6 of 12. Twice. I'll explain below exactly why Week 6, but for now, let's focus on the process at large and the limiting perspective that derailed it. I will call her R.

R had found great success within her company over the course of a decade, much of it accompanied by sharp, hard-working, persistent, and, in some cases, stubborn personality traits. And these are all useful qualities. No one makes a difference if they don't believe they're right most of the time, and if they don't have the conviction to insist on their rightness when bosses or colleagues fail to see the advantages of executing said belief.

So, this is in no way a dismissal of her character in general, but it's to point out, yet again, that the tools and habits that got us to where we are today may not be sufficient to get us to where we want to be. And if we cannot take on the habits and practices of those who've been where we want to be and do so even amidst discomfort, inconvenience, and self-doubt, we're doomed to fail or default to what we know and who we've been. Again and again.

R started both programs with incredible fervor. She was highly engaged, attended group calls well prepared with appropriate questions on content, and highly communicative within the group chat. This lasted three weeks. On Week 3 and 4, life things happened. There were unplanned work trips that altered her diet and training schedule and, in her mind, left her in a position where adhering to her prescribed protocol wasn't possible.

Eventually, she asked what to do when adhering to protocol isn't possible, and this is, I'm sorry to say, the beginning of the end for all of us.

The protocol was designed and customized to her personal conditions based on a consultation. In that consultation, she underestimated the very real conditions that work placed on her life and stated far greater control over schedule than would be possible. Twice. In her first program, this came as a surprise to her, I believe. In the second program… well, it came as a surprise to her.

If you're consistently surprised by something, it isn't the thing's fault.

She started deviating from her diet, and, due to inconvenience or fatigue shortly thereafter, started reducing her prescription or rewriting her protocol based on how she felt. She asked again how she could manage the protocol when she was unable to manage the protocol. And this is perhaps the single most misunderstood principle of this craft:

You don't train as and when the rest of your life is working; the rest of your life works when you train. You must make space for your own growth process.

It's very much a chicken and egg scenario, where most people believe training is a discretionary luxury rather than the thing that sustains you and makes the rest of life flow properly.

The Dalai Lama once said that everyone needs twenty minutes of meditation a day, unless they're too busy, in which case they need an hour. Training is the stuff that gives you the energy to sustain when times are tough. It gives you the mental peace and acuity to perform well, consistently, and under pressure. It's not just something you do with leftover energy once you've blown your load on the "important" life stuff. It comes first. It is urgent.

The core of who and what you are and the quality of and commitment to training has a direct and long-lasting impact on everything from your family relations to your career. Don't put it in the closet. Place it on a pedestal. But I digress.

So, R's fallacy was in assuming that the process of Weightlessness training didn't take into account her particular life constraints. She assumed that she was different, and that her reasons for deviation from protocol were valid. If she were right, Weightlessness training would be an inadequate system indeed. And from her perspective she was right, because she never overcame her circumstances and found a way to show up despite them.

It was a domain misunderstanding that led to a lack of trust in a process that claims to help individuals find a sense of weightlessness in life. There's no qualification there. It's not just promising that result to California housewives with eight hours of free time each day, or detox retreat trainees who make time and space for it. It's promising it to everybody. But there are compromises in the implementation process, in showing up, that make even the most appropriate protocols fail miserably.

This is an important consideration for those with personal constraints. For you don't learn to shoot in battle. And you don't rebuild a ship at sea. Just because a system teaches you to do something doesn't mean you effectively learn or implement it in chaos from day one. There's a reason military men go to basic training before they're sent to war. It's because none of them would have the wherewithal, focus, or fortitude to learn to shoot while under enemy fire, let alone basic skill and strategy.

Training is a laboratory that allows you to develop, test, and try new skills. Life is the battlefield where those skills get tested by fire and applied to survive or flourish. Don't confuse training and application. You must have a foundation, some modicum of awareness and control over your skills before you can appropriately implement them under fire. This is the one step back before the two steps forward.

Weightlessness provides the tools we need, really need, regardless of circumstances. Does this mean it provides all tools necessary for all cases? Nope. Again, that would only make sense if life were a static-closed system. This would be domain confusion. Weightlessness doesn't aim to provide all tools for all situations, period. It provides the minimum number of tools that we cannot do without and still expect to live a healthy, flourishing life (if not perform at our peaks). For this, we don't need many tools; we need strong compliance and the right ones.

The busier we are, the more stress we have, the more urgent it is that we comply with our training prescriptions without exception… and trust the process. The process is demanding, to be certain. But the training itself offers almost immediate payoff that cannot be further gamed or hacked. This means that when you're tired, trust the process. When you're busy, trust the process. When you think you know your body and would prefer to play your workout or nutrition by ear today, stop the nonsense and trust the process.

The process (within all good methods and programs) knows you better than you know yourself, at least in their respective ways. It has seen your personal circumstances and those that are far more convoluted. It has distilled the essence of your needs into a neatly packed protocol.

You may still have unanswered issues or challenges, but those cannot be properly identified and combatted without a well-laid foundation.

When you're entering a process that goes beyond rote knowledge acquisition and requires different habits, practices, and principles that exceed your experience and current understanding, do not assume that the process itself will be comfortable or convenient. You'll have to do things you don't want to do, things that won't feel natural or comfortable. Don't assume at those times that you know better, that you're different, or that the system doesn't work for you. Trust the process!

Consider Your Environment

We've all heard the saying that you're the average of the five people you spend the most time with, and likely the saying that you're a product of your environment. We are not independent, isolated creatures. We learn, grow, process, and change in relationship to our environments. They influence us far more than we realize.

If you want to be honest, don't hang out with criminals. If you want to be fit, don't surround yourself with fast food junkies. If you want to be successful, don't surround yourself with those who lack personal drive and ambition. Find your tribe. This is hard for everyone serious about change because we're not all blessed with the best resources, friends, families, mentors, careers, education, so on and so on. But we can affect all of these things to a degree, adding more of those we aspire to have, and reducing those that hold us back.

For everyone considering learning a craft or getting fit at home from a DVD, this is an important consideration. Some people manage very well at home, but most last only a couple weeks. The environment that's used for relaxing, eating, and working, doesn't always present the strongest motivation for hard physical effort. Sometimes, shifting environment, going to a park, getting a gym membership, or signing up to a committed change process, automatically shifts the mind and generates renewed interest and motivation. The latter option kills two birds with one stone, affecting both environment and tribe, thereby affecting you in a far deeper way.

Make Space For Your Head

Many people believe the process accurately diagnoses and prescribes their condition, but due to life issues, distraction, or a drop in motivation, compliance starts to wane. This often coincides with an attitude of self-acceptance, where the trainee relaxes if not reassess their governing reason or motivation for starting the process and starts to pat themselves on the back for achieving something, albeit not everything, and that's better than nothing.

The biggest problem with shooting for the stars and settling for the moon (prematurely) is the issue of nonlinear payoff that we discussed in The Uncertainty Scroll. It's quite possible that if doing 100% gets you to the stars, that 70% doesn't even get you out of the Earth's atmosphere. That may require 75% or 80%. The only way we truly know just how much it requires is when we pull no punches and go for the knockout. Giving 100% may deter many people from really undertaking a meaningful process, but it will ensure that of those who do, few will be delusional about what it takes to achieve life-changing breakthroughs.

For those who sign up to a committed process, there will always be internal conflict between the desire for discretionary choice and a disciplined execution of a plan. When we lose focus or feel the strains of life and the struggle of training, we all too often convince ourselves that one deviation does not an epic failure make. And we also think that we've got enough life experience to determine how much deviation or damage we can take without derailing the whole process.

I'm sorry to inform you, we're almost always wrong. If your first impulse is to seek comfort, and you listen to it, it is a slippery slope from there back to the problems and insecurities that led you to this path in the first place. And you won't have the evidence in hand to understand why.

Discretion gives us a short-term sense of control, but discipline sets us free.

To do this effectively may require you to create more space in your life for growth. If your intention is set, but your circumstances aren't permitting, then restructuring your schedule or environment is crucial. If, for example, you find your meditation is totally disconnected, distracted, or ineffective, yet you've set aside exactly fifteen minutes for it as planned, then you may need to ask what's happening at minute sixteen.

I've worked with many people who allot exactly one hour for their Weightlessness protocol (or any other form of mind-body or meditation practice), which always concludes with a meditation component. At one hour and one minute, they have a conference call with the boss, regularly. And they're confused as to why they can't clear their heads and meditate effectively. You must make space for training, and, therefore, yourself. It isn't just about executing a series of techniques; it's about assimilating new skills and habits that transfer to the rest of life.

Create space in life for your evolving self.

When something is precious, we don't just consider that thing, we consider how it's kept (reference chapter: "A Vessel With Holes" in *The Essence of Lightness* story). I recall walking behind an aiyi (auntie or caretaker) in Shanghai who was pushing a baby in a stroller. She was on her phone and pushing and, you know, multitasking, and didn't seem to notice the kid was passed out with his head rolled to the left and clearing the side of the stroller. She also didn't notice the glass door that was left fully ajar about ten feet ahead.

Low and behold, she cleared the door with the front of the stroller but drove the kid's head right into the edge of it. This is an example of NOT showing up, while believing you're doing a good job. *Wasn't my fault; someone left the door open.* Congrats, you're taking good care of something precious and some other person is responsible for leaving a door open. In fact, the child was strapped and secured quite well in the carriage, so she had that going for her too. But there was no goddamned space for the kid's head. I hope this metaphor is ridiculously clear. Even the best-laid plans fail miserably if we don't take responsibility for every part of their implementation.

Make space for your head or you may be in for a rude awakening.

Show the Fuck Up

Show the Fuck Up! is my personal appeal to those who begin to lose motivation. You started your process for a reason. You opened this book for a reason. It's easy to criticize a person we just met, or judge a book by its cover, but we cannot claim we understand the essence of either, and certainly not well enough to objectively categorize quality or character.

Many people put in 70% effort and judge a process or method as ineffective. Does this make sense? There is, first of all, an art to finishing unto itself, but in practice of your new path or craft, you must show up. This doesn't mean show up when you're excited to train, or super motivated. It means show up when you're tired. It means show up when you're injured (though focus on stuff that doesn't exacerbate the injury). It means show up when you're defeated. It means show up when it's hard. It means show up when you'd do anything for another hour of sleep, or a piece of chocolate cake, or any other potential conflict with the mission you set out on. It means show up for yourself.

Change is a Long Process, a Process That Occurs in a Moment

"Everybody breaks," I explained to each new tribe on Day 1 of their journey through Weightless in 100—the hundred-day peak performance program I ran for several years in Shanghai. "If you happen to be an exception, then you've got an extraordinary foundation in self-management and change processes. But for those who don't, it's important that we manage expectations. Your ability to complete this commitment with full focus and effort should not be contingent on a process free of pain. It's important that we orient ourselves around the idea that change often has fallout, and that growth requires discomfort. Because when you hit the wall, and you will, how you show up the next day determines who you become thereafter."

As I mentioned, I saw patterns to the process and could predict, to the week, when people would lose motivation, when they would struggle with identity issues, when the principles of Weightlessness would overflow and permeate the rest of life, thereby forcing deeper questions to surface on integrity and ownership, when some, if not all trainees would break, and when, fingers crossed, breakthrough would occur that would escort them to a better place where weightless moments were common occurrences.

In every tribe there was, by mere coincidence or otherwise, a subtle leader (for false leaders who impose their wills with alpha energy crack relatively quickly, while the quiet warrior patiently steers the group by example over time), a healer (someone who brought the group together emotionally), a loner (someone who held above all else their identity as an independent thinker), a cynic (someone who made known their skepticism of practices within the process, though who was really just trying to protect their sense of control), a quitter (someone who chases trophies and social approval but can't face their inadequacies honestly), and a hero (someone who fears loss and change, who bleeds emotionally during the process and avoids pain as and when it's possible, who doubts their own potential, and who discovers in one defining moment a strength that was never known and the warrior within who decides to stand back up over and over again).

The program was a microcosm of sorts that clearly manifested how people approach commitment in general, and how they perform under pressure in particular. The intensity of the training, the pace of the program, and the stress simulations were designed to get people up and running with robust tools as quickly as possible, and then throw them into aggressive scenarios that would challenge both the attention to physical detail and performance, as well as their ability to relinquish control and adapt to new, rapidly changing environments.

This was an escalating process that few made it through unscathed because when the body gets tired, the mind is exposed. And when your model fails to serve you and you're still forced to perform, who you really are begins to surface. Though my prior programs were 100 days, I want to be clear that this is one of many formats of applied principles of Weightlessness.

One might only take away from my program references here that you, the overcomer, will need a long enough commitment to realize those things the process can teach you about yourself. This might last 100 days, or it might become a multiyear journey into the depths of Weightlessness.

If the potential fallout from deep personal work wasn't so severe I'd happily overlook this foreshadowing of the growth/training process and let people discover these shifts along the way. But people consistently underestimate the difficulty of this process, and consistently overestimate their capacity to navigate the unknown. Thus, it's important that you're aware of pitfalls ahead of time so that if and when they arise for you, you'll approach them with a sense of familiarity and understanding.

While I'll be describing the changes and challenges faced with a 100-day Weightlessness program, these are universal patterns that anyone who attempts anything we could place in the personal growth camp will face. If the process is longer and slower in pace, we'd merely extend the timelines a bit. If it's shorter and even more intense, we'd tighten the timelines. But regardless, here are the pivotal moments and potential pitfalls in your process of change:

1. Exuberance. Weeks 1 through 3, you're excited to be learning something new, excited to be part of a new, edgy community, and excited for growth to come. You haven't settled into your new subject or environment yet, so there's an air of focus and effort by all as you find your right place within the group. You adhere strictly to schedule and diet and you give a lot of effort every session.

2. Familiarity and Deceleration. By Weeks 4 and 5, you've gotten acquainted with the location, the teacher, the trainees, and the process. And you're comfortable. You feel more secure with the subject and less exposed to judgment. And this is where your edge and focus starts to wane. You deviate from your diet. It's just *that*

one time, you tell yourself. And you start to conserve energy in training a bit more, thinking it's more about staying the course than killing it just today. And complacency, while not full blown, starts to surface.

3. Belly of the Beast. In Weeks 6 through 8 you'll face your greatest challenges, at best, a crisis of confidence, and, at worst, some form of breakdown or loss of identity. This may sound bad, but only through emptying your cup can it be filled. In this window, the fatigue of six to eight weeks of consistent effort sets in and there's no passion left for the process. You begin to crave comfort and security and avoid taking on the necessary stressors inherent in the growth process. And in an instant, despair, self-doubt, or a crisis of confidence sets in, and you realize you're nothing. You're not adequate, not knowledgeable, and not skilled enough to manage the pressures sucking the oxygen from the room. And you break.
4. **Breakthrough**. This may occur at the same instant of despair in the belly of the beast, or it may be a rapid acceleration of growth that occurs once the limiting walls of your prior self have been broken down. This window occurs between Weeks 8 and 11. This is where momentum begins to energize your body and elevate your mind. You begin to realize that the fatigue you felt at stage 3 was stemming from resistance to change, and now that you've relinquished control and have realized (after surviving the breakdown) that you're not made of glass, you feel unburdened of fear, fatigue, and anxiety, and you feel a surge of energy that you cannot wait to reinvest in the process now that payoff is obvious. You're no longer afraid to fail. You've realized the freedom that stems from self-discipline and control.
5. The Long Game | The Road Ahead. At the beginning of Week 11, you realize there are still four weeks left. You've seen incredible growth, mentally and physically, and you feel you've been gifted a new life in a way. You feel that you've achieved what you came for… and there are still four weeks left. This is the final demon to overcome—the belief that you've made it through to the other side already, that you landed the breakthrough you came for. This is where the lost art of finishing illuminates the true test of integrity and commitment. This is where masters are made. Continued in the next principle…

Finish What You've Started—You are the Canvas

There is a lost art to finishing what we've started. The long game is a mindset of mastery. All too often today, we're taught that the key to success is focusing on the 20% of effort that gets 80% of the results. We're taught that it's better to be a generalist than a specialist. While I'm not dismissing the advantages of having a general, well-rounded base of knowledge and skills, I do believe we're being fed bullshit.

In many ways, Weightlessness is an 80/20 type minimalist approach to mind-body development and peak performance. I've done the hard work and separated the wheat from the chaff in this very broad, all-encompassing domain so that you don't have to. It took me decades of study, trial and error, and a lot of blood and sweat. But my intention was never to cut corners. It was to focus on the minimum number of tools needed, those tools that we cannot overlook and still expect to be high performing, weightless individuals. But that 20% of meaningful information in your hands is meaningful because I burned the other 80% already; I didn't avoid it.

Doing only 20% of what's remaining, well, I wouldn't recommend it.

The mind of a craftsman is one that strives for perfection, regardless of whether it has learned to settle with *the good*. The mind of a craftsman knows that 20% is enough to fill out the form of a thing, but honor and integrity are found in the remaining 80%. And for many, this will be skimmed over and ignored if they adhere to the 80/20 rule because they'll never feel in a visceral way the depth of insight and meaning contained in the other 80.

But it matters.

I first started finishing things when I was in college. There was one particular day when I felt that finishing a book wasn't merely speaking to the quality or relevance of its content. It was demonstrating a fortitude and stick-to-itiveness in my approach to all things. Reading was a microcosm for life. I was cutting corners and doing enough to get by. I changed that. I told myself that I wouldn't open a book if I wasn't prepared to finish it. And with that, my comprehension of all subjects improved, not only because I was seeing the full story painted by the author, but because I was cultivating a habit of persistence past the point of intrigue. It forced me to struggle with concepts beyond a point of confusion or discomfort.

No matter what you engage in, if it matters, you *will* lose intrigue. Keep going.

I've been a hobbyist painter and sketch artist for most of my life and have dabbled in sculpting. What all artists learn quickly is that the broad brush-strokes at the onset of a new work make up the bulk of the presentation. They're also the most fun, as you splatter your vision onto a blank canvas and create something from nothing.

These early efforts rather quickly fill out the canvas and present something worth hanging on your wall. It's common for artists to show the rough concept sketch to somebody and receive a "wow" because it looks fantastic to them. The artist could, if they so choose, call it finished right then and there as what's there is enough to pass the litmus test of aesthetic beauty. But the artist knows better.

What happens in the hours to days to weeks thereafter turns something beautiful into a masterpiece. Most of the changes, if observed hourly or daily would be imperceptible in the same way observing a child grow daily shows no contrast. But if you see that child only occasionally, you're always amazed at the degree of change. I've painted many pieces that looked good enough to call finished after only a short time, hours to days. But it isn't just about the painting. How much of myself am I leaving on the table if I don't complete this once the work has become tedious, if not grueling? Sure, the painting might be acceptable as is, but what about the "artist" who accepts it?

In days to months, this difference means nothing. But in months to years it's the difference between experts and novices, masters and disciples. Over time, the other 80% becomes the true story. And in the game of mind-body development, in the game of Weightlessness, this story is no different. You can, rather quickly, implement the tools and principles of Weightlessness to have the body of your dreams and a mind that feels freer and more focused than you've ever known. But this is only the beginning. This is the launch point for the true work ahead. This isn't a game where you finish a painting and move to the next.

You're the artwork.

And if you neglect that other 80% of the journey, the tedious, monotonous, slow progressing 80%, then your canvas of life will always be empty of detail and depth. You'll find it challenging to adapt your skills in new situations, and challenging to maintain the physique or mental piece you've cultivated when stresses and pressures begin to rise.

Weightlessness does the hard work by filtering the information that can get you to an unburdened and powerful state, but your mindset ongoing is what makes or breaks that process and guarantees or jeopardizes those results. You're not a finished work. You're a work in progress.

The mindset that understands the cycles of growth and deceleration mentioned above can set strategies that allow you to survive the hard times, the times marked by boredom, fatigue, or tedium. They're hard. But rather than call something good enough, what if, just beyond those moments or days when training feels unnatural and unproductive and no longer worthy of the same dedication lies a deep and renewed passion for progress? What if true passion lies just beyond the belly of the beast?

The Dedicated Warrior Can Implement Many Weapons

Armed with a growth mindset and the right systems in place that allow you to stay the course, opportunity arises to implement key principles and tools that guarantee effective and long-lasting transformation. We'll examine the key principles of mind-body transformation next in The Transformation Scroll.

The Transformation Scroll

"

Antifragility is beyond resilience or robustness. The resilient resists shocks and stays the same; the antifragile gets better.
—Nassim Nicholas Taleb

The Transformation Scroll identifies the governing principles of mind-body transformation. These are not principles or facts exclusive to Weightlessness. They are well-documented, uncontested, scientifically validated principles of human growth and development that are true for all people at all times. If one doesn't start with the facts, then all methods of development are conceivably equal, and one cannot differentiate information from noise. The better we understand our nature, the easier it becomes to model growth. Greatest among these principles are antifragility, plasticity, and tensegrity.

Euthyphro Dilemma—A Useful Frame

In Plato's dialogue *Euthyphro*, Socrates asks Euthyphro if "the pious is loved by the gods because it is pious, or is it (the pious) pious because it is loved by the gods?" And ever since, Western theology has scrambled to rectify this dilemma within their own ethical systems, "Is something moral because God decreed it, or does God decree it because it is moral?" Christianity, Judaism, and Islam have yet to conclusively settle this dilemma for themselves in contemporary theology, for each horn of the dilemma has consequences that are less than desirable.

If God wills something because it is good, then there is something that exceeds or is external to God's will and power. There are many considerations here, but it does lead to a reductionist argument that makes God herself obsolete. If on the other hand, something is good because God wills it, then we cannot claim that there is reason for morality apart from the whim and whimsy of God's will. If nothing defines *the Good* apart from God's will, then there's an arbitrariness to *the Good* that can change and could do so in conceivably undesirable ways at least as far as our feeble species is concerned. It also would mean nothing to claim that God is good, other than to imply that she follows her own commands. But if she does, in fact, have omnipotence AND free will, then both she and *the Good* can become other than they are. There is space for not-good—for evil.

This isn't meant to be a theological discussion so much as it is a useful framework for how we assess the usefulness or truth in various systems of personal development. I only bring up this obscure dilemma because I've had many conversations on the system of Weightlessness (vs. other systems) as well as the techniques and tools therein. If we look at these factors on a superficial level, as mere approaches based on the whim and whimsy of a founder or a panel of experts, then there's little to say other than, *you do it your way, and I'll do it mine. My system does it this way...and I'm sticking to it.* That's great, but by what measure is your system an accurate model of us humans and the way we develop? How is it meaningful?

Many mind-body approaches to personal development are available in the world and some are less integrated than others. Of those that are integrated, few are useful. But to a devout disciple of them, you might as well be calling their God a hoax when you criticize their technique or their guru.

This is a postmodern tragedy because it means we can't speak to the truth of any one approach. It means people fundamentally believe in individual differences over and above species continuity. And while we certainly can see differences between individuals, my opinion is that these differences mean little until we get the similarities right. Until we know what makes us the same, we have no hope of identifying and capitalizing on differences. In the same way, if you want to make a great hamburger, you start by adding what's true to all burgers, most likely a patty and a bun, before going wild with fixings.

So, the next time you learn a new technique in martial arts, or a new pose in yoga, or a new breathing technique or embodiment practice, ask yourself *Does this work (i.e., is this true about humans) because guru says so, or does guru say so because it's true?* What's the integrative principle that makes it true? The personal growth world is wrought with teacher-student relationships that look like lord-servant relationships. In some cases, this may make some sense… but not most.

When you meet individuals who've dedicated five decades to self-mastery and they've done a good job, they are, in fact, different from your average Joe on the street. They move differently, they speak with precision, their eyes don't wander, and their presence has a preternatural element to it. But I'll submit this isn't much different from a high school basketball player facing off against Michael Jordan or Kobe Bryant. When we witness or experience something that exceeds our understanding or model of that thing, it carries with it the weight of the mystical. But this is a matter of degree, not of kind, and we must never forget that.

So, when your coach tells you to squat a certain way, or your guru tells you to breathe a certain way, or your somatic coach tells you to posture a certain way, by what measure do you filter these techniques and rules? The guru who tells you that exercise must be done this way because their teacher and their teacher before them all did it this way should be kicked to the curb. The coach who speaks to you of biomechanics and the guru who speaks to you of neurology and brain chemistry (with accuracy) are those who are at least sincere (we can't yet assess correctness) in their own training. They're likely a great starting point for your own self-exploration.

When a teacher can explain to you that a technique must be done a certain way because…x, y, z is in accordance with your physiology, then they have concluded, just like Socrates, that the gods will something because it is pious, and not the other way around. They are giving concrete assumptions, facts, and hypotheses by which their own teachings can be confirmed by you or tested and disproved through further scientific research.

You're in the game of the craftsman now, not the mystic.

As we discussed in the last chapter, when constructing a model, assumptions must be falsifiable. For that to be the case, they must be testable and transmittable in concrete terms. The days of "*Do this because my teacher and his teacher's grandfather's cousin discovered this in a cave and defeated a bear with nothing but the flick of his will"* are over. However, it's tempting for some to take this as an admonishment of all systems or practices within systems that are not supported with scientific evidence as, therefore, being pure speculation. This too is a mistake and not the point I'm trying to make.

Science is often a lagging corroborator. We must not forget this. We knew, for example, that gravity existed well before we had the calculus to prove it.

Science is decades, at best, behind most elements of human performance due simply to the complex, open system of human biology. This gap is becoming closer with the rapid growth in technology, but we're still not there. As such, we must allow for a place within all systems that speak of the void in less than scientific language, because true masters commune with the void on a regular basis, and the truths they discover there are often of no use to the novice.

Because *masters* are outliers in their respective domains, no ample data sets exist from which to extract reasonable objective conclusions. When you find a human who can generate ten times the electromagnetic current as your average Joe, or someone who can manipulate their autonomic nervous system at will like The Iceman Wim Hof, it's something worth considering on an anecdotal basis. But for the statistician, what can you do with a data set of 1? Not much.

The focus of all models should be on those things that we can empirically verify. It should be on those things we can test for ourselves, and research should we find the motivation. But it should not be limited to those things that can be proven under modern scientific analysis alone if the theoretical means of testing don't exist yet, for what's been proven is not all that there is. This doesn't mean it's mystical, it just means it isn't science yet.

We discussed in detail in the last chapter that reality exceeds our ability to model it in full. So, if you place absolute certainty in a model and don't allow for the uncertainties inherent in complexity to teach you further, you're dealing with a dead system. These unknowns should sit at the top of the pyramid of any good system. They should not be the foundations.

If a guru tells you that this works because when certain stars are aligned they make the waves in the ocean reverse and foam and this causes energy in your body to flow to the crown point so blah blah blah… charlatan. We must build a foundation of sound science and empirical evidence. We must will things, practice things, and teach things because they are true, and not the other way around. BUT, we must not forget that science is a lagging verifier. It tells us where to start, it cannot tell us where we're going with all things yet. And this is what keeps the game exciting.

Your Journey

Along your journey in Weightlessness, you'll be thrust into progressive series of practices that will test your sense of comfort and identity. It's important, as we've discussed, to recognize that this isn't for the sake of learning a new system, that is, learning something that pertains to life outside you. Each tool speaks to something essential about your mind-body complex.

These tools are not true or useful because Weightlessness or myself says so; Weightlessness dictates, cultivates, and integrates them because they're in accordance with contemporary science to the best of my knowledge. They're based on sound, corroborated principles of physiology and neurology. And, most importantly, they work time and time again.

While you may, at the end of the day, conclude that Weightlessness isn't for you, you don't have the luxury of being able to claim that what Weightlessness says about you is wrong (unless, of course, it is wrong).

Insofar as other systems capitalize on the principles in the pages hereafter, those systems speak truth. Insofar as they deviate, they don't. This doesn't speak to the omniscient comprehensiveness of the system, but the very thorough reductionist filters that are in place to focus on the few but very meaningful things we know well, things that play a strong role in our growth and development, and which we can implement methodically over time with predictive accuracy. Insofar as Weightlessness principles generate predictable and reproducible results, they are true. Insofar as the don't, they aren't.

But...the truth in some principles requires more effort and longer adherence to fully discover than others. Try to avoid the temptation of early cynicism.

I realize how frustrating, or even arrogant this may seem, but that's the risk we all take in seeking a common language of personal development and a science-based approach to integration. Hereafter will be the filters of personal development by which you can determine for yourself if the system you practice (should it be Weightlessness or otherwise) is reasonable or if it is astrological (speculative or anecdotal in nature).

This is an important distinction. If you are practicing yoga and you've got no principles of movement that underlie a specific position, how can you ever filter for yourself accurate from inaccurate technique, regardless of how many years you have in the game? If you're a martial artist who has no principle by which to assess the biomechanics of a punch or kick, how will you ever filter your instructor's teachings and corrections, or your students? How will you know if the theory of power is applied consistently from one technique to another—a sign of a coherent system?

In The Weightlessness Scroll, I present the foundational stage of development in Weightlessness Training known as The Weightlessness Spectrum, where we'll walk through a more personal storyline of your mind-body development, and the meaning behind each of the key pillars of Weightlessness. If it were not for the details about to be discussed, I couldn't expect anyone to accept that scroll as anything more than the philosophical musings of someone absorbed with their own perspective.

But I believe that if we can come to a common understanding of the foundations of mental and physical development according to key scientific principles, then the framework and conclusions drawn in The Weightlessness, Integration, and Lightness Scrolls will seem relevant, inevitable, and urgent.

Insofar as other systems of personal development embrace the principles that follow, they are also practicing Weightlessness to some degree, which, at its core, is more an organizing framework than a rote system. If you're becoming lighter in body and mind by any means whatsoever, you're doing something that honors your biological systems. But where they deviate, not only do they deviate from Weightlessness, they also ignore or misapply the science of mental and physical growth.

Weightlessness isn't the only path to the mountain peak; it's merely the shortest.

Diamonds are Formed Under Pressure—The Need for Deep Work

Many people think martial arts aren't for them. They're wrong.

Personal growth is not only about addressing personal strengths, weaknesses, and imbalances that are readily observable, or controlling those parts of us we believe we understand through introspection or analysis. We have deep, unconscious biological processes that weigh heavily on our ability to change, processes that can either hold us back or unleash our greatest powers, and sometimes, pressure is required to draw them to the surface.

Martial arts training is like no other domain of personal development. Many of the practices we take up in life can be somewhat detached from the core of our being. Martial arts, at their core, are about conflict resolution. The tools and principles therein are applied in the direst and most integral of circumstances. Our true essences manifest when we're confronted with conflict accompanied by the risk of serious injury. Your entire being integrates in a flash and organizes complex impulses that, with all hope, design survival. It's problem solving with skin in the game. It's 3D chess with love, life, and passion on the line. It's YOU unchained.

You may have the luxury of not asking the self-defense question. Many in this world don't, and many come to realize that just because you don't ask it, doesn't mean the risk of danger isn't forever present. Some think they can take up arms and carry a gun if they need to, overlooking one key factor; who you are at a shooting range is very different from who you are when your life, or the life of someone you love is on the line. Your mind changes in those moments. Your body changes in those moments.

At the center of conflict is still the sum of individual egos, knowledge, physical capacity, and experience. At the center of conflict is *you*. And as we all know very intimately, if you want the worst parts of you to surface, just add pressure.

In that sense, we can't escape Gay-Lussac's Law in thermodynamics, where heating a closed container leads to an explosive outcome. Those who are highly trained, psychologically, physically, or both, merely stand a better chance maintaining a sense of calm and allowing their higher faculties, their insights and intellect to weigh in on the complex chaos of conflict. But this is always a matter of degree.

When your present experience exceeds your model of how to interpret and navigate it, the dark shadows of your consciousness come to the surface because the rest of who you are merely isn't enough. Your inner Batman, a lawless vigilante with few inhibitions will surface, and he'll scare you. And he may be a genius billionaire, and he may be half retarded. This depends on your level of preparation.

All of us are hardwired to fight. We're as hardwired to fight as we are to love. The fight or flight response, when triggered by high-stress scenarios, alters neurochemistry and physiology in astounding ways, so much so that people who first experience an adrenaline dump don't recognize the person who took the stage.

Your prefrontal cortex, the part of your brain responsible for applied modeling and reasoning shuts down. Your hindbrain takes over with a cascade of reptilian responses. Adrenaline floods the skeletal muscles, speeding up metabolism, while at the same time, drawing blood and oxygen away from digestion to the skeletal muscles to fuel combat or flight. Did you every experience butterflies in the stomach due to nerves?

Those who have frozen while public speaking know this intimately. Vision narrows, hearing is subdued, and sensitivity to pain diminishes immensely. You become superhuman in many ways, dumber in others as blood leaves the brain and gut to fuel skeletal muscles for action. But you react from a place of honesty, whether that honesty is fear, anger, or creative problem solving. And for this reason, self-defense has been integrated into Weightlessness training as and when I've been able to fit it within a program for one reason only—it allows for controllable stress simulations that draw the subconscious mind to the surface.

Self-defense, while not internal to Weightlessness training, is, by far, the fastest route to deep, comprehensive breakthrough…or breakdown. I told my tribes on Day 1 that the premise of self-defense isn't to become proficient in combat within 100 days; it's to provide them with gross tools that allow for the expression of power and focus under pressure. You will, I warn them, be stressed. You need some vehicle with which you can trigger the integration of mind and body under duress, because only under duress will you dig deeper beyond your comfortable models of the world and use the entirety of your being to solve a problem to end your perceived conflict.

This generally unfolds over the course of six weeks of foundational blocking, striking, and movement. And as soon as people have a modicum of proficiency, I strike them hard and fast. Those who have little experience with physical contact or who operate in a world where they're top dog, often take this as a personal affront. They feel offended. They feel afraid. Their eyes scream it. And then their bodies begin to shake. Their breathing creeps up into the chest, and their movements become wild. In these moments, the quality of one's self-investment in concentration, awareness, sensitivity, physical power, and ego-transcendence manifest. Or they don't, and that person freezes. If this approach scares you, then you too may be limiting your deeper potential.

What's the use of working through superficial, marginal improvements if all it takes is a little bit of pressure for all your pains, fears, and insecurities to come screaming to the surface and override your most rational self's efforts at change? At such times, biology trumps intention. And at this level of self, the skeletons in the closet of past pains must be called out and faced in a visceral, embodied way.

With or without self-defense, deep work and conscientious training will elicit these moments of confrontation, moments that stand between the person you were and the person you can be. And in those moments, it's unlikely you'll recognize yourself.

A Piece of Plastic—Addressing the Mind-Body System

M had entered my program as a middle-aged woman looking to regain the health, vigor, and figure of her younger self. She was a very bright professional who believed Weightlessness had missing pieces to the puzzle and who wanted to test herself. She abhorred self-defense training, a cornerstone of the tribe experience, and thought that by half-assing it and holding back, she'd get through the program.

She thought this until she was asked to lie on the floor and defend herself and regain her standing position while pressure is applied—my arms coated with thick, heavy, Thai boxing pads. She had the tools, in principle. But when I stood over her and didn't allow her to merely stand up off the ground as we'd practiced, but insisted she fight for it under pressure as the technique was designed for, she fell back. And she became frustrated and angry. We did it again, and again she failed. And again the same, until she broke.

After thirty minutes of processing it all off to the side of the class, feeling helpless, wiping her eyes, and trying to collect her thoughts, I pulled out the tool for the next component of class, a plastic knife. Upon sight of this, she lost control and couldn't recover. She told me later, after days of consideration about whether to return to her tribe, that that moment under the pads, feeling overwhelmed, suffocated, and helpless unlocked a vicious memory she'd kept in the attic of her mind.

That memory was carved in a moment of powerlessness to help someone important. And in this moment, it all came back.

"What is this?" I asked her.

"A knife," she replied.

"What is this? Try again," I pushed.

"A knife," she replied, getting more worked up.

"One more time, what is this?"

"It's a knife!" she insisted.

"It's a piece of plastic," I corrected. "Nothing more."

It was a piece of hard plastic—no blade, no sharp edges. And she did know that. It in no way bore any resemblance to a real weapon other than loose outline. But when she looked at that piece of plastic in the context of a self-defense class, she saw only what it represented. Violence. Death. Her model of the world of conflict had no place for learning and growth; it was all evil. And with that, she was unable to see the relevance of learning movement, strategy, and technique that speaks to the intimate relationship between two individuals under stress.

But I ask you all, without facing these parts of yourself honestly, will you ever see beyond your model of the world to the realities right in front of you? Will you be able to think, act, and perform under pressure when your model of the world isn't sufficient to encompass your immediate experience, regardless of domain? Will you be able to enter the void of reality, or will you be stuck in the comfort of your own perspective, a perspective that shatters completely at the sight of a piece of plastic?

Before M left in tatters that day to pick up the shattered pieces of her deep mind over the days that followed, I pushed one last time to encourage her to face what just surfaced, "Why did this simulation elicit this reaction for you?"

"I hate violence."

"This isn't violence. This is only training with people you know and trust."

"It insinuates it. I want to practice compassion."

"What is compassion?"

"It's caring for others, loving and protecting them. Not fighting them."

"One last question, if, on the unlucky chance that you or I are ever physically attacked or one of our loved ones is attacked, which one of us, you or I, would have the ability to choose compassion in that moment?"

"What do you mean?"

"I mean there's a part of you so threatened by confrontation that you're unable to function. When deep confrontation occurs, there are a few options; engage or do nothing are the most likely among them. If you are ever threatened, mentally or physically to a similar degree, do you have the composure to be compassionate toward your attacker, to yourself? Or would your most blindly fearful and selfish impulses surface? If they surface, do you have the knowledge and control to defend yourself effectively without killing your attacker in return? What if that person was a misguided loved one who lost control? What we're doing here isn't violence. It's deep, personal work."

Now there are likely some people reading this who assume a third option of flight or running away is always available. I also address this assumption within the programs and remove it as a reasonable strategy for most people: We set up in an alleyway where you're attacked from behind. You don't know when or with what degree of pressure you're attacked, but you know in which way (an aggressive bear hug and a lift off the ground) and you have a programmed response we've worked on. You break the hold and strike and knee and elbow as hard as possible, and then you sprint 100 meters to a safe space. Despite this, everyone who is untrained shakes in fear. The uncertainty is what gets you.

Staring into open space and knowing you're about to be attacked elicits an uncontrollable, terrifying response the first several times. And something totally foreign happens, adrenaline floods the body and the legs become lead, so heavy and slow they can't be moved properly, and running becomes toddleresque. You gas out unbelievably quickly. You add to this equation that most predators are fit enough to prey on the weak; they can hunt and run. Their legs don't shut down under the same pressure. And in those few minutes, everyone becomes aware of how dangerous the delusion of fleeing to safety is.

M was determined not to let this defeat her, but it required more than a self-pep-talk. It required complete reorientation. It required a reframing of the world of combat, and self-defense training in particular. And it required a relinquishing of control in moments of duress, by far the biggest ask possible.

Six weeks later, with all six tribers squatting against the walls in a static hold for minutes on end until their legs trembled and their minds doubted, I called M back into the center of the room with everyone looking on. I ordered her to lie on her back and prepare to defend herself, just as we'd prepared. And she looked up at me with the focused eyes of someone reborn; she challenged me to do my worst.

She struggled and fought her way half way up only to get knocked back down again, sometimes into the wall, sometimes back onto the floor. But she fought, and with every misstep she refocused, fixed her eyes on me, adapted, and kicked harder, rose to her feet, and fought like hell until there was nothing left. Until her time in the center had expired.

At fifty years old, she realized the power of being empty of preconceptions. She realized that power stems not from imposing one's will, but from listening, adapting, and flowing in relationship to the living obstacle before her. She realized that the true obstacle was herself all along, as well as her true power. She learned to relinquish control, and, in the void, she found it.

Within any one transformation, many forces are at play: the will to change into a grander vision of self, the fear of failure to hit ones goals, and an ever-present source of doubt that hungers for comfort and security, for regression. You have angels and demons on your shoulders vying for dominance. The mind plays many games. But despite the internal dialogues and battles, other, more constant biological forces are at play. And these we must understand and capitalize on if we're to safely put pedal to the metal and become something more without the risk of injury or severe psychological fallout.

The Principles That Govern Your New Toolkit

The principles of antifragility, plasticity, physical structure and tensegrity, and integration are more than just pedantic theories about the body and mind; they're absolutely critical for designing holistic prescriptions that make us strong—really fucking strong—and free. They speak to deep capacities in the mind-body that generally elude our conscious awareness, but which can be cultivated through structured training.

Before we delve into them, it's important to set the stage for their relevance.

Many people are happy with a workout. And that's fine. But workouts are snapshots, not storylines. Workouts, while capable of being modified according to performance gains or declines, have a very narrow vantage point. A workout is unable to ask about itself, *Am I appropriate?* That question is presumed, and the answer is an affirmative *yup*! But by what measure?

One of the most common questions I get from students is regarding program design and prescribing their own Weightlessness workouts. It baffles many, and with the added complexity of balancing all three pillars—strength, flexibility, meditation—within The Weightlessness Spectrum, it means someone needs a way of assessing their current performance and prescribing targeted tools and exercises (discussed later in The Process Scroll) that ensure comprehensive gain.

Most arts and sports specialize in one of these pillars: strength (and conditioning), flexibility, or meditation. None that I know of organize them effectively in an integrated, principle-based, minimalist system of personal growth where the trainee can independently assess their mind-body state and prescribe relevant, holistic training prescriptions. And for good reason… it's difficult to do.

To work within the context of a given model is one thing. To take that model and extrapolate its principles into prescriptive, actionable steps is another. But it can be done. And the manner in which it can be done is by thoroughly understanding not only the tools of Weightlessness (described in The Weightlessness Scroll) but also the underlying biological principles that make transformation possible. This is critical in integrating two seemingly antithetical principles like antifragility, which suggests periodization of some applied tools, and plasticity, which suggests consistent, uniform application of others.

If you don't understand these principles and the nature of the tools involved, it's impossible to develop yourself methodically. Reversing them, for example, periodizing intense stress in the flexibility domain, can lead to serious injury. It can likewise lead to severe psychological damage if applied in the meditation domain.

On the other hand, consistent practice devoid of progressive stress-rest cycles would get zero results in the strength and conditioning domain. These are examples of principles misapplied; yet they're common mistakes. And they do lead to many injuries and plateaus respectively.

Embrace stress

Health and performance cannot be optimized without taking on stress. Your personal transformation is largely a byproduct of how you frame and take on targeted stressors that elicit positive adaptations. The great paradox of Weightlessness is that we all must add weight to unburden.

Stress-Adaptation and Your Antifragile Mind-Body

M not only survived the 100-day program but finished with flying colors, on fire for life, in her best physical condition, and with a focus and clarity she couldn't remember. She wasn't the same person who entered my training studio three and a half months prior. Her incredible transformation was noticed by all. She was receiving hot-mom compliments left and right. But her biggest shift was somewhat hidden. It's the shift that occurs amongst extreme individuals the world over when they fast for 20 days, when they hit a wall in business, or when they fight in combat. It's the realization that true strength is about letting go. In the absence of self, there is incalculable energy and focus available for problem-solving, survival, and appreciation of the now. We all have this capacity.

In Nasim Taleb's *Antifragile,* he highlights three categories of how things respond to stress or disorder: fragile, robust, and antifragile. A piece of glass is fragile. If it's dropped on the ground, it shatters. A brick or a sponge are indifferent to stress (up to a point). The human body, airlines, and Silicon Valley are antifragile, and when exposed to stress, disorder, or failure, they respond by overcompensating and becoming even stronger.

Examples of antifragility in the human mind-body: your immune system becomes stronger when exposed to a pathogen, muscle overcompensates to stress-based tears, and bone calcifies and rebuilds stronger when its fractured. Likewise, your brain adapts to fasting by increasing the number of mitochondria in neurons (and new neuron growth from stem cells), and your body by releasing fat burning, muscle building hormones that allow for more ready assimilation of nutrients post-fast. Strength in body and mind isn't a process of balance, or even of building. It's one of methodically increasing the stresses and pressures placed on the body and mind, breaking down, and then providing the building blocks (nutrition) and time (rest) for the magic of your biology to build a more resilient version of itself.

M's body was 15 pounds of muscle heavier, and 25 pounds of fat lighter. Her body was built week after week by applying stress in a variety of ways, tearing muscle, stretching tendons, and burning calories. And at the end of it all, she wasn't a broken mess. She was stronger. She was much stronger. Her body overcompensated for the hours upon hours of grueling physical conditioning. She burned excess fat to fuel the increasing demands of performance, and her body constructed new tissue, adding myofibers to every muscle in her body to be able to manage more strain.

She was a living, walking antifragile machine. And once she realized this strength, her mind began to open. She didn't need the same self-protection mechanisms she'd assimilated over her lifetime. She became more patient and less judgmental. She learned to let go under pressure instead of resisting it. And her mind too learned to cope with a type of stress that she vehemently feared in the most debilitating of ways. She didn't break, she didn't merely adapt, she supercompensated.

The mechanisms of transformation are hardwired into our biology. The example above of M's psychological shift is a microcosm of widespread biological processes in the body that we can only define as antifragile.

Break the Mold...or Become It.

The condition of our minds and bodies is largely a byproduct of repetition—of thought or action or both together. Change and personal growth are not merely the application of positivity and willpower but may require windows of discomfort that breach old and/or create new neural patterns that free or focus the mind.

Growth Doesn't Arise in Your Comfort Zone

M's breakdown demonstrated the possible repercussions of embracing models of the world that aren't large or accurate enough. It excluded key things that could break her—known unknowns that one chooses to ignore. There was no physical threat. It was a breach of worldview, which ceased to prove accurate.

This can fracture the mind in astounding ways. You can see the neural synapses fire and break as the eyes flash everything from frustration to fear. Her paradigm had no space for simulated stress in this fashion. It was all lumped under a broad category of violence, and she wasn't about violence.

I won't call this self-defense, and certainly not violence, for she was in no real danger. But the mere act of holding up a mirror for her, of holding the pads insistently above her and making her fight for the get-up, was enough to insinuate her greatest fear—a complete lack of personal control, a feeling of helplessness. This is the power of the mind. When we truly insist on the rightness of something, our world narrows until that thing is all that there is… until it isn't.

The problem here should be clear and should challenge all of us to test our assumptions of the world, to seek greater degrees of social feedback on our ideas, and to research known facts and anecdotes related to our hobbies, interests, and indeed, livelihoods. Many claim they're not that into finance or investing. Many insist that job security is right for them. Many state they're not that interested in nutrition or fitness… How's that workin' for ya? Known unknowns that one chooses to ignore, that can make or break a person's quality of life, can have harsh consequences.

You don't like golf? I get it. Don't really care about Elon's mission to Mars? Okay, no problem. But if you don't eat right, you get sick and potentially die. Obesity affects every one of your bodily systems in a negative way, compromises your immunity, and exposes you to far greater health risks. You don't like finance and prefer to trust an indifferent corporation for the security of your future? How did 2008 treat you? This doesn't mean that if you'd managed these things yourself, and managed them well, that all would be hunky dory; it just means that blindly entrusting them to someone else or ignoring them altogether is not without risk—risk that can kill you.

There are just some things we don't get to avoid and still hope that life turns out okay. Studying them certainly doesn't guarantee success, but it sure increases the probability of not dying tomorrow. We all want cocoons of comfort that shelter us from the things we fear or the things we don't understand. But which is more likely to empower us in the long run—right perspective of known facts or delusional comfort?

And to be fair, we are hardwired for comfort. We are hardwired to repeat things that alter our neurochemistry in positive ways. That chocolate bar, that cozy movie, those drinks with friends, all release serotonin and/or dopamine that reinforce these actions as positive, useful-for-survival things to do, regardless of whether or not they are. It's just that our biology evolved in environments where serotonin release required more work to trigger. Large quantities of simple sugars, alcohol, and sex were much harder to come by a hundred thousand years ago.

M couldn't understand and certainly didn't believe me when I told her I too abhor violence. I had the misfortune of having a childhood bully. I remember one sunny winter's day, after a long, cold walk home, getting my books and then my face pressed into the fresh powdery snow. I remember getting home and telling my dad I needed to learn karate. At that time, the only knowledge most of us had about becoming your own hero came from *The Karate Kid*. And I figured if it worked for Ralph Macchio, then bring on the crane kick. And that was the beginning of my 30-year journey in martial arts.

But I never liked violence. I liked self-perseveration, self-sufficiency, and the ability to do meaningful things in life without fear dominating my decisions. I like the ability to protect friends and family should the need ever arise. And I like the bottomless well of insight and development that the arts offer over time. Reducing self-defense to liking violence is like reducing dance to tragic spasms on a wedding reception dance floor.

In those early days, M had no options, as her efforts were snuffed out and she fell helplessly to the floor again and again. Her model of the world failed, and, with that, her psyche fractured. But just as her body and mind proved to be antifragile, that impetus to expand her paradigm and accept the training as such allowed us to methodically address the plasticity of her mind.

Plasticity and the Habitual Mind

As we age, our thoughts, emotions, and actions are increasingly determined by habitual patterns of thought and action. These patterns are coded into the mind and body, literally. New thoughts and actions create new neural synapses. Breaking habits separates established neural synapses, and habitual patterns strengthen the synaptic bond, like adding layers of concrete atop a neural highway, making it harder and harder to change thoughts and habits (in body or mind).

Frequency and intensity (as in extreme emotional events and experiences like PTSD) of an event that produces a similar thought or emotional response causes the same neurons to fire. We can be blind victims of our environments and neurological patterns, or we can proactively design ourselves.

Neurons that fire together, wire together. Neurons that fire out of sync, fail to link.

This old adage refers to the plasticity of your neurology and the ability to change your mind by changing your behavior. This is the reason visualization is used by peak performers in all domains: Olympic athletes, executives, fighters, artists. *Doing* with the mind's eye creates the same neural networks and neuromuscular outcome as physically practicing a skill! This has been known for a long time by peak athletes, and less time by modern science. And it's a great reminder to those who think they lack the confidence or strength to do something. They're right! The doing comes first, the confidence after.

Nonjudgmental awareness removes emotional connotation from thoughts and events, thereby weakening synaptic bonds and liberating you from conditioned responses. It creates the space needed to choose a different response to common triggers.

Meditation is both the flashlight that illuminates these patterns, bringing them to the surface of conscious awareness, as well as the sledgehammer that destroys them, allowing for the experience of novelty and empowered self-design.

Plasticity, Meditation, and the Space for Change

Meditation is most commonly touted as a great stress reducer. But its true power is in the ability to unburden ourselves of fixed notions and concepts, especially those that bind us negatively to events and experiences that lead to disempowering states of mind. This is the birthplace of change and personal growth.

Meditation is a condom for thought.

It creates space between a thought and the impulse to feel, speak, or act on that thought. Not every thought has to make a baby. Most of us aren't aware of the speed at which a thought becomes an emotion, and an emotion an embodied response. We think of our boss and anger or fear arises. We think of chocolate and guilt or excitement arises. We think of our partner and fondness or resentment arises.

Most of us flow at lightning speed from thought to emotion the way a rat is conditioned to paw a lever for a little treat. It's habitual conditioning. Meditation creates time; it creates space between those two seemingly inseparable phenomena. It gives us the opportunity to observe ourselves without judgment and become intimately aware of generally unconscious impulses. And it gives us the power to change. It does so in two ways:

1. It deconditions bad habits through awareness and dissociates events and emotions, which allow for an objective, nonjudgmental filtration of conscious activity.

2. It habituates sensitivity and awareness, which allow for a higher quality of present experience. (This is where weightlessness resides in experience.)

Who we are is what we repeatedly do. This isn't just about one person's struggle with the topic of violence. It's about all of us. It's about who we are. And lest someone mistake the story above as something irrelevant for them, we all do this with countless triggers in life.

The person who has been laid off from their long-time job unexpectedly might experience the same type of emotional fallout. People often associate themselves with a function or a job. When that job is removed, so too is one's personal sense of purpose. This also occurs in relationships, if a man's girlfriend or wife tells him it's over, really over. His paradigm of the world had the two of them there together, living, laughing, and struggling. But together. When that relationship gets severed, so too does the mind that identifies with it, that builds a narrative around it, and that finds meaning in it.

We are an amalgam of associations, associated ideas, facts, memories, emotions, experiences, and sensations, all cross-linked firing neurons in synchronicity. To put it bluntly, there's no permanent YOU beyond the contents of your immediate conscious experience. And this reality can either be the justification for your stagnation in life, or it can be an inspiring impetus for change. There's no YOU; you get to design yourself as you wish.

For if thoughts and actions can bind us, they can also set us free. We have the power to shift. We're fully capable of getting back up on our feet after losing a job, of finding romance after lost love, and of learning to fight after breaking under pressure. If you can accept that the "I" within you isn't fixed, but is plastic, is malleable, and can be formed and molded into a variety of forms so long as you have the space to breathe and awareness of common patterns, then you have a tremendous amount of control over your own fate.

Structure Yourself

Learning to sit, stand, walk, and lift in the most anatomically correct fashion creates the greatest leverage against external forces that stress our frames, which both maintains the health and integrity of the body and makes the mind-body feel lighter. Mind and body integrate through sound physical structure.

Physical Structure is the Foundation of the Mind-Body

Structure is composed of the skeletal frame and soft tissues of the body, which collectively, at rest, have one function: to keep you from collapsing on the ground. At movement, good structure provides the greatest mechanical advantage, that is, leverage against a counterforce.

The strongest patterns of human movement allow us to apply the greatest degree of force within specific vectors. That force is applied against load. The better the structure, the more effortless your stability and force production… and the more healthy and powerful you become. We cannot look at the strength of a person, holistically speaking, independently from the structure of their physical frame, for the mind *IS* the body, not merely *in* the body. This is largely dissected in The Strength Spectrum within The Weightlessness Scroll that follows.

Structure is also the vehicle through which body and mind integrate, as we'll discuss in The Meditation Spectrum within The Weightlessness Scroll.

Let's look at a few key facets of sound structure.

Neutral Spine

A neutral spine is the single most stable position for movement in general. There are a few exceptions, but most are specialized movements that require higher technical development. For the general purposes of strength and flexibility training, it's the safest position with which to apply load, as well as lengthen (stretch) the body.

Your nerves are a set length; they don't stretch with the rest of your soft tissue. So when you put a kink in the kinetic spinal chain, your body acknowledges the risk before your brain does, and responds by tightening the surrounding tissues, as well as potentially signaling muscles further down the chain to tighten. Lower back pain and sciatica are common byproducts of this protective mechanism misapplied, if not the byproduct of more serious injuries.

When the spine is neutral, your CNS (central nervous system) is able to function efficiently, and signals to the rest of your body that you're safe, allowing for efficient coordination, the application of greater load, or relaxation to stretch. You cannot stretch if your muscles are tensing to protect you from poor structure (i.e., a lumbar flexion fault on a forward bend or front splits). Again, there are justifiable deviations at higher levels of flexibility training, like contortion; those are generally global deviations, like those mentioned below.

All nonspecialized training should implement a neutral spine as a means of honing structural alignment, facilitating integration, aiding in transitional movements, and protecting the spine. This is not merely relegated to load bearing exercises, but should be consciously observed in standing, sitting, walking, rotating, and picking things up off the ground in daily life.

Global Versus Local Flexion & Extension

We can extend or bend the back in two ways, globally or locally. Local flexion, when the lumbar spine or lower back bends out of sync with the other sections of one's back, causes great risk.

While flexion/extension in the spine may occur in both strength and flexibility exercises, it should come as a last resort, and should be global. In both lifting and stretching, hinging from the hips (rather than the back) is what separates all safe movement from risky movement. Only when one's range is maxed out when doing a forward bend for example, should they allow the back to round out to complete your full global reach.

However, I want to be clear; I'm talking about effective training, not necessarily global application in sports, where specific, more compromised positions may need to be acceptable to perform certain techniques, wrestling being a great example. In domains where there are not many rules, there aren't many constraints on movements. But these deviations shouldn't be considered strength training; they should be considered sport-specific applications of strength or sport-specific conditioning.

Moving with a neutral spine places the body in its strongest and most balanced position during controlled movements. The purpose of resistance training is to learn to apply load under optimal structural conditions, so that it becomes default programming and transfers over into unstructured scenarios. In so doing, we maximize safety, as well as the amount of load that can be placed on the body as a whole.

Torque

External Rotation is used to stabilize the hips in most squatting applications, including the deadlift. This is implemented in the case of the squat, for example, simply by applying outward pressure of the balls of the feet without actually moving or rotating the feet. The old adage of *screw your feet into the floor* has the consequence of lifting the arches of the feet and tightening the connective tissue around the hip joint, thereby creating stability and torque in the hips. This is a structural cue that bears great relevance both in strength training and in standing meditation posture.

External Rotation is also used to stabilize the shoulders in most pushing or flexion-based applications, including the bench press, whereas internal rotation should be used in shoulder extensions, like that of a diver or jumper's preparatory draw back of the arms before they leap and throw the arms up. The old adage of *bend the bar* while bench pressing, by applying outward rotational force (lifting thumbs toward face, pinkies toward abdomen) has the consequence of tightening the connective tissue surrounding the shoulder joint, thereby creating stability and torque in the shoulders.

Applying torque in these ways tightens connective tissue in the joints, stabilizing the spine. This allows for the application of stable power as well as the irradiation of tensional force throughout the body. In both power lifting and martial arts striking, this is the key to explosive power and rootedness on impact.

Force Application and Power Lines

Your power line is the line of force with the single greatest mechanical advantage, that is, leverage, when pushing, pulling, squatting, or pressing. It's your strongest point of reference. Nevertheless, very few people utilize it, falling much more easily into weaker structures that call into play the wrong muscles to perform a push or pull, for example.

The single biggest error within pushing exercises is lifting the shoulders toward the ears, which engages the trapezius muscles on the upper back, and which winds up creating internal resistance to all pushing exercises. It also puts more load in the anterior deltoids (front of the shoulders) and moves it away from the larger pectoral muscles (chest) and triceps, which should be the prime movers.

The setup for this is exceedingly simple to find, and rather difficult to apply consistently. To find your power line within the push (or pull), place your elbows at your side with your shoulders fully relaxed and drawn down, and lift your forearms to a 90-degree bend from the upper arm. Then, without tensing the shoulders or compromising your neutral spine, draw your arms back as far as they'll go. This line, for most of us, falls at the bottom of the chest where the nipples are.

This is extremely important. You should obsess over the implementation of this structural archetype.

The Significance of Load

If you have ever been physically injured, you've probably been told by your doctor *don't lift more than five pounds*. What does five pounds mean? Your body is made up of countless levers, each allowing coordinated effort to create movement. Holding five pounds. close to your chest with your elbows tight to your sides is very different than holding it out in front of you with straight arms.

The objective of strength training is to apply the greatest load in your strongest archetypal structures and movement patterns. The objective of performance extends well beyond this, however, and often involves the exertion of force in unleveraged positions. This is where injuries often occur. Effective training should not result in injury, it should prepare you for the instability and uncertainties found in daily life and sports.

Load is how we test the quality of physical structure, which, again, is coordinated leverage against a counterforce, either gravity or another force-vector. How much you lift isn't important in and of itself; its important because it signifies the quality and integration capacity of your mind-body in certain positions. Once you remove artificial load, the weight of your body becomes effortlessly light. We should view all strength training as structural development first, and force application second. Load is a test of mind-body limitations.

On Tensegrity

The role of fascia in the human body has wide-reaching implications for healing, holistic performance, and mind-body integration. We're moving beyond the mechanistic view of the human body and reframing it as a dynamic, integrated system in ready adaptation to and in communication with environmental forces. Tensegrity allows the mind-body to come alive with sensitivity.

Fascia and Tensegrity in the Human Body

The body, like the brain, has similar tendencies of plasticity. The tissue in the body we might refer to with similar properties is called fascia. Fascia is a 3D matrix of soft tissue, primarily made of collagen, that covers virtually every internal member of the body. It surrounds muscles, muscle complexes, joints, organs, and even lines the entire body just beneath the skin. It is one of only three holistic systems within the body where you could remove everything but that one system and still retain the optics of your entire human form. The other two systems are the nervous system and the vascular system.

The textbooks on fascia are not yet fully written, and I believe that what we'll learn about it over the coming years will transform the way we practice movement and medicine. But what we know of it already is enough to shift our paradigm of human development and performance.

My first martial arts instructor always said *practice makes perfect.* My second instructor always said *perfect practice makes perfect.* When it comes to training, the truth is somewhere in the middle, for as we discussed, the application of models requires a bit of tinkering, and the desire for perfection at each stage can often derail a working system.

When we're speaking of fascia, however, we can rightly say that perfection, or getting closer and closer to it over time matters a great deal. Fascia acts throughout the body as a tension member in the same way that cables on a suspension bridge act. The closer those cables track to intended architectural design, the greater the integrity of the entire bridge. If one or more cables snap, the bridge reorients to find a new structural equilibrium.

Before Thomas Meyers started disseminating his views on tensegrity, plasticity, and anatomy trains, most of us in the fitness and wellness community were working with an antiquated model of human movement that was reduced to biomechanics. Muscles shorten, pulling tendons that are fixed to bone, creating movement. The body in general, and movement in particular, for centuries has been viewed as mechanistic, the composite of many small, interrelated parts. It's not that we've come to discover that this model of human structure is wrong, it's that we've come to learn it isn't the whole truth. And what we've been missing has profound relevance for movement, healing, and brain chemistry.

The body is not merely a series of stacked building blocks the way a house is formed from layers of bricks. The bricks of a house act as compression members of support. They carry load individually and collectively and don't really act to redistribute said load elsewhere in the system. Thomas Meyers, drawing from the theories of the architect and systems theorist Buckminster Fuller, speaks of a different structural model of the body based on the principle of tensegrity, also known as tensional integrity or floating compression.

Tensegrity structures are fascinating and playful things, retaining a specific form but capable of extreme manipulation before springing back into homeostatic structures. Tensegrity structures are floating, in a sense, with no real fixed and firm component. The system is self-contained, stabilized by the balance of forces between hard compression members (like a stick or a beam) and tension members (like a string or a cable). A suspension bridge is one of many applications of this principle.

These structures have clear, defined forms, some of them roundabout, some rectangular, but all of them share the same properties. None of the tension members are touching one another, and none of the compression members are touching one another, yet they retain the integrity of their intended form. When you squeeze, alter, or press these structures or toys, they distort until the pressure is released, and then they regain their original form. Nothing gets broken or damaged (unless its heavily manipulated).

Fascia in your body acts as tension members both in coordination and at cross-purposes with your skeletal system. Many people who haven't really looked into the body often get this basic question wrong: *what holds the upper body up above the lower half of your body?* The most common answer is *the spine*. But the spine, if you remove it from the body is flexible and flaccid. While it is comprised of hard vertebrae, nothing but soft tissue connects segments of bone. It certainly cannot bear load and maintain its own shape independently.

Without the surrounding muscles, tendons, and the myofascial networks that sustain your upright form through balanced tension and compression forces, your upper body would collapse down upon itself. This is a principle that may seem academic at this stage, but it is one of the most central principles of Weightlessness training and must be mastered for sensations of weightlessness to manifest in life. For in this balance, the body becomes alive with mind (conscious awareness).

Fascia is a strain distributor. When playing with a tensegrity structure or toy, pressure added to one or more sides is redistributed throughout the entire system. The entire system bears this new load until the pressure is released. Fascia, likewise, displays system memory. When there is pressure or strain added to your living system, that strain is redistributed in order to reduce the impact of said strain on one specific part of the body.

This is an incredible evolutionary feat. Your body has evolved to mold to its environment even in temporary bouts of stress and strain. And as long as that strain doesn't cause structural damage, your form will reintegrate itself in a structured way.

Where does this form come from you might ask? Well, it's partly dictated by genetics and the internal structures you carry. But it's also heavily dictated by habitual movement patterns. That means the older you are the more you've molded yourself into your current form. For those who claim they aren't the flexible type, it's time to call bullshit. You merely don't live a lifestyle of flexibility. Your day-to-day doesn't necessitate significant range of movement, and you don't take it upon yourself to take mobility on as a life practice. It's really that simple.

There's no divine dictum that separates the flexible from the inflexible, the quick from the slow. It's practice, plain and simple. Practice, habit, daily goings-on are the stuff of your structure. Do you have bad posture? It comes from one thing only, you had bad posture yesterday, and the day before, and the day before that. You want better posture? Stand with better posture today, tomorrow, and the day after.

The constant force of strain acting on your body is gravity. The more aligned your structure, the lower the impact of gravity in the same way that a Jenga set stacked vertically and symmetrically can be stacked indefinitely, but one that is even slightly off center and imbalanced will collapse before long. Small misalignments make bothersome *somethings* out of seemingly *nothings*.

Over a short time, this pressure may not be noticed, but over years or decades, it becomes the mold in which you live, just as your thoughts and actions become programmed into your neural networks. At that point, it becomes very difficult to change. For this reason, flexibility is generally a longer, harder path than strength and conditioning. It's easier to create tension than to alleviate it.

Muscles, under periodic stress, quickly supercompensate and grow larger. Fascia is far more delicate and, under sharper periods of stress, will tear or break down. If flexibility is programmed with consistency and very gradual progression, your system will relax and learn to redistribute the strain of any particular stretch across your entire frame. If this is done quickly, you break, but done gradually, you remold your frame.

Effortless Symmetry and Planes of Movement

Our bodies have evolved to apply force in three dimensions. Whether you're moving or not, your frame is a tensegrity structure that stores energy and allows you to access movement in any direction. This likely seems banal, but it is fundamental to transcending specific training techniques and entering a world of limitless growth.

Due to the flexibility of the spine, as well as shoulders and hips built with ball and socket joints, humans have one of the greatest potential ranges of movement in the animal kingdom, limited only by our lifestyle choices and personal drive. Some speculate that a reason for our evolved brains was to originally accommodate this limitless range of movement, and therefore interaction potential of our bodies in the world.

Imagine the balance of force required to stabilize a frame with limitless movement potential. In order to push something along the sagittal plane, those muscles designed to pull must relax while the pushing muscles (pecs, triceps, deltoids) contract; otherwise, there's no movement. In order to do a shoulder press, which extends the arms overhead, the muscles involved in pullups (which pull the arms down and retract the shoulders) must relax.

At rest, however, opposing forces must find relative balance. In order to maintain a symmetrical static frame (standing meditation), you must attain an intuitive balance of forces along all planes, ideally with diminishing effort and tension. This can be done with dramatically different levels of tension and effort!

The novice stands *on top* of the ground, using tension to keep the body erect and compensate for structural imbalances. The master stands *on* the ground with relaxed, effortless balance and natural lift.

Masters float, novices resist.

The essence of sound structure is attaining an effortless balance of force to minimize the effects of gravity with as little tension (resistance) as possible. Herein also lies the secret of deep sensitivity and awareness. Tension is the enemy of both. This is central to Weightlessness and will be explored more deeply in The Weightlessness and Lightness Scrolls in the context of standing meditation and ballistic weight training respectively.

Your Feet Tell Your Story of Health

Weight distribution and alignment of the feet is no trivial matter. Your body is a connected whole; any weak link in the chain weakens the entire chain. Correctly moving from heel to toe with straight feet, even weight distribution, and a firm arch is the foundation of structural integration and a healthy body. This goes for standing, walking, and running. You should obsess about this and be frustrated (moderately) when you witness it around you. A bad footprint is the cause of a slow painful death. The feet are not isolated; their alignment is the first link in the kinetic chain of posture.

Mind-Body Integration

Integration is a phenomenon of embodied awareness, where one's cultivated sensitivity and sound physical structure (devoid of nonessential tensions and compulsive thoughts) merge in this present moment. This regulates the nervous system, enlivens the mind, and sets the stage for peak performance in all domains of life. Integration is designed in The Weightlessness Spectrum.

Tensegrity Applied: Healing and Performance

As regards both healing and integration, this principle of strain distribution is subtle but profound. Take, for example, a bed sheet that has been perfectly splayed. Now imagine pinching and lifting one small point near the middle. Is that the only spot that alters form? No. Ripples are sent out over the entire sheet as it redistributes the strain.

Now take, for example, one of those tangent ripples (still holding the center piece) and attempt to push it back down or flatten it back to par. It's impossible. It will either bounce right back or it will create a ripple nearby that performed the same function of redistributing that strain. This is how your myofascial system functions in terms of strain distribution. It's why both healing and peak performance are incredibly difficult to dissect and prescribe targeted solutions for. You can't merely address the series of individual pieces that are out of whack; you must address the system in its entirety. This is where a master's eye often outperforms a technician's analysis.

The magic of this system is in the profound interrelatedness of various trains that span the entire body, front and back, left and right, and contralateral to name a few. They are so interrelated that Thomas Meyers has cured people from chronic headaches by fixing their walking stride. Excess strain on the Achilles tendon carries tension up the rear myofascial train of the body, up and over the top of the head and can settle in as headache.

When we begin to see the body as a whole, healing shoulder pain by massaging the arch of someone's foot seems less mystical and more mechanical. The implications here should seem clear; addressing pain in the body by treating only the location of pain and ignoring systemic imbalance is an inferior, if not ineffective way of healing or growing. Many acute injuries can be managed by addressing the site of the injury. Most chronic aches, pains, and even larger feelings of fatigue, malaise, depression, and anxiety stem from system imbalances, the source of which is not so easy to diagnose and resolve.

The same can be said of peak athletes. We may be able to identify many contributing factors to an athlete's success, but if we can't comprehend the whole system and the interrelations of various parts (something Lightness addresses), it may be impossible to articulate the differences between first and second finishers, or even professionals and amateurs. We often call that difference *skill* or *experience*, but it's hard to define those terms. Those can often be reduced to the integration of the mind-body system as a whole.

You have two dialectical nervous systems: the sympathetic and parasympathetic nervous systems. The first helps you fight tigers; the second helps you heal. Your body can't tell the difference between real life-and-death dangers and stress or anxiety stemming from thought (as exemplified in the plastic knife scenario). In short doses, the stress response is profoundly valuable, but if it's chronically activated due to stress or anxiety, your body doesn't have an opportunity to heal. It's constantly prepared to fight.

Here's the kicker… your biology has a long evolutionary past. All mammals under stress and during combat round out the shoulders, lower the chin (sometimes curl the back), and close off the torso to protect vital organs and tissues along the front of the body. Animals (of which you are one) at full rest, and among fully trusted company stretch out and expose their vital organs and soft tissues. You can see this with all domesticated animals being petted.

Why does this matter? Because replicating those forms manifests those functions. When you're hunched or your shoulders are rounded, it's nearly impossible to breathe from the abdomen, which forces upper chest breathing, which generates a stress response and countless negative health effects if occurring consistently.

Activating sound structure, signaling that you are not under threat, allows the nervous system to relax, the breath to drop and regulate, and your parasympathetic nervous system to initiate recovery, healing, and growth. I'll detail this further in The Integration Scroll.

Antigravity Lift

This craft is not only called Weightlessness to describe the sense of psychological freedom that can be activated with conscientious practice. It also refers to the physical sensations of lightness that occur by improving strength, structure, and integration, as well as the profound sensation of physical freedom cultivated with advanced training (Lightness Training).

Equilibrium is not a static state. It's alive, the balance of opposing forces. This is what people miss about standing meditation… It's the secret to deep power generation stemming from extraordinary balance and sensitivity to tensional forces within, braced against the counterforce of the earth. Standing meditation is the laboratory for the study of tensional integrity in the body and the study of self-healing and integrated performance. We'll discuss that in detail within The Meditation Spectrum in The Weightlessness Scroll.

No matter how relaxed you are, fascia is always under tension as long as gravity is present. By programming symmetrical structure into the body, thereby reducing strains stemming from imbalance, total tension throughout your entire system can be reduced, providing natural, relaxed, and effortless antigravity lift.

Repetition and Self-Worth

Repetition is the making of a hero or a zero. Right practice cultivates meaningful patterns of movement and thought. Wasteful or structurally poor practices lead to a lack of health and well-being, both mental and physical. We must, to a certain extent, view the things we do in life as practice for tomorrow. Because each effort either builds a foundation of clarity, momentum and health, or of chaos. Mental masturbation, video game playing, TV watching, sports chat with the guys, and brainstorming can all be titillating fun and be useful stress outlets. But they are, all of them, molding the future you, for better or worse.

Your brain forms neural patterns that are going to make you better at doing those things and harder for you to deviate from those things in the future. Sitting for too long with no counteractive training practice will mold your body into a tight, heavy shell. Your hip flexors, hamstrings, and the fascial networks that integrate them will all shorten and mold to the form of a seated man. So when you start to complain about back pain, tight hamstrings or hips, you'll know you've sowed that ripple with the pinched strain of chronically shortened hip flexors and hamstrings.

There's no room in this discussion for what we like and don't like to do. And that makes it a very difficult thing to incorporate new patterns and actions in our day-to-day lives because, by definition, it predominantly lies in the realm of discomfort. For you to create capacity and mobility in the body, you need to place strains and pressures on it that require it to redistribute strain and remold itself. This is uncomfortable.

For you to create better work-life environments, personal development habits, or greater momentum toward your passion or purpose, you must accept a certain degree of discomfort if you have streamlined the neural highways of a more sedentary pleasure-seeking person. Breaching those synaptic bonds and paving new highways of thought and action will, again, by definition, require discomfort.

The default motivations of our mind-bodies are to avoid stress and discomfort, and to seek immediate gratification or ease. This is a lesson revealed by our neurology and physiology. Nature never predicted humanity would create environments so comfortable that reward signals to the brain could be triggered with little to no effort: that convenient chocolate bar, that effortless *like* on Facebook, both releasing dopamine and making us feel temporarily high on life, only to dip back into the void of meaninglessness left in its wake. Nature didn't prepare us for this. Humans evolved in and were molded by very different environments.

We live in a new world that doesn't acknowledge or respect, at least at the time of this writing, the deep and undeniable forces at work within us to seek comfort, yet grow (optimize health and performance) from discomfort and stress. We design our environments to make life increasingly effortless. But in so doing, we remove the stressors that signal strength, confidence, and a sense of self-worth. We embrace the ready rewards that leave us empty and dissatisfied moments later.

This leads many to chase immediate gratification, which doesn't come through disciplined training, investing, and commitment of any kind. We've been deceived by companies that study our dopamine response to stimulus, and manipulate our attention and gratification signals just like rats in a cage. But you can still manifest the truth kept secret in your DNA—that freedom comes from a disciplined approach to embracing stress, breaking the mold, setting your structure, and integrating your mind-body.

The Foundations Have Been Set

Thus far, we've addressed the perception of time and how it determines our priorities in life in The Time Scroll, ways in which we can orient our mindsets to perform in complex, uncertain domains in The Uncertainty Scroll, effective versus ineffective ways of showing up to a change process in The Change Scroll, and key principles of mind-body development in this, The Transformation Scroll. The foundations have been set for the integrated approach to mind-body development and peak performance that is Weightlessness.

The Weightlessness, Process, and Integration Scrolls that follow translate the principles and theories we've explored thus far into a practical, prescriptive framework of peak performance and integrated living.

The Weightlessness Scroll

You want to know how to paint a perfect painting? It's easy. Make yourself perfect and then just paint naturally.

—Robert M. Pirsig —from *Zen and the Art of Motorcycle Maintenance*

In The Weightlessness Scroll, the system of Weightlessness is explained. Weightlessness is a system in two parts: The Weightlessness Spectrum (foundational mind-body training) and Lightness (advanced training). The Weightlessness Spectrum organizes the pillars of strength, flexibility, and meditation into a progressive, prescriptive model of development. It integrates and optimizes our most precious mind-body resources, the hardware with which all life experience is filtered, to live with a sense of power, passion, and freedom. A sense of weightlessness. The tools and principles herein apply the principles of transformation previously identified within a minimalistic, holistic, and prescriptive change process. Your strongest self is waiting on the other side.

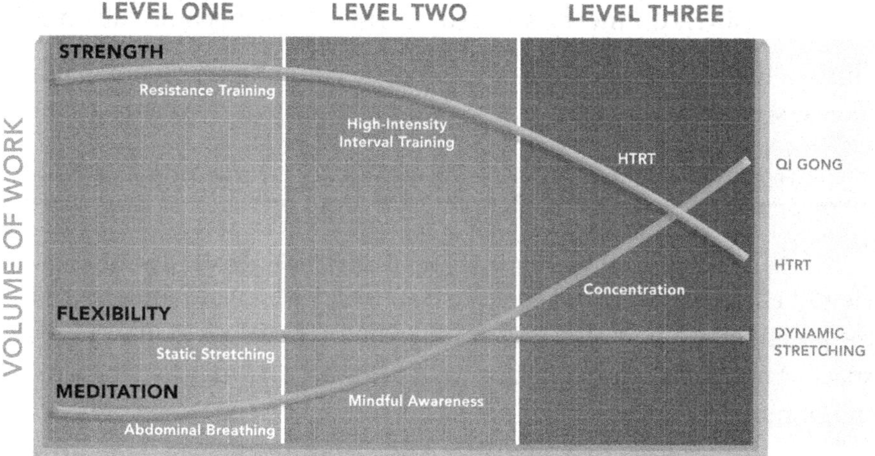

The first time the idea of a value spectrum occurred to me, my world opened up. And though it wasn't posited or framed in that language, I knew I could never approach ethics and epistemology the same way again. Reading Gandhi in my later college years, I came across a passage in which he qualified grades of nonviolent resistance. Perhaps the strongest nonviolent activist in history, up there with Jesus and Siddhartha Gautama, was Mahatma Gandhi, who was able to move Parliament by refusing to eat and liberated the Indian people from British oppression by marching en masse and surrendering themselves to British brutality.

Gandhi knew that the biggest challenge of nonviolence isn't accepting it as the greater good. In fact, most of us do know the power of love, and can at least believe that it may have longer lasting impact than violence or revenge. But when we're vexed or attacked, love is the last thing from our minds. In the context of preparing his warriors of nonviolence, Gandhi said, "*It is better to be violent, if there is violence in our hearts, than to put on the cloak of nonviolence to cover impotence.*"

He suggested that the value of nonviolence isn't absolute but presupposes a higher value of compassion. If someone is incapable of true compassion for their enemies, and they surrender themselves with fear in their hearts, then they're cowards and would be better off defending themselves and those they love using violence. He connotes nonviolence with true strength. A strong woman can sacrifice herself for her ideals. A weak man can claim self-sacrifice, but if he doesn't possess the resolve and unwavering strength and commitment to the path, then he's living a lie. First become strong enough to fight and love yourself. Only thereafter, do mercy and self-sacrifice truly become meaningful.

This Gandhian spectrum of non-violence could be charted something like this:

Nonviolence (from weakness) → Violence (from strength) → Nonviolence (from strength)

And within this one statement from a virtual modern-day saint, my view of ethics was transformed. For it speaks not only of values but also of the potential of a human being to adhere to those values in their time and space. And this is a rather large variable. In the Judeo-Christian tradition (if not most religious worldviews), right and wrong are absolutes. You're either on the wagon or you're off. And the difference is made up with sacrificial offerings. In the case of Christianity, that offering is Christ himself. So you find an awful lot of practicing Christians in a constant flow of self-deprecation and guilt, constantly praying for forgiveness. This is the opposite of empowerment and serves more to justify an inability to commit to one's values rather than provide relevant tools for unique and progressive developmental stages in order to empower change. In other words, it's a system that inhibits personal growth.

You're not always mentally strong or healthy or confident enough to choose what your best self would choose on any given day. With moral absolutes, your thoughts and actions are either right or wrong. There's no right-ish personalized solution that takes into account complicated grey zones in life, solutions that help condition your thoughts and actions to move in the right direction over time. If you desire the good but lack the knowledge or self-discipline required to act in accordance with it in full right now, then you're morally stuck.

Admittedly, value spectra are much harder to embrace and practice than moral absolutes because they require understanding of value hierarchies rather than mindless adherence to set laws. But for the warriors of personal development, I can't see another option.

There is an alternative to either-or dichotomies and binary constructs. Things are not necessarily wrong if they're not absolutely right. Not only does life have infinitely many options but we also aren't always US; that is, we change, we evolve and devolve, our minds are focused or distracted, happy or depressed, our bodies strong or weak, our health exceptional or compromised. We're in constant flux. So what practical good is an absolute if we're not capable of living with absolute knowledge and conviction in a constant state? Guilt. Guilt and control. The power of guilt and fear to maintain order. But this is not a path to mastery, merely an illusory path to perfection (or redemption).

Masters fail. Masters have failed more than most have ever tried. There must, in all paths to mastery, be degrees and admittances for error without guilt of failure. We must be encouraged to try, to fail, to get back up, and try again. And we must be capable of assessing our conditions well and prescribing appropriate methods that speak to those specific conditions. Otherwise, we're shooting in the dark, and success is a mystery. This is the value-add of the W-spectrum (Weightlessness Spectrum).

The Weightlessness Spectrum is a prescriptive framework for holistic personal development. There's nothing like it in any of the mind-body arts or fitness methods. And whether or not you adopt it for yourself, you should consider it seriously. For the greatest challenge in prescribing relevant training prescriptions are twofold. The first is the question of where you're going? If you don't know where you want to go, how in the world do you know what you should do?

You're shooting in the dark and asking how you should hold the gun... And this is why most people cannot adhere to a serious developmental plan; they have no higher paradigm for training to make sense. Going to the gym is independent and dissociated from the rest of life. Only when we can tie our physical strength, flexibility, and mental state to our overall performance in life at work, in relationships, and with personal passions will we have the resolve to carry on when excitement and interest wane.

The second part of this challenge is assessing where we currently are. We're not living in absolutes but in shades of grey. So most methodologies address this state by saying you're a beginner, intermediate, or advanced trainee, case closed. And for each, there is an intensity and volume of training just for you. And there may be some hope of this within the context of singular methods that address fitness only.

But what happens if fitness alone doesn't address your personal, holistic gaps or vices? Or what happens if you've addressed the fitness side, are boasting a six-pack, and you're miserable inside? How is it that someone can be called "fit," and still be stressed out, insecure, and fearful? Well it can and does happen, but is this true fitness? The irony is that the term *fitness* suggests some kind of edge over one's environment.

But this is a case where strength is not genuine; it's shrouding an abyss of insecurity.

Fitness is not about attaining a six-pack for summer. Fitness is about environmental adaptability and peak performance. You know your environment. You know the people you'll meet, the relationships you maintain, and the work you've committed to. This isn't jungle training or chasing down wild buffalo; it's modern day work-life. Fitness is the ability to crush these tasks and commitments and nurture relationships that lead to a greater sense of fulfillment in life. It's the ability to live with power, passion, and freedom. And this is a tall order by today's fitness standards. The current model of fitness is broken.

The W-spectrum gives us the missing pieces to the puzzle of personal development. It gives us insights and surgical prescriptions for immediate, actionable steps. And among the 4 pillars of foundational Weightlessness Training—strength, flexibility, meditation, and nutrition—neglecting any one of them could be a recipe for disaster. Developing all synchronously, however, is a recipe for becoming weightless: free of all mental and physical burdens that hold us back in life.

Weightlessness is not a workout. It's a process.

Weightlessness Training is not a workout; it's a process that aims to build true grit and resilience in body and mind and manufacture weightless experiences. I find that this point is particularly difficult to communicate to those in the fitness community, which is flooded with teachers and methods that seem to offer a singular solution to the complexity of human needs. At best, people get fit amidst confusion; at worst, they get sick, injured, or go nowhere… with confusion. Weightlessness training is different.

No single methodology trumps all others at all times. Some methods, by virtue of their simplicity or efficacy, trump others within specific contexts, but even among these, they're still relegated to a single position along the spectrum of human development.

We must know ourselves before we can prescribe our paths. As such, there are no identifiable workouts (until one begins Lightness protocols); there is only a prescriptive theory of development. This requires a greater understanding of the mind-body complex, no doubt, and that's not easy. But neither is understanding the human condition, and we must be willing to do a bit more work than the average Joe if we wish to be delivered from all the bullshit that weighs us down and keeps us from living and loving life.

Many people have asked me if they can try a Weightlessness session. At this point, it should be clear that's not something the system can accommodate. There's nothing to try in an hour or a day that provides insight into what *Weightlessness Training* is. It is, fundamentally, about you. It's about me. It's about you and I having the tools we need to activate our higher capacities and perform at our peaks in a holistic sense. This cannot be bottled in a workout and it isn't the same for all people at the same time.

All that exists in the world of fitness, so long as it adheres to sound biology and biomechanics falls somewhere along the W-Spectrum. You can practice yoga and still be practicing Weightlessness. You can practice Crossfit and still be practicing Weightlessness. The only difference is that you may not know you're practicing Weightlessness, how to assess where on The Spectrum you are, and how to progress from where you're standing.

The pillars of Weightlessness Training are minimalistic yet holy transferable to all domains in life. They are integrated in such a way as to provide perspective into our holistic performance. But it's quite possible that someone may have an extreme imbalance, be super strong but lacking concentration and focus, in which case the W-Spectrum will provide prescriptive insight into next steps until one's mind-body portfolio is balanced and peaked. At this time, Lightness protocols become relevant and the four pillars of Lightness become integrated and trained synchronously.

The identifying traits of Weightlessness Training are only visible at advanced levels when someone is working on Lightness. Prior to that, Weightlessness can only be said to be a developmental paradigm that organizes the myriad training methods into a coherent framework of personal development. There are distinct tools and techniques within the Weightlessness Spectrum, but the model, in general, resembles more a mutt than a pure breed.

Once one arrives at a balanced and integrated mind-body performance level, Weightlessness becomes best in show, and does so through Lightness Training, which places sensitivity as our greatest qualitative metric. More on that in The Lightness Scroll.

The secret to successfully assessing and prescribing surgical cures for our conditions lies in the natural developmental processes of three of our foundational pillars: strength, flexibility, and meditation. Nutrition is just as fundamental and important, but it requires no spectrum, merely a rudimentary understanding of real, unprocessed food, an understanding of hormone cycles, and consistent application. I've given the broad brush-strokes of this in *In Pursuit of Weightlessness.* So let's delve deeper into the interplay (and time allocation) of the three fundamental pillars (each a spectrum unto themselves) of Weightlessness.

Along the journey to integration, you'll notice that not only do the tools along each of the pillars evolve, but so too does their allotted time. This is due to our ability to maintain a quality of work relative to the intensity of practice. Flexibility does not require the same type of sophistication in programming that strength and meditation do, for it is essentially the practice of applied relaxation, and it doesn't necessarily benefit from longer durations or more severe sessions. It improves over time as one's sensitivity and capacity for relaxation improve.

Strength (and conditioning), on the other hand, is the prime mover of transformation at the early stages of everyone's journey. Without strength, stretching is a risk to joint health. Without strength one will lack the stamina and mental fortitude required for meaningful bouts of concentration and awareness (aspects of meditation).

So, we find at the beginning of the W-Spectrum an overweighting of strength, an underweighting of meditation, and a constant but minor time allocation to flexibility, at least in someone just starting out in the mind-body game. If someone has experience but is lacking in one pillar, the W-Spectrum will inform that person what to focus on to balance and integrate all three.

With time and personal progress, time allocated for strength decreases, while time allocated for meditation increases. As one becomes stronger, the capacity to exert more energy per unit of time increases (intensity increases), and this cannot be sustained to the same degree as moderate exercise. Stress causes adaptation… not merely volume of work. It also requires more recovery time. The inverse relationship between intensity and duration of exercise, and the direct correlation between intensity and time needed for recovery, are overlooked by many people. Unless one is taking anabolic growth enhancers, our bodies cannot sustain increased intensity without risk of serious breakdown, sickness, or long bouts of recovery.

In short, the strong show up to their workouts, embrace the acute stress required for adaptation and growth, and then rest, hard. They don't aim to do more and more. They look to do enough required, and no more.

As the body toughens and the mind gains resolve and discipline, one's potential to concentrate and remain present improves. All of us would benefit from a bit more effort toward breathing and presence as we currently are, but among those playing the long game, very few have the fortitude to apply a meditative mindset under stress and pressure without having previously conditioned the body and mind in the fires of physical training.

If you cannot face hardship without losing your shit, practicing meditation in solitude will not transfer into real life. If you cannot show up to the gym when you're tired after a long day, then you're not strong enough to be nonjudgmental and nonattached when circumstances challenge your personal preferences.

Meditation is the most meaningful experience in life, and the most challenging practice. It should be treated with respect and prepared for with bold resolve. Once an individual has laid the foundation of strength and acquired the ability to remain present for five to ten minutes (which is quite advanced), only then does the real work of mental development begin, as well as the heightened energetic practice of qigong.

Balancing and integrating the body and mind is a practice of self-mastery. In all domains in life, we have the ability to gain masterful knowledge and skill. Most of these domains are specialized, and knowledge doesn't necessarily transfer well outside those domains. Becoming a great golfer doesn't make me a good father. Excelling in business doesn't mean I'll take good care of my health. Becoming super fit doesn't mean I'll be happy. You might say these domains are software issues.

Weightlessness addresses the hardware issue, the core components of our being that manifest in every single activity we engage in.

Becoming holistically stronger, sensitive, and integrated makes you better at everything. Your mind and body are present whenever and wherever you are. Their development and integration dictate the level at which you show up and perform in life. Upgrade the hardware, and all of your software runs smoother. As aptly quoted in *Zen and the Art of Motorcycle Maintenance*, when the calligraphy student asked his master how to paint the perfect painting, the master replied:

> *You want to know how to paint a perfect painting? It's easy. Make yourself perfect and then just paint naturally.*

The remainder of this scroll is dedicated to dissecting the key tools and principles of each pillar spectrum—strength, flexibility, and meditation—while The Process Scroll to follow details their integration and application within personalized program design so that you can assess and self-prescribe your own Weightlessness workouts…forever. The Integration Scroll will address the larger topic of integration as it refers to life beyond training.

The Strength Spectrum

I ask not for a lighter burden, but broader shoulders.
—Seneca

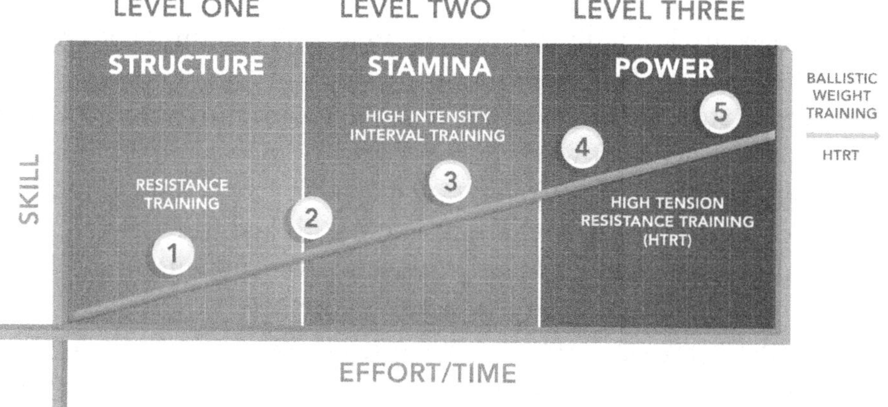

(The numbers within the spectrum can correspond to key metrics on the assessment in the next chapter. #3 might represent deadlifting your bodyweight for one rep, or running one kilometer in less than five minutes, for example.)

Strength 101: Baby Strength

The process of strength training begins at birth. Babies spend a good bit of time doing nothing, or so it seems. And with time, we see a bit of head stability, then a bit of rolling, then a pushup of sorts into a crawl position, and then a crawl. This pattern continues on and on, and therein lays the magical principles behind strength gain.

For months, if you look closely, you'll see *attempts*. Failed attempts albeit, but attempts nonetheless to achieve even a modicum of physical control. In those attempts, environmental stressors are sending signals to the baby's nervous system, signaling the baby's strength is inadequate to manage its environment. The successful aftermath of these attempts is an antifragile adaptation to the disorganized squirming that preceded. If there were no resistances, nothing in the environment to push back against us, all the growth hormones in the world would be ineffective at building enough strength for even basic calisthenics. This is why people with broken limbs kept in casts atrophy severely over time.

Our muscles are said to exert force in three types of contractions: concentric, eccentric, and static or, in gym lingo, positive, negative, and static. If you're doing a pushup for example, the concentric (or positive) contraction occurs during the push that brings you to the peak of the exercise. The eccentric (or negative) contraction is what controls your descent so you don't come crashing down. And a static contraction can occur at any point in the motion if you simply hold yourself at a given position for a few seconds or more.

Babies grow rapidly in part due to copious amounts of growth and other anabolic hormones they're blessed with. But it's also because they never stop moving, and in their incessant movement, they're trying things that don't work. Every activity or movement is laborious, challenging, difficult. They're putting max effort constantly to interact with their environments and acquire new skills and freedoms. They're constantly failing, and constantly growing, overcompensating for the degree of stress or difficulty a movement provides.

Modern science designates two primary types of muscle fiber in the body, fast twitch and slow twitch. In recent years, there's been greater distinction among types of fast twitch and speculation on super fibers that could be hybrids or the best of both, established through extreme circumstances and training methods. But for our purposes, the classic distinction of fast and slow twitch is sufficient and holds true.

Slow twitch fibers are responsible for those things in life that we can perform without much effort, walking, driving, and typing on a keyboard for example. They are said to be the fibers of endurance. Fast twitch fibers are recruited for actions that require fast, explosive movements, like throwing a ball or sprinting, or those that require considerable effort or force, like heavy weight training. They're said to be the fibers of power, and they certainly are the fibers of size gain. Both of these fibers require a faster rate of contraction to apply a greater degree of force.

Anything we struggle to do, so long as we can stimulate a contraction at all, will, by virtue of that difficulty, recruit the largest, strongest fibers we have: fast twitch fibers. Which means every attempt made by a baby to sit, twist, and push are akin to power lifting in adults. Which is why the feat of standing and walking in less than a year, starting from a state of virtual helplessness, is so miraculous. This strength curve is off the charts, and we see nothing like it for the remainder of our lives. For after, we can stand, move, kick, and throw; we more or less have the strength required for most of what we want. We no longer struggle to overcome intense forces, unless one is subjected to gymnastics, power lifting, or traditional martial arts at an early age, in which case this growth curve can be extended for a much longer period of time with diminishing rates of return.

By default, babies are constantly performing static and eccentric contractions. In order of absolute strength, we're capable of exerting more force during an eccentric motion than during a concentric contraction. And a static contraction falls in between the two.

If someone is incapable of doing a pullup on a bar, they can train this skill by standing on a chair and grabbing the bar with bent arms in a fully contracted position. Then when they step off the chair they'll lack the strength to remain there, but should have a modicum of strength with which to control the descent, during which they should be squeezing and pulling as if their life depends on it, making the descent as slow as possible until their arms have fully straightened. Rinse and repeat until strength has increased enough to hold a static position at the top for as long as possible before the challenging decent.

This is a terribly uncomfortable way to train, but it's, by far, the fastest way to rapid strength gains. The only down side is it does cause greater damage to muscle fiber (and connective tissue) and, therefore, potentially longer recovery is needed. So it should be used sparingly. Nonetheless, babies, with their surplus of growth hormones, struggle and break down against resistance and build at alarming rates until that grand moment when they can run and jump with ease. Their awesome grip when grabbing an adult thumb is a great example of applied static strength.

You'll further notice that babies and animals don't do what we'd consider standard sets and reps. They struggle a bit, and they play. If you've ever had a puppy, you'll recall their playfulness, and their attempts to do basic things like go up and down stairs, which, at first, is impossible. Within a few weeks they'll be dashing up and down the staircase with ease. They grow a little over the first few weeks, but their neuromuscular efficiency and strength both improve markedly. Children never do sets and reps of things early on. They just move with curiosity as impetus.

The first time a child stands, you see an uncoordinated mess that quickly results in a sore bum. Then the act is performed many times throughout the day (not many times at once) so that coordination and balance are honed. And then it's performed many times at once during play, or progresses into walking and running, which follows a similar pattern. This natural growth curve is captured and organized in The Strength Spectrum.

The Strength Spectrum

Structure—Stamina—Power

The first few steps are acts of crude strength. After that, skill is acquired, which allows for continued stepping and eventually running (acts of sustained strength, or strength endurance). And this marks the progression of development in all bodies over the course of learning any challenging skill:

1. Eccentric or Static Strength (And failed attempts)
2. Limit Strength (Gross—effective but not pretty)
3. Hypertrophy
4. Strength Endurance (Stamina—also often called *cardio*)
5. Limit Strength (Technical—effective and pretty)

The strength spectrum tracks progressions 3-5 on this list for the simple reason that a great deal of foundational development occurred organically before we ever proactively take on physical conditioning as adults. If someone were approaching fitness without much prior experience, their journey would still incorporate number 2—limit strength, as they learn new skills (and may even include 1 if they understand how to load advanced techniques with proper alignment).

Hypertrophy tracks to phase one of The Strength Spectrum—structure. Hypertrophy builds the "tension" members of the tensegrity structure that's your musculoskeletal frame. Rep ranges tend to focus on 8 to 12, which allows for heavy enough weights to stimulate an increase in muscle density and size without providing so much load that risk of injury is probable without superior technique. This is the zone and domain of bodybuilding.

This activates the ATP/CP energy pathway in the body, drawing from immediate stores of ATP from the skeletal muscles. This type of work generally lasts thirty seconds or less before ATP is exhausted, and rejuvenation cannot be accomplished without rest. Depending on the rate of lift, hypertrophic training can extend into the next pathway, the glycolytic energy pathway, and might exceed rep ranges of twelve or reflect slower lift cadences within the 8-12 rep range. This is where the greatest gains in muscle size can occur if workload is high enough (5+ sets per vector).

Strength endurance (stamina) tracks to phase two of The Strength Spectrum—stamina. Strength endurance within Weightlessness is generally practiced through high intensity interval training or circuit training. This stage assumes your structure is secure enough, developed at phase one, to be able to add ballistic movement and angle variants that both exhaust and challenge technique.

This takes several forms in application, but in principle it is comprised of intermediate bursts of intense exercise lasting from twenty seconds to a couple minutes with short recovery periods in between (either complete rest or reduced intensity baseline work). This could be the extension of work done in phase one into circuit training for example, which is akin to a child going from a few steps to running.

Reps in this range generally exceed twelve and could go into the hundreds, depending on training format if integrating techniques like burpees, high knees, mountain climbers, squat thrusts, and the like. This activates the glycolytic energy pathway in the body, converting glycogen stored in the muscles into ATP.

Energy pathways are not fully independent, but stack, first exhausting ready stores of ATP, then drawing and converting glycogen stores, thereby extending effort up to several minutes in advanced trainees. This might look like a back-to-back circuit of burpees (forty seconds), Bent rows (forty seconds), pushups (forty seconds), with ten or twenty seconds rest in between, followed by a one-minute rest after the full circuit is complete. Resistance (weight used) would have to be less than that in phase one and three, but the rate of effort forces all energy systems to work harder. This is the ideal zone for active (and rapid) fat loss and body transformation, though all phases can accommodate transformation with supportive nutrition.

Endurance training, whether high intensity training as just discussed, or steady state cardio that lasts for twenty minutes and beyond, both draw heavily on your oxidative energy pathway. This pathway begins to convert oxygen and mobilize body fat for ATP conversion. Weightlessness does not really emphasize steady state training for reasons of efficiency, but that doesn't mean that all energy pathways are not designed into the growth process, or that one can't integrate supplemental running or other forms of aerobic (cardiovascular exercise) into an otherwise progressive program. It just means you shouldn't do those things and neglect or bypass the other forms of resistance training that develop structure and power.

The Weightlessness Spectrum can be trained in exclusivity, or it can be used as prescriptive supplementation for other passions and skills—the yogi who needs more strength, the crossfitter who needs more meditation, the marathon runner who needs more base strength.

Limit Strength tracks to phase three of The Strength Spectrum—power. Power is that first form of limit strength developed in babies during first attempts at new skills, but in small doses with safe mechanics. Those who start strength training young could very easily start with and maintain this training ongoing. For most of us, however, there are risks to starting here and only training here, as it presents your frame with a tremendous amount of load (which can cause injury without sufficient structural development), and it doesn't produce the same cardiovascular benefits received from higher rep or longer duration training.

Don't expect significant caloric burn within this type of training (though added burn from extra muscle mass gained or the thermogenic effect of muscle creation from training is likely its best-selling point).

In Weightlessness Training, this takes the form of compound exercises lasting five to fifteen seconds (or 3 to 5 reps) though one-rep maxes certainly embody one's highest limit strength and can be done with sufficient skill. Testing the one limit max of any movement is by definition at the limit of your power potential and tests every part of you: structure, strength, connective tissue integrity, and mental focus. It will find weak links and break you if you're not well prepared.

Ideal for this type of training are compound exercises: deadlift, back squat, bench press or weighted dips, weighted pullups, and shoulder press or their bodyweight counterparts: pistol squat, one-arm pushup, planche, handstand or handstand pushup, etc. This approach carries forward as the foundational form of strength training within Lightness as well.

Limit strength activates the ATP/CP pathway, taking us back to ground zero for energy conversion. It draws from what's already present and burns out fast. If you can perform the movement for more than twenty-five to thirty seconds, it's no longer intense enough to fall into this category. This training is emphasized in Lightness Training for two reasons we'll review further in The Lightness Scroll: it improves myofibrillar density (strength) without a necessary increase in sarcoplasmic density (size) thereby increasing strength relative to weight, making you feel lighter. It also improves tensional integrity of connective tissue and bone density, allowing for max application of force without injury.

Samples of these strength progressions with specific exercise examples are given in The Process Scroll, as well as key metrics that help you determine which phase of training you should focus on, based not on desire or personal interest but on performance. It's important to remember here that the spectra of Weightlessness are technique agnostic. It's far more important that you adhere to principle progressions over and above specific techniques. This does require more knowledge and practice, but with them comes a sense of empowerment and ownership of your mind-body machine.

While some techniques provide exclusive advantage to level two—strength endurance—like burpees, running, and mountain climbers, the reason I haven't identified techniques for these phases specifically is that the techniques are largely the same as those used at other levels, i.e. key human movements along primary vectors, as I'll break down below.

A squat, pullup, or pushup can be perfectly integrated at any level of strength on the W Spectrum, *how* you integrate them is informed by your performance and skill level. At level one you might do a weighted squat for eight reps, or a bodyweight squat for the same number if you're starting out. At level two you might do bodyweight squats for forty seconds within a three or four exercise circuit. At level three you might load the back squat for a challenging set of three to five reps testing your limit strength. Same exercise, totally different implementation and consequent result.

Compound Exercises Reign Supreme

Compound movements apply force along key vectors. They're gross motor movements that allow for the greatest coordinated exertion of force by recruiting multiple muscle groups to perform an action. They also allow for the greatest applied load, a factor that is directly correlated with the recruitment of fast twitch muscle fiber within the movement, and, therefore, strength gain and muscular hypertrophy thereafter. They are integrated, high-leverage movements that translate directly to your performance in the real world independently of context, and they're essential for building a lean strong body, as well as power in all types of movement. Weightlessness strength training therefore focuses on compound lifts along five key vectors of force: push, pull, squat, press, and twist.

Isolation exercises focus on one muscle (or muscle system) at a time. These have taken over in the fitness industry and are often given as much attention as compound movements. Best known among them are likely biceps curls and triceps extensions. The problem is that small muscles don't allow for the same application of load and, therefore, don't stress your nervous system or stimulate the same anabolic growth response as compound movements, leading to one of the age-old rebukes: *If you want to grow your arms, squat!*

Our bodies seek homeostasis. Deep muscle damage or neural exhaustion is required to shift our antifragile systems into overcompensation and growth. Size isn't biologically efficient, so our bodies need a real reason to build it and keep it. Isolation work rarely provides enough stress to elicit meaningful growth and heighted performance if unaccompanied by compound exercises as a base or performance enhancing drugs.

Isolation exercises should only be considered marginally supplemental and physique enhancing in an otherwise well-structured, compound-lift-based program. They should be an afterthought unless being implemented for bodybuilding, rehab, or sport-specific needs.

Exercises should essentially be organized within a workout around energy requirements to train as hard as possible while being as fresh as possible. Big muscles require more energy than small ones. Compound lifts require more energy than isolation. Where this can get confusing in programming is when you've got multiple compound exercises in a single session. Trial and error and a bit of record keeping are of great value here to learn where your personal limitations are.

Let's say, for example, that you've got push and squat vectors in the same workout session. At higher levels of performance, you might merely say that one of these is a lagging vector for you, and you might place it earlier in the workout to ensure sufficient energy for it.

You might, alternatively, determine that the squat requires *so much* energy that everything after it is pretty much compromised... and, therefore, should be the last of the large compound exercises on that day, not the first. This would be a breach of the first rule (larger energy groups first) but might ensure that you can adhere to the second (train as hard as possible while as fresh as possible), for as you fatigue from any early exercises, your capacity for sustained tension and strict form diminishes. And with that decline, comes greater risk of injury and lower potential effort. This is where the insight of a coach or merely dedicated note-taking and performance analysis can answer the exercise priority question.

It's always possible of course to simply not compete with heavy lifts. That is, periodize them and train them on different days. This allows for higher levels of intensity and safety on both. But it may not provide as much conditioning if you have specific performance requirements or time constraints limiting training days overall.

If You're Not Pushing and Squatting, You're Not Training.

You were born to squat and push. You grew strong by living these forms with no instruction and very little effort. These are the two most essential movements, comprising up to 80% of your strength and conditioning needs. They are the backbone of any sound program. And great news for all of us, from absolute beginner to highly advanced trainees these vectors require nothing but your own bodyweight. We truly have no legitimate excuses *not* to train. You are your own gym.

When you've got the luxury of a well-stocked gym, the push or the squat can be easily accommodated at any strength level by any version of the weighted squat or bench press. As you get stronger, adjust the weight to suit your intended rep range. But as most yogis, gymnasts, and martial artists can tell you, weights are nice, but at the end of the day, your ability to move your body through space is what it's all about. So learning bodyweight strength progressions not only allows you to build strength without equipment but also generates confidence in the functional capacity of your body. Key progressions for the squat and the push:

Squat progressions—absolute beginner to highly advanced:

- Wall Sit
- Partial Squat
- Parallel Squat (to 90 degrees)
- Static Squat Hold at 90 Degrees
- Deep Squat (ass to heels)
- Partial One Leg Squat
- Supported Pistol
- Pistol (ass to heel)

Push Progressions—absolute beginner to highly advanced:

- Wall Push (leaning against a wall and pushing away)
- Knee Pushup
- Plank Hold (static or negative pushups from top position with elbows bent slightly)
- Full Pushup
- Wide Pushup
- Triangle Pushup
- Bicep Pushups (hands inverted and closer to hips)
- Assisted One Arm Pushup (assisting with other hand lightly)
- One Arm Pushup
- Planche Lean
- Planche Tuck
- Straddle Planche
- Planche Pushup

Improving Your Stress Threshold

Physical conditioning should be framed as a stress simulation—a laboratory where stressors can be applied methodically and gradually increased over time to accommodate improved capacity.

One could also throw themselves out of planes, fight, run marathons without preparation, speak publicly, or attempt anything else that frightens them, but some of these things could wind up exceeding your threshold by orders of magnitude, and may not necessarily increase your stress threshold, merely leading to systemic breakdown, injury, or sickness. So too could accepting the slow drip of work-life stress that disempowers and suppresses your spirit, but this will not necessarily increase your threshold in terms of acute intensity.

Strength is the only domain that allows for the methodical application of targeted stressors that allow for incremental and measurable progress. Again, the improvements made in this domain are not isolated to fitness but transfer to the whole mind-body system, impacting performance in all domains of life. We cannot ignore millions of years of evolutionary history where environmental stress was met with an embodied, holistic response. We carry that DNA, and we're built to become resilient to stress by taking it on.

Antifragility, Intensity, and Periodization.

The antifragile process that is stress-adaptation in the human body is innate. When the body is proven weak, it supercompensates and adapts. This is an inspiring process that ought to be considered fundamental to our humanity, and one that must be activated regularly for health, performance, and confidence to be mainstays. But it's not a free buffet.

An inverse relationship exists between intensity and frequency of training as exists between intensity and duration of a session. The truly intense cannot, by definition, last very long. But this doesn't require much analysis. You'll know it as soon as you feel it. Suffice it to say that in programming strength, as you increase intensity (in a workout prescription), duration should not be increased (if not reduced).

As we damage muscle in the strength training process or stress the nervous system with intense work or high volume, recovery time becomes even more essential. The relationship between these is inverted; meaning the more intense a session the more time you should take to recover from it. Many novice trainees (and many *advanced* ones too for that matter) get this wrong and continue to add more work and greater intensity the stronger they get without a corresponding reduction in frequency or duration only to get sick, injured, chronically fatigued, or simply plateau altogether.

Someone at phase one in the strength spectrum might be training all five vectors—push, pull, squat, press, twist—in the same session, three days per week. Because their capacity for work isn't at a high level, they can maintain this schedule and see results… until strength improves.

As strength improves, they must either reduce the frequency of training in cases where full-body routines are still employed or periodize body parts by separating vectors on different workouts, thereby allowing for greater intensity or more work per vector within a single workout, along with more recovery time between same-vector sessions. This might look like a four-day split, with upper body two days per week and lower body two days per week. It might also look like one to two vectors per day on a five- or six-day per week routine—far less overall work, but more frequent training.

Individual recovery and adaptation must be observed and measured to know how best to program your own growth. If you're lifting three days a week, are fatigued, and not seeing results, try reducing it to two days a week to allow for more recovery. Assess. Check your diet. Check your sleep. Monitor for another couple of weeks.

If you're training three days a week, are not fatigued, but not seeing results, try periodizing key vectors further, alternating push and pull days, squat and press days, but adding more sets to each vector. Barring working with a qualified coach, you'll need to study your own performance and look for patterns of progress, regression, fatigue, etc., and monitor nutrition and sleep habits.

Abdominal Breathing & Intra-Abdominal Pressure

The breath of relaxation and flexibility is also implemented in power based strength techniques by creating intra-abdominal pressure that irradiates tension from the core, stabilizing the midsection and spine, and adding power to the extremities. It's the reason power lifters hold their breath during the sticking point in a heavy lift (it's also the way strength athletes get abdominal herniations), and it's why martial artists kihap (shout) when striking, which forcefully contracts the abdominals and pressurizes the abdomen. Breath holding is acceptable in very short doses during heavy lifts to pressurize the system but must be quickly abandoned as rep range increases beyond three or more or within continuous, endurance-based exercises.

Strength as a Global Asset

The purpose of strength training isn't to get better at lifting weights. The purpose of strength training is to acquire an edge, an advantage in the real world that allows you to operate with grace and confidence. If we don't address the life question, there is no filter by which to say any method of training is better than another.

Even the recognition that strength is fundamental to performance in every domain, career, or craft, and the reality that we don't know with any certainty what life, career, or craft will throw our way is extremely insightful. It means we need enough strength to secure a formidable structural base and a confidence-building physique, but due to the lack of certainty regarding application we should spend as little time as necessary to accomplish it, lest we miss the forest for the trees.

The warrior mentality graduates beyond the various methods and manifestations of strength training and looks at the essence. More trainers and systems, regardless of level, believe that with no pain, there's no gain. They believe in the burn. They believe in the soreness, the sweat, and the suffering. That's what it's all about for them. They glorify puke day.

Warriors don't practice failing, they practice winning. In the beginning, it's impossible to avoid soreness, stiffness, and days of immobility. It's impossible to avoid failing in body or mind, along the path to holistic strength. But the gym goers who wear soreness as a badge of honor wrongly believe that if they're not sore, then they're not progressing. The warrior, who has been tested in the battle of life, knows that training is not an end in itself. For a mind-body warrior, days of soreness and stiffness mean days where performance is restricted. He's not in an optimal state of readiness.

For a warrior, the uncertainties of battle, and for a weightless warrior, the uncertainties of life, are what we need to address. Being tired and sore, needing days of recovery is a novice's approach. The warrior doesn't value soreness but freshness, readiness, and alertness. Always. And a warrior treats strength training as an efficient primer to maintain peak readiness, and nothing more.

Strength and Flexibility

As tension is to strength, relaxation is to flexibility.

We might summarize strength in our relationship to environment as one's capacity to resist or confront external forces. This is a complex equation that extends far beyond the strength of muscles, but looks at connective tissue, physical structure, leverage, mental focus, and grit. Strength allows us to face life without collapsing under its pressures.

Ignoring environment and only looking at the body, we might define strength as one's capacity to generate tension, both local and systemic.

If there's any downside to strength, it lies in the arena of residual tension, tension that accumulates in the body from the training process and which doesn't recede on its own thereafter. This can lead to lingering inflammation, poor range of movement (if not chronic stiffness), and a greater risk of injury. For strength to remain an asset and not become a liability, one must also be flexible.

The Flexibility Spectrum

The bamboo that bends is stronger than the oak that resists.
—Japanese proverb

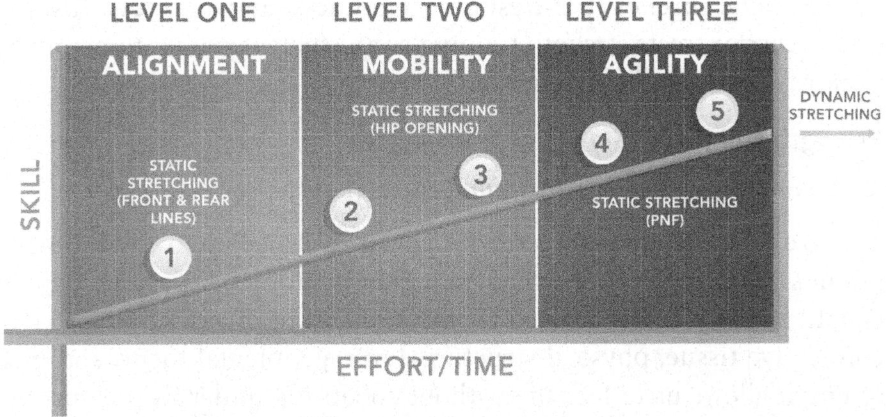

(The numbers within the spectrum can correspond to key metrics on the assessment in the next chapter. #2 might represent a forward bend with palms flat on the ground, while #4 might represent the front splits, for example.)

Flexibility 101: What is it?

Relaxation is to flexibility as tension is to strength. Flexibility is the correlate of strength. Learn to release tension, and flexibility will arise naturally.

Many people assume that the stronger you become the less flexible you'll become. But if we look at a diagram of myofibers (below), you can see that these two capabilities are not antithetical but are complementary.

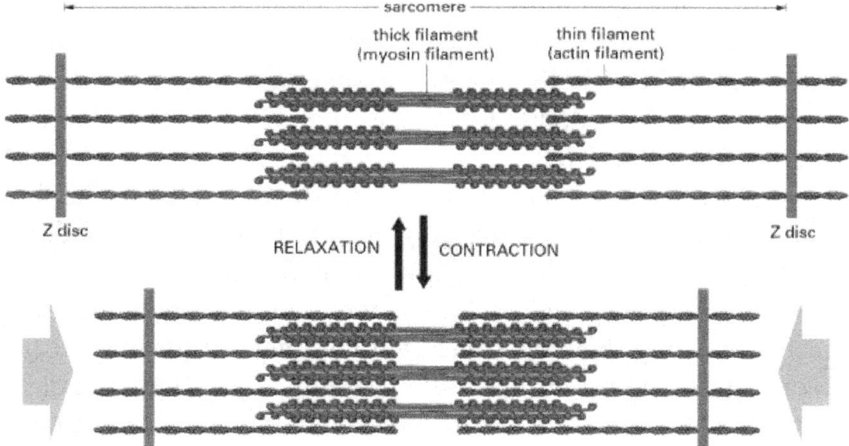

(Top image is a relaxed muscle fiber, where myosin and actin filaments are separated more than the bottom image, which demonstrates muscle contraction).

A muscle contraction cannot occur without a modicum of relaxation, for a muscle that is tense has nowhere to go. Tension is the close proximity of myosin and actin fibers to one another. Relaxation is their greatest distance apart. Flexibility is the skill (not talent) of activating length and distance between these fibers.

Consequently, one can see that the general view of stretching as "pulling" muscles with aggressive movement to gain flexibility makes no sense if one cannot release the tension that's inhibiting flexibility. In such a case, a trainee is at great risk of literally pulling or straining a muscle, tearing tissue that refuses to relax.

As we'll discuss later, nonlinear payoff from training pillars in tandem is particularly pronounced when flexibility and meditation (breath control, stillness, and concentration) are combined. The mind can learn to govern physical tension. And oddly enough, the body stores psychological baggage. The mind can be accessed through the body, and the body accessed through the mind. To approach this complex through only one pillar is to limit growth in that pillar. But for now, let's focus on where we came from.

Let's Not Forget Where We Come From

Animals in nature don't stretch for more than a few seconds, if at all. Nor do human babies, and they have extraordinary range. Flexibility has become relegated to an independent skill by many disciplines. Some people are fit. Some are flexible. Some are skinny. Some are fat. This type of categorical description becomes absurd when we look at animals in nature. This is relevant (in case it's not obvious) because we are animals, and even if not living within nature, we have a nature. Natural range of movement is defined, developed, and supported by environmental performance requirements.

Yogi's will spend countless hours on the sun salutation, which is a continuous flow from a standing posture to a forward bend, to a plank hold, to an upward bend (upward facing dog or cobra), to the downward facing dog, and back to square one. But when dogs wake up in the morning they too stretch with a downward facing posture, and sometimes upward facing, and this grand preparation for a day of running and playing lasts all of three seconds for each. Quick and dirty. Forward stretch, back stretch, boom, ready to go. Where's my ball to chase and leg to bite?

This is an observation that MovNat specialists target. MovNat teaches that fitness can only be activated and assessed in man's natural environment, through natural movement: lifting, climbing, running, leaping, balancing, fighting. Stretching? What the hell for? When moving in accordance with natural biomechanics, there's no need for stretching, and if there is… a few seconds will do. This is a proposition that, whether or not one agrees with it, should not be ignored if a person is conscientious about intelligent movement and personal development.

We human beings are animals. This is our starting place. Unless we first acknowledge and adhere to this simple fact, we're ignoring our most relevant fitness filter. And that filter, made glaringly clear here is this: Humans should not need to stretch to do things that humans do (i.e., run, jump, climb, lift, push, pull, balance, fight). If you're stretching prior to exercise, that's fine, just be prepared to justify it to those serious athletes with raw sinewy bodies and eyes of penetrating focus who are prepared to do all the above without it, who don't need it, for that is fitness at its best.

Then *why*, you might ask, if people are imbued with natural range of animalistic movement, does *Weightlessness* have such an emphasis on flexibility. The answer is simple, mere animals we are not. That is only our starting point. But… most of us have also forgotten our starting point.

Man as Existential Artist

Where this picture gets more colorful is when we start to ask questions about the meaning of it all, for just as humans are animals, we're the only ones we know of capable of deriving and creating meaning itself.

I feel the MovNat perspective is incomplete in two respects. The first is our biomechanical potential, which is, as far as the animal kingdom is concerned, virtually limitless. The ball and socket joints of the shoulders and hips allow for near complete range expression. The arms can, when trained, attain a full circular range vertically and horizontally. The legs, while more difficult to attain full range, can do nearly the same with full hip extension. Our spines too are capable of insane range that allows the highly trained and young children to fold backwards upon themselves. And this poses an interesting challenge to nature advocates because, given this natural range, how exactly do we define natural? There seem to be very few range limitations, except for lifestyle.

The second point lies in humans' unique ability in the animal kingdom to discover or create meaning in life. We're consciously aware of our own mortality, as well as our practical ability to affect our environments in countless ways. We are free (it seems) and, therefore, free to reject the need to focus on the natural range of cavemen or to accept the developed range of elite gymnasts, contortionists, and dancers.

Dancers and Yogis access a range of motion that I can only imagine was irrelevant for early man who needed to hunt, climb, sprint, stab, etc. But in this freedom of expression, we often find something worth living for, and an ability to express our hearts and minds in new ways, an ability to discover ourselves.

Wisdom of the Ancients

Grant me, if you will, that self-expression and personal growth have some merit along the lines of existential development. Then the next question is: by what criteria might we be able to filter the near infinite number of movements and stretching exercises to develop and express higher elements of our humanity, namely spiritual development and peak performance? And for this, I believe there are two arts that matter a great deal, yoga and martial arts, both of which have evolved over millennia under scrutiny and the discerning filters of genuine masters of movement.

Both of these crafts are empirical sciences of sorts, though no Western scientists would readily admit their principles as empirical facts. Imagine, if you will, the lifetime of only one man (or woman), admitted into a temple at the age of four and trained in martial arts for six hours a day, every day, for ten to fifteen years… to start.

At this point, their journey into the internal practices of insight and energetics begins and takes over a portion of the time previously relegated to physical training. They're learning dogmatic movement and theory that has evolved over thousands of years by lifetime devotees and grandmasters of the very same system, who, I might add, were ferociously focused on peak performance and, therefore, constantly assessing the tools and principles with which they built their bodies and minds. And while a real-world practicum may not have been required of all of them, Shaolin monks did come to the support of their emperors several times over the history of their craft, and tested their ancient theories in cold, hard, life-threatening combat.

Now, that's one person. Imagine a temple full of them and how this type of real-world experience and knowledge may culminate in the mother of all human development systems or, at least, one of the best. You'll find a very similar story in the annals of yoga, though instead of developing techniques for war, they were focused on its antithesis, peace.

At my first encounter of Shaolin kung fu, I was surprised at the simplicity and directness of the stretching—front and rear lines of the body with two to three global stretches—a quick and dirty approach to activating full length. I was truly grateful when, during my first day of Shaolin training at the live-in academy I attended in the countryside of Jilin province, the training hall echoed with screams of my classmates who were being pulled, stretched, and pressed into the deepest of possible stretches by the most unsympathetic of warrior monks.

The screams were chilling, and not everyone survived the first week. Some students left early after severe tears to the hamstrings or groin. But hey, not everyone was gonna make it anyway, right? The ones who do will be on the level. Such is the logic of those bred from birth to bend and fight. (I take issue with this perspective, as it suffers from severe hindsight bias… but the results do speak for themselves.)

My gratitude was not from the enjoyment of seeing grown men weep and break. It was because I was fortunate enough to enter the academy with full range, and so the monks left me alone. The reason their methods were so brutal was because, with the exception of a standing leg stretch on a balance bar that preceded partner stretching, all attention was focused on only four stretches, the intimidating fathers of all stretches: the front splits, the center (straddle) splits, the forward bend (toe touch/grab), and the back bend. Period. That's it. Four stretches. *Are you kidding me? And those… of all stretches?*

Unfortunately, the front splits are still accomplished in the Shaolin camp by force, which breaks as many warriors as it builds, by asking the student first to kneel on the ground and extend their front foot as far as possible. And then, as gently as only warrior monks can do, one monk holds your rear foot in place, another pulls your front foot away from you, and a third pushes down on your shoulders until you wish you were never born.

The center splits are not so different, with the exception of starting with a front facing position with legs apart and feet both turned up. The forward bend is nice, only two monks there. After sitting with legs together and fully extended, one monk pulls your arms forward, while another sits on your back and bounces until your hamstrings tear, your back breaks, or both.

And finally, my favorite, the back bend. For this, only one monk is needed to grab your waist and lift until your body folds fully backwards, and then they shake and bounce to remove all lingering tension and spinal stability.

It took me a few years to process what was really happening at that time due to the constant state of tension and fear in the air. But when I stepped back and looked hard at the method, cruelty aside, I saw the most efficient and practical means of accessing full range. And it can be summed up as such: stretch the front and rear lines of the body. Fully. They weren't concerned with specific regions or isolating muscles. Our bodies don't care about those things when we're sprinting, lifting or fighting. Our bodies need an interconnected and seamless transition through full range of the front and rear lines.

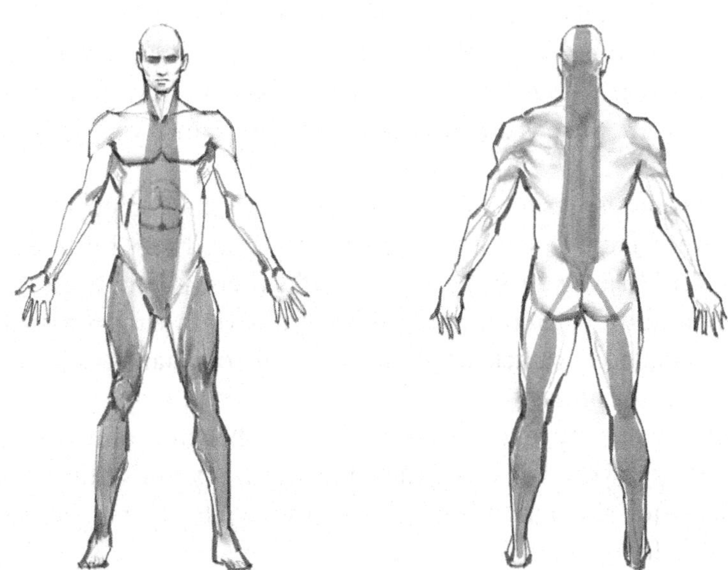

(Images indicate the superficial front and rear fascial lines. One can see the interconnected tissue from head to toe, and why muscle isolation is largely impractical.)

Fascia Revisited

This fully registered a decade later after long discussions with, and observation of, yogis. The most foundational asana in yoga is the sun salutation. And while the sun salutation doesn't go so far into the splits camp, it does focus on lengthening the front and rear lines of the body by way of the forward bend, the cobra, and the downward facing dog. Sound familiar? It was then that I fully understood the inherent logic behind the torturous methods of the Shaolin monks. If one can dismiss their lack of empathy with tight, tense foreign bodies and see into the direct, no frills approach to lengthening the front and rear lines of the body, thereby accessing full range, it makes sense.

Weightlessness Training begins with a similar emphasis on the front and rear lines of the body, with the supplement of center splits and hip opening exercises at later stages. This is the starting point, and the conduit to functional, dynamic flexibility developed in Lightness. What's most important is that we treat the body as an integrated whole and not the sum of many isolated parts. Flexibility only transfers to performance when myofascial trains, rather than individual muscles, are elongated in entirety.

On a practical level, we can employ our understanding of fascial plasticity discussed in The Transformation Scroll here. Recall that myofascia, as the tension member of the human tensegrity structure, is a strain distributor. Some have claimed that muscle is elastic, and fascia plastic. This isn't exactly right, but it's not a bad way to frame their differences.

Muscle, with sufficient mind-body connectivity, can be contracted or relaxed rather quickly. Dramatic improvements can be made in muscular tension in a short time if awareness of that tension and mental control over that muscle are well honed. This does create a sense of elasticity, where a great deal of range is accessible. Fascia is different.

The role of fascia is to maintain balance in the tensegrity structure that is your body. It does this by distributing strain across the whole system to alleviate as much strain or stress on the system as possible. This network of tissues in the body, unlike muscle, needs regularity and a consistent environment to settle into a state of balance. If you're not already flexible, this system will require the most time to redesign because its job is to keep you from doing exactly what you're trying to do, lengthen muscles and tendons, strain joints, risk injury, and alter what has come to be functional homeostasis.

Giving yourself time and space to relax, to sit in various forms that signify functional length, like the martial artist or the yogi, will give your fascial systems purpose to redistribute strain and release tension in the areas you're trying to gain flexibility. Repetition matters a great deal. Frequency matters a great deal. Even though our loose target for functional flexibility is full range accessed with a few short animalistic stretches, the road to get there may require longer bouts of relaxed position holding to reorient well-established structures. This is dramatically enhanced when flexibility moves beyond the domain of training and into the domain of living forms.

Live the Forms You Want to Embody; Don't Just "Train Them"

Flexibility, like strength, is best developed not through standard sets and reps within a workout, but through frequent repetition. It's quite likely someone who has neglected their flexibility for many years may need a window of concentrated practice to activate greater length, but this should be seen as rehabilitation, and not the aim of practice. If one needs five sets of stretching to get to functional length but spends the rest of the day walking around in a state of tension with duck feet and rounded shoulders, something is fundamentally wrong.

The value-add of flexibility is youth. It gives us free license to move again without constantly feeling stiff or fearing injury. Mobility is freedom. But mobility within a workout doesn't add much value to life unless it transfers. A martial artist who cannot throw a head-high kick without warming up and stretching has no business considering himself an expert in that kick. It exceeds his performance capacity when it matters. The same goes for a dancer, a gymnast, and any other athlete who may need to perform in uncontrolled settings.

The single best reframe for flexibility I've found is that of living the forms you want to embody. Don't merely practice them. Live them… do them. If you want to be able to do a forward bend with palms flat on the floor then do a forward bend, often, throughout the day. Good portions of the world's population, especially those in agrarian societies, use the deep squat as a resting, eating, and excretion position. Most Westerners in developed countries cannot even enter a full deep squat, ass to heels with feet flat on the ground and straight toes, without falling over or tearing something. Modern toilets… Toilets screwed up everything. We've removed the environmental necessity of that physical form (the deep squat) and lost the function.

You have to actually do the things you want to be able to do. Do them often. Use them. Make games and find reasons to use various, elongated stretching postures. Sit in the center splits while you watch TV. Sit in the deep squat while you're texting. Don't relegate these practices to external craft-based practices. Create a sense of importance or relevance for them, do them, and live them. They are you.

The Flexibility Spectrum

Alignment—Mobility—Agility

Weightlessness training in general, and Lightness Training in particular, is about unburdening the body and mind of all that holds us back. Physical tension, as we all know, limits range and has direct impact on blood flow, mental stress, and freedom of expression. As such, we're looking to traverse this landscape methodically, putting first things first, so that one at a time, we can kick those burdens to the curb.

Phase one—alignment—is a relationship. It speaks to the ways in which our physiology meets our environments and receives information or applies force. This correlates to phase one in the Strength Spectrum—structure. Alignment and structure are very much one and the same, though structure speaks to our ability to resist external forces, and alignment our ability to balance internal ones. Phase one is, by far, the most important phase of The Weightlessness Spectrum, the foundation that all capacities are built upon, including meditation.

Alignment is a highly nuanced study, but we can look at a few broad guidelines stemming from the principles of tensegrity and structure in The Transformation Scroll:

In standing, walking, squatting, and stretching, toes should track to knees and knees should track to hips. Straight feet, straight knees, square hips. This is a practice both in flexibility as well as daily movement. If you're walking with duck feet, you're going to have a hell of a time learning the forward bend, because you're stretching a few minutes a day and fucking it all up the rest of the time. For this to be a meaningful life practice, one that improves quality of life, principles need to be applied in the real world, not merely within a few minutes of gym time.

When you're bending, always create space first by extending joints or fascial trains before compressing. In the forward bend, for example, many people just bend down. This puts all strain into the lower back instead of where it should be, the hamstrings and glutes (and possibly the calves). To effectively train this technique (all others too), first extend your torso up, hinge forward and away from the hips while maintaining neutral spine, and only when no more range can be accessed with neutral spine should you fold fully into a global stretch.

In the hip flexor stretch and its big sister the front splits (and center splits as well), neutral spine and an untucked tailbone are essential. Tucking the tailbone and curving the back is a stress-based posture that triggers a tightening of tissue. To trigger a relaxed nervous system, one that will release tension throughout the whole system, it must receive and send clear signals through a neutral spine.

Eyes are your intention. In strength training, spot your target at eye level. If you look down, you fall down. If you look up, you fall back. In stretching the eyes set the position of the head, the head the position of the shoulders, and the shoulders the spine. Consider alignment something central to all aspects of life, where strength and flexibility both are the laboratories that allow you to perfect it. Consider not just the muscle stretched, but the whole system and its integration. Distracted gaze leads to loose kinks in the kinetic chain.

At phases two and three in The Flexibility Spectrum, we're looking to activate full length on the front and rear lines respectively (with center line hip-opening coming later from the center splits). These speak to orders of priority in development, both regarding safety and performance:

- Open the rear line and elongate the hamstrings to secure neutral spine within most practical movements (Forward bend)
- Open the front line of the hips (Hip Flexor Stretch)
- Open the inside of the hips and access full squat range (Deep squat)
- Balance the rear and front lines of the body (Front splits)
- Open the internal groin line (Center splits)
- Open the front line of the body (Back bend)

The Flexibility Spectrum, like The Strength Spectrum, doesn't preclude any movements, isolated or otherwise, that improve global range. It merely indicates the minimum necessary to generate full range in the body and in order of practical importance.

If someone feels they need more, they likely don't understand these foundational forms well enough. Most often, this comes down to an issue of 1) alignment or 2) concentration and effort. We'd all like to believe more (variety) is better because more is often more fun. But if we don't understand the essence, we won't understand what to do with any of it. Focus on unlocking global trains of myofascia, and all will be taken care of. Focus on hitting each muscle group, and you'll likely leave a lot undone and miss the performance factor.

Be patient.
Be precise.
Don't quit.

Where flexibility and strength have many synergies at phase one, and less so at phase three, flexibility and meditation grow far closer together at phase three than phase one.

Flexibility and meditation meet in relaxation. Each one amplifies the capacity of the other. To access full range in key global forms, you need to access a high level of mind-body relaxation. This relaxation is a vacuum where sensitivity and awareness come alive. Flexibility and meditation, therefore, become increasingly complementary the deeper one goes with each, and this is why we see them inextricably linked in the practice of yoga.

Abdominal Breathing & Relaxation

We discussed this in The Transformation Scroll, but it bears repeating—breathing determines mind-body state. Deep biological triggers are activated by things like physical structure (arched back versus neutral spine) and the location of breath (upper chest versus lower abdomen).

Upper chest breathing is the natural breath of fight-or-flight activity. Athletes use it to fuel intense work. Victims use it to escape from an assailant. Presenters often fall back on it before public speaking. Anxiety-riddled executives suffer from it unknowingly. And teenagers use it before asking someone to the prom. We should not vilify this type of breathing; it has many irreplaceable merits. In small doses, it fuels power and confidence. But if chronically applied, it creates anxiety, fear, and self-esteem issues.

Upper chest breathing signifies stress. And as we said, where there's stress there's resistance, and where there's resistance there's tension.

Learning to regulate the breath, to relax the chest and shoulders and to breathe from the abdomen triggers an antithetical response, one of relaxation and healing. Where abdominal breath can be implemented in power exercises with breath holds or shouts as discussed in The Strength Spectrum, in flexibility and meditation, slow, relaxed, and continuous abdominal breathing relaxes the nervous system and releases systemic tensions. Recall from above that flexibility is the correlate of strength—relaxed (stretched) muscles are simply ones without tension (contracted). Flexibility is the absence of tension.

The Artist Unleashed

Dance is one of humanities oldest form of self-expression. At its base is expression. At its peak is artistic freedom and mind-body unity. It is one of those crafts that call on each of our human faculties, and if competition is involved, even those deeper elements of stress and fear that accompany natural stressors in the wild. But here, we're playing in a realm where practicality of movement isn't really a relevant discussion. We're talking about art.

And while dance has lessons to teach on both strength training and presence, I find it a much more poignant attack on the critics of range. No doubt, one of the strongest signs of aging is stiffness. Look at any geezer on the street and if he has trouble bending, turning, moving with grace, he's either old, obese, or a terribly unfit zoo-human. His youth is gone.

Range of movement is one of the most empowering and liberating skills a person can have. And please notice I said skill, not trait. Flexibility is not preset or genetically predetermined (generally). Tension that impedes flexibility is a byproduct of physical tension, psychological stress, and the habitual conditioning of fascial trains to remain within narrow and fixed movement patterns.

Mobility is youth. An ancient yogic dictum states that someone's age is related to the flexibility of the spine. And sure enough, lower back mobility is where all of us start to feel the onset of aging first. We notice little things, like the hesitancy to jump into sports games or rush to play with the kids, nephews, or grandkids.

Rigidity in the body travels up to the mind and we find ourselves less open and saying NO a lot more than saying YES in life. That inability to express desired range of movement stifles the mind as much as the body, and fear of injury transfers into fear of the unknown. We stop pushing, trying, testing, and we settle. And instead of feeling light and weightless in life, we feel heavy, stiff, and burdened.

But some fierce creatives out there wear their passion on their sleeves, exposed, open. Dancers build bodies that develop range, not for the sake of range itself, but because range is freedom. That hard-earned freedom is an ability to express the mind without limitation, to release everything through the body and to be fully present and alive.

We are some of the most mobile creatures on the planet. Defining our humanness in terms of jungle play and guerilla warfare may be a relevant starting point for fitness and flexibility, but we shouldn't let it be the end. Humans aren't the fastest runners, the best climbers, the longest swimmers, but we are the most versatile and adaptable animals.

On top of that, we have conscious capacities that call into question what being human even means. We're self-aware and as capable of creating and affecting our environments as we are of cultivating ourselves. It's an incredible gift or profound mutation, depending on how you look at it. Use what your momma gave ya.

The Meditation Spectrum

I have realized that the past and future are real illusions, that they exist in the present, which is what there is and all there is.
—Alan Wilson Watts

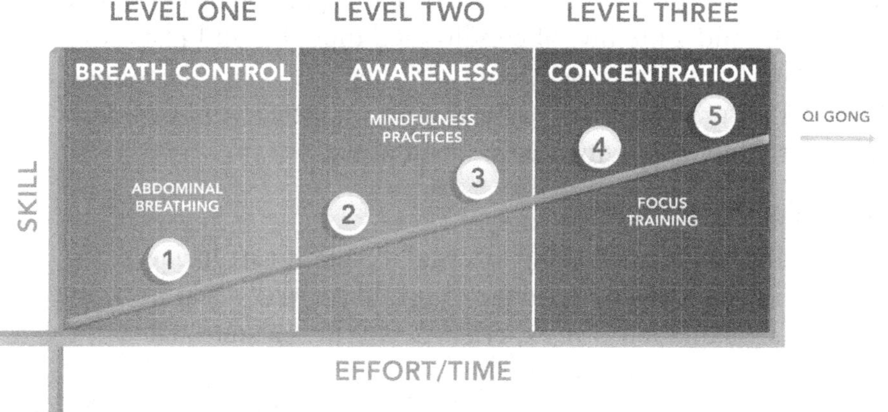

(The numbers within the spectrum can correspond to key metrics on the assessment in the next chapter. #3 might represent ten slow, constant breaths lasting longer than five minutes total, while #5 might represent a reverse count of 800 or higher, for example.)

From Breathing to Awareness

Let's begin at the beginning. When a newborn first enters the world and cries with startling power, you'll notice that the breath that fuels that wail doesn't come from the chest, but from the belly. And that little tyke doesn't drop this habit for quite some time. Infants continue to breathe with the lower abdomen as if still feeding through the umbilical cord for the first one to two years of life or so, and if lucky, a bit longer. Babies are masters of breathing, and our greatest teachers of meditation.

Babies run on base impulses that they're extremely committed to. When they cry, they cry fully. When hungry, they also cry fully and feed. When they grip, it's with extreme commitment and power. They have no pretense. What they do, they do in full. They haven't yet developed a worldview, and the host of mental associations that culminate in a well-formed egocentric identity.

They're masters at living in the moment. But they lack concentration, and with every new skill, word learned, value, or association, they move a bit further away from that natural gift of nonjudgmental awareness.

Awareness of the breath, in its continuity, is a step toward uniting with the transience of our experience. Life is present. It doesn't exist in memories of the past or projections of the future. It's right here, right now, in the words passing before your eyes, and the thoughts they elicit in your mind. And as awareness of the breath improves along with our ability to remain present and connected to the present, negative thoughts, judgments, and a lifetime of conditioned thoughts and responses lose their control over our present reality. We begin to notice the fullness and beauty of the present, undivided and interconnected. And we unlock our greatest tool for creativity, passion, and peace.

Meditation 101: What It Is.

Meditation is not a thing external to you. It isn't like learning golf, a new language, or any number of mundane skills that occupy your attentions. Meditation is an experience, a particular state of being, a state of mind that has no particular domain.

As a practice, meditation addresses your relationship with the stuff of your experience. It isn't so much what you're doing, seeing, or sensing, but how you're doing it. We might say that meditation addresses the quality of experience at large. It doesn't belong in a temple, a yoga studio, or a mountaintop. It belongs everywhere and may make a qualitative improvement to any experience, whether one is sitting in stillness at a temple, exercising, making love, facing conflict, or sipping coffee.

Our minds have two antithetical operations—I like to call them primal faculties—when sensing our present reality. These operations are simply to expand and take in (awareness) or narrowly focus and exclude (concentration). The first operation is the hallmark of mindfulness practice. It's an inclusive state of perception that aims to envelop the entirety of one's immediate experience. It aims to increase the quantitative data of the five senses (plus thought) right here and now.

As you're reading these words, are you also aware of your breath? Is your peripheral vision aware of the colors and forms of things around your book or reading device that are actually creating the form or your book/device? Are you aware of the pressure of your seat? Are you conscious of the temperature in the room? The degree to which you are intuiting these things in this moment speaks to your degree of awareness… in this moment. It may be the case, however, that this moment is better served by concentration than by awareness.

Concentration, the second of our mental operations, is a relationship with the present marked by exclusivity. You are observing the words in this sentence and, hopefully, immersed in them, but that happens at the expense of a wider potentiality of experience. Concentration excludes the infinity of potential data around you with the intention of fully grasping or merging with a single object of thought, sensation, or action. It's focusing on the flame of a candle or words on a page, it's pondering a calculus problem, and it's shooting the winning shot in the last second of a basketball game to the exclusion of all else.

Both of these states are nondualistic, which means that they are or, at least, can be non-ego-driven. They can be nonjudgmental and free of conditioned thought. And while they can be experienced or developed independently, they can, in the mind of an experienced meditator or in extreme life and death circumstances (or extreme sports) come together in profound ways. Awareness and concentration coexist within meditative experiences. To be clear on my use of the term going forward:

Meditation is nonjudgmental awareness, or preintellectual perception. It's a state of nondualistic experience—of presence.

It's important at this stage that you reread, if not commit to memory, the italicized definition above, as it's the point at which all dialogue in this domain tends to break down. Meditation, as a descriptor of various practices, is used and abused and retains very little practical meaning.

In discourse, when the Weightlessness trainee is in dialogue with a practitioner of any other method of mental development or meditation, they have a powerful filter by which to assess the validity of that practice. Insofar as the descriptions of those experiences are consistent with the definition above, they are descriptions of meditative experiences. Insofar as they are not, they are not.

The relevance of approach or practice within various methods can be further reduced along which neurological state it activates, or which primal faculty it cultivates: awareness or concentration, the constituents of a meditative experience.

Note: Currently devices can give immediate brain wave feedback to varying degrees of accuracy. Before long, these devices will be commonplace, and it's quite likely that having immediate neurological feedback will dramatically enhance a practitioner's ability to intuit and reproduce meditative brain states, marked by an abundance of theta waves in the prefrontal cortex and mid brain, as well as improved brain wave coherence across all parts. This will be a meditation hack like no other, but I speculate, while it may reproduce the state and phenomenon, the student may lack the skill to reproduce it without simple, repeatable, measurable metrics and practices like those that follow.

Because meditation speaks to the quality of experience, and not necessarily the type, it's quite possible that many approaches are valid. However, it's not because they are approaches to meditation that makes them valid; it's in their proclivity to access the states of mind described above. Visualization, for example, is not meditation. It's a great practice… just not meditation, for it's not preintellectual but a practice in which self-centered solutions are projected for rehearsal. This is an act of concentration without also being a meditative experience.

Transcendental meditation, heart meditation, yoga meditation, Reiki meditation, are not necessarily meditation just because the word meditation is applied. Each needs to be assessed and filtered along the definitional lines above, which defines the qualitative state of experience (and its constitutive elements) and not the permanent practices of a craft.

Each craft might have its own definitions, and that's okay. My priority here is to focus on saying something true about all humans over and above individual differences, so that when we come together we can elevate our knowledge and performance with mutual understanding, rather than allowing the application of the term to any practice whatever (causing confusion) with no clear definitional limitations.

This upsets some people sometimes, who feel this is a judgment on their personal practices or beliefs. But it's extremely important if we intend to do real work in this domain that we define our terms and understand the meaning of the things we're discussing, for practices break down with language.

A better way of assessing the valid application of the term in most cases is, rather than ask, "Is X meditation?" to ask, "When is X meditation?" for any and all practices and experiences can be. Again, meditation speaks to the quality of an experience (as present, undivided, and continuous) and not the substance or method employed.

Are heart or transcendental meditations meditation? Are tai chi or yoga meditations meditation? Well, maybe. Insofar as one is experiencing the present with undivided, nonjudgmental awareness they are (with an abundance of theta wave brain activity). If there are points of concentration (like the dan tian, heart, or third eye) to the exclusion of other points of awareness, they are not. But they might be qigong, which we'll clarify further in The Lightness Scroll. Does this mean they're not good practices? No, not necessarily. It just means that they are not, in and of themselves, meditation. With this clear dividing line, we're able to progress to the next level of conversation and assess the value add and relevance of certain practices over others.

Meditation is the most powerful tool we possess in life. The discussion above may seem extensive, but if we use the same word and mean different things, what are we talking about? And what does that do to the power of the practice and capacity for presence in our lives? Jedis love those light sabers. It would be a shame if the new light saber supplier in the galaxy used the word *light saber* to describe pickles. Well, not if he loves pickles too, I guess. But you get my meaning.

Identity and Ego: Neural Plasticity Revisited

Who you are isn't a static, fixed entity. You're a network of ideas, emotions, memories, and biological impulses. You experience this complex amalgam as a single "I" with concrete traits. But there's nothing concrete about you. Every seven years, most cells in your body are replaced by newer versions of themselves, which means that there are few parts of you that existed since childhood. What remains is a network fighting for survival on a biological level and fighting for meaning on a conscious level.

Your ego is a construct formed by countless conscious and unconscious associations. To establish relevance, most of your experiences establish hierarchical networks that help you make sense of the world, and which create a sense of order between you and your world. Everything from being told you're not the creative type, to cookies are bad for you, to your political views, are cross-linked in this network.

The neural synapses of this network are congealed with emotional connotation. This is why your memory of that argument at work makes you feel the same anger it did as the moment it happened, even though that experience is long gone and your mind is the only thing that gives life to it.

Most of us are afraid to consider experience devoid of ego, where there's no "me" in the experience. But consider this: you have more or less the same biology as many elite athletes, billionaires, entrepreneurs, humanitarians, world leaders, and countless self-made badasses. The difference? You think you're YOU, not them…

Imagine for just a few seconds the power of not being limited by your own beliefs, your limited hopes and stifling fears. Imagine the freedom of being who you're

not, if even for a few moments when it really matters. Meditation is that power.

Meditation IS Life

The ego—the person we know ourselves to be, as well as the unconscious associations and well-paved neural highways that lead to conditioned thought and habit… is the enemy of fresh, novel, and pure life.

Our operating systems (default mode networks) are so powerful that we can live a great deal of life without particularly noticing new things, without having "new" experiences. Knowledge acquisition is the accruement of various operating systems, worldviews, beliefs, habits, etc. These things, while very useful for survival, rarely address quality in life. And the more well formed the belief, emotion, or habit, the more each moment is merely a reflection of self, as if looking in a mirror.

We all remember that first sunset, the one that took our breaths away. Our first kiss. The first chocolate cake. The first holiday abroad. We had no preconceived opinions of these things, so the experience was brilliantly alive and impactful. Each successive chocolate cake and holiday abroad lost a bit of novelty due to our compulsions to compare: to call a sunset a sunset, a cake a cake, and measure each by some standard of the thing.

Meditation is the science of deconstructing those well-formed thoughts, judgments, and habits, and seeing this very moment as the first of its kind. It's seeing your lover as your lover, and not as a series of triggers and frustrations accumulated over time. It's seeing the sunset. It's tasting… the strawberry.

Ego-centric Experience.

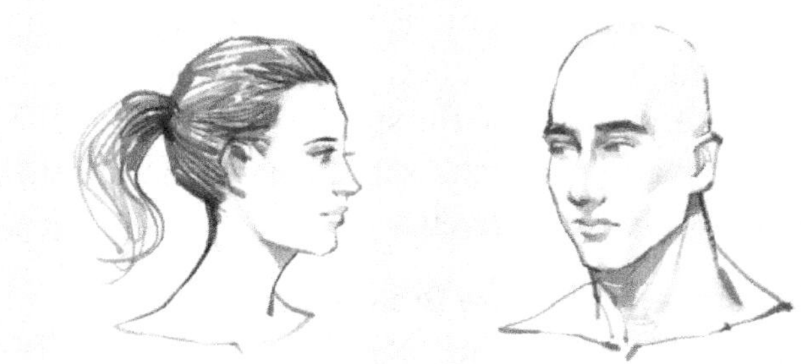

Clear Insight | Empathy | Love | Creativity

Meditation is the science of making every time your first time.

The Meditation Spectrum

Breath Control—Awareness—Concentration

One of the things that makes Weightlessness unique is the quantitative breakdown of meditative metrics. Meditation is, as we defined, a qualitative state of nonjudgmental presence. This makes it extremely challenging to derive practical techniques and tools, quantifiable practices that help us progressively develop the constitutive faculties of a meditative moment—awareness and concentration.

Abdominal Breathing and Integration

Preliminary to these practices in Weightlessness is basic abdominal breathing. The mechanics and coordination of abdominal breathing is the starting point of most meditative arts for three reasons. The first is that breathing is present, and awareness of breath is awareness of the present. The second is that abdominal breathing regulates the stress response, signaling to your nervous system that you're not under threat. The third is that awareness of the breath integrates body and mind in a single, unified act. Breathing is the beginning and the end of mind-body integration, the gatekeeper for self-control and peak performance.

Many trainees can activate the mechanics of this effectively on day one, some trainees with more tension (in mind and body) and less abdominal control require weeks to months. Very simply, sit or stand with a neutral spine with the center-top of the head drawn up (not elevating the chin). Relax your shoulders after setting your posture (posture to be detailed below shortly). And breathe in deeply using your diaphragm, not your chest.

The lower abdomen should expand and contract with each relaxed breath, even though the lungs don't extend so far down the torso. You should thoroughly practice this, making sure your shoulders remain relaxed and your chest doesn't take over. Once this is relatively comfortable, you can proceed to the specific tools within The Meditation Spectrum for cultivating awareness and concentration: slow breathing and reverse counting, respectively.

Cultivating Awareness Via Slow Breathing

Mindful awareness should be practiced in its simplistic purity ongoing. But those who've been in this game a while know all too well that there are few survivors, few who make it past a few weeks of practice. One of the biggest hindrances is there are no useful measures (until now), so the gifted experience the immediate benefits and continue, and those who need it most lose hope and say meditation isn't for them.

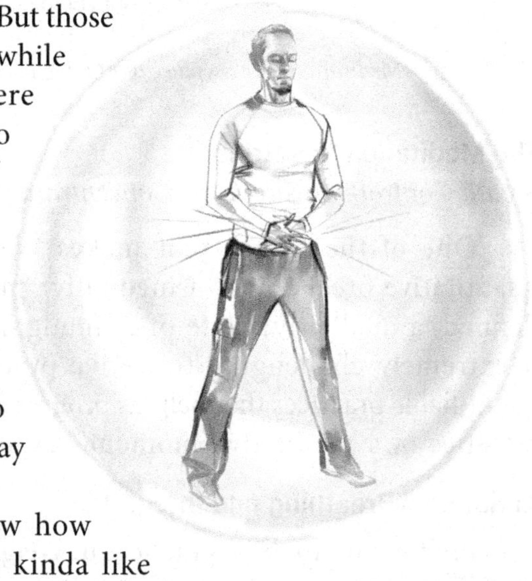

Hopefully, you see now how misinformed that is. That's kinda like saying arms are not for them. They're there, dude; learn how to use 'em.

So, here, we implement slow breathing, a practice that slows metabolism temporarily, activates the mind, relaxes the body, and stretches time. Within this practice, you realize there are moments within moments, data that goes otherwise unnoticed.

Referencing our metrics outlined next in the assessment in the The Process Scroll, I consider ten breaths in five minutes or less to be beginner level (level one). Ten breaths in five to eight minutes is intermediate (level two). To reach a high target of ten full, slow, continuous breaths (or fewer) in ten minutes (or more) one must either cultivate a high level of oxygen uptake and utilization (fuel for qigong—discussed in The Lightness Scroll), learn to release all points of tension so as to reduce energy requirements and, therefore, reduce the need for air, or do both. As tension is reduced, the body comes alive with feeling, and with feeling, awareness grows to encompass more information per unit of time.

The greatest advantage to this challenging practice is that it's exceedingly simple to get started and it's measurable. Within the practice of slow breathing, abdominal breathing should still be employed with a slow breath cadence, relaxed, and continuous. There should be no pauses or retention holds at the peak-in or peak-out of each breath. And the length of inhale should equal that of exhale. Yes, basically a really long, slow, extended breaths.

You will need to work through the drowning reflex that occurs early on in practice when you're testing your limits. It happens to all of us. But with time, you'll relax more, and that reflex will be subdued. You'll be able to extend the breath far easier without panicking and gasping for air. Breath cycles should be timed, with awareness placed on inhale versus exhale duration until they are consistently equal.

Moments Within Moments Revisited

As your capacity to stretch your breath is tested, you'll be forced to acknowledge points of tension within the body and mind that use energy unnecessarily. Lung capacity must improve along with oxygen uptake and utilization (on a cellular level). This is analogous to high altitude training, and, over time, will produce some of the same adaptations.

Tension in the body and a hyperactive mind waste energy, and these must both be stilled and silenced to attack the task at hand from both ends: increase energy via greater lung capacity and breath control, and energy demand reduction through the release of physical tension and mental waste.

Within this potent process of self-exploration, you'll quickly notice that time expands, or more simply put, you notice more. In stillness, your mind will intuit more and more data per unit of time. You'll discover moments within moments, and this has the psychological effect of lengthening time.

But what's more remarkable is that these moments, which cannot be emotion-filled or intellectually processed, are rather beautiful. They're unique. They're novel. They've never been before and never will be again. And all of a sudden, you notice that you notice. You taste life.

Developing Concentration Via Reverse Counting

Concentration is the ability to hold an object of awareness for an extended time. The quantity of concentration can be easily measured, and the quality improved.

Absolutely anything can act as a vehicle or focal point of concentration. In classical meditation and mindful awareness, the breath acts as that focal point initially, anchoring consciousness to something objectively real yet fleeting. But for many, asking them to observe the breath is a fool's charge, and many can't manage to do so for more than a few seconds.

The device we use within The Meditation Spectrum to maintain and measure concentration is reverse counting. Yes, literally counting backwards. It's simple. It's boring. It isn't easy. And it cannot be hacked. It's the perfect vehicle for practice. You actually have to concentrate.

You either hit the count without losing focus or you don't. Period. With time and skill, this practice is not as simple as it seems, and does develop a plethora of new sensations and abilities. The practice itself may even become meditative, centering, and rich as one progresses far enough. And great news, it transfers quickly into enhanced focus and confidence in daily life.

For this practice, begin with a reverse 100 count (seated or standing), *visualizing each number in the center of your forehead*, and speaking the number softly aloud. Do not overregulate your breath or employ slow breathing here.

It helps to speak quietly or merely mouth the letters while inhaling so it doesn't interrupt your natural breath or create a sense of panic. You should not coordinate breath with number count, this will hyperregulate your breathing and complicate general meditative practice down the road. Breathe regularly and count slowly, but continuously.

The first question I usually receive is: *Does it still count if I don't mess up any numbers in the count, but my mind drifted for a second and I don't remember counting them*? Oddly enough, this happens often in the beginning. And sorry to disappoint, no, it doesn't count. The point of the exercise is concentration; counting is just a device. If you hit the numbers without concentration it doesn't make you a genius; it means you're cheating yourself. Start the count over.

Every day to every other day attempt your highest count. When you have successfully completed the count in a controlled, concentrated manner five times with no mistakes, then you can increase your count by 100 (meaning you'd now count back from 200 to 0, and so on.). Continue this until you develop a 1,000+ count with no loss of focus (which is approximately forty-five minutes or more of straight concentration). If you make a mistake or find a lapse in concentration, penalize yourself and return to your previous count (the number before your latest increase), perform that count one time before attempting your highest count for a fresh attempt at five consecutive rounds (to be done at separate attempts on different days).

If this practice were taken on daily, it's quite possible for someone to reach a reverse count of 1,000 within ten to fourteen weeks...though not easy. After 300 counts, it become increasingly challenging, with new insights and skills manifesting every additional 100 count. Be patient with yourself and make space for this practice. It has wide reaching impacts.

A Meditative Moment

Slow breathing (which leads to awareness) and reverse counting (which develops concentration) are not meditation. They are merely devices that develop the different operating systems of the mind: expansion (inclusive) and focus (exclusive).

Meditation is not just a practice; it's an experience!

The myriad methods of meditation should not be considered the real thing. They are merely vehicles that allow us to activate a meditative mind. Meditation has no domain. It's the experience of life itself. It should not be relegated to a temple, a gym, or a secluded, quiet room. These are fine training environments for cultivating the stillness necessary to meditate, but they're not what meditation is or where it belongs.

In the same way that professional athletes strength train to gain an edge on the field, so too does meditation *practice* prepare us for the field of life. But the athlete never mistakes strength training for the game... it's only preparation. They still HAVE TO APPLY IT.

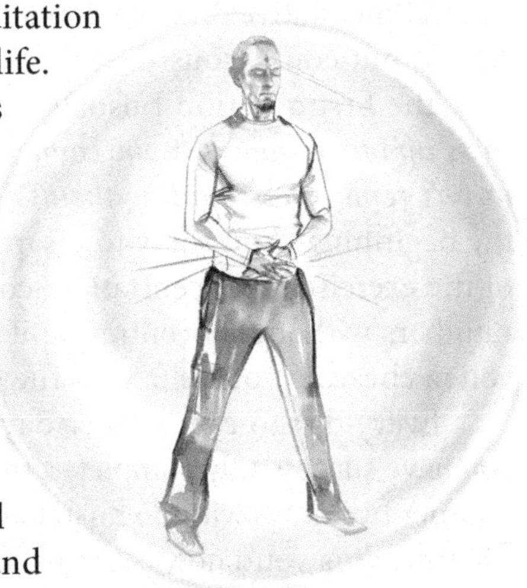

Meditation, as an experience, is the integration of awareness and concentration within a single timeframe. To repeat, it is an egoless state of nonjudgmental awareness, or preintellectual perception. It's pure, unfiltered, and brilliant with detail. Meditation, therefore, isn't really practiced; it's arrived at. Techniques and various efforts fall into the domain of preparation (similar to strength training), the cutlery that allows us to enjoy the banquet.

Setting Awareness Triggers and Applying What You Know

From isolated practice to mindful living

If you're fortunate enough to get past that first stage of meditative practice, the one whereby your ego relinquishes control for even a few moments and you simply are—you're not doing for a few moments, you're being—then there's hope for real change. But this real change doesn't occur in the isolated environment of practice within a safe space, a temple, a dojo, the park, your meditation room; it happens in the midst of regular life, in conversation, when ordering at a restaurant, when tasting food, when learning a new skill, and every other event in life. If you're gifted or advanced enough, this transference of skill just happens. For the rest of us, we need triggers.

A trigger is anything that you associate with the performance of a new act or behavior in an attempt to generate a sense of relevance and routine around it. Our brains are built to repeat those things that help us survive. The more relevant an action is (the more necessary it is), the more conditioned it becomes. This is ironic because meditation is essentially an unconditioned, novel state of experience, but if we can forego that paradox and implement this tool, magic does indeed happen.

Anything can act as an awareness trigger… walking under a certain doorway, opening a car door, turning on your computer, and hearing a text message beep. As long as you're able to associate that trigger with the behavior you'd like to repeat (awareness), anything can serve as your reminder to ask yourself:

AM I AWARE OF MY BREATH?

Why We Stand

Standing meditation IS the integration tool of Weightlessness Training. It's far more challenging than any of the strength training and conditioning exercises you'll face. It will test your mind in ways you don't expect. Take it seriously. Respect it. Be Patient.

I saw a client about six months after finishing a 100-day program. She said she was still meditating, but that she was doing seated meditation because she preferred that. This is fine. It's understandable. You'll prefer it too. It's easier. But this is real work here. Deep work. And it isn't always about preference.

There's simply no other way to do what standing meditation can do for you. So meditate as you wish. All practice is good practice! But don't assume that one form is an equal stand-in or replacement for another… it isn't. We're comparing hot dogs to steak here.

Standing meditation is the laboratory where we study the nuances of our complex mind-body system. We observe imbalances in our physical structure, chatter in our minds, and idiosyncrasies in our breaths. We become aware of excess tension in various parts of the body, which, by necessity and in accordance with tensegrity structures, creates ripples of tension elsewhere that may lead to pain, poor posture, or psychological insecurity.

In identifying and releasing the points, while, at the same time, consciously attending to your antigravity anatomical alignment, the energy required by your system to sustain its basic operations drops precipitously. That energy can be felt immediately, and can be spent on both internal healing processes as well as stress-adaptation processes ala strength training. It can also manifest in sustained, bottomless energy throughout the day.

Integration is not an easy thing to define, or to access. It's the sum total of your various systems and faculties coordinating effort simultaneously. As we age, we move less, think less creatively, and avoid the stressors that force holistic performance.

When a child goes to pick up a toy, you'll see an entirely coordinated movement. Eyes spot, head turns with shoulders and hips. Arms extend, legs squat, hips bend. Everything lifts together. It's obvious the need for such effort diminishes as we get stronger. There's no need for you to bend from the knees when picking up a pencil. But we can see in all children a mind-body integration potential that we still contain deep within our biological and structural potential.

So what does this have to do with meditation?

We've talked above about the neurological and psychological happenings within a meditative moment. It's fair enough to say that if that stuff happens, then you're good to go. But the Weightlessness practitioner knows well by now that this moment is only half the equation. Meditation today may be easy to access. Tomorrow? Well that may necessitate far greater wherewithal or mind-body connection if environmental stress or personal health tests one's ability to forego judgment and monkey-mind chatter. It may also require greater physical strength and conditioning, which is why strength is prioritized in early Weightlessness training. A strong, weightless mind requires a strong, physical temple.

Standing meditation does a few things that seated and lying meditation don't, which is why it has been the preferred method of practice for qigong practitioners and Chinese martial artists for millennia. Let's recap what we learned in The Transformation Scroll regarding your physiology that may be relevant first:

- Your structural frame is built to resist gravity, among other forces.
- Your nervous system relaxes, triggering healing when it isn't stressed.
- Strains require the whole system to compensate. It does so by adding tension to redistribute said strain.

Weightlessness doesn't focus solely on accessing egoless nonattachment or relaxation. These are fine add-ons and extremely valuable. Weightlessness is focused on the whole system.

Presence is an embodied phenomenon, not purely a psychological one.

Stop reading for two seconds. Wherever you are, whatever you're doing, stop. Sit or stand straight, shoulders back and down, head drawn up, abdomen relaxed, eyes straight yet soft and taking it all in. Take five relaxed, full, deep abdominal breaths.

Did you not just feel a significant shift in what we could describe as your mental state or mood? Perhaps you even felt a shift or increase in wakefulness or energy.

We dramatically underestimate the degree to which our structure affects physiology affect psychology (and vice versa!). Jordan Peterson, in his *12 Rules for Life: An Antidote to Chaos,* discusses battle-losing lobsters that carry their losses in their physical posture. Incredibly, loser lobsters slouch and winner lobsters puff up and "walk tall." He shared that a dose of dopamine will correct a loser lobster's posture without it needing to win another battle, which would normally be the case. It's mood and physical structure are inextricably linked… as are yours and mine.

We have extremely similar nervous systems (shared with most of the animal kingdom), and can reverse this cycle, can game it, if you will. Your mind takes these success-failure cues, that is, the hormones and neurotransmitters that directly affect mood and psychosomatic states in the here and now and associates them with physical responses. When you shift your structure, you disconnect that negative feedback loop, you relax your nervous system, and you open the door to change. Setting your structure and breathing deeply is like taking a small dose of antidepressants.

This is why we need a living embodiment practice that allows us to connect with the present and shift our states. Standing meditation is that practice.

When your system is stressed, it signals hormones and neurotransmitters that empower action. They allow you to stay sharp and fight if needed. But they don't allow you to relax or heal. Because your body supports its upright posture, not through the stacking of independent concrete blocks, but by delicately balancing tension and compression members in a floating system, each disturbed piece of that system has repercussions for the rest. These repercussions manifest in one specific way: tension. Tension is created elsewhere in the body to reorient your frame to avoid pain and discomfort, which itself creates the need for further compensation elsewhere, and so on and so forth.

Standing meditation is the means of eliminating compensations that justify strain and imbalance and store stress in the body. They must be reversed for rejuvenation to fully take place. Since your body is built to stand up, and to do so, it must resist gravity to a certain extent, the reduction of the force of gravity on your frame is directly correlated to reduction of strain on your system. This is very simple, though it may not seem so at first.

Look at someone texting while standing on the subway, or an old man walking with a cane. You'll see from the strain on the back of the person's neck who's texting, and the strain on the lower back and shoulders of the old man, that a lot more effort to sustain their postures is required than if their parts were stacked vertically atop a symmetrical frame. We've all played Jenga; this is Jenga 2.0.

Sensitivity lies in the distributed brain, not in the brain. Your mind isn't in your head. Your brain proper is in your head, but the mind (the distributed brain) is distributed throughout your body via the nervous system, a system that gives direct and instantaneous feedback between you and your environment, much of it unconscious. This feedback can be dramatically augmented through mindful attention, and mindful attention can be dramatically augmented through relaxation and a reduction of tension.

Tension is the enemy of sensitivity.

How do we improve relaxation and reduce tension? Well, we reverse the self-preservation mechanisms just mentioned. We reduce the need for strain distribution by realigning and balancing the body. When the body is stacked effortlessly, tensions that arise as compensation present or past are no longer needed.

When we release those tensions, we find a natural balance stemming from right anatomical alignment, relaxation and sensitivity. And when we relax, we heal. We actually begin to feel improved efficiencies in neural signaling in the form of bioelectric tingling and heat in regions of the body. This is the origin of qigong, a practice we'll explore further in The Lightness Scroll.

To sum these points, standing meditation is integration practice. Integration allows your system to heal and to coordinate power. Both of these are the byproduct of increased sensitivity, which stems from a reduction in tension throughout your system. The reduction in tension, or rather, the increase in relaxation, is the natural consequence of optimized tensegrity of your free-floating structure. When you're aligned effortlessly against the forces of gravity, you relax, you release, and you heal.

How to Stand: The Anchored Buoy

So how do we do it? Apply these structural cues in the order listed to 1) create balance, symmetry and natural lift and 2) to release tension from your frame, allowing your relaxed tensegrity structure with effective stacking to maintain your posture with diminishing degrees of tension over time.

Represented by the first figure in the image below:

- Feet parallel
- Externally rotate feet (apply force, not actually rotating the feet) to create torque in the hips
- Tighten quadriceps and hamstrings
- Tighten your glutes
- Tighten your abs
- Externally rotate shoulders
- Lift crown point, elongating your entire frame
- Place tongue to roof of mouth just behind the palate

Represented by the second image below:

- Relax all muscles and loosen all joints, relaxing—face, jaw, shoulders, abdomen, thighs, knees, ankles, feet—working back down the body.
- While leaving your head drawn up, allow your frame to sink in relaxation, creating space within your body, like an anchored buoy drawn between sinking and lifting forces—lifted by the buoy above yet rooted by the anchor below.
- Maintain your stacked structure with diminishing degrees of tension over time. Maintain awareness of and survey for tension that may creep back in.
- Sense. Feel. Be present.

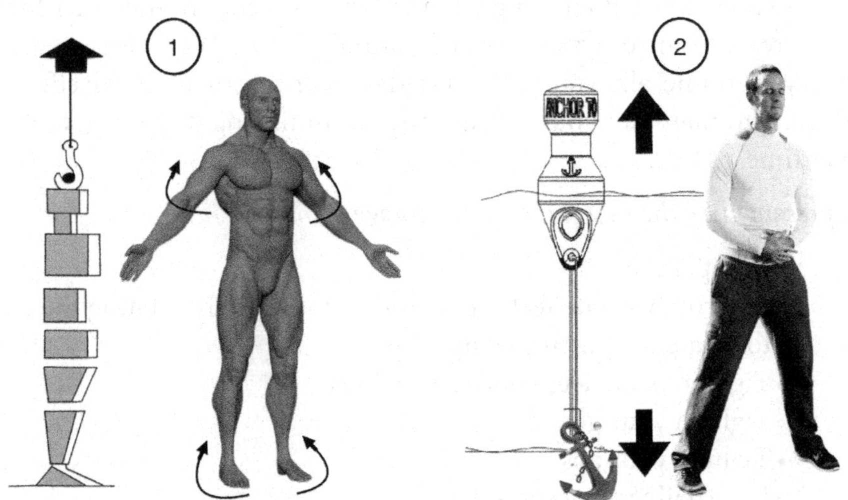

(Image 1 represents the framing sequence that aligns and stacks the body as it's built—to resist gravity. Image 2 retains that alignment while eliminating all the tensional factors used to set it. Your frame is an anchored buoy—floating yet rooted.)

As we progress from unstructured frames (which isn't an absolute thing; we continuously float in and out, largely dependent on self-awareness and structural conditioning) to structured standing, the ever-present force of gravity on our frames, itself a constant stressor, is diminished.

As it diminishes, less tension is required to remain upright. As we release tension that is no longer needed to support our upright frames, maintaining alignment through balance and symmetry, our mind-body comes alive with awareness and sensitivity. This is the birthplace of rejuvenation, health, presence, and performance.

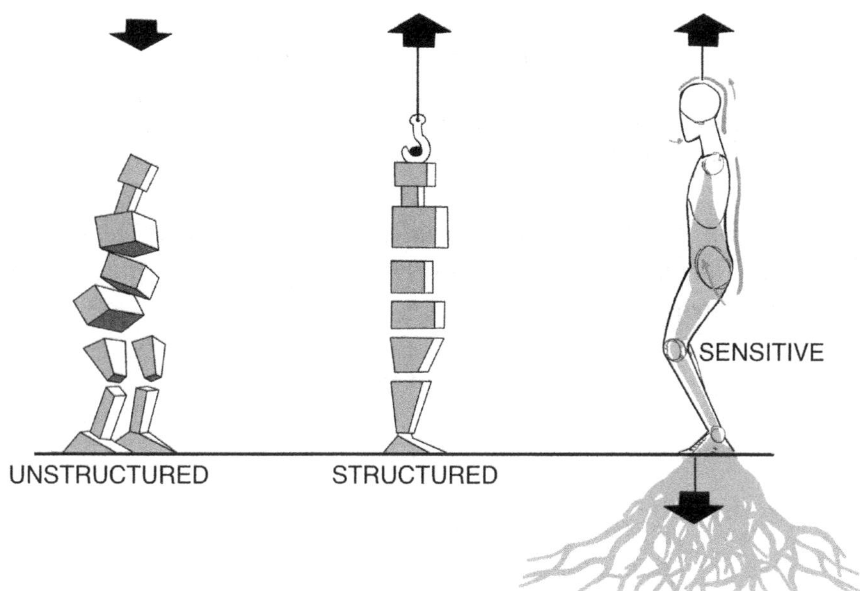

Now that we have this monster tool in our toolkit, we can discuss its myriad applications beyond the incredible benefits mentioned. In The Integration Scroll, we'll discuss integration a bit further, and we'll look at the role of structure to affect perspective, mood, and state. Shift the body to shift the mind.

If Meditation Is About Presence, Why All the Details?

Someone might fairly ask why I reduced meditation to a very simple act of immediate presence in *In Pursuit of Weightlessness*. And this is well worth clarifying. In particular, one chapter, titled "How to Meditate," had these sparse instructions:

You.

Yes, you!

At the end of this brief chapter, you're going to set this book down for exactly one minute. You're going to breathe your fullest breath in years. You're going to experience the vivid beauty of the world directly in front of you, the world you have been overlooking.

You'll sit quietly.

You'll listen carefully.

You'll feel...everything.

Tension will fall from your shoulders.

You'll see what's in front of you. You'll notice all details. You'll forget all names and descriptions.

For one minute, you'll sit quietly and judge nothing. This is the last minute of your life. The only minute that matters. Don't fill it with nonsense. Be with it, intimately.

Observe your breath.

Listen.

Feel.

Empty yourself. Open your heart. Let in the beauty of the moment, your moment, your last moment, let it in.

Be.

Clearly that's a very different *how to* than the tools and methods I present above. And if you've read that book and are feeling frustrated that the method above is a thesis by comparison, I want to assure you nothing has changed. At its core, meditation is as simple as we have it in this passage.

It's simple, its direct, its free, but it ain't easy. *In Pursuit of Weightlessness* was heavily focused on the *why* of meditation and explored a variety of meditative moments through true, taboo experiences I had over the years, including a night on the streets in Florence, Italy; an insight from an ex-con; high on hallucinogenic mushrooms; and a chance encounter with a Thai prostitute. They were all examples of meditative moments in its purity.

The tools and structures presented in the book you're reading now don't negate the simplicity of a meditative experience. They merely add color and credence to the harsh realities of life that wreak havoc on our bodies and minds. It's *that* simple to meditate; it just isn't that easy.

It isn't that easy when we're busy, stressed, fearful, anxious, injured, and any other negative state that pulls our minds in a million directions, preventing us from sitting in stillness for even a few peaceful moments. This is reality, and reality can be harsh.

It takes precise tools and a lot of practice to show up and extract more quality and beauty from the present, and even more practice if life is more stressful or volatile than usual. Volatility and stress are triggers that encourage reliance on prior patterns and habits, stuff that's worked before and just may work again. They make it harder to remain actively present and open to what life presents, open to change, nonjudging, and instead we often default back to a heavily filtered, judged reality, unless… unless we have a marked stress-threshold cultivated through strength and conditioning, a well-stacked physical structure that facilitates relaxation, and a high level of awareness and concentration cultivated through meditation.

When times are good, the short passage above may suffice. You've got few inhibitions to momentary insight. But I want you prepared for war, so that, rain or shine, good days or bad, you can extract as much quality as you want from this life. Live the shit out of it. Be weightless.

Presence and Personal Power—Arriving at the Threshold of Lightness

One might argue there are two ways to view power. One commonly accepted definition is that of an individual's ability to exert their will over their environment. An alternative view is that of one's ability to act in accordance with the nature of things – to see clearly and to act with integrated purpose.

There is tremendous power to sensing the way of things, to being aware, alert, and concentrated, and physically fit enough to act in accordance with one's intuitive impulses. In sports, we call this "the zone." Hippies call it going with the flow. Taoists call it effortless action. Artists call it passion. Lovers call it love. But regardless of domain, it's one's ability to sense and act in accordance with nature. It's nature proper. It's the river flowing downhill, rolling off rocks, finding paths of least resistance, and ever flowing, ever adapting. This is the power of warriors and sages. This is the power of Lightness.

Your Process

You now have the key mind-body principles and tools of The Weightlessness Spectrum—of personal transformation, peak performance, and integration. In the next scroll, The Process Scroll, I'll help you translate these into practical, actionable, and personalized prescriptions that design your own growth process.

In The Integration Scroll thereafter, I'll discuss how these tools apply to life beyond training, and the subtle steps that help translate your cultivated mind-body capacities into improved presence and performance in life.

The Process Scroll

“

Change does not roll in on wheels of inevitability but come through continuous struggle.
—Martin Luther King, Jr.

The Process Scroll is your personal manual for change. It takes all that you've learned thus far and thrusts you into your own journey of transformation. We deviate here from the philosophy, the biology, and the abstract theories of Weightlessness to personalize the process for YOU. Today matters and your future is the sum total of your efforts today, tomorrow, the day after that. This is a practical, actionable framework for your personal transformation. One hundred days from now, you could be looking back with regret, or looking forward to what's to come with a whole new set of tools. Take the leap.

The premise of this book isn't to dissect and scrutinize the science behind each aspect of development, though I hope that each chapter bleeds with both clear empirical validity as well as well-researched and filtered scientific information. Each pillar of Weightlessness, the science and principles of transformation, the foundations of nutrition, and the essence of Lightness, if elaborated in detail, would take up tens of volumes.

We've all read books on nutrition, fitness, and meditation. Each one is a comprehensive analysis of that particular domain but fails miserably in drawing relevance and integration to the whole person. This last detail is the premise and focus of this book. And between this scroll and The Integration Scroll that follows, I aim to remedy that issue.

As such, I'll be alluding to energy systems in the body, priorities in movement, and aspects of mental development that the student must research if they really want to understand in depth. There are limitations to what a book of this nature can cover with integrity without becoming a compendium of all science everywhere. But I'll leave many breadcrumbs in these pages that can serve as launch points for those who want to delve more deeply into particulars, while I'll focus my energy here on how exactly all these worlds culminate in one human being for greatest impact and upside. And that is through intelligent programming of a Weightlessness process.

So, let's start at the beginning. Assessments matter. Plans matter. Imbalances matter. We're about to discuss all of these in detail, along with supplementing your program with the appropriate level of nutrition. But none of them are the whole picture. We'll be discussing a plan that looks at a 100-day commitment, though it could certainly apply to a shorter or far longer timeframe.

As we progress, let's not forget that while training and nutrition are critical factors in cultivating weightlessness, they're not the whole. Don't mistake the finger for the moon. The other twenty-three hours of the day are the true domain of Weightlessness; training is merely preparation. And nothing, no amount of strength training or meditation or stretching trumps your personal answer at the end of the day or, to be more accurate, in this very moment, to the question:

"Are you weightless?"

Nutrition Filters

In *In Pursuit of Weightlessness* I go into detail regarding calorie shifting, carb cycling, intermittent fasting, and insulin control that I don't care to repeat here for the sake of offering fresh content. I'd refer you there first as a consistent, descriptive resource.

Weightlessness nutrition provides a structured approach that leads to intuitive self-regulation after a short time, empowering you to design your body and enhance your performance without yo-yo dieting, guilt for eating something you think is bad, or fear of unwanted weight gain. I'd also refer you to Ori Hofmekler's works: *The Warrior Diet* and *Burn the Fat, Feed the Muscle* for some of the science behind fasting and calorie shifting that complements this approach.

Here, I'll focus strictly on implementation—the *How To*. The Weightlessness approach to nutrition isn't meant to be a rote, follow-along diet. It's meant to be a principle-based, progressive plan that leads to an intuitive ability to eat for both health and performance. The crux of the diet is, like nearly all other effective diets, consuming real food and insulin management. Many people study the diet or practice Weightlessness for a time and make the mistake of thinking Weightlessness nutrition is a restrictive diet that falls on the extreme end of self-control. It isn't.

WEIGHTLESSNESS NUTRITION

STAGE 1: DETOX & METABOLIC RESET	STAGE 2: BODY TRANSFORMATION	STAGE 3: WEIGHTLESS NUTRITION
APPLY ~2 WEEKS	APPLY FOR 4–6 WEEKS (OR UNTIL OPTIMAL BODY COMPOSITION)	ONGOING (CONTINUE WITH PRIOR BASE)
• VEGETABLES, MEAT, FISH, OR EGGS . . . ONLY • EAT UNPROCESSED WHOLE FOODS • WATER, BLACK COFFEE, AND TEA OKAY • NO PORTION OR FREQUENCY CONTROLS • NO SUGAR OR GRAINS NOTE: YOU MUST ACTIVELY INCREASE YOUR FAT INTAKE (WITH AN EMPHASIS ON OMEGA-3S): FISH, AVOCADO, WHOLE EGGS, BUTTER, OLIVE OIL ARE OKAY. THIS FACILITATES KETOSIS.	• CONTINUE WITH STAGE 1, BUT ADD: • CARBS POST WORKOUT • ONE DAY PER WEEK CHEAT DAY • SKIP BREAKFAST ON OCCASION FOR MORE FAT LOSS	• FRUIT, BEANS, LEGUMES, YOGHURT, NUTS, SEEDS CAN ALL BE REINTEGRATED IN SMALL QUANTITIES AS DESIRED. • LISTEN TO YOUR APPETITE, EAT WHEN HUNGRY, BE MINDFUL OF GENUINE CRAVINGS. • DAIRY IS OK IN SMALL DOSES (IT'S A GOOD WEIGHT GAINER, NOT GREAT FOR FAT LOSS.) • GRAINS AND SUGARS CAUSE INFLAMMATION IN THE BODY AND SHOULD BE CONSUMED SPARINGLY.

All of us should aim for stage three nutrition—a relaxed, intuitive way of eating the things you like while maintaining health, body composition, and performance, which isn't an altogether separate diet from stage one and two but is rather a compounding and smart application of both as needed. Once you gain a visceral feeling for the effects of grains, sugars, and processed foods on your body composition and performance it becomes very easy to regulate as needed. Normally, we adhere 100% to stage one or stage two for four to eight weeks (if also training, stage one might only last two weeks before moving to stage two). We do this so that we've got a long enough data set to monitor the effects of adding food types and see concrete shifts in body composition and performance.

Patterns matter. They enable us to move from rote rule following to intuitive on-the-fly adjustments as needed. These stages are not exclusive states, and this is an important, all-too-often overlooked aspect. When comfortably at stage three, meaning you're content with your body composition and overall mental and physical performance, it doesn't mean you abandon all reason and eat like an idiot. There are always needs for corrective measures when you loosen the reigns.

So what might this look like? This might mean that once you achieve a body composition you're happy with and want to loosen the reigns to enjoy life a bit more, occasionally revisiting stage one or two might be necessary to detox or burn a bit more fat. But by now, you should note that these aren't distinct, independent plans. Each stage teaches you how to eat (for a time) to elicit certain responses. It means if you eat too much one day, then the following day you may need to reduce grains and sugars, or even intermittent fast until dinner to compensate.

It also means that if you're preempting an unavoidable gluttonous anomaly like Thanksgiving dinner, that you can go into it with a caloric deficit. How do you do that? Intermittent fast beforehand or reduce grains and sugars for a day or two leading up to it. The former approach works on the mathematics of calorie metabolism, and the second on insulin control as a means of energy storage reduction.

This isn't yo-yo dieting as compulsive self-sabotage. It's intelligent nutrient management to sustain metabolism and performance. The better you understand the role of grains and sugars, and high-calorie or deficit periods, the more intuitively you can navigate unplanned anomalies without falling off the wagon and needing to return to a strict, drudging phase of eating. That compulsion last mentioned is yo-yo dieting in the worst sense, for one lacks the ability to eat without guilt. You must trade guilt for knowledge if Weightlessness will grow in your life to include diet and nutrition.

So, a basic self-assessment goes as follows:

1. Do you feel lethargic, stiff, heavy, and/or distracted and cloudy headed? Are the whites of your eyes a color besides clear white?

If yes, then begin with stage one for two to four weeks. (Four weeks is only recommended if training volume is three days or less per week, and you're getting sufficient sleep. Stage one isn't designed for long-term fat loss. If sustained, you'll likely experience a drop in metabolism and energy.

2. Do you have more than 10-15 pounds to lose in order to reach your body composition target but don't feel the symptoms from stage one?

Then utilize stage two. The addition of grains (notice I'm not saying carbs…all vegetables are carbohydrates, as are fruits, beans (much of), legumes, etc.), ideally complex ones, can dramatically improve workout recovery, sleep, and overall energy when consumed post training.

3. Are you looking to make the most dramatic gains in the shortest period of time?

Utilize stage two.

4. Are you feeling any other symptoms, like leaky gut, acid reflux, poor digestion in general, lose stool, constipation, anxiety?

Cut coffee and everything else but water and stick to stage one for two to four weeks (max).

Stage one can, in the beginning, offer rapid fat loss benefits, but these won't be long-lived. You will, at some point, experience a decline in energy and metabolism UNLESS you are actively eating a very high-fat diet. This is easier said than done, and most people don't take the time to study the matter enough to make sure they're getting ample vegetables and healthy fats. The hack for this issue is stage two.

Stage two is the sustainable fat loss and body composition optimization plan. Don't assume that just because you see immediate results with stage one, that it's your all-purpose savior when you feel guilty about gaining fat. It isn't. There's a reason stage one is referred to as a detox process, while stage two is a body transformation process. Stage two is far more effective for sustaining fat loss without calorie shifting (or fasting) in stage three (i.e., regular intermittent fasting).

5. Are you content with your body composition and overall performance? Do you have less than 12% body fat as a man? Less than 17% as a woman?

Then you're free to be at stage three if you like, so long as energy seems sufficient and the mind seems clear and focused. This implies that you understand the premises of stage one and two and can implement them as needed for corrective purposes or peak conditioning.

Programming Within the W Spectrum

This is consistently one of the most challenging aspects of studying Weightlessness according to most of my clients. Even after years of regular practice, and even through several 100-day immersions, designing or augmenting one's program in a way that is consistent with the W

Spectrum still presents challenges. And fair enough. It's one thing to design a progressive strength plan, or a flexibility or meditation routine; it's altogether different when you're looking to design integration and peak performance while still acknowledging individual differences and starting points. Let's look at the process.

1. Assess Yourself

We accept tests, assessments, and feedback in almost all domains in life, especially those of a professional or occupational nature. We understand that assessments improve self-awareness and performance. Yet, we avoid them like the plague when it comes to physical or mind-body performance. If this sounds like you, please consider this for yourself:

How can you get where you want to go if you have no accurate insight as to where you are?

Today, countless free resources online, programs, diet plans, and even mindfulness apps are available. And these are indeed great resources. But how do you determine if/when they're relevant for you in your current state? There are progressions to development, certain things that beginners need more than experts, and vice versa.

One of the main reasons few people make progress on bodybuilding routines is because most professionals are taking potent anabolic steroids and have far more developed muscles. So when a novice hits a professional's routine, rather than see progress, they tend to see little results and experience ongoing fatigue. Without the drugs, which artificially sustain anabolism, your muscles fail to hypertrophy without less frequent training and a calorie dense diet.

There's also no balancing of powers. The logic runs that if weight training is good, then more is better. If stretching is good, then more is better. If meditation is good, then more is better. And this may even be true up to a point, given zero life contexts.

But the reality is that we all tend to focus on our strengths and neglect our weaknesses. It's exceedingly difficult to get most gym buffs to stretch and most meditation practitioners to embrace high-intensity training. How do you determine, based on your current, holistic performance, if your time is better spent emphasizing and progressing strength or flexibility, given very real time constraints, or meditation over flexibility for that matter?

The W spectrum is designed to answer just that. It doesn't merely address what you ought to do to extract the most payoff from the least amount of work, but it tells you when and in what proportion to do it. This is invaluable feedback and direction for those of us with limited time and high performance goals (in the broadest sense).

For even though more strength training could get results, you may be limiting your personal growth dramatically by prioritizing it. You're a multidimensional being whose integrated performance trumps your capacity in any one pillar by heaps and mounds. You may meditate daily, but if your strength and conditioning metrics are at level one, it's unlikely you'll manage to activate a meditative mind under pressure.

The assessment below contains a few metrics in each pillar. Conceivably, other metrics could have been chosen, and one or two of these could possibly be replaced, BUT, they serve the requisites to a very high degree of testing well-rounded pillar performance and integration. In other words, it's an excellent working model—not an absolute one.

Each of these exercises should be executed according to the guidelines that follow and should adhere strictly to the biomechanical and structural guidelines we covered in The Transformation Scroll. 10 full range pushups with neutral spine and palms centered at your power line trumps 30 crummy pushups any day of the week. And there are a million ways to make them crummy. So… don't cheat!

WEIGHTLESSNESS SELF-ASSESSMENT

STRENGTH TEST	LEVEL ONE	LEVEL TWO	LEVEL THREE *
☐ RUN 1 KILOMETER IN...	>5 MIN	<5 MIN	<4 MIN
☐ DEAD LIFT	<BODYWEIGHT	BODYWEIGHT X 1 REP	BODYWEIGHT X 5 REPS
☐ 100 BURPEES (NO PUSHUP) IN...	>12 MINS	<12 MINS	<8 MINS
☐ PUSH UPS	<20	20-30	30+ OR 1 ARM PUSH
☐ DEEP SQUATS (ASS TO HEELS - 3 SECOND PAUSE AT BOTTOM)	—	5-10	10+ OR 1 LEG SQUAT
FLEXIBILITY TEST	**LEVEL ONE**	**LEVEL TWO**	**LEVEL THREE ***
☐ ACTIVE STRAIGHT LEG RAISE | ARMS OVERHEAD	NO	YES	YES
☐ FLAT PALM FORWARD BEND	NO	YES	YES
☐ DEEP SQUAT | HEELS ON GROUND	NO	YES	YES
☐ FRONT SPLITS	NO	NO	YES 170 DEGREES+
☐ CENTER SPLITS	NO	NO	YES 160 DEGREES+
MEDITATION TEST	**LEVEL ONE**	**LEVEL TWO**	**LEVEL THREE ***
☐ 10 BREATHS IN...	<5 MINS	5 MINS+	8 MINS+
☐ REVERSE COUNT OF...	<500	500+	800+

*LIGHTNESS CANDIDATE

(Note: Many of these resources will be provided at www.weightlessness.co for those who want to print out and work through them!)

Guidelines for the Assessment:

- Perform each of the strength exercises in the exact order shown within the same session. This not only tests individual metrics but also compound performance. Rest exactly three minutes between each exercise.
- Take no more than 3 sets to reach your max dead lift, resting no more than two minutes between each preparatory set.
- For the pushups and squats, any pause at the peak of either exercise counts as a rest and means the set is over. Reps must be continuous or they don't count (that's not the same for the burpees, which should be completed in full, with a little rest as possible).
- Skip any exercise you don't know or aren't comfortable with. Any skipped exercises default you to level one of strength.
- Rest five minutes and perform the stretching techniques. If you can perform the first three, you're at level two. If you can perform all five, you're at level three. There are no gradations; it's a pass-fail test. All should demonstrate key structural cues—neutral spine, untucked tailbone, hip-knee-feet alignment, etc.
- Your slowest breath count and your highest reverse count can be tested externally to your strength and flexibility test. You should not perform the breathing test after training; it will give a false, low read.
- For slow breathing, take ten slow, continuous, even breaths (equal inhale and exhale length) and time them. Make sure you're using abdominal breathing, keeping the chest relaxed. Sit or stand with erect posture.
- If you don't already know your highest reverse count, it's unlikely you're at level two or three. Test a reverse 500 count. If you falter, you're at level one. Most will start at level one. If you can manage 500, you can attempt level two prescriptions, but if they aren't consistent within training, revert to a count of 300 or lower.
- Plot your overall performance on The Weightlessness Spectrum:

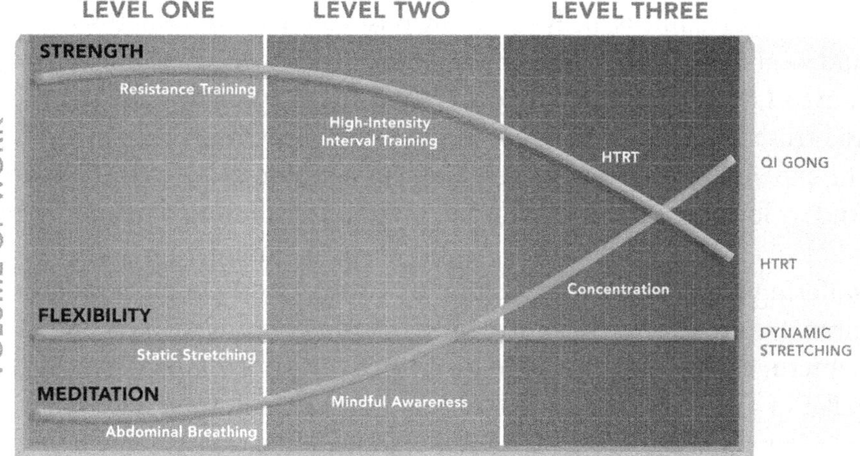

(Note: You're only as strong as your weakest link. If you can deadlift or run at level three, but cannot do the deep squat due to range and flexibility, you're at level one for both strength and flexibility. If you can test to level three concentration but slow breathing cannot exceed five minutes for ten breaths, you're at level one for meditation.)

Crutches and Liabilities

Over a lifetime of effort to find our places in this world, we gravitate toward those domains and activities that we find a rapid modicum of control over. In so doing, we tend to hone and then heavily rely on one pillar at the expense of others. As long as I've been in this game, people who enter my programs with equal performance at level two or three across all pillars are extremely rare. Generally speaking, the higher performance metrics for strength or meditation come at the expense of the other.

Those who emphasize strength embrace and cultivate the stress side of the Tao of Weightlessness. Those who've developed a capacity for meditation and, with it, breath control and sustained and focused awareness have cultivated the sensitivity side of the Tao. These are, outside of the weightless individual, antithetical values in practice.

Tension is the enemy of relaxation, and awareness the antithesis of tension. So, we find our niche and ride it out for years until environment, work, and social relations make it clear that our toolkit is insufficient.

Some people never challenge the status quo enough to make the realization that they need to develop untrained pillars. There's simply no obvious correlation.

This dynamic is likely more obvious if we discuss strengths as assets and weaknesses as liabilities, but for the purposes of cultivating a growth mindset, the word *asset,* while accurate, doesn't provide enough insight. The truth is that, over time, we come to rely heavily on our strengths at the expense of our weaknesses. We lean on them as we would a crutch. And as long as we can rely on them, no one will notice that we're not whole. We won't even notice. We just keep on, dominating if we're lucky, suffering if we're not, and assume that we're good people because our strengths are strong. But you're only as strong as your weakest link. And sometimes, you must remove the crutch, or underemphasize a strong pillar in order to cultivate and learn to integrate new tools and resources.

Your weaknesses are liabilities. Some define assets in the financial world as things that put money in your pocket every month and liabilities things that take it out. According to this definition, real estate that doesn't earn income or have cash flow, a house you live in, for example, wouldn't be considered an asset, while a rental home would be. Liabilities bleed you. They hold you back. They counteract the power and influence of your strengths. Again, this may never be felt if you seclude yourself from a variety of stressors or have a high degree of control over your environment. But for the problem solver, the innovator, the warrior, the lover, these weaknesses will be exposed in the worst of ways at the worst of times.

The Weightlessness Spectrum is a model of both integration and performance. It contains the metrics and structure needed to peak-out each of your primary pillars. It also contains the filters by which you can determine not just what you ought to do, but when to do it, and to what degree.

We all need meditation. But is it of immediate priority for you? Well, not if you're at level one in strength. Is strength a crutch you rely on, but with meditation, you're a laggard? Then to balance and integrate your mind-body portfolio, you shouldn't aggressively focus on strength metrics, which you find the most exciting; you should somewhat reduce that emphasis for more meditation and flexibility work until they catch up. This is hard work.

Integration is a byproduct of balance and performance. It's a brilliant manifestation of honed mental and physical faculties that create a sense of ease and power in daily life. Some say experience becomes far richer. Some say their insight, awareness, and influence at work grows tremendously. And some talk about the sense of mind-body connection, a unified will, where thought and action are one and the same.

Integration can be designed, but it cannot be forced. It isn't a skill; it's a manifested state of experience that stems from the cultivation of skills within each pillar. We must never forget that our biology didn't evolve in modern contexts. Our DNA evolved and our epigenetic expressions adapted over millions of years in environments that rewarded mobility, physical power, awareness, insight, focus, and holistic, integrated action. We cannot find our true selves, our path forward, without embracing the past within us.

2: Appropriate Your Plan

While this continues to be one of the most challenging aspects of practicing Weightlessness independently (according to long-standing trainees), it isn't as bad as it seems. You're armed with an explicit lighthouse that is your assessment. And here's the great value add of the assessment: it's also your prescription. This doesn't mean your program should be reduced to practicing the test; it means that the assessment should heavily dictate how you prioritize both individual technical gaps as well as pillars as a whole.

As you know now, The Weightlessness Spectrum is a progressive, prescriptive framework of development. Each level of performance within each pillar develops new skills that are—and this is very important—PROGRESSIVE. This is what many people overlook not just in Weightlessness but also in most training methods.

I'm asked all of the time if people should run, if they should do HIIT training, what I think about jumping rope, and what I think about kettlebell training, to name a few. There's no way for me to say anything intelligent on this abstract. All movement is good (unless it's not). If those people are asking about the exercises alone, sure, they're all fine. If they're asking if they're appropriate for them at this particular time, well that's a different question altogether and one that requires a personal assessment.

The scope of Weightlessness isn't to prepare you for all possible physical contingencies. It's to give you a strength and performance edge. If someone wants to run a marathon, for example, and they didn't grow up in the Tarahumara tribe in northern Mexico, then they're undertaking a specialized form of training. I say specialized despite the obvious biomechanical proclivity the human body has toward running, because going from an untrained state to running twenty-six continuous miles places an extreme amount of stress on your frame and your cardiovascular system.

Everyone worries about their cardio. They worry about conditioning the muscles. They're unaware of the bone and tendon conditioning required to run long distances without injury. And while most people can condition the stamina aspects of a long run in just a few months to half a year, bone and tendon adaptations may take far longer. This then becomes a specialized practice.

Kettlebell training is similar. Most movements within kettlebell training are gross motor movements that work full range ballistically. Is this bad? Not in and of itself. Is it bad for you? Probably. Swinging heavy weights quickly without sufficient structural development is a recipe for serious injury. And yes, many people get injured practicing them. Kettlebell practitioners don't often discriminate on their audience; they frame the training as a common good. But in its place of origin in Russia, kettlebell training was designed and integrated for elite performance, in particular for those preparing for combat, where the body needs such ballistic preparation. Ballistic weight training IS integrated in Weightlessness training, but not prior to Lightness Training due to the inherent risks. Risk is relative.

Weightlessness will, however, help condition the foundations of long-distance running and kettlebell training as well as the power mechanics inherent in all other forms of movement, but it avoids the specifics so as to be of the greatest possible value for the greatest number and reduce the risk of injury. It's important that you take this into account in your program design.

The point at which your program deviates from broad vectors and minimalistic efforts, for example the point at which you add aerobics, kettlebell training, boxing, football, etc. is the point at which you're now practicing two things: Weightlessness + name your craft. This is perfectly okay, but it does make it harder to identify prime movers of performance with added variables. Make sure that what's designed into your W protocol is simple, measurable, and holistic, and remain aware of how outside, specialized practices impact your targeted, measurable performance metrics.

I'll give three sample workouts below. These are general samples and don't take into account any individual differences. In a healthy individual at each of the three levels of performance, these would generally serve well as they are. That is, they could get you to the next level of performance if you adhere strictly to them for four to six weeks. None of them are intended to be lifelong routines. Each is a graduated version of YOU.

They signify meaningful changes and shifts in your mind-body portfolio that simply cannot be hacked, meaning that someone at level one could simply not accidently test at level two, and implement a level two workout fruitfully. Sure, you could practice level two and level three workouts, but if you haven't cultivated the structural stability designed in level one, or the anaerobic capacity in level two, then you're unlikely to make good use of a level three workout across any of the pillars without injury or fruitless practice, for level three assumes you have developed prior foundational skills.

Further, these assume someone is balanced across all pillars. Your personal program would need to take into account your crutches and liabilities and emphasize lagging metrics/pillars if you had a marked imbalance.

Note: To remind, Weightlessness isn't a workout; it's a process. So, the prescriptions below should not be interpreted as *THE* Weightlessness prescriptions. There are many ways to skin a cat. These are samples and will serve most people most of the time. The further you delve into the theories that preceded, the more variance you could include without compromising progress, including calisthenics-centric workouts that meet the load/resistance objectives listed or other forms of meditation. But the following will serve as minimalist prescriptions that take into account all mind-body considerations at each of the three levels on The Weightlessness Spectrum.

Level One Prescription:

WEIGHTLESSNESS LEVEL 1 PROGRAM		
WARM-UP Superset (3 sets)	Jumping Jacks - 1 min Supported Deep Squat Hold - 1 min	
STRENGTH 4 sets of 12 reps each	PUSH (Recommended: Push-Ups) PULL (Recommended: Bent Rows) SQUAT (Recommended: Weighted Lunges) PRESS (Recommended: Shoulder Press)	
CARDIO & TWIST | CORE	Burpees x 15 Plank - 1 min	Superset (4 sets)
FLEXIBILITY 3 Cycles	1st Forward Bend 3rd Deep Squat	2nd Hip Flexors 4th Front Splits
MEDITATION	Reverse Count from 100 Mindful Awareness - 5 min	*Rx | Supplement:* Highest Reverse Count or 10 Slowest Breaths

What this workout teaches you about program design at level one:

The strength and conditioning component of a level one workout focus on structural development with an emphasis on hypertrophy. You'll see similarities here to many bodybuilding workouts, with higher rep ranges per set and relatively low rest times (under one minute). All exercises are compound movements, and there's little need for wide variety at this stage. Because your musculoskeletal system is relatively untrained, meaning the muscles lack contractile force and stamina, and the bones and tension members that hold together your structure are not well conditioned, you're essentially performing the same, consistent workout a few days a week. This may not seem sexy, but it's, by far, the fastest way to building meaningful structure and integrity in the body.

A rep range of 10 to 12 implies that your frame cannot safely handle power-based loads. We stick strictly to the primary vectors, doing no more than one compound movement per vector, and seek to maximize muscular fatigue with mid to high rep range. We keep the sets under five per exercise so that you can get right back in the gym two days later and repeat the process.

If you do too much, you cannot effectively do it again. We want you to do it again, and quickly. There's no additional attention paid to core development (beyond the planks listed) or cardio because isolated abdominal development isn't required to stabilize the fundamentals in this rep range (and the core gets developed indirectly through compound exercises), and it isn't safe to do endurance-based activities if you don't have the structural integrity to hit level two metrics.

The flexibility component at level one is bare bones. Are you sitting a lot? Are you considerably overweight? Do you feel all around tight? This simple routine is rehabilitative. The bar is low, but meaningful. Even those at level three should always maintain these three stretches, which essentially reverse the negative effects of hours of sitting. The hip flexor-hamstring complex is in a constant shortened position when seated. This conditions your myofascia to distribute strain according to that default posture. You've molded yourself into a sitting, squatty person. The forward bend, the hip flexor stretch, and as an extension the front splits (which is little more than a combination of the first two stretches) allow you to remold this structure. The deep squat is integrated as preparation for level two, and as a hip-opening, ankle-mobilizing primer.

The meditative component is foundational. Mindful awareness is central (ideally in standing meditation posture), and with it, the mechanics of abdominal breathing. This should be done at least every workout, if not daily. Reverse counting and slow breathing can also be integrated at this stage but should not take precedent over the foundational standing meditation practice. They should each be given a few honest attempts each week and can even be done at odd times like on the subway or waiting for a meeting at work. But first, one must learn to activate diaphragmatic (abdominal) breathing to reduce tension and stress throughout and set the foundation for more aggressive practices.

Level Two Prescription:

WEIGHTLESSNESS LEVEL 2 PROGRAM		
WARM-UP Superset (3 sets)	Jumping Jacks - 1 min Deep Squat x 15	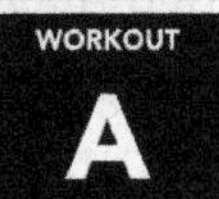
STRENGTH CIRCUIT 4 sets of 40 I 20 seconds (1 min max rest between sets)	PULL | 40 secs (Recommended: Bent Rows) REST 20 secs BURPEES | 40 secs (No Push Up) REST 20 secs PUSH | 40 secs (Recommended: Push Ups) REST 20 secs TWIST | CORE | 40 secs (1 Leg V-Sits)	
FLEXIBILITY 3 Cycles	1st Forward Bend 2nd Hip Flexors 3rd Deep Squat 4th Front Splits	
MEDITATION	Reverse Count from 100 Mindful Awareness - 5 min	*Rx | Supplement:* Highest Reverse Count or 10 Slowest Breaths
WARM-UP	Run 9 mins + 1 min Sprint	
STRENGTH 5 sets of 8-10 reps each INTERVAL 8 sets of 30 I 15 secs	SQUAT | (Recommended: Dead Lift or Weighted Squat) PRESS | (Recommended: Shoulder Press) CHOOSE ONLY ONE: BURPEES, HIGH KNEES, MOUNTAIN CLIMBERS, TWIST HOP (FOR EXAMPLE): BURPEES 30 secs on, REST 15 secs, BURPEES 30 secs on, REST 15 secs	
FLEXIBILITY 3 Cycles	1st Forward Bend 2nd Hip Flexors 3rd Deep Squat 4th Front Splits	
MEDITATION	Reverse Count from 100 Mindful Awareness - 5 min	*Rx | Supplement:* Highest Reverse Count or 10 Slowest Breaths

What this workout teaches you about program design at level two:

In the strength and conditioning component of level two we apply our new understanding of periodization. You're stronger, fitter, and therefore more capable of applying greater degrees of stress on the body. In other words, intensity is increasing. And as we discussed in The Strength Spectrum, there's an inverse relationship between intensity and frequency, and intensity and duration.

So you'll notice that while set number increases for strength sets, rep ranges also decrease slightly, AND you're not training the same exercises each workout. You need more time to recover, and due to the added intensity within each workout, you simply cannot cover everything needed within a 40- to 50-minute window.

Level two is also designed to emphasize both anaerobic endurance and aerobic conditioning. The simplest way to consider this progression is that if level one is where we learn to do something properly one time, level two is where we do it two times plus. We're not just adding stress to our bodies, we're sustaining it. Some call this strength-endurance. Some call it cardio. Both are fine descriptors and scientifically accurate. But simply put, we're learning to endure sustained stress.

This is as much mental as it is physical. As such, the two most efficient methods of sustaining stress, each of which equally valid insertions at this stage, are circuit training (adhering to 5 vector guidelines—shown in workout A) and high-intensity interval training (which may include calisthenics techniques that allow for sustained cardiovascular output, but may not be formal, load bearing movements such as jumping rope, mountain climbers, burpees, squat thrusts, high knees, wind sprints, etc.—shown in workout B).

The mechanism by which we elicit the cardiovascular response is reduced rest times. Condensing workload into a shorter timeframe places much higher requirements on cardiovascular performance. Everyone who first attempts interval training feels this. This takes time to build up, but the objective is simple: Do the same work in a shorter time by reducing rest and recovery times. This means, by necessity, that total workload may also need to decrease, but it doesn't mean total stress on the system (intensity) is reduced.

The flexibility component at level two is more of the same, with the addition of level three targets for practice and preparation. At this stage, the forward bend, the hip flexor stretch, and the deep squat should all be proficient (though deep squat may need further technical development regarding neutral spine, splaying the knees, and ankle mobility). But we add in here front and center splits, with an emphasis on front splits first.

If you're on track and hitting metrics here, then stretching within your workouts doesn't need to be too time-consuming. They should come between strength and meditation practices, and should work through the key stretches, holding each for only a few breaths, until three or four cycles are complete. If, however, your stretching is lagging, you'll need supplementary at-home sessions when you sit in these positions until they open up for you, as discussed in The Flexibility Spectrum.

The level two meditation prescription, while including all three key practices (mindful awareness via standing meditation, slow breathing, and reverse counting), should emphasize slow breathing practice, which is our awareness tool. Level two assumes proper abdominal breathing technique (developed at level one), as well as foundational mind-body awareness. It looks to enhance that mind-body connection along with conscious control over physical tension.

The practices of standing meditation and slow breathing (usually seated upright) are perfect complements in the mindful awareness game. Slow breathing as a skill, however, also has extraordinary anti-stress effects. As the breath drops and elongates, tension falls from the shoulders, and the mind and body have to relax in order to reduce oxygen requirements. Thereafter, healing begins and energy increases.

Level Three Prescription:

WEIGHTLESSNESS LEVEL 3 PROGRAM

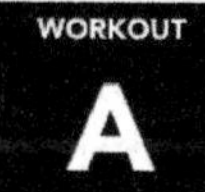

WARM-UP Superset (3 sets)	**Jumping Jacks** - 1 min **Deep Squat** x 50 **Push Ups** x 50	
STRENGTH 5 sets of indicated reps (except CORE) Rest 2-3 min between sets & exercises. Adjust weight to match desired rep range.	**PUSH (1) |** (Recommended: Bench Press) (reps per set) 15,10, 5, 5, 5 **PUSH (2) |** (Recommended: Dips) (reps per set) 15, 10, 5, 5, 5 **PULL |** (Recommended: Pull Ups) (reps per set) 10, 8, 5, 5, 5 **TWIST | CORE |** V-Sits x 50	
FLEXIBILITY 3 Cycles	1st **Forward Bend** 2nd **Hip Flexors** 3rd **Deep Squat**	*Rx | Supplement:* 5 Cycles Front & Center Splits
MEDITATION	Reverse Count from 100 Mindful Awareness - 5 min	*Rx | Supplement:* Highest Reverse Count or 10 Breaths

WORKOUT
B

WARM-UP	Run 9 mins + 1 min **Sprint**	
STRENGTH 5 sets of indicated reps (except SQUAT and CORE)	**SQUAT |** (Recommended: Dead Lift) (reps per set) 10, 8, 5, 5, 5 **PRESS |** (Recommended: Shoulder Press) (reps per set) 10, 8, 5, 5, 5 **JUMP SQUAT |** 4 sets of 15 reps (<1min rest btw sets) **TWIST | CORE |** Crunches x 50 Twist Hops x 50	
FLEXIBILITY 3 Cycles	1st **Forward Bend** 2nd **Hip Flexors** 3rd **Deep Squat**	*Rx | Supplement:* 5 Cycles Front & Center Splits
MEDITATION	Reverse Count from 100 Mindful Awareness - 5 min	*Rx | Supplement:* Highest Reverse Count or 10 Breaths

What this workout teaches you about program design at level three:

At level three we're at the precipice of Lightness Training, and we're beginning to incorporate Lightness principles. The strength and conditioning component at level three is what we can cleanly place in the strength training camp, less so the hypertrophy camp. We're not focused here on building and shaping, and we already have a strong structural foundation, so our prime focus is myofibrillar hypertrophy (which has more density, but less volume than sarcoplasmic hypertrophy).

We want to strengthen and increase the contractile force of our muscles *without* a significant increase in overall bodyweight or size. This maximizes strength to weight ratio and produces the effect of physical lightness. This is best accomplished by low volume (reduced reps), high-intensity resistance training within the five vectors.

You'll also notice a meaningful shift in load application for each set. This doesn't necessarily correlate to rep range and, therefore, often confuses those new to legit strength training. Max effort strength training is truly a mind-body practice, and one that takes on a tremendous amount of stress. Your objective—I've said this many times, and it's worth repeating—*is not to get a workout*. Your objective is to get stronger.

At higher levels, this is done primarily by applying greater amounts of load within key compound movements, thereby recruiting and damaging a higher ratio of fast twitch muscle fiber. This isn't a volume game; it's a skill and precision game. Sets 1 and 2 are progressive primers. They should feel easy, and build confidence for set 3, which is your all-out, tear-the-house-down effort. That's right, one set (set 3) is your heaviest, hardest, ball-busting effort. Use set 3 to aim for your personal records each session. Those that come before are primers (warmups), those that come after are there to ensure max muscular fatigue.

You'll also notice that rest times are longer that those in the previous levels. This is by design. When lifting heavy, we can only draw from ATP directly stored within the muscles doing the work, and this is well exhausted (in theory) within fifteen to thirty seconds of max-effort work, and much faster if we're going for one-rep max.

In practice, this may burn out even faster with very intense exercises like a one-rep max of a deadlift. There's no opportunity to rejuvenate or produce more energy without some rest and breathing. You may have phenomenal cardio, and after performing your max lift, you may feel like you're breathing fine within thirty seconds. This doesn't mean your muscles have had time to convert glycogen into the volumes of ATP needed for another max effort lift.

Some of my clients who try advanced workouts get frustrated for the long rest periods. If this is you, you're not ready for strength development in particular and advanced Weightlessness Training in general. You'll need to put yourself in conditions that seem wasteful or unnecessary sometimes to tap the body's higher potentials. This is a perfect case in point where you "knowing your body" is totally irrelevant. The regeneration of ATP in volumes that allow for max effort takes time. You can't "know it" until you conscientiously do it. We need to move beyond a *workout* mindset and into a *strength* one.

The workout above has multiple exercises for a certain vector. It may be justifiable (though not necessary) to increase set volume (not rep volume) by incorporating multiple exercises per group. I'd recommend your performance is heavily monitored and focused on increasing the number of max efforts in one key lift in each vector every week to ensure you're not replacing productivity with variety.

Some people can productively handle more volume than others. Some need very little. Your strength metrics and general energy (and body feel) during the other twenty-three hours of the day will be your guiding light for this. If you can improve your metrics weekly with a low volume routine (which implies neuromuscular and musculoskeletal adaptation and development) and you've got enough energy outside the gym for work, family, and friends… why add more?

If you're doing more work, seeing results, and lack energy the other twenty-three hours a day… why not see if you can hit your metrics with less work? But if you're doing the extra work and not hitting metrics, you need to audit everything you're doing. This is a failing program.

Flexibility at level three is predominantly focused on hip opening via the center splits and opening the front line of the body through back bends. Level one addresses the hip flexor/hamstring complex. Level two goes deeper into the front and rear lines of the body from the core down with the front splits, and primes the center splits with the deep squat. At level three, we look to activate full range of mobility for the legs and the front line of the body.

Excellent complementary stretches to integrate are the butterfly stretch, the cobra (to prep the back bend), and hanging (from a bar). This is not exclusive work. You can always add supplementary stretches, but these are of central focus. While the backbend is not considered a prerequisite for Lightness like the front and center splits, it should be integrated and trained at level three to prepare for rear dynamic stretches.

The meditation metrics at level three are, pardon my French, fucking brutal. You cannot game these. They are monster metrics and ones that are chosen due to their surgical precision in developing different mental faculties. Each offers magical insights, capacities, and perspective shifts, as well as prepares you for the more challenging game of qigong within Lightness Training.

You have by now built the foundation of standing structure, breathing mechanics, and capacity for mind-body connection and awareness. At level three, while continuing to progress all of the above, we focus more on high levels of focus and willpower. Reverse counting is our vehicle for both. This doesn't mean we neglect the other practices. Slow breathing and standing meditation are still staples. But progressing to an 800 plus reverse-count (ideally 1,000+) with great consistency is an altogether different state of focus.

Balancing Pillars

If you're not an expert in the mind-body development domain or if you're simply human, then your performance in each pillar is likely unbalanced with the others. As we discussed in The Weightlessness Scroll, we all tend to put our focus where we feel rewarded for our efforts. This is human. Few people actively seek environments that challenge their sense of security and self-esteem. But the deleterious effects of swimming in small ponds with weaker fish or no other fish at all should seem obvious. It's absolutely impossible to avoid delusions of grandeur and false confidence.

The assessment you've taken will dispel any delusion you may have coming into this game. And if it does open your eyes to the crutches you've been relying on or the liabilities you've been neglecting, take it as a gift rather than a shot to your ego. At this stage, you and I don't need to be the best; we need to be honest. After being assessed, many clients over many years have asked how they did. My only response was that we're here looking for honesty so that we can design *the better*. We're not comparing you to anyone else. We're comparing *you* today to *you* tomorrow.

No matter where you are, you're here now. And this is a phenomenal starting point. But no one is the same. And this needs to be accounted for. I've worked with athletes at level three in strength who cannot pass level one in meditation or flexibility. I've worked with experienced meditators who cannot pass level one in strength. And I've worked with everyone in between. We rely on our strengths. We neglect our weaknesses. Integration arises once we remedy those imbalances.

The good news is that if you're capable of programming each pillar individually, then it's rather simple to program all together. The assessment IS the prescription.

If you're at level three in strength and level one in meditation, where should your focus lie? Yes, meditation. Implement a maintenance strength prescription until meditation catches up. If you're at level three in meditation and level one strength or flexibility, same question. Yes, emphasize the other two. This is an objective assessment. There's no room left for personal preference. Once you're aware of considerable imbalances, it's your first priority, rather than progress your crutches (those advanced pillars you've come to rely on), to elevate and minimize your liabilities.

If you're at level two, let's say for flexibility and meditation, and level one in strength, it's perfectly reasonable to continue to train, program, and progress on your crutches, but its critical you progress your strength as well and, ideally, with greater attention. If you wind up progressing to level three on flexibility and meditation while strength remains at 1, then you're not programming efficiently.

If all move up in tandem, then you're in a reasonable range of effective program design. If strengths are getting stronger, and weaknesses remain as they were, it's time for a training audit. It's okay in such cases to overweight your weakness, or to add additional work outside of your prescription if, for example, meditation is a lagging metric. Do it every day, no problem. But don't pat yourself on the back if you move from level two to level three in strength, but flexibility remains at level one.

A quick reminder: The same does NOT go for strength. Adding more doesn't mean better results once a reasonable program is in place. Always remember that stress requires periodization for recovery and adaptation, while sensitivity (cultivated through meditation) requires consistency. Meditation often benefits by increased frequency, while more frequent strength sessions can cut into recovery and stall adaptation/overcompensation (unless volume is adjusted down considerably).

With such imbalances, you'll need to mix and match some of the pillar prescriptions above, and fill your workout with the appropriate level for each. This is rather easy when, again, the assessment IS the prescription.

A Much Needed Reality Check

The reason for The Weightlessness Spectrum, well, one among many, is that it not only gives us a sliding scale of progress but also tells us that there are no static achievements in this game. There's no such thing as maintenance; we're in a constant state of internal flux. We may not see it or feel it from day to day, but there are antithetical forces, hormones, and neurotransmitters that keep your system in tight balance. On a small scale, these changes are difficult to observe. Over weeks or months, they're glaringly obvious.

Every time you relax for a couple weeks, or deviate from your diet, or experience illness or injury, your performance changes. YOU ARE NOT ALWAYS THE SAME PERSON. You might have been at a level three in strength before, but if you just got over pneumonia, you're quite likely at level one. If you broke your ankle and are just now getting back to the gym, level one. Have you experienced a serious episode of stress or burnout? Level one meditation (even if you crushed your level three metrics last year!). What you did on your best day in the past means fuck-all. You're here now; own it.

Many find this frustrating, especially those who prefer a pat on the back over an honest mirror. Many find it hard to start off at a lower level than they last remember. But the reality is those people either rarely start up again because the pressure of performing at your previous peak is daunting, or they jump into a workout they believe they're at and get injured.

This is one of the largest inhibitors in meditation practice. It's extremely difficult to continue after time off because you remember the ease of connection and the stillness you could activate before. And now you know you'll have to face the monkey mind again. It's also hard for many people when they've let that fitness slip. The bro-ego takes over and stacks the bar with too much weight or cranks that treadmill up to top speed.

Be humble. Be honest. Stay hungry.

No absolute status of performance exists for any of us. Your level is simply how you perform on any given day (or within a period of days). Back in my fighting days, I'd use as a measure of my ability not what I could do on my best day, but how I performed on my worst, how I performed when I was sick with fever, hungry, injured, or heartbroken. These are the true measures because they account for real volatility in life.

Your best deadlift and your calmest mind are illusions that give a false read on who you are. Slow down, be patient, and subjugate your desire for progress to the objectivity of a holistic assessment over time.

3: Implement Your Plan

I've had tremendous success with 100-day committed programs. I think there are a few reasons for this and why you should consider that timeframe for yourself. First, given normal daily life, it's rare to find people who can put in full-time training. On four days a week for six weeks most people can experience tremendous body transformations. That's also a good timeline for meditation to reach a deep and practically relevant level. But it's not enough time for both. Adding pillars compounds the time required for each independently, unless someone has hours a day to dedicate to training.

100 days is also not so long that it becomes a monotonous, casually ongoing, long-term commitment. It's short enough to keep the edge, long enough to transform your life. And with that, it's long enough to acquire more than mere results, but to internalize many of the skills of performance within each pillar that will allow you to carry on and own Weightlessness for yourself. In short, it's a good place to start.

Does this mean you can't trial a program for four weeks? Nope. Does it mean you can't make this a lifelong vocation? Not at all. It just means that you can't expect life-changing results stemming from mind-body integrative training in four weeks, at least not results that stick. And it means that open-ended engagements almost always fizzle and fade.

Define your personal targets.
Choose an appropriate timeline.
Schedule it.

Stress-test it against the reality of those days when fatigue, stress, frustration, or indifference creep in because they will. And remove all obstacles that could become excuses for you to skip, alter, or reschedule your sessions. If you cannot keep a commitment to self, how can you expect to keep one toward anyone/anything else in life? It starts with showing up to self.

A reasonable plan on paper might look something like this (after taking the assessment):

Training

- Current Status: strength level one, flexibility level two, meditation level one
- Target in 100 days: Level two to three in strength, level three flexibility, level two to three in meditation
- Target for the next four weeks: level two strength (deadlift bodyweight. 20 plus pushups.)
- Don't just show up. Be there fully and fight for gains.

Diet

- Physique target: Lose 20 pounds of fat.
- Current Mental State: Cloudy. Tired.
- Target: Phase one detox for two weeks. Phase two transformation diet for four weeks. Reassess.
- Actions: Throw away sweets and simple sugars. Stock freezer with meat for the next month, hit the market or have veggies delivered twice a week.
- Fast until noon two days per week (nontraining days).
- Plan meals three days in advance during the work week.

Execution

- Train three days a week for first two weeks, then four days a week for four more.
- Train first thing in the morning, before breakfast. No excuses.
- If too tired one day, I go to the gym and breathe and stretch. I do not abandon ship. I show up to *me*.
- After first two weeks, apply phase two diet five days per week minimum. Relax with friends on the weekend.
- On Friday of week four, I take the assessment again. I repeat at the end of week eight and week twelve.
- My workout prescription is one hour; I do not plan any calls or meetings within thirty minutes of completion so as not to distract my meditation.

Inhibitors (What do I need to remove or avoid to succeed?)

- Avoid drinking alcohol at work dinners. Claim I'm on medication or have explosive diarrhea.
- Make sure the fridge is stocked so I'm not tempted to go to something bad.
- Limit social engagements for three to four weeks just to get my routine established.
- Leave work on time so I have time to rest and recover, and energy to train.
- Limit my conversations with Gretchen because she leaves me feeling stressed.

There's no single right way to write a plan, but one thing is certain—you need one. Assuming you'll assimilate the wide range of complex practices that we're discussing without structure and space to train effectively isn't reasonable. The more concrete your plan, the better. The more honest and aware you are about the real conditions of your life, the better.

If you travel for work, you shouldn't have a plan that doesn't fully assume and account for those constraints. Nothing should be a surprise. Make space for yourself. A workout is not just a workout. It's a stress stimulus and a point of connection. Put yourself in the best position so as to put everything you have into the workout, to train as fresh as possible. Consider the time and space around your workout so as to make it most effective, including diet, sleep, and tightly scheduled plans leading into or following the workout.

Last but not least: show up to your plan. No excuses.

4: Rinse and Repeat Every Four to Six Weeks

People who avoid honest feedback aren't serious about growth. The assessment is honest feedback. It's a phenomenal accountability tool to make sure you're showing up to your plan, as well as honest feedback as to the quality and intensity of your practice. On a very basic level it's good for us to hear "try harder" when we're not seeing the results we set out for.

After taking the assessment every four to six weeks, rinse and repeat. This doesn't mean you reassess your 100-day targets, it means you check your alignment with those targets. If you've progressed to level two in strength, you're in a new workout program for at least the next four weeks. Congrats. Same with the other two pillars. Give yourself an hour on the assessment weekend to review your original goals, to go over the assessments and plot your progress, and to audit how you've been showing up.

It's okay to be gracious with yourself if you've executed on plan (specific written plan) 100% and results weren't as expected. But if you fall short of your plan, you should take a hard look at why. And consider what you might expect from any plan if execution of it is the challenge. In such cases, more realistic targets should be set, or a doubling down and refocusing of efforts is called for. But try not to fall victim to the "I did my best" delusion (or the "something unexpected came up delusion"), when effort to execute is insufficient to get the results you're after.

I promised you something in The Transformation Scroll. I promised you discomfort. The nature of growth, both psychologically and physiologically is that discomfort is necessary. You know this. Remind yourself of this. And don't fall victim to thinking you don't have what it takes, that you're not sure if you've set the right targets, or that it's just not fun. Focus and finish! Practice finishing. Embrace the discomfort and double down.

5: Day 100

Celebrate. No matter how you performed, celebrate. Give yourself a needed release from the strict schedule and structure you've adhered to. Consider taking a week off and resting to allow full physical recovery and to remove the mental pressure to perform. Allow yourself to reorient and embrace training as something you get to do, not something you have to do. After 100 focused days, a disciplined routine can become rather tedious or rote and feel obligatory. Shake those cobwebs off. You've set the stage for a new beginning, one in which you're starting from a better place!

6: Day 101

Throw down a blank piece of paper and at the top write:

Targets for the next 100 days:

From Your Process to Life Integration

You now have the process diagnostics and prescriptive framework to integrate the pillars of Weightlessness and design your own growth plan. In the next scroll, The Integration Scroll, we'll address that elusive quality of integration, and introduce a few additional tools that help translate your elevated mind-body performance into better performance in life.

The Integration Scroll

> *Many things have a plurality of parts and are not merely a complete aggregate but instead some kind of a whole beyond its parts.*
> —Aristotle

The Integration Scroll addresses the intangible, unquantifiable attribute of cohesion of parts. An elusive gap exists between effort and insight, which is attainable but not coachable. That's where weightlessness lies. It's up to you, the Weightlessness practitioner, to do the work and then to ask that hard, honest question: Am I weightless? The gap between yes and no is everything in life—the gap between happiness and depression, determination and lethargy, active presence and anxious distraction. It's your conscious choice to apply what you've learned as if today were your last. Time, change, and transformation are of the essence—choose.

A Story of The Whole Person

Dynamic systems and domains, as discussed in The Uncertainty Scroll, are complex. One of the reasons they're complex is because to understand a part, possibly even all parts, doesn't mean you comprehend the whole.

Life has many things like this. You can read a book on how to ride a bicycle and understand the various actions required to get it going and stay going. That doesn't mean you can ride a bike. Humidity accumulates, clouds form, the sky darkens, temperature drops, and rain falls. Each of these phenomena is well understood, yet we struggle to understand the interrelations of factors well enough to predict rainstorms.

The same can be said of businesses, networks, and the human body. The network effect is a magical property of goods or services that connect a lot of people. The effect looks at the impact of each additional user on the value of that good or service to other users. Facebook, Twitter, LinkedIn—all obvious examples. It does no one any good to be the only user of Facebook or Twitter. With every additional registrant, the value those networks brings to me goes up. Recruiting your base faculties, fine-tuning your mind-body resources, is no different.

A Whole Beyond its Parts

This is an excellent frame from which to consider the mind-body. The robust pillars of Weightlessness run deep. And each, by their own contribution not only enhances that particular facet of the person but also augments the value and impact of the other pillars individually and collectively. Strength is a measure of resilience to stress. One's resilience to stress can be tackled from two angles—by increasing one's threshold to it, or by minimizing one's stress-response to or the perceived significance of a stressor. Strength attacks the former, meditation the latter.

Meditation as a practice, cultivates nonattachment. This allows one to extract the highest value from a day, from a moment within a moment. This skill is augmented through relaxation practice, which is synonymous with flexibility. The skill of meditation is also retarded by fear and stress, emotional states that can be heavily deconditioned through strength training.

Hopefully, this circle is beginning to fill in a bit. Flexibility is the antithesis of strength, in principle, but also in practical function. Strength without flexibility is stiffness stemming from residual tension if not inflammation. This is a recipe for sickness and injury. Flexibility without strength is mobility without structural integrity. This is a recipe for injury.

Further, as we've said, meditation is the means and the end of Weightlessness. But fortitude conditioned through strength training is necessary for the deep work of meditation. One may activate a high level of meditation in stillness, but strength and the fortitude that stems from it allow for the transference of meditation into dynamic or stressful environments.

While the development of each pillar will enhance both the other pillars as well as the whole person, there does seem to be a magic-sauce element of integration that eludes some trainees, in which the parts are shining but the system isn't quite buzzing. That buzz should manifest as confidence, as presence, as influence. You know, a general sense of badassery.

Progression along The Weightlessness Spectrum should generate more weightless moments and the ability to shirk off nonweightless ones with rapid mind-body realignment. As odd as this may sound, that difference seems to lie in the desire of trainees to simply be presently aware and apply what they've learned. With that awareness comes a sense of weightlessness—basking in the glory of their awesomeness—or an opportunity to troubleshoot.

We can paint a pretty close picture sometimes, but we can never fully reconstruct highly complex, dynamic experiences by adding together what they seem to be made up of. So too is this the greatest challenge in mind-body development.

I can give you a roadmap.
I can teach you the tools.
I cannot make you weightless.

That's something you have to do on your own. I can, however, provide a few more filters and reflections on what may separate a diligent practitioner who is still anxiously awaiting that elusive experience of fully integrated, weightless moments, and the practitioner who owns that gap for themselves and can activate that psychology and mind-body unification at will.

There is a strong possibility that if you practice the pillars and move through the metrics outlined in this book with conscious awareness and reflection, that integration will arise naturally. It did for me. It has for many of my students. But again, the whole doesn't necessarily equal the sum of its parts. Weightlessness, the experience, is something greater than the sum of various techniques and capacities.

Each pillar contributes to a unilateral facet of your being. But adding multiple pillars at the same time isn't a 1+1 equation. It provides a nonlinear payoff far exceeding the straightforward sum of strength plus meditation, for example, which could look more like 1 + 1 = 4. That gap, that added upside that isn't purely mechanical is made up, as far as I can tell, from one's awareness to their environment and their simultaneous awareness to their emotional responses to said environment.

If that sounds very similar to applied meditation, that's because it is. And it's reasonable to ask how you can be meditating if you're already not. And the answer is through conscious inquiry and frequent self-reflection.

Inquiry

We're quite fortunate that we don't need to be meditating in order to realize we're not having a meditative moment. Otherwise, it's unlikely we'd tip that scale despite serious effort and training. But we can tell, with practice, when we're reacting emotionally, when we're acting on autopilot, or when our judgments are heavily outcome-oriented and egocentric.

This doesn't mean there's no place for ego. It means that if you aren't aware of the origin of a thought or impulse you're exposed to its potential fallout. It means you don't get to own your decisions fully, to understand them, and to grow beyond them if they aren't serving you. Awareness is a vehicle for change.

We need to create space for alternate responses in life, for if we continue to do what we've always done, as we all know, we'll continue to get what we've always gotten. So we need to cultivate awareness, on the one hand, of external triggers and, on the other hand, of internal conditioned responses. And we need to create space between those two, triggers and responses, and feel the undetermined and changeable nature of their relationship. Viktor Frankl, the Austrian neurologist, psychologist, and Holocaust survivor had profound realizations about freedom and choice while confined in a Nazi concentration camp.

> "Between stimulus and response, there is a space. In that space is our power to choose our response. In our response lies our growth and our freedom."

Inquiry isn't critical self-judgment. It's personal investigation without an agenda. It's openness to the honest world beneath the surface of your *self* that's guiding your thoughts and actions. It's watching a movie, caring about the main character, but not wishing for a Hollywood ending. We don't need to fix the world right now; we just need to see rightly the way our thoughts and reactions manifest in the present.

Let's look at a few real examples of how this has played out with clients, with my assisted inquiry:

CLIENT: I can't handle the pressure of this program.
ME: But you're head of the class in fitness. What's wrong?

CLIENT: What if I don't hit my targets? What if one of the others hits their target ahead of me?
ME: What if they do? Is this about them?
CLIENT: No, it's about me. I just need to hit my targets, or I'll feel like a failure. I can't handle that.
ME: What about that can you not handle?
CLIENT: If I can't succeed at this, then what can I succeed at?
ME: Is success only about hitting a target? Or is it learning? Growing? Are you confusing the specific target with the overarching objective? Are you missing the forest for the trees?
CLIENT: Maybe.
ME: Let me ask another question. Right now, just between you and me in this room, where is success?
CLIENT: What do you mean?
ME: Well, that thing you're afraid of. Where is it? Is it in this room?
CLIENT: It's in my head.
ME: Okay, is it something that's already happened and is causing you pain? Or is it something that hasn't happened and hasn't caused you pain?
CLIENT: It's purely in my head.
ME: Okay, knowing that, at this moment, right here and now, there is no threat or danger. Can you join me here for a moment? Can you sit straight, relax your shoulders, and breathe into your abdomen?
CLIENT: Okay.
ME: Now, survey your body. Survey your breath. Open your senses.
CLIENT: —Adjusts posture, breathes into abdomen, senses.
ME: Are you weightless?

The response could go either way to this. If the answer was sincerely yes, then they're working through their baggage and are on the right path. They see that connection is possible. If the answer was no, then the process begins again with the question *why not*? Rinse and repeat.

There's no way around this. You must want to change. You must prefer weightlessness to feeling burdened. This is the beginning, not the end. If you prefer the comfort of your discontent—the devil you know, so to speak—it's unlikely all the training in the world will deliver you a different outcome.

And another:

CLIENT: I haven't been meditating; I'm far too stressed out.
ME: I'm sorry to hear that. Question: when you're stressed, are you aware of your stress in real time?
CLIENT: Sometimes. But generally, my head is down, grinding out work. No time to think. Sometimes, not even enough time to eat or sleep properly.
ME: Do you want to change?
CLIENT: Yes.
ME: Okay, in those times that you find yourself aware of your negative state, what's stopping you from breathing, from being present and stepping beyond the stress?
CLIENT: I'm just too stressed out. I don't have a clear enough head to practice. When I practice, it's useless.
ME: Sure, but there's practice and then there's application. If you're aware of your mental state *in real time*, you have the freedom to choose whether or not you'll continue to carry that burden forward or release yourself.
CLIENT: But how can I do that if I cannot even think?
ME: Do you want to change?
CLIENT: Yes.
ME: Then you choose. If you're aware of the stress, the negativity, that's the beginning. If you don't have awareness, start asking yourself regularly if you're aware of your breath, your state of mind, your physical structure. If you're not aware enough to do that then set triggers, buzzers on your phone or messages that remind you to reflect on your condition every hour. Find a way back to the present. Once aware, correct your posture, relax your shoulders, and drop your breath. Stop everything and connect for a few moments.
CLIENT: It doesn't work. I'm not mentally in the right place.
ME: How do you think you get in the right place? By doing what you always do?
CLIENT: No.
ME: You need to be willing to fail, to lose some of the time, in order to win. You must be willing to show up to fruitless efforts some of the time before they become fruitful. You've conditioned yourself to survive but not without a lot of stress. Fixing this is simple, but it's not easy. There's no amount of training that can fix an unwillingness to apply what you know when it matters, when it's most relevant.
CLIENT: But how do I do that?

ME: Assuming you're aware of your negative mindset in real time, you CHOOSE it. You don't make excuses. You don't merely carry on. You stop and breathe for even a few seconds. And if you're not aware, you need to set reflexive triggers to stop what you're doing and inquire.
CLIENT: I'll try that.

Everyone is in one of two camps when they're discontented. They're aware of their discontent in real time, understanding the nuances and details of it. Or they're unaware and lost in negative thought or mental chatter.

Awareness is the beginning, but it must be accompanied by a will to change. Change isn't complicated, but it is hard. It requires work, repetition and right action. Once aware, inquire within. If you're unaware and spiraling downward, awash in random negative thought, try to change your environment and set awareness triggers.

This isn't only a mechanism for self-correction from identifiably negative states. It's also the process of self-mastery in this domain, and peak performance in general. This domain doesn't have universal metrics for integration; it's very context dependent. We have the preparation tool, standing meditation, but there are no metrics that signify one's ability to first apply their awareness and then to care about changing.

This requires repetitive, soft inquiry into your state of being, your physical structure, the location and depth of your breaths, physical tension, and negative (or positive) egocentric judgment. And then, once aware of your current state, release the tension, let go of your judgments, and reunite with the present moment.

And one more:

CLIENT: My relationship with my family has really improved over the last month. I've been much less aggressive and found I've been able to listen better.
ME: That's fantastic.
CLIENT: It's made me realize how practical meditation is, and how much my relationships can improve when I show up differently. But I still yell at my son over stupid things. I get so angry when he doesn't listen.
ME: Right. It sounds like you're having significant shifts. What do you feel is lagging regarding your son?
CLIENT: I just don't understand why he does some of the things he does. He doesn't listen.

ME: At those times, how does this affect you? What's going on in your mind?
CLIENT: I just get angry, and sometimes lash out.
ME: Why do you feel angry? Do you feel threatened by something?
CLIENT: Threatened? I don't know. He's my son. I don't think so.
ME: If not threatened, then why the anger? Are you protecting something?
CLIENT: Maybe I don't feel in control.
ME: Control over him or yourself?
CLIENT: If I'm honest, maybe myself. Maybe I fear losing control.
ME: That sounds reasonable.
CLIENT: Why would I fear that?
ME: We all carry a lot of baggage. We find ways of surviving, often from youth when we're not so aware of the mechanisms we employ to manage various triggers, responses that we carry forward unconsciously. They were probably very reasonable responses once, but they may not serve you going forward.
CLIENT: I've been angry a long time.
ME: It's not going to change quickly. You'll snap at your son again. These patterns are in you. But you're in a place now where you can be aware of those bubbling impulses before things escalate, at least some of the time. With practice, I think you can manage it quite well.
CLIENT: Keep breathing?
ME: Keep breathing.

These are straightforward examples of identifying negative states or responses, stepping back and observing with nonjudgment, and discovering a new set of possible responses. I'm using negative examples here because, most often, weightlessness is the consequence of removing inhibitors, not of adding more skills or knowledge. Weightlessness, as I've defined it, is the art of unburdening. When you remove the tension in your body, the judgment from your mind, weightlessness is well within reach.

The process above doesn't need a facilitator. Self-inquiry follows the same pattern; from self-awareness, to investigating our emotional responses to environmental or internal thought triggers, to aligning our actions with our higher selves. A simple set of filters for self-inquiry might look something like this:

- Am I weightless?

  No
- Why?

  Reason X
- Is Reason X true or is it my interpretation/feeling of a set of facts?
- Is Reason X causing me direct pain in this present moment? Or is my suffering a result of events not meeting my expectations and desires?
- What purpose does this expectation or desire serve in me? What good does it do (presumably there is value in carrying it forward)?
- Would I be better or worse off if I relinquished this desire in this moment?
- Are my feelings based on something present (and urgent) or past?

Nearly all suffering stems from past pains carried forward or fear of the future. Not the now...remind yourself that this moment is something fundamentally new.

- If another person is involved, am I trying to fully understand their motivations?
- Is this issue imposing itself on me right now? Or am I choosing to give it credence and carry it foreword?
- Could this moment be considerably different, less burdensome, or more beautiful if I ceased to carry it forward?
- Am I aware of life directly in front of me—of my immediate present?
- Is my physical structure weak or empowered?
- Am I aware of my breath?
- Am I weightless?

  Yes?
- Yippee!

  No?
- Rinse and repeat.

For those at higher levels of performance, where integration under pressure is a priority, like an executive entering a meeting with sharks, or an athlete before a contest, physical inquiry is equally important. Your mind, as discussed in The Transformation Scroll, takes direct neurochemical cues from your physical structure and degree of tension. In volatile, dynamic, high-stakes scenarios, masters will not survey the mind as above; they'll skip to the last two questions and survey the body.

Even though modern humans are relatively domesticated, neurotransmitters, such as serotonin and dopamine, operate according to very primal rules. We discussed the example of the battle-losing lobster shrinking and withdrawing, a response so unbelievably close to the human response to failure or self-doubt that its uncanny. The winning lobster, meanwhile, puffs up and peacocks, filling out its frame with dominance and confidence.

That's act one of the play. Act two gets a little more interesting, because, as you could guess, a defeated, self-doubting lobster has a lower likelihood of emboldened battle than the confident lobster, and it, therefore winds up in a self-fulfilling prophesy. It carries this weakness in its structural frame until it finds a weaker lobster still to dominate, while the stronger lobster carries its bravado until it meets a bigger badass who whups him. To really put things in perspective, lobsters aren't self-conscious. They don't know they're depressed or conquering. They don't walk around with pride or self-doubt. They embody it.

And so do you!

And just as a losing lobster's physical structure can be remedied with antidepressants, the same ones us humans might take, so too can you release those same neurotransmitters by embodying the physical structure and relaxed breath patterns of your most winning self. To shift your mental state instantly, employ the structural signals of strength and confidence highlighted in The Meditation Spectrum, those for standing meditation: neutral spine, shoulders drawn back and relaxed, crown point of the head drawn up, face relaxed, and abdominal breathing.

Get Your Power Back

When D entered the last of my Shanghai tribes, he went through my standard intake consultation, at which time, he told me that he lost his power. Approaching forty years of age, recovering from a recent breakup, and CEO of a fashion brand, D had realized a loss of self, of confidence, of the power to insist on his visions at work and go after what he wanted in life. By objective measures, he was very successful, by subjective metrics he was far from weightless.

At the onset of every 100-day tribe I led in Shanghai, I selected a target for each trainee that takes into account their current mind-body status, their personal self-assessment and life targets, and my own intuitive consolidation of all factors. From experience or other, I tend to have early intuition around setting course to expose and conquer demons and fears to elicit growth. D's target wasn't sexy, but it was profound. The man lost his power. I prescribed him the deadlift to get it back. He had 100 days to lift two 40kg dumbbells for five reps. This was a lot, considering he entered the program struggling to lift less than half that weight with good form for five reps.

Like most, D didn't really connect with his target right away. He didn't ask about it much, just showed up and executed. He followed the process trajectory I outlined in The Change Scroll to an absolute T. He hit the belly of the beast right on schedule, and by week eight I had to tell him that, at his inconsistent pace, I saw two options unless he corrected course. He would either quit or he'd get injured. No need to sugarcoat things; transformation is hard work. And by week eight he'd gotten over his excitement, he got comfortable and began to lose momentum, and thoughts of quitting surfaced.

And once that occurs, trainees don't often admit those thoughts. They don't want to acknowledge failure or a lack of drive as first offense. They start to challenge the process or question the target. And he did. "Why did you choose the deadlift, again? Can we change the target?" Most often, this comes with a request for a flexibility or meditation target, but the trainee doesn't realize, of course, that those are far harder than the strength targets set for them.

These dire straits don't worry me as they once did because I know that, while increasing the probability of fallout or failure, it's the only true way to breakthrough. One must come to realize the inadequacy of the tools at their disposal before they relinquish control, open their minds, and commit to the unknown without the desire for security. D was right there at the brink and, though he didn't tell me until later, was ready to quit when I texted him the warning shot.

"You said you lost your power, D; I chose this target to give it back to you."

"Is there any other way to get it back?"

"There's no other way. We're in this."

The deadlift is the single most meaningful exercise for a number of reasons. It requires more muscle recruitment than any other exercise. It alone, possibly with the addition of the incline chest press (bench press) would be enough to build an incredible physique to 90% or so of balance and strength. It's a heavy hitter. On top of this, though, it delivers something far more informative about our physical structure and capacity in the real world.

The deadlift, at its core, teaches us how to pick things up off the ground without injury. Boring, I know. But the deeper one looks, the more bottomless the well of benefit. It alone allows us to test our physical structure under maximum load. If there's a kink in the armor, the weight reveals it. There's no way to really cheat it. The weight either leaves the ground, or it doesn't. And when lifting near one's capacity, even a five-pound addition in weight can shift the experience from one of severe challenge to lifting an anchor attached to the Earth's core. And that's where mind and body integrate in a single, coordinated effort to perform at the limits of strength, structure, and focus.

Many wrongly assume the journey of transformation begins on day one. It doesn't. The journey begins at first failure. It begins the first moment you realize you may not be able to do what is expected of you… what you believed you could manage. You may not be able to realize your targets. Your dreams. That is truly day one. And the decision you make in light of that failure designs the future you. It's a defining moment. When you try to pull that weight and it doesn't budge, not even a little, it's demoralizing, castrating in a deep way. Will power isn't enough. *I actually have to grow as a person.*

D triggered his lower back about six weeks into the program and lost even more confidence in his ability. It wasn't symptomatic in a way that made me nervous, as I've worked with clients to train through and rehab a wide variety of injuries, but he was nervous. And like the defeated lobster, he showed symptoms of psychological defeat and started holding back for fear of injury.

At this time, fear of failure in the grand sense sets in followed by thoughts of quitting to avoid failure, because people often assume that if they choose to stop because interest and focus wane conveniently when things get tough, it isn't really quitting; their priorities just changed.

Nice try. Now lift the goddamned weight you set out to lift.

But D didn't quit and on the last week of the program, he lifted those 40kg dumbbells for five textbook reps with a lions roar. He finished with no back pain, a strong back, and a transformed physique. His nightlife improved dramatically, which he was grateful for. But that's not all. A week later, D met with the owner of his brand and discussed his future with the company. D listened to their plans for him, and with a newfound confidence told them what he wanted instead. They weren't happy, but D realized he wasn't made of glass and could demand his worth. He found a sense of calm amidst the uncertainty of that negotiation, and in his future.

Shortly thereafter, he told me, not without deep gratitude, that he stood in front of the owner and made no compromises. He did so without attachment to outcome and with full commitment to himself. He was strong enough to state his needs and accept the consequences. "I know why you gave me the deadlift," he told me. "I found my power again." D learned that the confidence and focus of the mind are inextricably linked to capacity in the body, and that structure in the body signals competence and confidence in the mind. He learned that one's influence is entirely contingent on his integrated being.

Influence

In my last remote tribe, during the two-weeks when we focused on the principles of meditation and neural plasticity, I had the group watch a video of a troop of wild gorillas passing through a small village. The video was taken by one of about ten tourists who were frozen in place and exhibiting submissive postures. The silverback, a massive and majestic creature was twice the size of every other gorilla. The gorillas slowly sauntered into the village and organized just behind one of the tourists. I mean *just* behind!

The baby gorillas were curious about the human in front of them, poking and pulling his ears, climbing on his back, and bouncing about. The silverback stood for a few moments before sitting, peering over his shoulder, observing, sensing, influencing. The tourist was awestruck as it was, but when the silverback took a seat behind him with the others, a mere arm's reach away, he was absolutely petrified. The beast let down his guard and sat quietly, occasionally pulling one of the youngsters off the tourist in front of him. The silverback knew it wasn't respectful.

A minute or two later, the silverback rose, and without a grunt or gesture carried on the path. One after another, the others rose and followed. He gave no orders. He showed no aggression. His mere presence dictated the movements of his troop and the actions of every human present. Sure, he could have ripped everyone there to pieces, but he led from a place of complete self-control. It wasn't just fear or respect of his power. It was respect for his character. Yet another example of capacity in the body being foundation for the mind.

The following week, one of the women in my program, a tuned-in executive and a minority in her male-dominated company, decided to experiment with her newfound insight. Inspired by the gorilla, she decided to see if shifting her own state within the meeting could elicit a response from the room, if her presence could become influence in similar fashion.

She corrected her posture, released the tension from her shoulders, and connected with her breath, all the while maintaining connection with her environment and the speaker at the time. As she did so, she noticed that others in the room started to shift in odd ways and reorient, some of them toward her. As they did round-robin feedback, she noticed a considerable shift in their attentiveness to her, as well as openness to her contributions. She recalled it to us almost as a mystical experience. It wasn't.

Your biological system was sculpted millennia ago in the unforgiving harsh realities of nature. Do you think you're not hardwired to react to extreme presence and power? Do you think you're not capable of profound influence? The nonverbal cues of self-control and influence are deep within us, whether we can articulate what they are or not. We note with intuitive precision the confident lobster, the powerful gorilla, and the trustworthy executive. These are embodied states of presence. The embodied state of power and influence in human beings is the story of this book: a strong yet relaxed body and an aware, focused, and determined mind, integrated in this moment with sound structural integrity and heightened sensitivity.

This was one of many similar stories that have been shared over the years from Weightlessness meditators at level three (of the Meditation Spectrum) and beyond. We've heard of similarly impressive shifts from tribers going into fund-raising meetings as entrepreneurs, in government meetings, public speaking in front of a thousand people, and in career-changing conversations. Make no mistakes; the domain of Weightlessness isn't relegated to gym training. It's the stuff of life, the quality of presence and power that you bring to every facet of life.

Are you weightless?

Set your structure. Fix your gaze. Sense. And breathe.

The Eyes

"If you look down you fall down. The body always follows the eyes," repeated my first martial arts instructor. It was one of those simple cues that was easy enough to identify, but hard to appreciate the depth. The eyes permeate every aspect of your being. They dictate your physical structure. And they dictate the quality and focus of your psychology.

We've all had that conversation with the shifty, scattered individual, feet tapping on the ground, knees bouncing nervously, and eyes fixed on nothing. We don't fully trust this person. We feel very quickly that frenetic energy affecting our own. Regardless of what we tell ourselves, we know that a loose gaze means loose resolve. He might be a good beer buddy, but he's unlikely the right business partner, confidant, or leader. We all know this so deeply that we feel it in our guts; we just don't always know why.

Once upon a time, early man was rewarded for long, expansive vision and strong focus. These skills supported the spotting of threats and opportunities and allowed for the execution of protection or exploitation. While all of the young gorillas jumped and poked and looked around, the silverback surveyed and assessed, moving with caution and confidence. His priorities and position within the troop was manifested in his gaze: cold, clear, ready, and unwavering.

One has no chance of integration without addressing their eyes. The spirit of the person is in the eyes. Fixing the eyes organizes your physical structure. One should consider the training process a laboratory for organizing and integrating the components of will. When doing squats, where are your eyes? When running, where are your eyes? When at rest, where are your eyes?

Over the years, one of my key mantras in class is "eyes up." It's one of the hardest things to correct in people, and it's of highest priority. Once fatigue sets in during squats, for example, if the eyes are downcast, the head tilts. When the head tilts, it rounds the shoulders. When the shoulders round, it strains the back. When the back is strained, the hips close off and the knees buckle. This is no trivial matter. They literally dictate your entire frame. And once all of these elements deteriorate, the mind inevitably quits. Where the eyes fix, not just when you're fresh but also when you're tired, matters a great deal.

The eyes that remain up and penetratingly fixed on a point are the eyes of an indomitable person. This person should not be underestimated or overlooked. And you can confirm this for yourself, not only in the gym, but also in life. You likely know someone like this already, but if not, look for it. And when you recall or discover them, look carefully. You'll notice a presence behind those eyes. And you'll notice subtle impulses within you to submit, trust, or fear. The eyes don't merely take the world in. They speak.

Are you weightless?

Set your structure. Fix your gaze. Sense. And breathe.

The Breath

Your breath is both sword and shield. It's your most potent weapon in the battle of self-control, and it's your greatest protector from an unhealthy body and a burdened mind. The breath is that *one* tool that connects your mind with the unconscious processes of your autonomic nervous system that regulates everything from mental state to healing to physical power and performance. Connect with your breath in the present and unburden yourself of all else.

Are you weightless?

Set your structure. Fix your gaze. Sense. And breathe.

Arriving at the Precipice, a Master Awaits

In the preceding scrolls I built a case for Weightlessness from the ground up, looking first at the uncertainty problem, and at how our perception of time affects our priorities in life. I addressed how we show up to processes and commitments that matter, and the principles that give rise to fruitful transformation. And, thereafter, I presented the art and method of Weightlessness, laid out its implementation process, and addressed that elusive quality of integration that brings forth your most empowered, weightless self.

And now you're at a precipice. You're free to turn back and focus purely on The Spectrum. It will serve you forever. But if you turn the page, a new world awaits, a world that may not be recognizably different from the one you inhabit now, unless, of course, you've already done the hard work and have executed (and not just read about) the principles and practices discussed thus far—have embodied weightlessness for yourself. It's a world where nothing necessarily changes, but where everything is different. It's a world that marries arrival with process, life with practice.

You're entering the world of mastery.

The Lightness Scroll

A ship is safest at harbor, but that's not what it's built for.
—John A. Shedd

The Lightness Scroll unveils the specific principles and skills that allow us to tap our deepest potentials. Lightness, as the advanced developmental methodology of Weightlessness, moves beyond progressive, prescriptive, quantifiable workouts of The Weightlessness Spectrum in order to focus on consistent, quality-centric protocols designed to cultivate the highest of human virtues—sensitivity. You might consider this scroll as author's notes on or an appendix to The Essence of Lightness short story and the imaginary Qing Gong (Lightness) Scroll Grandmaster Flash discovered in The Wisdom of the Ancients. This scroll should serve to fill some of the theoretical gaps and scientific foundations to training approach and provide practical implementation guidelines for the modern mind-body athlete. Herein lies the path to mastery. Proceed at your own risk.

The Pillars of Lightness

The Pillars of Lightness—High-Tension Strength Training, Dynamic Stretching, Qigong, and Ballistic Weight Training—must be trained in tandem through Lightness Protocols to safely design mind-body lightness. The pillars below assume the foundations discussed within The Weightlessness Scroll, and that someone has tested to level three of The Weightlessness Spectrum before undertaking advanced training. At the end of this scroll, I'll organize these pillars into balanced Lightness Protocols for the advanced mind-body athlete, but first let's dissect each.

Pillar 1: Strength Training

It isn't quite clear from the description in the Qing Gong scroll whether the masters' description of five-vector strength training is merely emphasized or is to be practiced exclusively, but I think we can derive a couple key principles from what is here.

The first is that the focus, above all else, is on the intensity of exercise while utilizing mechanics that allow for greatest leverage. In other words, apply as much load as possible within the strongest movements possible. They are clearly not approaching conditioning from a bodybuilding perspective where muscle hypertrophy is preeminent but are looking to maximize the contractile force of the muscles while strengthening the connective tissues—maximize the integrated strength of the system.

This makes perfect sense in the athletic domain, where tensional forces are applied rapidly and often in unpredictable ways. Muscular strength is great so long as it doesn't exceed the integrity of connective tissues supporting joints. If it does, strength becomes a liability.

The second principle we can derive is one of stimulation over exhaustion. This is a difficult line to ride, but those with foundational conditioning should be able to quickly test and measure gains and recovery. The biggest issue I've seen in teaching Lightness is that trained athletes don't generally approach conditioning in a methodical manner. It's often haphazard in the form of throwing shit at a wall to see what sticks.

For this method to take hold, it's not just about adding high-tension resistance training but also adding it in the right volumes AND reducing most other work so that recovery, performance, and overall energy and readiness in life are not compromised. This is far more than athletic training with on-off cycles designed to peak out for an event. This is the long game, where performance in life on average overrides performance in the gym on any one day. Maintain that perspective.

Regarding Intensity

Working within five compound vectors ensures maximum effort potential and, therefore, maximum muscular tension, but that potential must be activated with appropriate resistance. With a sole priority of increasing strength, the number of applied repetitions per set could theoretically span from 1 to 12. This is a very loose stipulation without considering the pace of the lift and the quality and range of form.

One long static rep for example could create as much time under tension as 5 to 10 repetitions and reap the same results. So different methods of applied strength will require different analytics. But in most cases, a steady, heavy lift cadence in the 1-to-12-rep range is suitable for increasing strength in healthy individuals.

However, the impact on both muscular strength and hypertrophy are affected differently even within that narrow range of 1 to 12 repetitions.

There are three (and possibly more) types of muscle fibers, the recruitment of which are largely determined by the resistance we're struggling against. Type 1 fibers are slow twitch and largely called into play when doing low resistance, higher duration movements and normal everyday activities. These are the muscles of refined movement like walking, brushing your teeth, pouring tea, cycling, etc., anything that can be sustained a while or for which there's not much felt resistance. These fibers dominate aerobic activity.

Type II fibers come in two forms but share a common trait (so we'll lump them together for our purposes). They're built for short, fast bursts and rely on ATP and glycogen as fuel, depending on duration of the set. They burn out before oxygen can contribute to the conversion of ATP for sustained activity. Training with heavier resistance for shorter durations ensures that fast twitch fibers will be activated over slow twitch fibers. These are the fibers of power, and they also have much higher hypertrophic growth potential than slow twitch fibers (and stimulate the release of anabolic hormones that facilitate growth), which is why you see bodybuilders lifting heavy weights instead of jogging all the time.

Below, you can see how training in various rep ranges affects both muscular growth as well as strength in various ways. And note, particularly, that strength and size are not necessarily coincidental. This is what Lightness Training wants to capitalize on.

Muscle Growth Vs. Strength Gain

Repetition Range	Type I Growth	Type II Growth	Strength Gains
1-2 repetitions	Very Low	Low	Excellent
3-5 repetitions	Very Low	Low to Decent	Excellent
6-8 repetitions	Very Low	Good	Good
9-12 repetitions	Low	Excellent	Good
13-15 repetitions	Decent	Decent to Good	Endurance
16-25 repetitions	Very Good	Low	Endurance
25-50 repetitions	Excellent	Low	Endurance

As you can see, the trend is such that training in the 1 to 5-rep range is ideal for maximizing strength gains without a necessary increase in size (though some hypertrophy can occur). Training in the 6 to 12-rep range is a good compromise for increasing both strength and size, and it should not be surprising that this is the range of bodybuilding. It is also heavily emphasized in The Weightlessness Spectrum at level one to allow for structural development without the risk of injury under heavy weights.

Advice focusing on this range of training has completely dominated the fitness industry and has unfortunately distracted the masses from the plethora of benefits stemming from both very heavy resistance training as well as high volume calisthenics (though the latter seems to be making a comeback with high intensity interval training). Training beyond the 15-rep range begins to maximize aerobic capacity and stamina but is at a point of diminishing returns for both strength and size gains for most of us—which largely emphasizes type II muscle fiber recruitment.

The Weightlessness Spectrum integrates all of these in a continuous, integrated, prescriptive framework in order to build a formidable physique atop a strong technical foundation. Lightness Training, on the other hand, retains only 5-vector training in the 3 to 5-rep range as a potent, minimalist approach to maximizing strength. Concentrating on this range of resistance training provides the greatest chances of becoming really strong without a corresponding increase in bodyweight or size.

This was once a well-understood approach to athletic performance, and I believe it to be nature's modus operandi, because a super strong yet relatively light individual is extremely fast (for the object against which they're exerting force, in this case their own bodyweight through space, is considered light and can be moved effortlessly). The faster the individual, the more powerful they become, for power stems not only from strength and size, but also from acceleration. A good strength-to-weight ratio, whether you're throwing a ball or leaping with your own bodyweight, creates the sensation of effortless movement. Hence, strength is of preeminent importance when addressing an individual's *lightness factor*.

Five-vector strength training accomplishes this feat with maximum efficiency, and minimal time investment. The purpose of strength training is not to get good at lifting weights, but to establish an edge in the game of life. Training shouldn't take priority over living. Every athlete on the planet knows that the stronger you are, the better you perform. This should be done with as much impact, but as little damage to the body as possible so that recovery time is rapid, and daily energy remains high.

Most people will notice that they feel fresher after a single vector workout than before they started, contrary to the objective of many entering a gym, which is to feel like trash after training, to feel sore as hell for the following two days, and to need days of recovery thereafter. This is the approach of a novice. But the warrior always keeps something in reserve and knows that strength is only as useful as your ability to apply it. If you're stiff and sore and tired all the time, you're useless. If you're strong, fresh, rested, and limber, you're ready to hunt.

This reduced load volume also prevents excessive residual tension from accumulating in the skeletal muscles. They generally don't experience as much wear and tear, soreness or fatigue, and, therefore, are able to return to a state of relaxation much easier. This is a critical factor in Lightness. It's not about your performance within the set; it's about your readiness in life. Balancing these factors is a master's game. The novice is still focused on destructive play.

How

Select at least one vector per session, but no more than three: squat and press, for example. Select an appropriate weight, defined by time under tension (according to the masters in the Qing Gong Scroll, approximately fifteen seconds max, or five seconds on the low end). Generally, three to five reps mirror the count (time) allocation the masters speak of, but it's interesting that they focused on duration over reps. Many exercises are trained and tested under static contraction, ones that reap tremendous proprioceptive, strength, and agility benefits. Among them are the handstand or handstand pushups, the planche and planche pushups, the one-leg static squat and the one-leg pistol, to name a few.

Movement isn't required for maximum muscle recruitment and adaptation. You can test this for yourself right now by holding a pushup (or one arm extension with elbow slightly bent) or a squat (or one-leg squat at 90 degrees) position for ten to twenty seconds. Your body will tremble with effort and your muscles will burn with contraction. This opens the door to many creative applications of high-tension vector development and many techniques that transfer to bodyweight performance (which require more balance and technical training than weight-based resistance training).

To translate this for general protocol programming, perform five sets of five full-range, controlled repetitions of one compound exercise (like a shoulder press or handstand pushups within the press vector). Rest between sets until recovered; three to five minutes works well for most. Focus on training as hard as possible while fresh as possible rather than digging into last reserves. Once this is accomplished with a certain weight for a certain vector two or three workouts consecutively, attempt a heavier weight for two or three of the five sets (you may not hit five reps in those attempts, and that's okay), until you can manage it for all five sets. Rinse and repeat.

The most difficult part of this type of training is only doing this type of training. People are obsessed with volume and variety. They're obsessed with *feeling* like they've worked out. These are not meaningful metrics of performance, and, ironically there is no direct correlation between those subjective factors and a subsequent recovery and adaptation.

Doing more doesn't mean you'll be leaner. It doesn't mean you'll be stronger. It doesn't mean you'll look or feel better. Again, nature has one preeminent metric—power. This is most readily activated by low volume, high-tension resistance training and a diet that supports lean mass. Ironically again, for those willing to take the leap and embrace this minimalist form of training, you'll notice very quickly how your strength and performance increases and your body composition improves. Go figure. Less is often more.

If you're including strength within a Lightness protocol on any particular day, you can reduce this to one or two vectors per workout in order to recover faster and spare energy. Protocols should be practiced four to six days a week, so you'll have plenty of time to cycle through each vector at least once if not twice per week. If you're only including strength a few of those six days, then you could hit that third vector each strength session, for example.

Frequency and volume matter far less than the intensity of the workout. If you lifted only once every two weeks, yet your strength metrics have increased, meaning the total weight lifted in the same time, then guess what? You've done enough to elicit an adaptive response and an increase in strength. This will seem counterintuitive at first, but it's the way things work. As long as your diet is acceptable, your newly gained strength (and possibly mass) will sustain health and metabolic function with great efficiency. Muscle will not atrophy in such a short time, given adequate nutrition, nor will body fat accumulate (as a result of perceived undertraining).

That is particularly relevant within weight training, but we may consider greater frequency (maintaining intensity) for skill-based bodyweight movements, where structure and integration are as integral to strength as the contractile force of the muscles. Practice still makes perfect.

Pillar 2: Dynamic Stretching

Dynamic stretching has a subtle, but extremely important contribution to Lightness. Rarely will it play the role of a technical tool as in martial arts kicking techniques or dance, where the practice and the application are very similar. The role of dynamic stretching in Lightness is to disinhibit the body and to release, as I like to call it, the emergency break.

Our bodies are brilliant. Almost every bodily system is designed to sustain a balance of dynamic antithetical powers. Our hormones work in complementary yet antithetical ways to support metabolism, healing, adapting from stress, sleeping, and much more. Our musculoskeletal frame is built of countless levers that counterbalance prime movers and antagonistic muscles to coordinate and produce movement.

Made of checks and balances, our bodies are built to adapt and grow... but within reason. Too much strength without the ability to control it will tear the body apart. Too much flexibility without strength will jeopardize the integrity of joints and connective tissues. Too much insulin without a healthy sensitivity to it will result in obesity. But kept in check, our bodies find balance and power.

So how does dynamic stretching play a role? Regarding internal checks and balances, strength is unequivocally good. However, strength applied beyond the limits of structural integrity (including required ranges of movement) results in injury. Sprinters for example, are prone to tearing hamstrings. This could be overexertion and due to the strain of contraction against the counterforce of the ground. But it can also occur as the leg extends forward, stretching beyond its comfortable limits and preparing to land in the next step.

Our bodies have a reflex known as the stretch reflex (or myotatic reflex), that signals to the nervous system a muscle is being stretched too rapidly. This signal doesn't make it to the brain but communicates with the spinal cord for a more immediate, and more instinctual response to danger: *Shut this movement down!* And it does. The muscle in question seizes or cramps in hope of preventing over extension and sparing the muscle. This spares body parts in the weekend warrior but dramatically limits the well-trained athlete. Dynamic stretching conditions the body to calm the hell down, and not panic when being stretched at a rapid pace.

For most gym rats, this will seem completely irrelevant. But for peak performance athletes and weightless warriors, you'll recognize in this skill the ability to unlock much higher degrees of power, speed, and agility. It's one thing to be strong, but another to be strong with few limitations, with no fixed, short-range of movement.

Everyone believes strength is a good thing. But what's the use if it only allows us to bench press or squat more weight? Where's the application? As per our discussion of building a machine for an uncertain journey, we don't know the application clearly. But we do know with certainty that, at some point, we'll face a bumpy road, or need to activate a greater degree of power under volatile, unbalanced, and unstable circumstances—for this is life. Readiness requires flexibility in body and mind.

How

There are five dynamic stretches within Lightness, each responsible for unlocking a myofascial train. The front-rising kick activates the rear train of the body in the same way a forward bend would. The inward and outward crescent kicks similarly activate that line with the addition of hip opening and contralateral trains. The rear-rising kick aggressively opens the front line of the body, and the side-rising kick unlocks the internal line of the groin.

As the masters of Lightness highlight for ballistic weight training, *dynamic stretching is also the dynamic application of static principles.* Dynamic stretches move through a full range of movement into a fully stretched state without compromising well-established structural alignments. Each begins with a preparatory step or setup that first spring loads the movement to decrease the duration of the stretch-shortening cycle of the concentric phase, thereby increasing the speed of the rising kick.

To fully activate this, the body must be stretched or bent counter to the movement (and muscles) in question in a relaxed extension. In the front-rising kick, for example, the front line of the body should elongate, lift, and stretch in order to generate elastic energy in the myofascia of the front line as well as secure extended alignment before compression occurs. This creates a natural spring in the body that assists the kick without the need for as much muscular force or tension.

As the kick rises, your body should remain relaxed and should coordinate with an exhalation not unlike receiving a punch in the gut. Release about a third of the air in the abdomen from the pressure therein, rather than a full exhale. As the kick rises, the body (and length of spine) should straighten (or remain straight), not curl in upon itself due to lack of global range. Alignment should resemble the same established through our static stretches under The Weightlessness Spectrum (and in particular, The Flexibility Spectrum within) where the tailbone is untucked.

The first stage is to activate and disinhibit the stretch reflexes associated with the front and rear lines of the body. Dynamic stretching greases the grooves of movement, not just for a single muscle, but for the full range of your myofascial trains. I don't mean to be a tease, but these techniques should not be learned from a book… I've left them out intentionally so as to spare people unnecessary injury (but supplementary resources can be accessed from my website).

Static images also cannot do justice to the dynamic mechanics of these stretches. I teach them in the real world, as do most kicking martial and dancing arts. While there may be technical variance between them, there are only so many ways to activate dynamic length, and good coaches in several arenas will provide that instruction. What I've given you here is the conceptual blueprint, a checklist by which you can audit your own developing technique.

Pillar 3: Qigong

You Are a Walking Battery

Qigong is the practice of energy cultivation and manipulation in the body at the direction of the mind. To be crystal clear here, the energy we're referring to is bioelectromagnetism. The avenues into this practice are breath control and breath manipulation, sensational awareness, and concentration.

Energy work has a bad rep due to the abundance of communities and gurus who prefer to sell mysticism rather than science. It isn't clear to me why they do this, whether it's because they're trying to appeal to those who are attracted to magic, or they're just too lazy to research their crafts and identify prime movers of healing. But there's no need for this anymore. We know far too much about the body to chalk health, healing, and internal development up to that cosmic juju in the universe.

Bioelectricity is tangible, its measurable, its internal to every metabolic process within the body, and can perform most if not all functions attributed in Chinese medicine, qigong, and most healing arts to that elusive energy known as qi. It doesn't do it by magic but through organic, biological processes that convert chemical energy (ATP) into electrical energy. This is discussed more in the Energy Analects below.

Bioenergetics is a massive rabbit hole. The more that I study it, the more I realize how vast the topic is. On top of that, there are a lot of things that are just unknown. We know, for example, that bioelectricity is central to all cellular processes in the body. We don't know how fluctuations of it to the X degree affect cellular metabolism or general health to what degree... we're far from understanding the causal relationship between specific voltages within certain bodily systems and corresponding responses. We just know there is one unequivocally. And some scientists (a few names listed below) are trying to dissect that causality with precision.

But let's not get lost in the unknown, for what is known and common knowledge at present is still very enlightening.

In most cells, the resting bioelectric potential is 50 millivolts. Your cells produce electricity when charged ions (sodium and potassium) move across cell membranes against an electrochemical gradient. This is the basis for bodily functions like motor, autonomic (controls breathing and heartbeat), or sensory signaling along the nerves. This includes muscle contractions and brain function.

Your body can do literally nothing without electricity, which should make self-evident the fact that, if energy is insufficient or signaling impaired, overall energy, immunity, and health will be compromised. This is why qigong has been practiced for millennia in China and around the world by healers, yogis, and martial artists to combat every illness and disorder under the sun as well as improve physical power, memory, and mental acuity.

Those who put in a fighting effort with their qigong practice over time will find that, at times, regions of the body, such as the lower abdomen, the palms, or the center of the forehead get flushed with heat. Sometimes, they feel associated swirling or vibration. Heat is a direct byproduct of increased electrical activity, as the accumulation or conversion of energy affects neighboring tissue.

What

Do a simple test with me. Squeeze your fist as hard as possible and hold it for five seconds.

Congratulations, you're a qigong master!

Joking aside, how do you think that just happened? Thought from your brain mobilized current in the body, communicated that intention through your nervous system to the muscles of the hand and forearm, and fired those muscles in a specific sequence to create and sustain the fist squeeze. Your mind moved energy. It's not a very sexy way to frame it, I know, but it's real and it happens constantly ongoing. Electricity is the source of life in the body.

What we're talking about in qigong is essentially more of the same, with far greater mental control, and without the need for muscular contraction as an end result. Qigong is the practice of generating and manipulating bioelectricity with the mind directly.

Qigong is, at its base, a concentration practice. As we discussed in The Weightlessness Spectrum, concentration and awareness are not exclusive but complementary. Concentration allows one to sustain awareness of focal points or fluctuations in the body, without distraction. Awareness allows one to transcend compulsive thoughts and judgments and, therefore, persist with a concentrated mind in intuiting real and present information. Qigong, at its root, completes the circle and draws concentration and awareness together in mind-body connection.

But this isn't all. Qigong addresses more than the psychological phenomenon of meditation. It goes into our physiological makeup and, through awareness, unites us with the subtle energy that sustains us from one moment to the next. And through concentration, it allows us to accumulate, develop, and manipulate that energy through willpower and intention alone.

In highly skilled qigong practitioners, healing, both internal and remote, telepathy, and telekinesis (the projection of energy to move objects) are all theoretical potentialities, even in modern biology and physics, though still far from accepted by mainstream science. For the skeptics out there, you can research a few mind-blowing applications of electricity toward healing, including:

- Regrowing of limbs/bone in animals—Robert Becker
- Cell regeneration of tissues, organs and limbs—Dr. Michael Levin
- Healing frequency of cells—M.B. Reilly
- Muscle growth—EMS (Electric muscle stimulation)
- Cancer treatment—Yoram Palti
- Colloidal silver on wounds
- Improving memory and intelligence—tDCS studies at the Mind Research Network

How

In the *Essence of Lightness* short story, Flash finds three qigong progressions within the first section of the scroll titled *The Pillars of Lightness*. These are the most essential progressions to work through, slowly. Very. They should not even be remotely considered before the meditation metrics (slow breathing and reverse counting) in The Weightlessness Spectrum (and the Meditation Spectrum therein) are well mastered. Without them, you'll waste a lot of time and likely conclude qigong is mental masturbation. To acquire skills that most people don't have, you'll need to do things that most won't do.

***Intermission**: Give that section in The Essence of Lightness a quick reread.*

The first thing to keep in mind is that you're already an energy-making machine. The progressions detailed are essentially progressing from a point of awareness of said energy to accumulation, then to distribution, then to channeling.

There are two primary movers of qi in these practices: focal point concentration and visualization. We might also include physical tension, but I've elected to focus on the essence of development here. I had you squeeze your fist a moment ago, and in so doing, you moved energy (or converted chemical energy to bioelectric impulse).

Most of us are unconscious of the process and oblivious to the sensation of charge produced. With added conscious awareness, tension can be integrated and coordinated with the breath to accumulate energy in various parts of the body. This is something I practice and occasionally teach... but it should be considered tangential to the foundational progressions. If it's something that interests you, integrated tension techniques can be found in the works of Dr. Jwing Ming Yang.

As for Lightness progressions listed in the scroll, tension is only lightly added in drawing up the perineum within Small Universe practice. This is a very difficult thing to do without hindering relaxed breathing at first and, quite frankly, isn't essential (but it does add a modicum of control in directing energy). As awkward as it is, the perineum, the muscle between the legs that keeps you from peeing yourself, should be lightly tensed during inhalation to block energy flow and accumulate it as its drawn (visually) in from the nose and passes to the dan tian or the perineum itself. Releasing it upon exhale opens the flood gates and allows for the circulation of energy up to the crown point, third eye, and philtrum point where the Small Universe cycle begins anew. This should only be integrated at progressions two and three, and it adds considerable difficulty to the coordination of tension and relaxation in the body.

In each of the three progressions, the trainee should be ever conscious of tension in the body, while constantly enlivening the senses. The mind dictates where energy should accumulate and move—from concentration on the dan tian in the first progression, to circulating energy down the front line of the body upon inhale and up the rear of the body on exhale in the second progression, to resisting the collapsing room with nothing but will (body empty of all tension and force) in the third progression. All of the structural cues cultivated in The Meditation Spectrum should be second-nature at this point and tacitly supporting the energetic process.

[Remember—Tensegrity is cultivated through alignment that produces natural, effortless lift. Proper alignment removes the need for stored or sustained physical tension, and without tension, the body comes alive with sensitivity, and dramatically improves neural signaling (which is inhibited by tension and inflammation in the body). Do not overlook standing meditation as a critical foundation to advanced energy work.]

What's more important than the specific practices, just like we discussed back in The Weightlessness Scroll, are the principles of progression: accumulation, distribution, and channeling, in that order. We all want to jump to the sexy, but sexy doesn't come first. Salads and squats do. Be patient. Stay hungry.

A relatively fast progression through these three (assuming one has already tested to Lightness in all Weightlessness Spectrum metrics) is three months for the first, three to six months for the second, and six months to several years for the third. These are extremely loose timelines (some are gifted and move quickly, some struggle for years) and only listed to remind the reader that these aren't weekend trophies, they require patience and dedication—the long game.

Other energy enhancers that can complement your qigong training include:

- Fasting—which elicits energetic upregulation to compensate for the lack of nutrition, a detoxified body and mind for greater mental clarity and efficient current flow, and heightened sensitivity to internal movement.

- Hyperventilation—which is a good precursor to any of the three progressions if done correctly, focusing on intake over expulsion (ideally with longer and deeper inhales than exhales), increasing electron availability, ATP generation, and energy conversion.

- Exercise—which increases energy conversion to fuel work and primes the body to do so with greater efficiency. If one can relax quickly post training, the lingering, heightened metabolic charge also makes for easier awareness of current flow in the body.

- Cold—which causes vasoconstriction but which, over time, will open veins and enhance circulation in order to maintain body temperature or sustain heat in certain regions. Ice baths are great for general energetic practice, while icing a region of the body like the hand might be useful in regional awareness and manipulation required for channeling.

Of Jedis and Sith Lords—Reflections on the Dark Side of the Force

I'll try to avoid the "*with great power comes great responsibility*" spiel because, hey, we all love a good villain. But I'll point out that fine line that masters of antiquity have warned their students about. The tools of Weightlessness don't discriminate. Ideally, they're used to make you your best self, and that includes compassion toward others. But that isn't a given. It's a choice.

Despite freedom to choose, some training triggers actually make it harder (more complicated) to choose the light: an over-nurturing of yang—the tension building side of the training equation. This takes two forms, strength and conditioning on the one side, which can be counteracted with flexibility, and willful concentration practice on the other side (reverse counting or other concentration practices), which is egocentric.

The key meditative tools within The Meditation Spectrum (slow breathing and reverse counting) are qigong practices, because they manipulate breath in the first case, and concentrate attention in the second, both of which move energy in the body at the direction of the will. I just don't often call those practices qigong, as it's easy to treat them as strictly mechanical skills that cultivate awareness and concentration respectively. The point at which these practices become meditation and not merely willful effort, is the point at which the technique of each becomes well honed, and nonjudgmental awareness envelops the exercise. As we discussed, meditation is a phenomenon that stems from awareness and concentration coming together. Back to those good ol' definitions!

We might accurately describe that phenomenon (in addition to it being the definition of meditation within Weightlessness) as passive qigong, the transitional phase of training that bridges The Weightlessness Spectrum with Lightness Training. In my time with Grandmaster Shi de Jian at the Shaolin Monastery (which was the nonfiction part of *The Essence of Lightness* story), and other monks at other times, passive qigong was always emphasized over active qigong.

It has always been considered the true practice for those individuals focused on spiritual enlightenment, while active qigong (accumulation, distribution, and channeling) has been the way of the warrior or mystic healer. And given what we've learned about our primal faculties, this makes sense. Awareness is inclusive, concentration exclusive. Concentration, the empowerment tool of martial artists and healers is volitional. There's no way around that, at least for quite some time within the training process. Stay with me here.

As such, there's no way that the practice of active qigong is not internally dictated and, therefore, egocentric. Again, just to be clear, awareness is a passive, receptive practice. It's an openness to and nonjudgment of environmental information. Concentration excludes a great deal of data in favor of concentrating on or manipulating a subset of it. That point of concentration is a predetermined (prejudged) subset of data to the exclusion of other "less valuable" points of data.

Awareness is ego-transcendent; concentration is ego-tolerant, if not augmenting. Whenever we embrace our identities and act in accordance with values and suppositions, we reinforce the neural pathways that create meaning and context. Sitting down and visualizing, or pushing your mind to concentrate and focus, is not natural (at first). It's not passive. There is very much a *you* doing the work. And with successive progressions, this *you* will pop up every time the work gets harder and you test your edges.

Just as Michael Jordan had a reputation for being an egomaniac on the court, and nobody wanted to play against him, so too can this type of training to become the best *you* augment the identity that's hungry for more… more knowledge, more skill, more power. And, therein, the Jedi becomes the Sith lord.

There was a time in my life when I threw the baby out with the bathwater and stopped practicing qigong for nearly a decade because I was convinced that energetic manipulation was off the true path. Thank you very much, Jiddu Krishnamurti.

I now believe it can fruitfully coexist in the mind-body of a Lightness practitioner so long as that counter practice of awareness (nonattachment) is dually cultivated. As flexibility is to strength, so too is awareness to concentration. Both must be present for a balanced mind-body.

Awareness without concentration is soft and compassionate, but potentially powerless, leaving the practitioner at the cold discretionary forces of an indifferent world. Concentration without awareness is hard and self-centered, and potentially aggressive (if not evil), potentially converting the tools of Weightlessness and the power one cultivates into vehicles of malice.

So… be a Jedi… I guess.

Pillar 4: Ballistic Weight Training

Have you ever seen a pro baseball player preparing to bat? You'll often see him swinging a bat with a circular weighted ring attached to the end of it, adding resistance to his masterful swing. A few moments later when he's up to bat, he removes the weighted ring, focuses all his attention on the pitch, and swings through a full range with a bat that feels as light as a feather. Your body is the bat. We want to establish the same sense of lightness with our limbs that the ball player activates for his bat. The resulting *lightness factor* stems from improved neuromuscular coordination, a shortened stretch-shortening cycle, and stronger connective tissues capable of supporting ballistic movement.

On Coordination

We discussed in The Weightlessness Scroll the correlation between flexibility and strength, both of which resemble opposite ends of the relaxation-tension spectrum. Ballistic weight training greases the grooves of this interplay, allowing for efficient and, therefore, rapid contraction of muscle fibers. On a broader scale, holistic and integrated coordination improves by way of identifying and removing all tensional sticking points.

The added weight forces our neuromuscular systems to find paths of least resistance, thereby improving coordination and making it easier to accomplish the task at hand.

You might consider this the integration tool of Lightness, drawing on the explosive fast twitch fibers developed with strength training, with the safe range of dynamic stretching, with the neural efficiency cultivated with qigong, coordinating all systems against marginally greater resistances.

Ballistic weight training should be a reflective, fully conscious practice in which the trainee is connecting mind-body-breath within a single, unified action. While weights are highlighting deep points of tension, consciousness should envelop these with deep awareness of the mechanics of movement.

This is a not a throw-the-ankle-weights-on-and-call-me-weightless type of thing. This is meditation in movement. If you're listening to music, you fail. If you're pondering relationship or work issues, writing your next book in your head, or just getting through the workout, you fail.

Ballistic weight training is to lightness what standing meditation is to the Weightlessness Spectrum.

On the Stretch-Shortening Cycle

Strength training addresses the ability of a muscle or group of muscles to contract and create tension synchronously. But without a conversion tool that allows us to utilize this strength practically, strength will never become power, a process that requires acceleration and range.

Our bodies are built of volumes of levers, where muscles apply force on bone to create movement. Where these two intersect, we have muscle tissue built with less flexibility but capable of great load, tendons. Strength is born of tension. Power is born of mass times acceleration, or the rate at which tension is created; therefore, power application creates greater demands on the whole structure than does strength training alone.

Within every ballistic movement—you can check this for yourself—you'll find a very natural counter movement that precedes the intended committed action. Before a basketball player leaps, he dips. Before a baseball player throws, his arm retracts. This has the effect of stretching a muscle or the group of muscles responsible for generating force before they shorten (or contract), spring loading the tendons with elastic energy. The faster this transition can be made the more powerful (and explosive) the action.

This very short transition is called the stretch-shortening cycle, and quickening it is the secret to transferring strength into explosive power.

Sprinting and leaping, both fully committed ballistic movements, activate this stretch-shortening cycle with every stride or repetition. Adding weight to the ankles or torso slows this process down during training, but it provides greater load and stretch on the muscles and connective tissues, requiring greater concentration, coordination, and muscular force to overcompensate.

This process tricks your neuromuscular system into finding a short cut to coordinated, explosive power that one would be hard pressed to find without natural athletic ability or years of plyometrics. But! It does take time and dedication for these adaptations to occur safely.

On Enhanced Connective Tissues

Over the long term, ballistic weight training is the process of learning to live in the body of a heavier person. If this process is undertaken religiously for a long time, one's body will, by virtue of contrast to training in bondage, feel as light as a feather. You'll feel weightless.

Part of this is building the internal connections; strengthening tendons and ligaments methodically over time until they can accommodate the forces of a false, heavier body. Connective tissues require much more time to adapt to stress than muscle, and a long-term approach is, therefore, necessary if one is fully committed to activating *Lightness* safely.

How

Choose one or more *Lightness vehicles*—running or leaping being the most likely candidates. These are gross motor skills innate to our physiology and biomechanics that cover a wide range of myofascial recruitment and that transfer to most other human power movements.

Add a small amount of weight to the ankles and possibly the torso when leaping. Establish a base of relaxed, sustainable movement with abdominal breathing. This could mean a light five-to-ten-minute jog, jogging in place, or light, relaxed kicking. Scan the body for tension continuously and maintain (awareness of) abdominal breathing with constant awareness of tension throughout the body, releasing it when and where it creeps in.

Perform one all-out effort at 90-100% until performance declines and fatigue sets in (but not failure... never to failure). This would generally last less than one minute for your sprint, or six to twelve reps for leaping with several recovery breaths and moments between each, all the while maintaining abdominal breathing and as little tension as possible.

This process should last *less than* 15 minutes daily (including dynamic stretching), and could last less than 10 as you become more experienced. Make small, incremental additions to the weight you carry and the height you're leaping, but not to the duration of training. Every few weeks to few months (over time additional gains will be slower), add eight to sixteen ounces to each ankle, and possibly a few pounds to your weight vest if leaping.

This can be adapted for athletes of all types by applying the same principles. Runners use parachutes and ropes around the torso, and rubber bands around the ankles to provide resistance. Football players lift with chains attached to bars that increase resistance as exercise leverage improves. Boxers use small dumbbells when shadow boxing, and dancers use ankle weights through full-range movement in training. These are sport/craft-specific, specialized applications.

If the athlete knows their craft well enough they'll have no trouble with the creative application of Lightness principles therein, but for the general all-purpose mind-body athlete, weighted running, leaping, and dynamic stretching are your workhorses. They're the foundation that should not be overlooked or replaced.

It's crucial that the weight you carry be managed without generating more tension, and that it feels natural (a part of you) by the time you increase it. More important than the quantity of weight carried is your ability to sustain a state of fluid power and conscious awareness of movement, marked by relaxed movement and activating tension only for explosive bursts.

If you find yourself struggling to maintain your technique against the weight, you're off the path… If you find yourself upper chest breathing, you're off the path… If you can sustain your maximum effort for more than a minute, you're off the path and need to adjust resistance, height, or personal effort.

Where there's struggle, there's resistance; where there's resistance, tension; and where there's tension, *there's no sensitivity.*

Tension is the enemy of sensitivity.

In the game of Lightness, less is more. We're looking not for more work, but for a quality of movement marked by extreme sensitivity and coordination. This is ballistic meditation. It's integration with balls and passion. One must be willing to play the long game, to be patient, to look the fool for a time and remove one's ego in order to make profound gains. It will take time. But in that emptiness of self is the life we're all looking for.

After finishing your intense exertion, spend fifteen to thirty breaths in active recovery. This should also be a practice in sensitivity as well, surveying the body for any remaining tension and assessing one's alignment and structure. You should stand naturally in something resembling standing meditation posture, with the head drawn up as if by a string, with relaxed shoulders, parallel feet, and bent knees. Breathing can occur through the nose or mouth, but breath volume in (inhalation) should exceed that of your exhalation. You're actively recovering and replenishing lost oxygen.

This isn't the time to get lost in music or ruminate on nonsense. This is training. Survey your body actively and use recovery as active sensitivity training. This breathing style would qualify as hyperventilation like that discussed under qigong above, though triggered here through exertion and embraced during recovery with added awareness.

A primary principle of Western conditioning, strength training, and sports performance is *progressive overload*, which states that our bodies require higher degrees of stress than we're used to in order to elicit an adaptation. That is, we must overload our muscular or neuromuscular system to elicit overcompensation and growth. With ballistic weight training, we're looking for progressive training, but not overload in the same sense.

Overload requires time for rest and adaptation and often accompanies training to failure. We don't want to sacrifice tomorrow for today; we want to be ever ready, ever fresh and prepared. Warriors don't practice failure. They practice winning. Overload is a spectrum game; the game of Lightness is incremental and imperceptible increases in resistance. We're looking for deep, not superficial adaptations that provide form without function.

Weightlessness is preparation for the battle of life, that is, life outside the gym. Students value hard work and will exhaust themselves in the pursuit of knowledge. The master values smart work and always keeps something in reserve for challenges unforeseen.

The Energy Analects

To recap what I perceive to be an extraordinarily simple but accurate representation of energy conversion, the masters highlight the origin of chemical energy in the body from food and air sources. They're insistent on these factors being well sorted before adding to them specific manipulations or practices for enhancing performance.

Make no mistake, they implore that the quality of food (and digestion) and air (and breathing) are paramount in energy cultivation. Practicing qigong without a healthy gut and effective breathing (and likely substantial physical structure and conditioning) is like adding high-octane fuel to a busted old Pinto with a leak in the gas line. It's unlikely to take hold no matter how much you put in.

Fascinating enough, the masters lump fasting and hypoventilation together as a way of framing supercompensation in cellular capacity. Overconsumption and hyperventilation are lumped together in terms of metabolic upregulation or increased energy conversion. It's interesting to think of these as biological survival mechanisms, and I believe they make perfect sense if we frame them in this way, simply:

In deprivation, the body relies on storages BUT increases capacity. In excess, the body converts energy, heals, and builds performance structures.

Even the most basic life on the planet follows very similar survival principles, with single cell organisms conserving energy for self-healing when deprived, and reproducing or multiplying when fed.

The composite of the characters rice and air that make up the character qi has been contemplated by Sinologists for millennia; with interpretations ranging from qi as potentially material or immaterial to it being the vital essence of all things in the universe—the tangible and intangible. But it's never seen as a simple equation. Leave it to a warrior to see things practically.

Energy here isn't being discussed in a mystical sense, as was often the case in Chinese medicine prior to this century, but in a matter-of-fact, straightforward sense. You put gas in the car and it goes. Gas is energy. Food and air are energy in this case.

We know that carbohydrates (rice in the masters' parlance) are not the only fuel source for the body, but they do make for the most efficient, readily convertible energy source. They burn faster and can be stored directly in muscles themselves as glycogen. So long as glycogen is present, fats and proteins will only be converted to ATP in small amounts, if at all. This may seem at cross-purposes with my previous writings on Weightlessness Nutrition that frame grains and sugars as reluctant friends, so let's clear a few points.

I don't personally discriminate against energy sources as a general rule, assuming they're not processed. Humans are energy-making machines and different fuel sources have greater relevance in different contexts. The Weightlessness nutrition structure is a progressive model of assimilating macronutrients to gain an intuitive awareness of insulin response in the body. This allows us to optimize health and body composition without needing to count calories or weigh macros.

It's my priority more to understand the impacts on energy, both immediate and sustained, which is a complex equation that must take into consideration meal composition, energy output and intensity through training, and overall health and body composition. I dissect this in the prequel, *In Pursuit of Weightlessness.*

Carbohydrates are the anaerobic (heavy weight lifting / high intensity training) athlete's fuel, no doubt about it. They burn hard and fast, and they replenish energy quickly (fruits, nuts, beans, starchy veggies, and legumes also falling into the category of carbohydrate sources—not merely grains and sugars). Is this all or nothing? By no means.

Your body is an energy-making machine and can make awesome use of most types of natural food. But for those who require faster recovery or more energy, you just can't make up that gap with noncarb sources easily if you're doing regular, anaerobic training. You can certainly maintain optimal health, but not aggressive daily training or recovery from intense training without significantly more rest between sessions.

But it shouldn't surprise the reader that The Energy Analects point at this fuel source as being preeminent in the creation of qi; though, admittedly, it could also be circumstantial due to rice being a staple in the Chinese diet for thousands of years.

Metabolism is an incredibly complex thing, with back doors and workarounds that keep your dynamic system constantly doing what it needs to do to get the job done. So there's no "one way" for energy creation. The process of converting biochemical energy from nutrients is called cellular respiration, and it takes several forms. Whether we're looking at glycogenosis with carbs, lipolysis with fats, deamination of proteins, or oxidation of all three, energy will be created so long as food (nutrients in the cells, blood stream, or stored body fat) and oxygen are present.

But let's look at the oxygen-glycogen equation a little more. We know, or at least we should, that we can create energy both with and without oxygen for at least short periods of time. Divers, sprinters, fighters, and other elite, anaerobic athletes all know this. But without oxygen our conversion of glucose to ATP is poor, very poor, which is why high intensity exertion cannot be sustained for long without a rest. In fact, in the presence of oxygen 34-38 ATP are produced per glucose molecule. Without oxygen? 2. Yep, sixteen times less.

For years, VO_2 max has been the gold standard for measuring performance capacity of an athlete. It measures the maximum amount of oxygen utilized, generally during aerobic exercise to measure cardiovascular performance, but is equally improved through high intensity interval training (if not more). This is based on the theory that increased oxygen consumption leads to an increase in ATP production in cells.

The most prominent Guru in the breathing game today is the Dutch Iceman Wim Hof, who has proven extraordinary feats of autonomic nervous system control like generating body heat while submerged in ice for over an hour, hiking Mount Kilimanjaro in shorts, and suppressing his immune response after being injected with endotoxins (benign bacteria that would normally elicit a severe feverish reaction). He's also taught thousands of others to repeat his feats and demo them under scientific observation.

Wim is the most renowned these days, but breathing techniques like his have been employed for thousands of years by mind-body masters around the world to tap their unconscious metabolic processes for increased energy conversion and improved health and performance. Wim uses a hyperventilation technique for several minutes followed by a max breath hold during out-retention (holding breath after full exhale). This is an age-old yoga practice, but again, is commonly found in a wide range of mind-body arts, including some martial arts. It has one, if not several, key measurable impacts: it improves VO_2 max, the amount of oxygen one can consume and utilize and therefore convert into ATP.

Consider this, hyperventilation increases oxygen intake and affects something called oxygen saturation. That's where blood cells are carrying a bit more oxygen than baseline. During breath retention, or rather, when you stop breathing and run out of air, vasodilation occurs (veins dilate) and the corresponding rise in CO_2 levels causes blood cells to release oxygen into muscle cells to fuel work.

Consider how brilliant this physiological response is. With sufficient air, your body converts more energy, and with insufficient air, your veins become larger to carry more blood (with less oxygen) to various cells. This was always thought in Western science to be a wholly unconscious process… until recently.

Hyperventilation accumulates energy and excites the body.
Retention releases energy and, if sustained, depresses the body.

This occurs even within a short session of practice. Sustained practice creates the same adaptations as high altitude training—an increase in red blood cell count and improved oxygen utilization due to reduced oxygen availability in the air. It also has pronounced and long-term impact on VO_2 max.

So, to draw these together clearly, deprivation leads to both immediate and longer-term adaptations that allow one to take in, deliver, and convert more oxygen to ATP (the chemical energy currency of the body). And as we've discussed, qi, or bioelectric energy conversion requires ample ATP for faster healing, improved cognition, and increased strength.

ATP is the chemical energy responsible for, well, everything. If it's production exceeds metabolic burn or aerobic output, in the case of hyperventilation or air packing (as free divers do just before they dive) where more air is taken in than expunged while at rest, there's a theoretical surplus that will increase the electrical potential across cell membranes by adding energy (ATP) to the sodium/potassium pump. You can test this for yourself right now.

Take three minutes and breathe fully and deeply, continuously for thirty breaths, emphasizing the inhale over the exhale. Fill the lungs as much as possible. You'll notice right away an improvement in mood and an increase in mental clarity and energy. You may even feel stronger with improved clarity and color of vision. Instantly.

This isn't magic. You've just taken in more oxygen to fuel ATP and electricity conversion, and the billions of neurons that sit in your brain and throughout your body are screaming with happy sauce.

Rice (glycogen) + air (oxygen) = qi (bioelectromagnetic energy)—the source of life.

Sensitivity

> *Shape clay into a vessel; it is the space within that makes it useful. Cut doors and windows for a room; it is the holes which make it useful. Therefore benefit comes from what is there; usefulness from what is not there.*
>
> —Laozi

Sensitivity Defined

Lightness, like weightlessness, isn't a fixed, objective state of being; it's a living state. The protocol discussion above is an entirely different orientation to training than most. Where practices open the door, they give us access to living states of power and freedom, but they don't comprise them in and of themselves. Lightness is a craft that requires a craftsman's mindset. This isn't a simple game of effort = reward. This is a game of conscientious effort = integration and sensitivity.

One can assume that this state is inherently rewarding, but sensitivity doesn't discriminate. This isn't some bullshit secret, positive affirmation nonsense. It's quite possible that an increase in sensitivity could lead to more felt pain and suffering. This is a warning to the reader. You cannot determine the specific contents of what you sense. That's the world's job. You can, however, determine how much of it you feel and how much of it you attach yourself to or choose to hold onto. That's the craft of Weightlessness in general, and Lightness in particular.

The less attached you are to the specific outcomes of your actions and, at a deeper level, to your own sense of self, the less negative events will impact you in devastating ways—like the farmer in the parable in The Uncertainty Scroll who watches his life unfold around him yet remains uncompelled to judge the positivity or negativity of each seemingly important event. This is the only way to contain Lightness safely, for with attachment and a low stress threshold, the sensitive creature will be prone to anxiety, depression, and fear.

Second, the discussion of sensitivity here should be read with the strictest of material interpretations. It shouldn't be translated as an overt emotional tenderness with a proclivity for hurt feelings. It's a literal application of the term toward receptivity to information or data.

Michio Kaku, the theoretical physicist, has a definition for consciousness that I feel fits that of sensitivity far better. He defines degrees or levels of consciousness as direct expressions of awareness to sensate data. Things that have zero responsiveness to the world, of which there are not many, have zero degrees of consciousness. As we go up the spectrum of sensation we find higher degrees of consciousness. He states that a thermometer, for example, in that it's sensitive and responds to one environmental factor, temperature, has one degree of consciousness. Congratulations, thermometers, you made the cut!

Hopefully you, like me, can see the definition start to break down if we cannot substantiate a difference in kind vs. a difference in degree here. The consciousness of humans does seem like an altogether different kind, not just degree, than that of a thermometer. But his definition works remarkably well for sensitivity, and this is consistent with Lightness Theory.

A thermometer senses temperature. It responds to higher temperatures by expanding mercury within a glass casing. Simple. One input, one response.

Single-cell organisms, while infinitely simpler than all complex life, are still infinitely more complex than a thermometer. The protist, for example, is shown under scientific observation to be capable of learning, and this is without a brain or nervous system. Regardless, bacteria reproduce in a variety of ways, heal, replicate, and convert energy. These marvelous feats, even in very simple creatures, occur through environmental interaction and feedback.

Now leap forward about 4 billion years, from the first single-cell organisms to… us.

Overlooking the complexities of cellular metabolism if you'll allow, and merely looking at direct sensate data received on a momentary basis, the human brain has 80 to 100 billion neurons that communicate with one another and send signals throughout the body via the mechanisms we discussed previously—electrical impulse. To boot, the heart contains about 40,000, the spinal cord about 100 million, and about 500 million neurons in the enteric nervous system of the gut… which makes the phrase "listen to your gut" a lot less preposterous from a decision-making standpoint. There's a whole lotta data there.

Sensitivity refers to the volume and coherence of those data signals (feeling or touch-based information) along with those stemming from the other senses: sight, sound, taste, smell, and thought itself.

Let's take this and apply it to what many perceive as mystical powers in martial arts, namely, the effortless throwing of opponents or tremendous leverage some tai chi masters display over their larger opponents.

The inability of some masters to be uprooted when pushed by many others at the same time may be explained by a higher sensitivity to, and an ability to redirect or disperse, force from an opponent. This is so obviously possible when moving slowly, applying pressure against another person's arm, that it's baffling why extending this same logic to highly skilled athletes isn't a natural and logical leap.

Standing meditation cultivates a deep awareness of structure and sensitivity to the ground, as well as other incoming forces, allowing for appropriate, coordinated responses.

The ability of a master to coordinate his movements against the fixed force of the ground can and will profoundly increase force potential. All athletes know this, for if their angle of force is off—a high jumper in leaping, a sprinter in stride—then they waste energy and botch the show. The same is true among martial arts experts in relation to one another; we're just dealing with greater complexity and multitudes of force vectors.

The empty, sensing body will feel and react far faster than the full, tense one.

Your Inner Homunculi

Third, your homunculus can evolve. Wilder Penfield, in the 1930s revived an ancient creature, a fully formed miniature human from sixteenth century alchemy, as an iconic representation of the somatosensory brain map (regions of the brain associated with sensation in the body). He was one of those renegade surgeons who cut away parts of the skull to zap parts of the brain with electricity to see what would happen. You know, one of those guys. He did this while they were awake and conscious, which could be done because the brain has no pain receptors. Then he'd remove parts of the brain that weren't working right. *You won't be needing this...*

From extensive sampling in a similar manner Penfield created a brain map that showed which regions of the brain corresponded to sense and function in which regions of the body. And he discovered disproportionate spatial real estate in the brain to that of the relative body part size. The tongue-taste region of the brain for example might take up more brain real estate than back-sensation or feel, even though the surface area of a person's back is far larger than the surface area of the mouth and tongue. This is not hard to understand, but it has interesting implications.

The Penfield homunculus was a creature whose features were proportional to the ways in which we sense and interact with the world, with massive hands on twiggy arms, gigantic lips, mouth and tongue. You might portray a cobbler with larger hands, and a musician with larger ears, for example. It was a visual representation of sensate experience as mapped by brain space allocation.

This cartoonish figure has been the subject of many sculptures and paintings, sometimes funny, sometimes freakishly haunting. But it does reinforce the fact that we live in a world of bias, dictated in large part by key data centers rooted in biological impulse. Those impulses correspond to regions of the brain allocated to processing that data.

We'd like to believe we're all rational, balanced people, but the truth is that most of the information we receive for processing and interpretation isn't intelligently or even broadly selected. It's dictated by and received according to the primal curiosities of your one-year-old self, the self that wanted delicious things to eat, new things to touch and feel, and to get rid of that uncomfortable waste in the intestines. It isn't evenly distributed, unbiased perception receptive to all available data. It's preselected and reinforced through unconscious habit over a lifetime.

Why does this matter? It matters because your homunculus can be retrained, your body map can change, and, with them, your sensitivity to information in and around you. A musician to sound, an archer to sight, a chef to taste, a wrestler to touch, a dancer to proprioception, each master's in their own domains, elite representatives of masterful sensitivity with key biases.

They have taken that piece of real estate in the brain, invested heavily in its development, and have transformed their inner homunculus. Penfield proved that brain maps are not static; they evolve as your relationship with your environment evolves, as your complex feedback system receives data and reinforces patterned responses.

Daniel Kahneman, psychologist and behavioral economist, in his book *Thinking, Fast and Slow,* describes one type of optimistic bias as *What You See Is All There Is* (WYSIATI), which describes the proclivity of people in decision making to focus on known knowns, to rarely consider unknown knowns (perceived relevant but lacking in information), and to altogether disregard unknown unknowns (unknown information with unknown relevance).

We might say the latter two are the central focus of The Uncertainty Scroll, while The Weightlessness Scroll details known knowns with little uncertainty. To his credit, Kahneman places accountability on the decision maker, not only on our unpredictable world. We can own much more of our experience than we do and can access much more information.

Our experiences in the world then are highly self-selected, and this generates biases that reinforce habitual patterns of thought and action (which reinforce your homunculus). This bias keeps the ignorant in ignorance and the overconfident exposed to hefty and unforeseen risks. It also keeps us feeling like "us" and makes change a very complicated process.

Sensitivity (and Lightness Training) is tapping directly into the Matrix. It's seeing, sensing, feeling without bias, or at least with diminishing bias to environmental information over time. With this comes novelty in life, comes accurate perception, comes incisive and relevant decision making, and the mind-body coordination to act with power.

That Tai Chi Tho

In the martial arts world, this complex process of right perception and intelligent response is honed over years of contact fighting and meditation, but there's perhaps no greater tool in all of martial arts than that of tai chi push hands, or similar sensitivity tools in other systems (like those found in Wing Chun or Filipino boxing).

In the chapter "That Tai Chi Tho" in *The Essence of Lightness* short story, push hands represents the highest embodied practice of sensitivity (and personal power). It tells the story of Flash's progress, from a state of powerlessness at the will of Grandmaster Caz to becoming his equal. This was only possible through his cultivation of sensitivity, his intuitive reception of real sensory and proprioceptive information and his coordinated, embodied response.

This is no simple practice, despite how seemingly innocuous it is. And, in my opinion, it's well worth contemplating, if not actually learned for everyone everywhere. I've had the pleasure of training with remarkable push hands players in both Shanghai and Tai Chi village itself in Henan province while filming a documentary on Grandmaster Chen, purportedly the only living inheritor of Small Frame Tai Chi. The ghostlike sensation I describe in Flash's practice sequence I've experienced firsthand. It leaves one feeling truly powerless, where everything you think you know and are capable of is suddenly rendered useless.

Every act, even every intention of aggression finds no home and is quickly redirected, pulling your mind from a point of confidence to total helplessness. When you receive the master's push, it feels like a mystical surge of energy that uproots your footing and sends you flying like an awkward rag doll. The master feels the base of your feet through the slightest touch of your finger. He feels the slightest gap in your integrated structure through first contact.

I can only say it's bizarre and validates every far-fetched assumption of mysticism in the martial arts from ages past. I won't toot my own horn here, but I'm no slouch in the martial arts game. I'm a serious lifer with over thirty years of experience, and I say that only to point out how insanely skillful some push hands masters are at reading another individual on a deep systemic level. The sensitivity and awareness they demonstrate is hauntingly dark.

So, Flash's process was one of opening, of learning to receive, of maximizing yin rather than yang. His path to matching Caz's power was not one of tool acquisition or an increase in physical power or force. It was through emptying himself of bias, both psychological and physiological, and learning to listen deeply to the most minute sensate data available to him: the angle and degree of force, the point of his opponent's diminishing power, his own tensegrity in live-action against the force of gravity, his own structural alignment against the earth, and his breath.

There is infinite complexity in martial engagement. On a simple level, we can imagine how two arms are an advantage over one, how greater strength is more valuable than less, how good technique trumps bad. These are superficial but meaningful points of data. Add to that awareness. Add to that great structure. Add to that sensitivity of more and more and more, and it's not so hard to imagine how masters are to novices what adults are to children in this game of physical dominance.

The master of Lightness cultivates the capacity for unbiased reception of data to a high degree. We're designing a far less self-centered way of interacting with our environments, a way of sensing more of what is actually there, right in front of us and coordinating our mind-body legions against it. This true insight and coordinated response is a warrior's magic bullet against selfish bias and inappropriate action. Flash needed it to survive the 18.

A Vessel with Holes

Lightness isn't the place for people to work out their personal baggage, that's back in the Weightlessness Spectrum. Lightness is for those who have laid the groundwork already.

Both my last book and this one (I suspect) paint an aspirational view of Lightness training. But I want to be clear. It's for everyone in principle insofar as we all grow from the implementation of smart stressors and we liberate our minds with concentrated bouts of awareness in the same human ways, but it's not for everyone in practice, because not everyone does the groundwork.

This takes many forms. I get emails from those who have read *In Pursuit of Weightlessness* and gone out and bought a pair of ankle weights, and I get people signing up to my remote Weightlessness Process who want to jump right into Lightness when they're struggling to hit level two metrics in The Weightlessness Spectrum. Lightness is not the place you seal your holes. Lightness is a craft that will attack your gaps and inequities. If you've left them unsealed, it can break you. It's only after you've laid that foundation designed in The Spectrum that Lightness becomes a safe playground.

Cultivate and Balance Your Pillars

Examples. Had a client who couldn't hold a static squat (horse stance) with proper knee-ankle-hip alignment and neutral spine who started self-prescribing ballistic weight training. Why? Because he wanted that speed. What happened? He got injured. If you cannot splay the knees and maintain neutral spine while in a static squat for one full minute (or longer), global strength and the integrity of your connective tissues is insufficient to stabilize ballistic movement with added weight. Walk before you run.

Seal your holes.

If you cannot deadlift a weight equal or greater than your bodyweight with proper form, you WILL injure yourself doing weighted dynamic stretches in one of two ways: you'll tear your hamstring or slip a disk in your lower back. These are two sides of the same body mechanics, flexion and extension. The deadlift shortens (tightens the rear train of the body) while dynamic stretching extends it dynamically (relaxes the rear train… up to its peak point).

Without sufficient strength in the rear train of the body, rising kicks will uncover and attack whichever weak link is left—lower back strength, neutral spine gaps, glute-hamstring pull strength, even upper back strength. If you cannot deadlift your bodyweight, you cannot add weight to dynamic stretching. If you cannot stretch dynamically, sprinting and leaping with weight presents a great deal of risk, as you load your limbs with elastic tension but don't know how to release it quickly.

Seal your holes.

If you cannot perform the full splits (within a narrow margin) with an untucked tailbone, you WILL tear your hamstrings, strain your Achilles, slip a disk, blow your knee out or experience plantar fasciitis or any number of other aches, pains, and injuries stemming from muscle strain and tendon wear and inflammation. If one thing should be totally self-evident at this point, it's that you're an integrated being. All these systems are related. A runner's stride, especially with added weight, tests the rear myofascial train of the body in extension, and the frontal plane (lower abs, hip flexors, and upper quads primarily) in flexion.

Seal your holes and balance your pillars!

The Healer Without Energy

And yet another, okay, several trainees here, who wanted to learn "*healing*" in one energetic practice or another, but they could not 1) understand the correlation between the metrics within The Weightlessness Spectrum and other modes of effective healing, and 2) could not perform the metrics in The Spectrum to a high degree. They also could not, which is a whole other debate, define *energy* in the term *energy healing*. Some call it Reiki. Some qigong. Some faith healing. If your answer to the question of "What energy are you healing with?" and "How are you cultivating it?" is *idunno*, then we have more serious problems.

You're in the domain of placebo (if lucky) or make-believe (if not lucky), but not science. Not even in the domain of empirical science with isolated variables and testable hypotheses on an individual level. There are many known energies including thermal, solar, sound, elastic, gravitational, electric, radiant, chemical, magnetic, and radiation, to name a few. If you've got access to some undiscovered special sauce when the greatest minds on planet Earth don't even have it on their radar... something is amiss. Do better. Look deeper into your craft.

Slow breathing and reverse counting, while enhancing awareness and concentration respectively, are also basic forms of qigong, in that they are self-directed practices that move attention and, therefore, energy. They address fundamental operations of the mind, but they also improve oxygen uptake and utilization in the first case and intensity of focus in the second.

Improved oxygen uptake and utilization (from slow breathing) means a greater quantity of free electrons available for the production of ATP, the chemical energy that supports the generation of bioelectricity. These are real, known energies responsible for healing (among everything else) in the body—chemical and electromagnetic.

Concentration, on the other hand, accumulates energy. We've discussed the neural communication between thought and tensing muscle to form a fist. This is the movement of *electricity* in the body.

Maintaining the thought alone without a corresponding act also improves neural signaling; hence, the advocacy by all coaches, both athletic and otherwise to practice visualization and rehearsal. Thought alone has been proven to enhance technique and performance. How? It moves energy in the body and refines neural signaling just as well as actually doing the real thing.

So, if you want to put somebody on a bed, light the incense and play that serene Balinese music, laying your hands on a stranger after a weekend certification class, be my guest. But on my playground, healing takes time and practice—lots. To have a body that can produce and carry charge at will takes practice. To empty yourself of tension so your neurology can carry out energetic transfer at will takes practice. To be compassionate (and selfless) enough to give yourself to another without looking for praise or admiration takes practice. Learn to breathe and concentrate first without the pressure of performance for others.

Full disclosure: I don't claim to be a healer or energetic guru of any kind. This isn't about that. I'm a student of Lightness and will likely be forever. The discussion above is a well-researched, science-based approach to tapping our deeper potentials. Use it if it helps you; discard it if it doesn't. But always maintain focus on the basics (outlined in The Weightlessness Scroll). While I've had corroborating experiences in the domain of energetics that make the theories above very tangible to me, I don't often share them. Qigong is very hard work that I occasionally honor and more frequently neglect. Higher skills (healing and "seeing") can easily become an aspirational distraction, causing us to neglect foundational training and right living. Sincere self-study of our mind-bodies in the world trumps mysticism any day of the week.

Seal your holes… And if you've still got time, dance in the void.

The Integrity Gap

Perhaps the single biggest hole, the greatest barrier to personal growth and one that requires constant attention, is the integrity gap. It goes something like this:

You've started a change process, joined a self-improvement program, started a new fitness regime or diet, or just committed to make changes for the better. After a couple weeks, something pops up that you think prevents you from honoring your commitment. You believe it. You accept it. It's just a small thing, after all. Then it happens again. You believe it again. You accept it again. A bit later, you stop showing up or you get injured. You believe you need complete rest. You accept it. There it all goes. I've said it before, but it bears repeating often:

Weightlessness is not a fitness system. It's not a workout. It's a process. It's a philosophy of life that informs best practices in good times AND bad.

I believe in safety first. I'm not suggesting you do things that activate or trigger an injury; I'm suggesting you don't use that as a point of self-pity, an excuse to derail the *real* work you need to do. You can always train. That may not mean training physically, however. But you can still show up.

You hurt your knee? Can't squat? Okay… but pushups don't use that knee much, right? Chin-ups and seated shoulder presses don't use that knee much. Why are you staying home, is the rest of your body perfectly sculpted already?

Your back is hurt, and you can't do much lower *or* upper body work without aggravating it. Fair enough. Can you sit in the splits or practice standing hamstring stretches, with an elevated foot to prevent arching the back? How about reclining hamstring stretches with a belt? Still no? Okay, can you breathe?

If you can breathe you can train. And you can always breathe.

To reiterate a phrase I heard early in my martial arts career: If you can breathe, you can train. Everything else is an excuse. You think this game is about fitness? Does your knee hurt? Does your back hurt? You gotta rest?

You're in the wrong game! That's not what this is about. This is about life. This is about being the guy or gal who does what they say they'll do because it fucking matters, and it doesn't stop mattering just because it's inconvenient today to follow through, or because you don't have the self-discipline to prioritize meaningful things without overcommitting yourself. Not feeling well or being busy is not a get-outa-jail-free-card for life.

This was never about that. Fitness is central to the process of self-development because it's the only safe environment of methodical applied stress. It conditions our stress systems and improves our stress thresholds. But it isn't the whole game.

This game is about you! It's about how you show up in life, and how you navigate uncertainty in times of change. Saying you're gonna make changes and do the work required therein doesn't mean you're gonna make changes so long as it's convenient and nothing pops up to distract you or derail your plans. That's inevitable. That's guaranteed. It means you're gonna wait for those moments to confront your true self, and you'll work through them. This is the meaning of showing up. This is integrity.

If traffic makes you late, is it the traffic's fault? Leave earlier next time! If a meeting runs over, is it the meeting's fault? It's either yours if you have the power to end it on time, or it's bad planning to schedule your training appointment (or any other priority) without a safe transition window. If a phone call runs over, is it the phone's fault? If you're in pain, take responsibility for what isn't in pain. Own your shit. Show the fuck up.

Now, there are indeed occasional emergencies that exceed bad planning, self-pity, or laziness. To name a few: relative or friend in the hospital, personal illness (respect your community, coach, and personal recovery here; don't train sick in general or risk passing it to others), car gets a flat tire, car gets stolen, terrorist attack, so on and so forth.

The key here is to hone your sense of responsibility for the things that *are* in your control and learn to let go of (though still take responsibility for) the things that are not. It's nobody's fault the conference meeting wasn't serving anything but pizza and donuts, it's yours for not considering that possibility and taking precautions. Learn from these mistakes. Give yourself one mistake, but don't repeat them.

If the integrity hole isn't sealed, no amount of training matters. If you're harder on others than you are on yourself and believe in showing yourself grace when you break commitments you've made to yourself, then you're not ready. This hole is a big one, and it will derail a Lightness protocol ten times out of ten. The Weightlessness Spectrum is built for this particular aspect of self-exploration. Not everyone makes it through, and that's what makes it an extremely effective vetting process.

I have pain in this spot.
I didn't sleep well last night.
I had a work meeting.
I'm in a tough spot with my partner.
I know that stuff already, so I don't need to do it this time; I'm a super genius.

Seal your holes.

The Knower Who Doesn't Do

I know that already. The person who gets the thing but doesn't practice that thing with conscientious mind-body effort is a poser. I transgress here occasionally myself; teacher syndrome, practicing less from the head of the class because you're teaching and you "get it," is a dangerous pitfall. The more we learn, quite often, the less we feel we need to practice it.

If someone told you they know how to ride a bike because they read a book about it, but have never attempted the act before, would you put money on that person's first ride? We live in an era where the black box of human development is mostly worked out. This doesn't mean we know its inner workings; we don't. Brain neurology is far from fully dissected, but an important question is: *Are we at a point with physiology and neurology as a whole that we understand inputs and outputs with little variance*?

And we are. We know what makes muscle grow, what strengthens tendons, what remolds fascia, what breaks synaptic bonds and lays down new neural pathways. Point being the science of transformation, while not 100% dissected, is dissected enough so that what we don't know isn't preventing us from masterful implementation of core principles. The stuff we do know… that's the stuff we gotta actually do. And you can't *get* it by reading about it or hitting a few weekend classes.

Last point to hit this home. I had a client who *got* the science of neural plasticity and *understood* its relevance toward mindfulness meditation and nonattachment. That same person made clear that he got it, while at the same time claimed he couldn't meditate effectively or still his mind without distraction. We have here a bicycle-from-a-book problem, and an integrity problem to boot.

This isn't something you can actually know without also being able to do. It doesn't work like that. If someone told you they knew how to ride a bike and, within two seconds, toppled over, you'd call bullshit. This is why this game is tough… integrity gaps of this nature are hard to self-assess because we're often prioritizing and focusing on the wrong information—information that is true, but isn't relevant. It's a very difficult thing to point out to someone that they're attached to *knowing* the concept of nonattachment while being unable to nonattach from their compulsive thoughts in life.

What exactly is *known* in this case? And is it the right information to care about?

Do you need to seal the integrity hole? Nope, not for me anyway. We all need to face that beast for ourselves. But warning to the wise—it's worth addressing now and always. To quote a good friend and Weightlessness veteran, most people want hot dogs, but we're selling steak here. Steak is always gonna nourish the body better, but that doesn't mean it's for you.

A lot of people prefer hotdogs to steak, cereal to whole grains. It's a standards conversation. If you don't see that Weightlessness is not *just another* option, that it uniquely addresses deep problems we all face in life in a substantive way, and you're happy to see people in a group aerobics class with no structural training or technical oversight leaping sloppily because "it's better than sitting on the couch," then Lightness isn't for you. I still love ya, but it ain't for you… yet.

Weightlessness implies things about the nature of movement. If you're willing to accept extremely high-risk activity because you can't see that its high risk or because you think it's an acceptable risk, then there's a disconnect. We don't need to lower our standards because many people prefer hot dogs and cancer to steak and health. This isn't binary; there are many shades of grey. And making it either-or doesn't give credence to the notion of smart, methodical, incremental progress.

We need to move in the right direction. Aerobic training is at level two in The Weightlessness Spectrum because those without sufficient structural conditioning will get injured throwing their bodies around. But we do move on from it for deeper strength and structural purposes (in prioritization, not fully in practice).

Seal your holes.

The Black Belt Who Doesn't Train

There's no such thing as a black belt who isn't training.

Last but not least, a black belt who isn't in shape enough to perform the techniques and skills of his art isn't one. This is also hard to communicate to people in a modern world of certificate and trophy collection, but things fall apart here if we don't apply this basic litmus test of performance.

Some people go through Weightlessness programs multiple times. Most get this premise, some don't. Some remember the glory days when they performed at level three with this or that metric, even though they've stopped training or neglected their protocol altogether for months. Some then enter the program believing they're ready for advanced work because they once were but haven't shown that within the last few months. You're the level you perform at. In the mind-body game, we are what we do.

If you're injured, you're most certainly at level one for strength and conditioning. Is this bad? Not at all; it means that because you want to apply speed, stamina, and limit strength again, you need to first ensure the integrity of your structure so higher skills are safe.

You hit a 1,000 reverse count before but can't manage 300 now without losing focus? Your concentration level is at 300 (level one). Period. This is where The Spectrum becomes prescriptive medicine, and not merely a way of assessing skill.

Movement is medicine. Stretching is medicine. Breathing is medicine.

Apply the appropriate tools at your current level, heal, and grow. Don't attach yourself to a static view of your prior performance. It means fuck-all. You are where you are today. And that's okay! That's awesome. You're awesome. Empty yourself. Humble yourself. Be present. And get to work.

This applies to me as much as anybody. If I take time off, which I do, I do not EVER start up again with Lightness protocols, not even level three Spectrum prescriptions. I ease back in for one or two weeks and work through The Spectrum as my metrics dictate until they clear me for the next level and eventually Lightness. If you don't want to start over, don't ever stop. But be honest about where you are so The Spectrum can heal you.

Lightness Protocols

A review of "The Long Game" chapter in *The Essence of Lightness* short story would be advised here to reinforce the psychology of training and commitment to protocol required, both in doing what's prescribed as well as ignoring what isn't (for a time).

A Word of Caution

Don't mess with the special sauce. I believe I've made a strong case in the preceding pages as to the importance of *not* leaping into Lightness Training (pun intended) without sufficient preparation. But I want to highlight the risks of picking and choosing pillars, as many have done. I get it; ballistic weight training is sexy (for some). It does add that quickness relatively quickly. And it's certainly more interesting than stretching and breathing. BUT! Consider for a moment the consequences of only doing ballistic weight training and neglecting the other practices…

I've stated before that Lightness is in part the process of living in the body of a heavier person and learning to coordinate your energies against greater resistances. Imagine the tension and force required to move that body through space and to control it effectively. Without a balance of forces, and the ability to release tension within and after ballistic weight training, a skill that's cultivated in dynamic stretching as well as qigong, you're taking on the tension required to move without the relaxation required to release. These tensional adaptations will last quite some time. This will make you feel light indeed, for a short time, until your body stiffens and its function disappears.

Likewise, dynamic stretching with added weight and without the strength to stabilize the rear train (from deadlifting, ideally) will tear your body apart.

Lightness protocols are sacred.

Balance requires all four pillars. Pillar selection matters. Order of execution matters.

Entry Level Protocol | Advanced

Perform four to six days per week. Movement elements should not exceed thirty to forty minutes per session. Cycle through sixty to one hundred days of training, then rest for a full week. Each cycle should result in higher leaping and heavier weights for all exercises.

Lightness

Jog for ten minutes. For the last 100 meters (up to one minute), sprint at 90 to 100 percent effort. Begin with three pounds on each ankle. If you struggle against the weight, it's too heavy for you. It should be imperceptible. Your stride should be light and free of tension. Your breathing should be abdominal, not upper chest. If you cannot sprint under these conditions for a time, you are not yet ready for fruitful Lightness Training. The emphasis here is not in getting it done, but in how you do it. This is a long journey.

After a short rest, proceed to weighted box jumps. Add three pounds to each ankle and ten pounds to your torso. Perform only one set to fatigue, allowing for deep meditative breaths in between each repetition.

Dynamic Flexibility

Perform short rounds of static stretching to ensure lingering tension from the previous exercises has dissipated. In particular, work through the key stretches of The Weightlessness Spectrum.

- Front Rising Kick: 5 sets of 3 reps each – Each set is higher and faster
- Side Rising Kick: 5 sets of 3 reps each - Each set is higher and faster

Strength

*Alternate the strength and meditation components from session to session. Do **A** one day, **B** the next, and **C** the next. Strength can be trained 3 to 6 days per week. It's also okay on a 6-day protocol week to practice strength 3, 4, 5, or 6 times. But remember, the more frequently you train, the more you need to reduce training volume per session.*

Strength A

- Vector: Pull | Suggested exercise—Weighted pullups
  - ▹ Reps per set: 5, 5, 5, 5, 5
- Vector: Push | Suggested exercise—One-arm pushups (assisted)
  - ▹ Reps per set: 5, 3, 3, 5
- Vector: Push | Suggested exercise—Pushups (controlled)
  - ▹ Reps: 100 (made up of sets to failure)

Strength B

- Vector: Squat/Pull | Suggested exercise—Deadlift
  - ▹ Reps per set: 5, 5, 3, 5, 5 (set 3 uses your heaviest weight)
- Vector: Press | Suggested exercise—Shoulder press or handstand pushups
  - ▹ Reps per set: 5, 5, 3, 5, 5 (set 3 uses your heaviest weight)
- Vector: Pull | Suggested exercise—Bicep curls (for men. Women may not want the extra volume / bicep growth)
  - ▹ Reps per set: 10, 8, 5, 5, 20

Strength C

- Vector: Squat | Suggested exercise—Barbell squat or pistol squat
  - ▹ Reps per set: 8, 6, 5, 5, 5 (set 3 uses your heaviest weight)
- Vector: Twist | Suggested exercise—Cable wood chops
  - ▹ Reps per set: 10, 10, 10 (each side)
- Vector: Twist | Suggested exercise—Cable crunch
  - ▹ Reps per set: 15, 10, 6, 8, 10

Meditation

- Slow Breathing: 10 slowest breaths
- Qigong: Progression #1—fifteen minutes
- Awareness Practice (Standing): five minutes

Lightness Notes:

At this stage, you should be very in tune with tension in your body. Maintain static stretching as needed, based on what you've learned through the earlier stages of training. You may not need much if you've activated both front and center splits already. But it's okay to add static stretching after your meditation, or at other times of the day as you have a short break. Regularly putting your body in extended positions is the best way to remold your form. I also highly recommend hanging from a bar as much as possible, and back bends should be integrated at this stage if you have knowledge of safe form.

Don't consider static stretching a protocol; just integrate it whenever and wherever you can. This goes the same for meditation. At this stage, you should be very connected to your breath, and practice will wind up spilling over into daily life. When you're walking down the street or sitting in a business meeting and realize that your mind is aware of the *dan tian*, that you're relaxed and you feel energy within while simultaneously being receptive to your environment, then meditation becomes a living practice outside of training. That's when you go from training to being.

Veteran Level Protocol | Very Advanced

Perform six days per week. Movement elements should not exceed forty minutes per session. Cycle through sixty to one hundred days of training, then rest for a full week.

Lightness

Jog for eight minutes. For the last 100 meters (up to one minute), sprint at 90 to 100 percent effort. Add five to ten pounds on each ankle but if you struggle against the weight, it's too heavy for you. It should be imperceptible.

After a short rest, proceed to weighted box jumps. Add five to ten pounds to each ankle. Perform only one set to fatigue only (likely 6 to 15 reps), allowing for deep meditative breaths in-between each repetition.

Dynamic Flexibility

You should no longer need static stretching prior to dynamic movement.

- Front Rising Kick: 3 sets of 5 reps each—Each set is higher and faster
- Inside Crescent Kick: 3 sets of 3 reps each—Each set is higher and faster
- Outside Crescent Kick: 3 sets of 3 reps each—Each set is higher and faster
- Side Rising Kick: 3 sets of 3 reps each—Each set is higher and faster
- Rear Rising Kick: 3 sets of 3 reps

Alternate the strength and meditation components from session to session. Do ***A*** *one day,* ***B*** *the next, and* ***C*** *the next. Strength can be trained 3 to 6 days per week. It's also okay on a 6-day protocol week to practice strength 3, 4, 5, or 6 times. But remember, the more frequently you train, the more you need to reduce training volume per session.*

Strength A

- Vector: Pull-Push | Suggested exercise—Muscle-Ups
    - ▹ Reps per set: 5, max, 5
- Vector: Pull | Suggested exercise—Weighted pullups
    - ▹ Reps per set: 5, 5, 5, 5, 5
- Vector: Twist | Suggested exercise—Hanging Leg Raises
    - ▹ Reps per set: to failure, to failure, to failure (performed slow with squeeze at top)

Strength B

- Vector: Squat/Pull | Suggested exercise—Deadlift
    - ▹ Reps per set: 5, 5, 3, 5, 5 (set 3 uses your heaviest weight)
- Vector: Press | Suggested exercise—Handstand pushups & hand balance work
    - ▹ Reps per set: 5, 5, 3, 5, 5
- Vector: Squat | Suggested exercise—Pistol Squat (1-Leg Squat)
    - ▹ Reps per set: 5 sets of 3-5 reps

Strength C

- Vector: Push | Suggested exercise—Planche Work
    - ▹ Reps per set: 5 sets of 5 to 15 second attempts at highest planche progression
    - ▹ Planche Leans: 3 sets of 15 to 30 seconds
    - ▹ Weighted or 1-arm Pushups: 3 sets (of 3 to 5 reps)
- Vector: Twist | Suggested exercise—Crunches (w/ twists integrated)
    - ▹ 200 Total

Meditation

- Qigong: Progression #1 – ten minutes
- Qigong: Progression #2 – five minutes
- Qigong: Progression #3 – five minutes

Review the qigong progressions in *The Essence of Lightness* short story in Part 1 under "The Pillars of Lightness" section where qigong progressions are listed.

Theoretical Lightness Metrics:

There are not now and will unlikely be formalized metrics in Lightness Training due to the overarching emphasis on qualitative movement and presence rather than objective, quantifiable metrics. However, we could look at a few indicators of elite performance that would serve well as guiding lights over time:

- Strength: Planche
- Flexibility: Suspended splits
- Speed & Agility (from ballistic weight training): 3-step horizontal wall run, or the 5-step corner-turn wall run
- Meditation: 10 breaths (or fewer) in fifteen minutes (or more)

The Mastery Scroll

> *Lightness didn't invent anything...*
> *lightness reinvented everything.*
> *—Grandmaster Caz*

The Mastery Scroll is a reminder that Weightlessness is a process of becoming, not arriving. Your reward for doing good work is more challenging work. You now have the tools; it's time to internalize them. This doesn't just mean within grandiose visions of self with farther-reaching metrics, but in the applications of basic yet deep principles to the small, seemingly inconsequential daily actions in life. Weightlessness is a craft to be lived. You're no longer naked and afraid. Whatever the process reveals, you accept. You work with it humbly and conscientiously, tightening your circles of applied theory and bearing responsibility for your personal sense of weightlessness in life. Be weightless.

In the Mind-Body of a Master, Present and Future Are One

The Tao of Weightlessness Revisited

The Samurai, after decades of precise technical training and tens of thousands of hours of meditation has the fortitude, grit, focus, and presence to see with crystal clear insight the blade of grass amidst the mind-shattering pressures of battle. In the mind-body of a master, stress (resilience to) and sensitivity not only integrate, but also amplify one another.

The samurai, the master, in preparing for future stresses today has attained a presence and focus that transforms the grueling work he *must* do into the life-giving vehicles he *gets* to do. In the mind-body of the master the polarities of survival and quality, stress and sensitivity, within the Tao of Weightlessness become a unified whole.

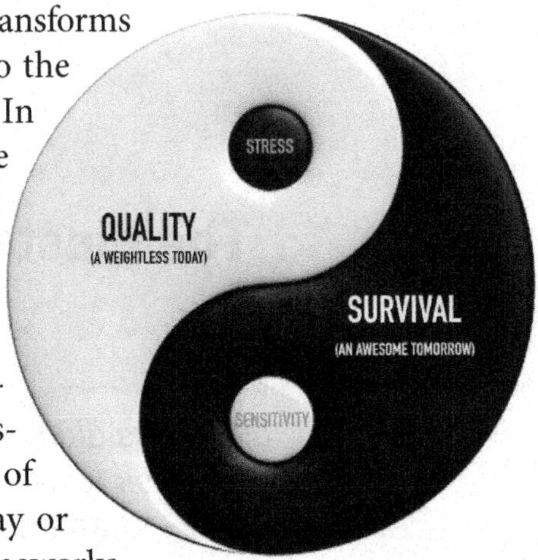

In The Time Scroll, we discussed how our perception of passing time leads to the prioritization of one frame above the other—today or tomorrow. Rarely do these two frameworks merge in real time, though in Lightness, this is possible. The challenge, as has been discussed in The Uncertainty Scroll, is that inherent risks of the unknown can kill us (literally or metaphorically) and fear of that unknown tears us from the present.

On the other hand, delusion around the risks inherent in complex-dynamic domains such as life allows us to underestimate future volatility and the suffering it can cause. So we shrug off the unknowns of the future and delight in the present. The master has learned to bypass this dilemma, not in principle but in the daily practice of making every mundane act both an end in itself and an investment in the future through conscious presence.

Albert Camus posed an existential challenge regarding the myth of Sisyphus—prankster-god condemned to an eternity of rolling a boulder up a hill only to watch it roll back down again. *One must imagine Sisyphus happy,* he said. This question, this position, wasn't really about the fatalist dilemma of Sisyphus, but was very much about you and I and the way in which we view our existences and the meaning of our choices.

Of that life of monotonous mediocrity, Camus wanted us to ask ourselves what *we* would do, and who *we* would be. That punishment, that torture was such only because Sisyphus was wholly conscious of his plight, and incapable of altering it. Sisyphus had no freedom except for the way he chose to view his plight. His fate was sealed but his mind was his. In the strain and agony of completing his charge, is it possible that awareness, focus, confidence, self-respect, self-worth, and dare I even add freedom, are possible?

In embracing the burdens we carry with full, integrated presence, they can become our liberation.

How We Frame Our Burdens Is How They Frame Us

A hero is only as great as the greatness of his villain. We love, in the Judeo-Christian tradition, to worship the hero and condemn the villain. But in so doing, we dishonor the process that makes the hero heroic. We can't escape the reality that if you want a great hero, leader, savior, you need a really big problem for them to solve, for he is nothing without it—not even himself. In the process of overcoming the challenge and defeating the villain, the hero becomes the hero. Not before and certainly not *just because*.

In the process of self-mastery, we need to be equally concerned with the kind and degree of villains we take on. With the kind of burdens we accept. We must be conscious that the Joker made Batman, that the boulder made Sisyphus, and that our burdens will define us. If we are present and aware of those burdens as we take them on, they lose power over us. What's more, they empower us. And rather than continue to be the rocks that make us sink, they become the life preservers that lift us up to that fresh breath of air.

The violent interplay between tomorrow and today, stress and sensitivity doesn't exist in the conscientious master who bears no attachment at cross-purposes with his burdens. He's not the devil-may-care hedonist who burns his opportunity for a bright future by soaking up ephemeral pleasures today. And he's not the sad martyr who burns the majesty of this current plight by preparing, investing, sacrificing for the future.

All actions provide the opportunity to manifest weightlessness, for who we are is cemented in everything, every small thing that we do: the listening, the standing, the sitting, the sensing, the eating, the walking, the positive acceptance of discipline and structure, the ownership of elected obligations, the knowing embrace of the unknown. Every act is dually present and preparatory if we allow it.

Making sure that we haven't drifted too far into one or the other timeframe at the expense of the other requires frequent auditing of our actual choices, big or small, the only true reflections of personal priorities.

Am I sacrificing my future for greater comfort today?
Am I resisting or embracing my burdens?
Am I aware of my breath, my present reality?
Am I weightless?

Uncertainty Is the Only Certainty—We Still Have to Make Decisions

Uncertainty Revisited

The not knowing is what kills us. It retards our logic and ability to plan for the future because we cannot effectively plan for something that could be five days or fifty years in waiting. It kills quality moments from day to day because we step outside of time to solve its lingering uncertainty. Yet we, like Sisyphus, have to make sense of it all and push ahead. Without knowing how much time we have in life, determining which timeframe to focus on in life is impossible. But we know it's likely to be some of each: more present and some future, and we would do well to optimize the quality of our experience in the present and our probability of having quality experiences in the future.

The biggest inhibitor of mind-body development and performance isn't in technical development; it's in our underlying paradigms that make any technique or tool relevant in the first place. Humans are awesome at things we deem both important and urgent, but god-awful at things we don't. With the visceral urgency of a finite existence, the uncertainty of tomorrow, and the loss of potential life from moment to moment, we don't have much useful information.

But, as Sherlock Holmes in the *Hounds of Baskerville* noted (reference in The Uncertainty Scroll), sometimes the absence of evidence *is* the evidence to take note of. Uncertainty is negative information that we can use to make meaningful decisions about living a quality life, one that isn't consistently and chaotically oscillating between two selves torn over future fears and ambitions, and momentary pleasures. These selves can coexist with power.

This living paradox can coexist in the master of Lightness.

I've been asked more times than I can count if running is good… if swimming, if bicycling, if hiking, if eating nuts, beans, and tofu (and on and on) are good for you? The only response I've had, if I'm in the mood that day to attempt to answer a loaded question, the depth of which cannot be addressed with a simple yes or no, is to ask in return: *Good for what?*

If you ask ten different people what the best car is, you'll get ten different answers. Some prefer sports cars, some prefer SUVs, some prefer luxury, some prefer hybrids or alternative energy cars, and some prefer NASCAR or F1 racecars. If you're lucky, one of those ten people may not answer, but ask in return… *Best for what?* And now we're getting somewhere. We're getting to the beginning that is. *Well... where are we going?*

So you explain further, rather vaguely, that you're going on a journey together. You'll need to pick the best tires, a cool design, and probably a killer stereo because eyes gravitate toward that bling first and substance second. And since this one-out-of-ten responder is pretty sharp, he investigates further: *That's all well and good, but where exactly are we going? Are we touring cities? Are we going off road? How many miles will we need to run on one tank of gas? Will there be bandits we need to speed away from or risk of being shot at? Will we need to spend any nights in the car? How can I tell you what tires are best without defining the road ahead?*

You think long and hard about this question. You know your original question still has merit because you know you'll need tires, a cool design, and probably a good stereo, but you're not entirely sure where you're going. So you ask yourself a deeper question: *What do I know about where I'm going? And, more importantly, can the things I don't know, can't possibly know, kill me?*

While you don't know precisely, you do know a few things true of all paths. You know you'll face some good times and bad, regardless of the path you take: rough roads, broken parts. You also know that good roads don't require a lot of planning. If you can survive the bad roads, good roads tend to take care of themselves. And you know that, while you're most likely to remain on paved roads under stable conditions, the truth is that you're not sure if you'll go off road for a time, have to outlast a fuel drought on a particularly long stretch, possibly hit ice and snow, get into a fender bender, and who knows, maybe get shot at once in a while by evil bandits.

So, you know one thing with certainty: there will be volatility—unforeseen and unpredictable. But! But you don't want that to dictate all your experience along the way and prevent you from enjoying the smooth roads with incredible views that allow you to blast the Allman Brothers and feel the wind flowing through the windows. So how do we make sure, despite it all, that those incredible moments are experienced no matter what?

While many of the negative potentialities do exist and pose a challenge to the machine and, therefore, your journey, you still walk away from that conversation with a level of depth and understanding that surpasses most who will undertake the journey of life. It's unlikely you'll need the most powerful engine, as you're not planning on plowing through warzones or spending all your time off road. If you know you are, by all means, put the Navy Seal of engines in there. But you know you'll need a powerful engine regardless, capable of carrying you through such circumstances should they occur, resilient to volatility and stress, albeit crudely.

You know you'll need a machine that can navigate clean paths, yet agile enough to handle the occasional rough road or dangerous obstacle to avoid a collision. It doesn't need F1 precision steering, but something in that direction couldn't hurt. You also know that there will be fuel stops along the way, regular energy supplies spaced out over your journey, but you can't see any downside in making your car as energy efficient as possible, while allotting extra space for a backup tank if possible. You know if you put that hot-sauce fuel, the artificial stuff, into your engine, it might perform well today, but is likely to break down tomorrow.

You can also be sure that at some point, parts will break and building a machine of highly specialized parts requiring specialized skills to fix is also unwise, as who knows when or where this may occur. So you determine, at least as a starting point, that while this machine should look and feel good, it must rely on a minimum number of robust parts, built in the most fundamental of ways with the crudest tools. While this won't make for the most specialized car in any one domain, it will make the most resilient and versatile car across all domains. This will allow for the greatest chance of staying the course and experiencing all the beauty that is sure to present itself along the way.

In our ignorance, in the complexity and uncertainty of life, we find the deepest insights into the road ahead, and the vehicle required to allow us to enjoy the trip.

So we return to our original question: *Is it good to run? Swim? Bicycle?* Sure, man… its better than lying on the sofa. But where the hell do you want to go? Humans aren't really specialists. We're king generalists and we live in complex environments wholly foreign to that natural environment that engineered our genetics. We have no individual assets that rival any other animals in the kingdom, save for intellect, and this only equalizes things well when we find a way to reduce or fully eliminate the need for physical performance from our environments, which, sadly, many of us have. Sadly because we lose something inherent to who/what we are the more we reduce the role of the body in any activity. But that can be reintegrated through conscious applications of structure and awareness in basic living.

Humans aren't the fastest runners, the strongest lifters, the most graceful swimmers or capable of surfing the wind. But we can build strong muscular engines, agile mental steering, and impressive energy systems that take in amply, assimilate, convert, and expunge with great efficiency so that general energy and health support our efforts and dreams, rather than become liabilities. We're not born with the hardware to be the best at any one thing. We are born with the hardware to be the best of all things, to reign by way of balanced and integrated mind-body assets developed with the most basic of nature's tools: Stress and sensitivity.

This is a practice of perspective that must be regularly audited—the practice of embracing the unknown. It's not a practice of dismissing what we know, but one of *not* dismissing what we don't. Like the parable of the farmer's son recapped in The Uncertainty Scroll, future events far outside of the farmer's control had more to do with determining the positivity or negativity of happenings today than the events themselves.

This is perspective that can remain fresh and alive and empower us to see what's here and now without getting lost in myopic interpretations of current events. We can mold ourselves to become resilient to these unpredictable events, yet sensitive to see novelty and beauty within them. This is a combination of thorough mind-body preparation, and frequent auditing of personal perspective:

How could what I don't know affect my interpretation of what I see?
Affect the way I feel about this person in front of me?
Affect the way I treat this person I love?

Positive Stressors and Useful Idiots

Change and Transformation Revisited

A useful idiot is someone who accidentally supports a cause, a pawn of sorts. They're idiots because they're ignorant about the realities that underlie their influence. And they're useful because they bring about desired change—for someone else. Stressors, those things that trigger biological or psychological discomfort, are no different.

We often feel like the things that frustrate and burden us are malicious or designed. We take personal offense from them and grant them power to affect our moods and actions the way we might with a puppet president. They're almost always not designed or malicious. They're just idiots, blind to their purpose and impact, and affecting us to the degree we allow them. As such, the same idiot, the same stressor, can be either good or bad in our lives. *We* are the determinants.

Our villains define us, yes. But our response to the villain, to stress, to that useful idiot, says a lot more about us than the idiot. The stuff that burdens us in life is indifferent to us for the most part. It's within us, a psychoemotional response to external stimulus. Insofar as we can learn to face it with full presence and without suffering, we create the opportunity for change in ourselves. In The Integration Scroll I quoted Viktor Frankl:

Between stimulus and response, there is a space. In that space is our power to choose our response. In our response lies our growth and our freedom.

During the Holocaust, a Sisyphusian plight of the highest order, Frankl identified that gap between experience and interpretation that left him in control, if not of his circumstances, at least of his own mind. Examples of such extremity are useful because they leave the rest of us with very few excuses not to take responsibility for our circumstances. Torture has a way of putting things in perspective.

It's very easy to look outward and identify factors that cause your suffering just as Sisyphus could blame the boulder or Zeus for his condemnation, and Frankl the concentration camps or the guards carrying out their orders. If we can conceive of a world where each of these characters chooses the other thing, that self-ownership, that responsibility for personal perspective, then we have to raise the bar on how we show up to our own plights, which are far less oppressive: that off-hand comment, that shitty driver during rush hour, that lost business or work opportunity. Is there space between those stressors and our power to choose the best version of ourselves? Are we open to change?

Change is the process of showing up when times are hard.

It's easy to be virtuous when the world awards you a desired outcome. It's very difficult to stay true to commitments and personal values when reality doesn't meet your expectations. When things get tough. When the stressor burns deep. When the villain is stronger than you expected. But that *responsibility* for self, that ownership isn't granted any of us; it's taken.

We must decide how much responsibility we want, the size and degree of our stressor-villains. Some stressors build us up, and others break us down. And the hard part of life is that they're often one and the same, determined more by our responses to them than the objectivity of the stressors. Some villains make us victims, and others make us heroes, determined not by the villain but by the dedication and commitment to cause manifested in our response. The more we choose to bear, the more we can bear, and the stronger we become.

In the aftermath of this struggle against increasing resistance with a deepening sensitivity, we find our lightness of being.

All burdens are not created equal. We choose the burdens we are willing to carry for the most part. And those burdens either give meaning to our lives or they take it away. So it's our first charge to ask: *Am I carrying the right burdens*? As we discussed above, to honestly address that question we need to face the uncertainties of life in an honest way, for that's how we suit means to end. (Hint: If you're training Weightlessness you're carrying at least some of the right burdens!). If the answer is no, eliminate those burdens with cold resolve and add some of the right ones.

Secondarily, assuming the answer to that question is yes, the next question is: *How am I carrying those burdens*? In terms of Weightlessness, that first question is addressed within The Weightlessness Spectrum, where you take up the torch of meaningful mind-body practices that empower you, the practices that build resilience to unpredictable stresses-to-come and that cultivate sensitivity to beautifully fleeting, present moments in life. These are the broad brushstrokes; the all-purpose tools for calibrating robust parts.

Lightness answers the second question regarding *how*. This is a qualitative question, and one best answered by increasing one's sensitivity, or we might say, increasing awareness over and above one's felt burdens to a high degree. This isn't in the broad brushstrokes; it's in the minutia. It's in the how-we-do-the-little-things that determines how we do *all* things.

That differential—of awareness over burdens—that is embodied sensitivity, is where weightlessness awaits you.

The student is concerned with building up; the master is concerned with carving down. The student is concerned with the deadlift and standing tensegrity. The master is concerned with the subtle applications of integration and influence within meaningful real-world experiences, the small daily actions and interactions that embody the true battle against the only villain who matters—the self.

The open mind that maintains perspective on the long game and the role of stressor-villains in personal transformation is a mind available to change. In this perspective lies power to act with purpose. You must frequently audit your approach to stress, with which perspective you embrace or tolerate it.

Of those positive stressors—the one's that help me grow—am I approaching them with an open, growth mindset? Or am I treating them like negative burdens in my life?

Of those unnecessary stressors—the ones that only weigh me down—am I tolerating them and suffering for it, affecting those around me with my personal baggage? Or am I actively working to reduce their impact on my life, to eliminate them?

That "Feeling"

Integration Revisited

The experience, *the feeling*, must coincide with (or precede) the intellectual grasp of the essence. Imagine, you meet someone who confesses they've never been in love. They have an idea of it, have read about it in poetry and literature, but have had no firsthand experience and no attachment to a partner beyond their physiological needs and camaraderie.

It's hard for most to imagine. What would you say to someone of this rare ilk? What more could you do than repeat some of the most poetic, heartfelt descriptions. Without the sensation itself, that all-consuming, gut-wrenching, earth-shattering emotion simply cannot be described or encapsulated with words. In fact, the harder we try, the further away we really are from understanding the thing itself, like trying to explain the flight of an arrow by tabulating its points of trajectory.

Mind-body integration is very much a preintellectual phenomenon that cannot be constructed or reconstructed from descriptions of its composite parts. The skill of the master to integrate, to feel, stems only from hard, conscientious effort over time. Just as with love, there's no amount of technical knowledge sufficient enough to represent the sensation itself. And this leaves us all with a strange accountability to self, for there are no true external metrics and facts that bear meaning without a corresponding performance capacity in the mind-body, without the skill to manifest weightless moments.

This will rub some the wrong way. It will particularly rub cynics and "intellectuals" the wrong way, as I'm burning intellect for the moment. I think intellect holds a critical role in the filtering of relevant information, tools, and metrics in this domain, but in the game of integration and true presence, it's only a finger pointing the way to the moon.

Intellectuals often mistake the finger for the moon in this case, and lazy cynics don't believe they need to put in the work after they "get" the idea. And if this might be you, I'd like to again ask one question: *If someone told you they could ride a bike because they'd read ten books on it but never actually attempted to ride a real, physical bicycle—to balance, to steer, to accelerate, and brake—would you believe they could get on a bicycle right now and demonstrate that integrated skill with proficiency?*

There is something poetic in systemic integration that cannot be reduced to the knowledge of parts.

My second chain whip master of Shaolin kung fu, himself a monk of the warrior tradition and a national champion of wushu in China, seemed to float when we leapt, and moved with such ferocity and grace that it was breathtaking. I asked him how he maintained some of his elite skills with a seemingly low level of training—he really didn't practice much at the time I knew him—and his reply led to a paradigm shift for me. His answer was simply: *You must acquire the feeling.* He did the hard work. He got it. It stayed with him. It's something beyond the training, beyond the tools.

You must acquire the feeling.

The point isn't to simply study and practice for the sake of practice. Nor is it simply to maintain. Practice is a means to an end. The purpose of study and practice is to internalize that thing in a visceral, intuitive way so that the skill inherent in that practice manifests constantly across all facets of life.

The principle, the *feeling* of that thing, is no longer external to you in the way you know the answer to 2+2 or perform any number of complex things effortlessly—the way you walk up stairs, use a fork and knife, or ride a bicycle. At one time, these were exceedingly complex activities to coordinate or abstract numbers to ponder. But now, you can climb stairs without any attention whatsoever and in a million random ways. It's not something you need to train, it's something you just do because you *get* the thing in a deep way (stairs go up or down, I want to go up or down, take a step) and the doing maintains and strengthens the skill with little additional effort. The skill, in this case, is lived rather than practiced.

Life *is* the practice.

In the integrated mind-body, the trajectory of the arrow is alive, the bicycle is ridden, and love is. In the master, physical structure stacked with effortless tensegrity, with abdominal breath and concentrated awareness, integrate in reproducible moments of presence and power. In moments of weightlessness.

For this, there's no simple hack. It requires deep personal work and frequent auditing of personal perspective. Integration is not only a phenomenon; it's an active practice. In any moment wheresoever you find space, scan your structure. Find your breath. Sit or stand with natural lift and sinking relaxation. Breathe into the abdomen. See, hear, and feel what's present. And ask…

Am I weightlessness?
Yes? Awesome! (You likely won't be asking if you already are…)
No?
How about now?
Still no? Align your frame, drop your breath, release, and sense.
And now?
And how about now?
Still no? Slap yourself in the face. All you have is this moment. Wake the fuck up.
And now?

Crossing the Threshold

The day I was awarded my first black belt in martial arts after five years of training over twenty years ago, my instructor handed me that symbol of expertise outside of a national conference and qualified it at the same time, "*Now your real training begins.*" After five years of training, attaining the rank that everyone who first enters a dojang dreams of and hearing that I'd reached the level of… a beginner? This was a paradox that took me quite some time to understand, let alone embrace. In the five years prior, I wasn't mastering a craft, I was laying the bricks and mortar, building a foundation from which the real temple might just have a chance of standing atop.

To internalize *Weightlessness* a threshold must be crossed that only the initiated can truly appreciate. This is part of the game. It's part of all games where mastery can be considered a thing. Until that point, perspective doesn't exist to make sense of it all.

Just as my first five years in martial arts laid the foundation for the rich world of mind-body development that opened up for me thereafter, so too is The Weightlessness Spectrum instilling the raw materials, the structure, the awareness, the physical resilience and mental nonattachment, the knowledge required to enter a whole new world of holistic development. And while there are further lessons and tools in Lightness Training, the whole person can be well accommodated by The Spectrum alone.

In effective systems, this threshold should not be a placeholder on a continuous spectrum of development, it should be categorically different, a world from which one can never return. This is the world of perspective, of integration, and of sensitivity. It's going to the depths of things you thought you understood and discovering an ocean at the bottom of a well. It's accepting again and again, forever, that beginner mindset.

There never was anything but the foundations. The black belt is a white belt in disguise, but with heartfelt passion and purpose. You learned everything that mattered on day one. Now you're ready to actually practice it without expectation or desire for more. Ready to do it for its own sake, because the tool is no different from you. Its role is that of a mirror reflecting your true self.

Lightness Training takes on new forms and skills that we might consider advanced practices, but it's critical to remember that they are ways of deepening the well, of connecting to self. But they are of the same well!

In structure, Lightness Protocols are far simpler and deceptively easier than the progressive workouts of The Weightlessness Spectrum. But they will not bear results for the dabbling or whimsical mind. They are minimalistic and simple, adding nuance to strong structural foundations. And because of their poignancy, the tools of Lightness are few, but extremely deep.

Lightness isn't for the uninitiated. Anyone can adopt the four pillars of Lightness as one can pick up a staff or sword and swing them around, but to those who haven't done the real work, embodied the foundational tools of The Weightlessness Spectrum, their movements will look like those of children at play. Without the requisite preparation, the four pillars will go unappreciated and completely misunderstood. They'll fail to produce the intended senses of power and freedom, and worse, they'll have little impact save for the risk of injury, boredom, or self-delusion.

Worse still, the trainee will be none the wiser because they've loaded their vehicle with a good stereo and a cool design but they haven't looked under the hood. So they'll play and dabble and, with time, transition to the next fad. Regardless of whether someone chooses to cross that threshold and take on the craft of Lightness for themselves, the essence, the white belt stuff that matters more than anything else is contained in The Spectrum. That's the stuff that if we don't do well, quality of life deteriorates. But if we do well in them, all aspects of life improve and weightless moments manifest.

While we're all free to choose and dabble and taste, we don't *need* more hobbies or specific methods of fitness (or mind-body development), for your biomechanics dictate one most efficient way to squat. We don't *need* different breathing or meditation systems, for your central nervous system dictates how synaptic bonds form and break, and how breathing affects stress and recovery. We don't need a million varieties of movement for your tensional integrity dictates how all humans resist the forces of gravity to stand and move. While we can and should embrace movement play, hobbies and various practices, when it comes to that mind-body growth and performance system that feeds us over time, we don't need to dabble and dabble. We need something more.

We need a system that doesn't allow us to excel under certain conditions with certain rules in certain domains of life. We need a lawless system that allows us to stand above it all, to build our raw assets with the most crude, robust tools and strategies, tools that cut to the very depth of what it means to be human in every sense. Tools that allow us to master ourselves. Tools that allow us to be weightless.

You have those tools. It's time to cross the threshold.

Now your real training begins.

The Master of Lightness

> *When you reach the end of what you should know,*
> *you will be at the beginning of what you should sense.*
> *—Kahlil Gibran*

Grandmaster Shi De Jian was quite the storyteller it turned out. I for one was inspired to learn about the origins of his monastery and the legends of the masters of Lightness. And I certainly didn't expect him to be such a connoisseur of old school American hip-hop. But you know, it's the little things in life.

I can't say I knew what to do with it all, then or now, as some of it seemed fantastical. But there were parts, insights and beats that definitely struck a chord. It's particularly tough to filter fiction from reality when in the presence of someone who defies what you understand to be natural limits. In all my years of training, these types of moments are worth living for. They tear that veil of impossibility to shreds and show you fiction is closer to reality than perceived reality itself.

Over my short stint at the Shaolin Monastery, I saw living warrior monks training on landscaped stone patios before purple sunsets, humble temple dwellers pacing slowly up endless stairs, and visitors from around the world coming for Master Shi's healing touch and herbal remedies. All of it felt like the right thing in the right place at the right time.

"Everything is Zen," said master Shi in response to a question I raised on the intersection of Zen and martial arts. "Everything is Zen. Everything is kung fu. We never stop practicing, look," he said, pointing across the monastery.

Across the way, meandering up the liberally spaced stone steps of a seemingly endless stairway was one of the female chefs. She was one of a number of PHD students who had waited three years for the privilege of cooking master Shi's food every day just to draw a little bit of his presence. She was moving very slowly with a concentrated rhythm, swaying gracefully from side to side with every step, not unlike a speed skater's full body drifts from one leg to the next. It was surreal—watching a slow motion version of a scene in real time. Nothing else mattered but that moment, that step.

“She’s aware of every step. She’s aware of her movement. She’s aware of her breath. Everything is kung fu. Everything is Zen,” he reiterated.

The man who lived in a mountain cave for thirty years, who conditioned his body on concrete pillars morning and night, danced on perilous rooftops, shook bedrock with a stomp, and kindly offered to put his finger through my sternum emphasized only the basics in our time together. He delighted only in the basics. Walking. Eating. Listening. Training… and breathing.

It isn’t just about what we do—the specifics; It’s about how we do them.

I have no doubt Master Shi had secrets upon secrets, and skills that defy logic. He surely had disciples who dabbled in these things. But for him, in him, the three treasures of Shaolin: health, martial arts, and Zen were everything. The integration of a healthy, sensitive body with a free, unburdened mind in our most simple moments of active living, *the breath,* is the greatest treasure of all.

For the master, this was the essence of Lightness.

Epilogue

...and preview of *Law of the Die*

Not long after the Grandmaster Flash's freedom challenge, the Furious Five stood before the Shaolin council with pride, inspired by Flash's impudence. He was a true master, so far as they could tell. A true leader not swayed by the status quo or earthly temptation like several of the nine before them, some of whom were walking hypocrites.

And after Flash's unforgettable demonstration, one thing was very clear: he had more to teach. A lot more. So, when the council asked whomsoever may want to leave of their own will, whomsoever wanted to use this window of discord to reconsider their vows and follow Grandmaster Flash, they could do so at this time only.

This was a calculated move by the council to allay the risk of dissension by opening the floodgate quickly so to speak, in order to contain the remaining pool of monks, the beggars who kept the coffers full. Something like this could create a chasm in the loyalty of those remaining, with itching doubts and thoughts of rebellion, and they deemed the risk of offering free departure to the monks who wanted to leave as the less risky of their options.

The legend would become an indelible discordance if those monks who Flash inspired were bold enough to form bands within the temple but not brave enough to challenge the 18.

It's fine, go now; we'll have an easier time regrouping after this shameful loss with the truly pious who remain. It's time to step back, show restraint and compassion, and, with time, the noose will tighten again, stronger than before.

The Furious Five took the council's one-time offer posthaste.

***

A warm winter's day, Flash hung his over-robe on a hook on the wall next to a blood-stained chain whip with fresh maroon tip, and sat down at a wooden desk before a floor-to-ceiling carved wooden door, opened and revealing a lush and vibrant valley.

His room wasn't much more exciting than his temple quarters, a humble barnyard storage construct in the foothills of Songshan Mountain, converted to accommodate the living solitude of a monk without a tribe, and one built to weather time. The Spartan walls were far less stifling than those that housed him in years past, and the door had a sharp red within its rugged frames—a color that had taken on new meaning for Flash of late.

Flash could feel his energy relax and disperse throughout the valley. He could follow it wherever he so chose. He was responsible only to himself now.

Flash wondered daily if he'd known his best childhood friend was a Wu Tang plant, would he have allowed them to grow so close? Would Flash have even reported him at some point? Things had become so foggy of late, and ever since Flash rolled his first die his moral compass was far from calibrated; good was not without bad was not without good, at least insofar as convention was concerned. In other ways, he felt far more connected to the essence of things, could sense which loyalties truly mattered, perhaps were even worth dying for.

At the behest of RZA, who had more clout than Flash would have imagined, the Wu Tang Clan did indeed have his back after his departure from Shaolin. This led to safe passage beyond Shaolin territory and the humble, yet protected living quarters he now resided in. This came with a mixed bag of fortune and folly, however, that continued to test Flash's honor as well as his sense of lightness. Help did not come without expectation it seemed.

The world beyond the temple was more hostile than Flash had imagined, and after his victory, students, challengers, and opportunists befell his path to learn from, defeat, or exploit The Master of Lightness. Monastic life had prepared him to face himself, but it didn't teach him how to navigate the complexities of the world beyond. For that, he relied on a device of chance.

Flash took with him the three treasures of Shaolin, stored in memory and neuromuscular habit, a living embodiment of Shaolin's deepest truths. Truths so precious the Guardians had risked their lives to protect them.

Flash's mastery of the treasures: Zen, health (medicine and qigong), and martial arts was at levels and depths that few had ever known outside the temple walls. But he now held one more, quite possibly the most powerful of them all—the treasure of infinite possibility—the die.

As The Master of Lightness sat with brush in hand before a blank canvas, reflecting and organizing his thoughts, the silhouettes of five figures approached Flash's barnyard storage convert from a distance. They had weapons in hand: spears, swords, sabers, and darts, and were dressed in Shaolin protector gear.

Grandmaster Flash ran his brush through ink, and placing it over a fresh scroll began to write:

Law of the Die

THANKS FOR READING!

If the ideas and principles in this book appeal to you and you would like to go deeper in the study and practice of Weightlessness, you can subscribe to my free newsletter and find information on upcoming training programs, workshops and new releases:

www.weightlessness.co

PLEASE CONSIDER:

As a self-published author I rely on word of mouth to market my books and creative content. If you feel this book has been of value to you, please recommend it to someone you think may benefit from it as well. Every review also directly impacts the book's ranking on Amazon.com, while giving prospective readers the information they need to make a decision. I would really appreciate your review on Amazon.com. Thank you!

For those looking to go further down the Weightlessness rabbit hole, the following books will help fill out the canvas:

In Pursuit of Weightlessness (Weightless Trilogy #1)

...is a journey through the trenches of mind-body fitness. It explores principles of peace, power, and enlightenment under the iron fists of Shaolin monks, high on hallucinogenic mushrooms, amid unexpected homelessness, and through random dice-dictated experiments. In it, you'll learn exactly what's required to transform the body, unburden the mind, and become weightless.

Law of the Die (Weightless Trilogy #3)

Can good luck be designed? Two unlikely heroes with little in common are bound to one another across time by the most unlikely of fortunes. Should challenges exceed their abilities they'll embrace the power of randomness and roll the dice, and in so doing provide insights that allow you and I to navigate uncertainty in our own lives.

For the Children: *Here Now Breathe*

...is a story for children about the challenges we all face, big or small, and a reminder that the secret to being strong and weightless in life is already within us. It introduces mindful awareness as a tool for managing fear, pain, and change.

CONNECT WITH ME

Follow me on YouTube: youtube.com/user/ShaolinRopeDart
Connect with me on LinkedIn: linkedin.com/in/tomfazio/
Follow me on Instagram: weightlessness_by_tom_fazio

Made in the USA
Middletown, DE
31 July 2019